W9-BBF-023

The Republic

UNIVERSITY OF CONNECTICUT — GROTON, CONN. — SOUTHEASTERN BRANCH LIBRARY

JUL 8 1969

CHARLES A. BEARD

THE REPUBLIC

Conversations on Fundamentals

NEW YORK: THE VIKING PRESS

COPYRIGHT 1943 BY CHARLES A. BEARD

ALL RIGHTS RESERVED

COMPASS BOOKS EDITION

ISSUED IN 1962 BY THE VIKING PRESS, INC.

625 MADISON AVENUE, NEW YORK 22, N.Y.

DISTRIBUTED IN CANADA BY

THE MACMILLAN COMPANY OF CANADA LIMITED

PRINTED IN THE U.S.A. BY THE COLONIAL PRESS INC.

Note: Except for the name of the author and the names of public figures and other persons easily identifiable from the context, the names of all participants in the conversations and persons mentioned in them are wholly fictitious and do not represent any actual persons, living or dead. The name of the town or city or community in which the conversations are supposed to have taken place is likewise wholly fictitious and does not represent any actual town, city, or community in the United States.

Table of Conversations

Introduction

ONE morning last autumn, while I stood at my study window watching maple leaves make burnished swirls in the wind, and pondering some ancient lore, I was surprised to see Dr. Robert Smyth and his wife Susan drive up my lane. They had come to my home with friends on several occasions in the late afternoon for free-for-all conversations about things in general. At such times we had all been accustomed to frank and direct speech. In this relation with the Smyths I had learned that they were well informed about many matters and had a lively interest in public affairs. I had also found that they were both vigorous personalities, forthright in expressing their opinions, and that the Doctor had a tendency to flare up when he did not like things that were said. But all such encounters had been mere neighborly pastimes after the day's work was over, and the Smyths had never broken into the precious hours of my mornings.

They had never seemed to have time for that. The Doctor is a practicing physician in our city and is also engaged by the management of a neighboring factory to superintend the health of two or three thousand industrial workers. His wife, besides taking care of a household and four children, is active in community affairs. She led in raising money for the city hospital and has long served as secretary of the Board. For these heavily burdened people to be off duty during the golden hours of the day was something of a shock to me.

Knowing that it would be a surprise, they explained the unexpected visit as soon as I had opened the door. "We can only stay a minute," they said almost in unison. "But we have an urgent problem and we can state it quickly."

As soon as we were seated, Dr. Smyth began: "You surely know how hard it is for busy men and women to keep up with public affairs as issues, opinions, and decisions. We find little time for reading, and have relied mainly on weekly magazines, newspaper reports, and the radio. In trying to learn what is going on and what we as citizens should think and do, we use the radio a great deal.

We turn it on while we are eating or resting, or at odd moments, to hear summaries of the news and public speeches.

"Well, after listening to a long string of talks on the American way of life, democracy, liberty and constitutional government, the four freedoms, and America's responsibilities to the world, we decided that we ought to be better equipped to understand and judge such speeches. We reached the conclusion that we ought to have some experience of our own with a critical analysis of the opinions, assertions, and declamations that are blared at us day and night.

"They all seem hazy to us. There are glaring contradictions in them. Indeed, most of the discussions we hear amount principally to mere assertions and counter-assertions. Many radio commentators are supposed to give us the facts, but I have sense and knowledge enough to discover that they are giving us *selected* facts strung on hidden opinions. When views are frankly expounded they are usually cast in very abstract terms, such as individualism and collectivism, or world-order and isolationism. Accustomed as we are to dealing with concrete matters all day, we have little practice in analyzing these abstractions and finding out whether they have an anchorage in precise knowledge of public affairs. We have not developed for ourselves, amid the tumult of opinions, any standards of judgment, any positive ideas, any body of criteria or convictions to which we can cling with assurance or confidence, by which we can test the validity of the torrent of words poured out over the radio and in print. If I were not skittish about vague language I should say that we have no philosophy of life and history by which to check thought and assertion.

"We know enough to know that individuals and groups of persons who set themselves up to instruct the country stand on fixed convictions of some kind and that the various convictions on which they operate are as contradictory as the opinions which they thunder at us. Frankly, we are thoroughly discontented, amid the uproar that goes on around us, with our ability to cope with it. Books pour out from the press. Many of them are greeted by the reviewers as offering the solution of this or that, and they make a big furor for a few days, perhaps a few weeks, seldom for a longer time. Some of our friends are so busy chasing from one new thought to another that they seem to us as mad as March hares. And, having observed enough of that kind of business, we want to clarify our own thinking and to discover some solid ground to stand on, if there is any."

"Yes," Mrs. Smyth interposed, "before the fifth speech in the current series on American affairs was finished, I just shut off the stream of words. Robert and I then sat and talked the rest of the evening about the practice of listening inertly to everything that comes over the air. We felt that we did not understand much of what was said, although we thought we understood the words; that at the end of a speech we were more often wearied and confused than enlightened and informed. Toward midnight we decided that we ought to study more ourselves instead of drifting to and fro in the winds of opinion, or grasping at ideas the way a drowning man grasps at straws. Speakers and writers so frequently turn public questions into blacks or whites and refuse to admit any grays or middle ways. They try to make everything a fight, and we do not want to be victimized by that type of thinking."

"You know," said the Doctor, taking up the story, "that we have dipped as others have, into books and the more serious magazines that deal with current affairs and intellectual problems. We have read some of Spengler. We know something about Freud, as medical persons should. We have been entertained by Mencken. We both had courses in history at college and still thumb over new books on it occasionally. We glance through the speeches of politicians—or statesmen, if you prefer to use that word. But we undertake no systematic study to get a basis of judgment about the opinions of others or to correct our own fleeting impressions. And we don't know just how to proceed best in a study of public affairs with reference to the criticism and formation of opinions.

"You have devoted many years to exploring American history and have written books and articles about the Constitution, civil liberty, democracy, and other subjects in line with present-day discussions. Would you let us drop in one evening a week for a kind of elementary course on current issues in government and democracy? We don't mean formal lectures. We should like to interrupt with questions to test the things you affirm."

"I shall have a lot of questions," added Mrs. Smyth. "My opinions do not always square with Robert's. My experiences have not been exactly like his and I often see things from a different angle."

"You do me neighborly honor by your proposition," I replied, laughing heartily. "You must be hard up for a consultant in this case. Many years ago I asked the late Justice Oliver Wendell Holmes whether he had any principle to guide him amid the tangle of legal opinions, and he answered: 'About seventy years ago I learned that I was not God.' "

"Some radio speakers talk as if they thought they were," Mrs. Smyth remarked.

"It is true, my good friends," I conceded, "that I have been studying history and government in the United States for about fifty years, with intervals for travel and study in other parts of the earth. But I have come to realize that in fact I know little. History and government are far from simple subjects. We can know something about them. We can refuse to give up in despair when we find how frail our knowledge often proves to be. We can keep on trying to learn more. The same rule applies to hospital management and medicine, I suppose."

"Indeed it does!" Mrs. Smyth exclaimed. "But in keeping up the battle we win many victories and escape sinking into dry rot."

"In the field of history," I continued, "nearly every day a new document is likely to turn up and spoil something that I thought I knew. In the government of mankind so many unforeseen personalities, events, and contingencies appear that judging them by rules derived from past experience is hazardous, to say the least."

"Yet," the Doctor interrupted, "some features of history and government must be well established and agreed upon. Otherwise public affairs would be a senseless chaos. Otherwise there would be no use teaching the subjects, as you have done, or writing about them. Anyway, our orators and politicians are always appealing to what they call the lessons of history and American principles of government."

"Yes, Doctor," I granted, "some things are fairly well established and agreed upon in history and government—indeed many things important for private and public life."

"Then let us discuss those things," my visitors proposed. "We take risks every day, even with lives. So if you will give us a chance, we will take the risk of being misinformed and misled."

"That is all very well, and generous," I answered, "but where or, rather, with what do we start, and close to what supreme line of interest shall we hold our discussions? If we do not fix a center of gravity, so to speak, we can talk and talk till the crack of doom and at the end our chatter will be as jumbled as all the radio speeches, magazine articles, and newspaper reports mixed together."

"As I come to think of it," Mrs. Smyth remarked, "it is the lack of any center of gravity that permits us to be blown about by the storms of opinion. What is our center of interest? It is above all our country, America. We are both Americans by birth, education, work, and affections. Our ancestors were immigrants—English, Scotch, French Huguenot, and what have you. We have never taken much interest in them and have never had any communication with our relatives across the sea, if we have any now. I do not say that it is a virtue or a fault, but honestly we are more concerned with the fortunes of America than with those of our ancestral homes or other countries. Please don't regard us as blind isolationists, whatever that may mean, but as Americans whose strongest affections are centered here."

"That suits me," was my response. "Suppose then we set down or fix as our center of concern the Republic, our Republic, as strengthened, developed, and governed under the Constitution of the United States. Whatever may be the future of international relations, most Americans, I take it, will agree that our Republic, including all the values associated with it, is to be maintained, and that the civilization which it represents is to be continuously advanced."

"Admirable for us!" my guests exclaimed.

"I promise not to be too rigid in procedure," I assured them. "I'll allow you both all the elbow room you want, but I shall gently steer our discussion by the center of intellectual interest we have chosen—the Republic, under our Constitution. This is all on the understanding that you can turn me off any moment, the way you do the radio. When do we begin? What about next Friday night?"

"We shall both be here at nine o'clock," they agreed.

"As you have no telephone in your house I shall be safe from interruptions by my patients," said the Doctor with evident pleasure as we parted.

The Republic

We, The People . . .

THE Smyths arrived for our first session on the stroke of the hour, in a serious mood, as if they really meant business. On a signal that they were ready, I started our explorations.

BEARD: According to our understanding when you came up last Monday, I shall set the theme, and you are to break in as abruptly as you wish any time you feel moved to do so. We shall save time by reducing what are called courtesies and accomplish more at our sessions. How far we shall get tonight is uncertain, of course, but my starting point is 'We, the People . . .'

DR. SMYTH, breaking in: Oh! You are beginning with that. That is nothing but rhetoric from the Preamble of the Constitution. I studied it in high school long before I began my battle with the manager of the factory over the health and safety of his employees. It means nothing in my young life. It's for politicians—and statesmen, if we have any, for lawyers and for the lobbyists who promote the special interests of capital, labor, and agriculture at the national capital. Besides, the words in the form they take in the Constitution are largely due to an accident. You say so, yourself, in one of your books. And anyway the men who wrote them were not democrats and did not believe in the people. If I am not mistaken, you say that, too, somewhere.

MRS. SMYTH: Yes, and the original Constitution was made by men for men in what they thought was a man's world. Women had to battle for nearly a hundred and fifty years to get a place among 'the people.'

BEARD: All right. I shall face both objections. I start with those words not merely because they stand at the head of the Constitution. My reason is that they are also historic words and words of strangely prophetic nature, illustrating the force of ideas in history.

In the eighteenth century, they were as revolutionary as any modern phrase which makes timid citizens look under their beds at night for bogies. Indeed there are many Americans who loudly profess their devotion to the Constitution and are mortally afraid that the Second World War will be turned into the people's war. 'We, the people' are vibrant, elusive words. They do not yet have a settled place in American thought or in that of several countries belonging to the United Nations. But they have gained in power since 1787 in the United States.

These words did not mean to the men who cast the Preamble in 1787 what they do to Americans now. Consequences and collaterals that the framers did not contemplate, outrunning their vision, have filled the Preamble with sentiments and practices that would have astounded them. It was a curious turn in affairs, almost an accident as Doctor Smyth has said, that put 'We, the People of the United States' at the opening of our fundamental law. The men who made the final draft of the Preamble did not call themselves democrats, or believe in the people, in any modern sense. As an example of a critical and philosophic way of examining current dogmas accepted without question, let us look briefly into the history of these opening words of our Constitution.

As late as September 10, 1787, seven days before the convention that framed the Constitution had finished its work, the Preamble of the draft then read:

> We the people of the States of New-Hampshire, Massachusetts, Rhode-Island and Providence Plantations, Connecticut, New-York, New-Jersey, Pennsylvania, Delaware, Maryland, Virginia, North-Carolina, South-Carolina, and Georgia, do ordain, declare and establish the following Constitution for the Government of Ourselves and our Posterity.

The Preamble, in its final form, as it now stands in our Constitution, with one little word omitted, was drawn up by the Committee of Style appointed by the convention to shape up its work for the last review. But the convention had adopted a resolution that, when ratified by nine states, the new constitution should go into effect as applied to those nine states, leaving the other four out in the cold; and it thus would have been a mistake to name all the states in the document, for some of them might have decided to stay out of the Union.

DR. SMYTH: Just what I thought. The words were not intended to mean the people of the United States as one people, but actually the people divided into as many independent groups as there are states in the Union. That is exactly the way it was put by my old Uncle Henry, of South Carolina, who was standing near to Edmund Ruffin when the first shot was fired on Fort Sumter in 1861.

BEARD: Well, there is no doubt that the words now mean 'We, the one and indivisible people of the United States.' It is a case of men's building better than they knew—or of an incidental matter before the Committee of Style leading to one of the strangest and most momentous prophecies of all history.

DR. SMYTH, grunting: That is all right with me, if you don't get mystical. Now what about the democracy of the business?

BEARD: I am not being mystical. I just want to repeat the statement that words, which were intended in 1787 to mean something else, have come, in the course of our history, to mean 'We, the People as one people.' If you want to put mysticism into the phrase 'come to mean' or to take it out, I won't object. No doubt fundamental problems of philosophy are tangled up in the interpretation of *come*. But let us get back to our Preamble.

The Committee of Style, which shaped up the Preamble, was composed of Alexander Hamilton, William S. Johnson, Rufus King, Gouverneur Morris. and James Madison. They were responsible for ——

DR. SMYTH, impatiently: Wait a minute. I know something about those men. Nobody can say that Hamilton had anything but contempt for the people. He is the fellow who said, 'Your people are a great beast,' or something like that, and thought it, whether he said it or not. And as a Yale man I dimly recall hearing something about our alumnus Johnson. He was too much of a Tory to lend any aid to the cause of the Revolution. While George Washington and his men were fighting for our independence, Johnson lived in retirement, most of the time in a farmhouse in Bridgewater, Connecticut, which Raymond Moley has bought for a summer place. After the Constitution was adopted he became a Federalist, though a bit quiet as president of Columbia College.

Then take Rufus King. He was a Harvard man. I don't want

to appear prejudiced, but King was a Hamiltonian—to the bitter end, was he not? He was the last candidate that the grouchy old Federalists ever put up for President. A democrat, a man of the people? I should say not. I know little about Gouverneur Morris except that he was a high Tory Federalist, despised the French Revolution and Thomas Jefferson, and was about willing to break up the Union of 'we, the people' during the War of 1812. Of the five men who fixed up the Preamble to the Constitution, Madison is the only one who could be set down as caring a hoot about the people. Maybe he didn't either, but at least Jefferson chose Madison to succeed him as President and I suppose that little Jimmy must have been all right on the score of the people.

BEARD: You remember an amazing amount of your course in American history at Yale, Doctor.

DR. SMYTH: Oh! That's a good joke on you. Just to show my erudition, I looked up in the Dictionary of American Biography the names of four or five men who took part in making the Constitution, including Johnson and Morris. Of course I had heard about Madison and had somehow stumbled on King. So don't take my learning too seriously.

BEARD: Anyway, substantially all that you say about the men who fixed up 'We, the People of the United States' for the Preamble is true enough. The men who put 'We, the People' into the Constitution, with a few exceptions perhaps, feared the rule of the people and would have been horrified if they could have foreseen all that was to happen under their Constitution in the next hundred and fifty years. As to the suffrage, it again is actually a case of men's building better than they knew, or at all events preparing the way for outcomes they did not approve. With poll taxes and other limitations on the suffrage, we have not yet achieved universal democracy, but we have gone a long way in that direction since 1787.

MRS. SMYTH: Is there any evidence that your great men were building anything for women in the Constitution?

But Sue, the DOCTOR remonstrated, there weren't any feminists at the end of the eighteenth century. What could you expect?

MRS. SMYTH: I know very well that there weren't any women then who called themselves feminists. Still there were women who did their own thinking and feeling and who protested against the cool way in which men insisted on determining all their legal rights.

Why, [turning to me] in a history of the United States which you and Mary Beard wrote, you tell about protests by Mrs. Abigail Adams and Mrs. Hannah Corbin. I do not call myself a feminist. I do not claim to know exactly what the word means. All I am say-ing is that, in the early days of the Republic, women who had worked hard for its independence objected to the manner in which men proposed to fix their legal rights and political privileges. Can you put your hand easily on that passage from Abigail Adams?

When I had found Abigail's letter, dated March 31, 1776, to her husband, John Adams, then in the Continental Congress, Mrs. Smyth read this paragraph from it:

> I long to hear that you have declared an independency. And, by the way, in the new code of laws which I suppose it will be necessary for you to make, I desire you would remember the ladies and be more generous and favorable to them than your ancestors. Do not put such unlimited power into the hands of the husbands. Remember, all men would be tyrants if they could. If particular care and attention is not paid to the ladies, we are determined to foment a rebellion, and will not hold ourselves bound by any laws in which we have no voice or representation. [Another prophecy! commented Mrs. Smyth.] That your sex are naturally tyrannical is a truth so thoroughly established as to admit of no dispute.

Mrs. Smyth, commenting: Such sentiments and opinions were abroad at the end of the eighteenth century and the brave men who made the Constitution paid no attention to them.

Beard: I do not deny the truth of either statement, Mrs. Smyth. But there is a queer thing about this man-woman business and the Constitution. Men did draft the Constitution. Men ratified it. No doubt about that. Yet, if I may go into details, I will point out some strange phases of this question of male and female under the Con-stitution, which may surprise you.

The word man, even in the generic sense, appears nowhere in the original Constitution or in any of the amendments; nor the word woman, not even in the woman suffrage amendment. The word man almost got into the original Constitution. The prelimi-nary draft of the document, as turned over to the Committee of Style by the convention on September 10, 1787, contained this provision:

The legislative power shall be vested in a Congress, to consist of two separate and distinct bodies of men, a House of Representatives, and a Senate. [But the Committee of Style substituted the section]: All legislative powers herein granted shall be vested in a Congress of the United States, which shall consist of a Senate and House of Representatives.

I admit that the word he is in the Constitution several times. For instance, it says: 'The executive power shall be vested in a president of the United States. He shall hold his office during the term of four years.' The Constitution also provides: 'No person [not 'no man'] shall be a Senator who shall not have attained to the age of thirty years. . . .' But the he, as used, has been interpreted to mean woman as well as man. Otherwise how could a woman sit in the Senate or House of Representatives?

Where the rights, privileges, and immunities of the people were treated in the Constitution, the word citizen or person was used, and deliberately used to cover the people, even Negroes, who were then usually chattels, but are now among the people covered by the Constitution.

Only in one place does the word male appear in the document. That is in the Fourteenth Amendment adopted, after the Civil War, in 1868. Leaders in Congress wanted to provide against state legislation depriving Negro freemen of the right to vote. Only men then voted anywhere in state and federal elections. So the draftsmen of the clause stipulated that when a state denies the right to vote 'to any of the male inhabitants of such state . . .' its representation in Congress shall be reduced in the proportion that the number of males deprived of the vote bears to the whole number of adult male citizens.

Women, led by the indomitable Elizabeth Cady Stanton, Susan B. Anthony, and others, struggled hard against the introduction of the word male into the Amendment. They were demanding the vote for themselves then. Most of them had halted their agitation for the suffrage in order to support Lincoln, the emancipation of slaves, and the Union. It was a bitter pill for them to receive as a reward this provision of the Fourteenth Amendment, which they opposed to the last ditch—in vain. In time, however, in 1920, the letter and spirit of that limitation were killed by the adoption of the Nineteenth Amendment. Women can now vote, hold office, and claim all the rights and privileges given to anybody by the Constitution, as you know. Still the word woman is not to be found in its text.

DR. SMYTH: That is a strange story about the Preamble and the way the words of the Constitution have acquired meaning in the course of our history. Isn't there a touch of symbolism in it?

BEARD: I do not myself recall having seen it stated anywhere, Doctor, exactly as I have put it. But we do not have to go into symbolism. The framers of the Constitution intended some things clearly, anticipated others, and prepared the way for many things they neither wanted nor contemplated. I did not tell the story for any mere historical or antiquarian purpose. My primary concern is with the people of the United States as in truth brought within the scope of the Constitution and as having rights and duties under it —real, everyday rights and duties. So leaving symbolism out, let us get on with the people.

There are about 135,000,000 of us, the people, right here in the continental United States. The people are a fact, or facts. Our continental boundaries are facts. The earth we stand and labor on is a fact. Whatever you think of the Constitution as a piece of paper for lawyers and politicians, all the people on this land, within these boundaries, come within the purview of the Constitution today; they have rights, privileges, and duties under it, and owe more to what it stands for than you or any American thinker has yet imagined, or at least set down on paper. This nation ——

DR. SMYTH, snapping: This nation! We, the people, are not a nation. The United States is what Theodore Roosevelt called a boardinghouse. We have a conglomeration of peoples that have come here from the four corners of the earth. Most of them, or their ancestors at least, had lived in serfdom, servitude or barbarism; had been ruled over by kings, aristocrats, tough fellows, or freebooters. Most of them had never had any real experience in managing their own affairs; or, if they had, they had made a mess of things where they were. And now they are here. Big blocks of them stick together like primitive tribesmen. They vote together. They intrigue together. They make the demagogue politicians bid for their votes and play their games. And whenever their relatives anywhere on earth get into trouble, these tribesmen think that the rest of the people should drop everything else and save their relatives from the consequences of their own folly. Do you call this a nation?

Of course, the tribesmen in playing their games never proclaim the honest truth of their purposes; they always cover their doings with high-sounding phrases; but they are tribesmen just the same. They profess to be working for the brotherhood of man or something of the sort, but they are really working for the brotherhood of their tribes. There are at least six tribes in our factory. Each has its labor boss and its political boss. I know the people all right. These tribesmen who came from Europe, some of them at least, brought with them what they call culture. They have made contributions to arts, sciences, letters, and folk-dancing. Their vocal chieftains boast of their superiority right in our faces. But they have made no contribution to the institutions of self-government and liberty. Unless my courses at Yale in English and American history were all wrong, every single institution of self-government and liberty we possess was developed here by the old Anglo-Saxon stock.

BEARD: Now it is my turn to be brusque, Doctor. I note what you say about the origins of our institutions of self-government and liberty. But it is surprising to hear a good Democrat like you talk in the language of Alexander Hamilton, whom you just decried for his lack of democratic feeling. You have contacts with the tribesmen, as you call them. Unquestionably, many people follow bosses blindly. Still, that is not the whole story of the people. During the early days of the Republic, peoples of many national origins worked together in our country, in peace and war. On battlefields, in council rooms, in civilian labors and sacrifices to support the armies of the war for independence, English, Scotch, Irish, Dutch, Germans, Jews, Welsh, French, Swedes, and Negroes—bond and free—took part, and forwarded the great cause which brought our nation into being. This is a fact of history. It can be ignored or slurred over, but it is a fact.

Furthermore, it was early recognized that all these tribesmen, as you characterize them, were one people in the sense that they were all Americans. Let me read you a passage on this very subject from an old book here on my shelves, Hector St. John Crèvecœur's *Letters from an American Farmer*, published in London in 1782, the year before American independence was formally acknowledged. Crèvecœur may be called a typical American of the eighteenth century, even though he went back to France to die. He was born in

France in 1735, received a part of his education in England, migrated to Canada, made explorations in the regions of the Great Lakes and in the Ohio Valley, came to New York in 1759, became a naturalized citizen, traveled around in the colonies, married Mehetable Tippet of Yonkers, and finally settled down on a farm. He is one of the most fascinating figures in our history, and a first-rate literary man besides.

In one of his *Letters*, Crèvecœur asked: What is an American? His answer fills several pages but these quotations give the main points:

> Whence came all these people [in America]? They are a mixture of English, Scotch, Irish, French, Dutch, Germans, and Swedes. From this promiscuous breed that race now called Americans have arisen. . . . In this great American asylum, the poor of Europe have by some means met together, and in consequence of various causes; to what purpose should they ask one another what countrymen they are? . . . Urged by a variety of motives, here they came. . . . In Europe they were so many useless plants; . . . they withered, and were mowed down by want, hunger, and war. . . . Here they rank as citizens. By what invisible power has this surprising metamorphosis been performed? By that of the laws and that of their industry. . . . What attachment can a poor European immigrant have for a country where he had nothing. . . . What then is the American, this new man? He is either a European, or the descendant of an European, hence that strange mixture of blood, which you will find in no other country. I could point out to you a family whose grandfather was an Englishman, whose wife was Dutch, whose son married a French woman, and whose present four sons have now four wives of different nations. *He* is an American who, leaving behind him all ancient prejudices and manners, receives new ones from the new mode of life he has embraced, the new government he obeys, and the new ranks he holds. . . . This is an American. . . . We know, properly speaking, no strangers; this is every person's country. . . . Europeans become Americans.

It is too bad that we haven't time to read the entire letter. It is so crowded with wisdom and wholesome truth, and so charmingly written! And this is the way, my friends, that some first-rate American thinkers, including Dr. Benjamin Rush, looked on your tribesmen when our nation was young. They regarded them all as Amer-

icans. The naturalization act of 1790, requiring only two years'
residence for citizenship, was evidence of their spirit.

DR. SMYTH: Oh, I concede that there is something in the handsome theory. But if you come down to brass tacks, you see that
your precious Crèvecœur mentions only seven nationalities, all from
northwestern Europe. And he says nothing about the Negroes—
and there were more of them here in 1782 than there were of the
Dutch or Swedes or Germans or Irish or French, or all of these
nationalities put together. Anyway, being an American was relatively simple then. Now we have twenty, thirty, God knows how
many, nationalities represented in the people.

Besides, the real leaders of the early Republic did not believe in
this asylum business. I see that you have R. L. Garis' book, *Immigration Restriction,* on the same shelf with Crèvecœur's *Letters.*
Hand it here and let me read you two quotations from that book,
the first from George Washington, written when he was President,
and the second from Thomas Jefferson's *Notes on Virginia,* written about 1782, as I remember from college browsing.

What did Washington say on immigration? Here it is:

> I have no intention to invite immigrants, even if there are no re-
> strictive acts against it. I am opposed to it altogether. . . . I want an
> *American* character, that the powers of Europe may be convinced we
> act for *ourselves* and not for others. This, in my judgment, is the
> only way to be respected abroad and happy at home.

Now for Jefferson on immigration [Dr. Smyth went on]—this is
what he said:

> Every species of government has its specific principles. Ours, per-
> haps, are more peculiar than those of any other. It is a composition of
> the freest principles of the English constitution with others derived
> from natural right and natural reason. To these nothing can be more
> opposed than the maxims of absolute monarchies. Yet, from such we
> are to expect the greatest number of immigrants. They will bring with
> them the principles of the governments they leave, or if able to throw
> them off, it will be in exchange for an unbounded licentiousness, pass-
> ing, as usual, from one extreme to the other. It would be a miracle
> were they to stop precisely at the point of temperate liberty. These
> principles, with their language, they will transmit to their children. In

proportion to their numbers, they will share legislation with us. They will infuse into it their spirit, warp or bias its direction, and render it a heterogeneous, incoherent, distracted mass.

You can quote your French Crèvecœur. I prefer Washington and Jefferson. We violated their warnings, and Jefferson's prediction has come true. I do not say with Hamilton that your people is a great beast, but rather with Jefferson that it is an incoherent and distracted mass. I know that Congress has attempted to correct, by recent immigration acts, the mistakes of a century. I know too that the State Department has often played fast and loose with the immigration laws, keeping out friends of the Republic and letting in enemies, for instance, White Russians, German Nazis, Italian Fascists, and Communists. But it is all too little and all too late to transform the boardinghouse into a nation.

BEARD: With your particular facts, Doctor Smyth, I do not quarrel. Your opinions you are entitled to propound; that is in our agreement for our fireside seminar. But even to your opinions I have an answer. You claim to be a realist in everything, including your medicine. If you find a sick man you do not say to him, 'Your grandfather ought to have come to America in 1607 or 1620,' or 'your grandmother ought to have been a Scot.' If there is any chance of saving his life, you do not roar at him, 'It is too late.' You try your level best to find out what is wrong with him; you choose the medicine best adapted to restore him to health; and you prescribe a diet and a regimen of life for him. You may fail to cure him, with all your skill, but you stick at the task. I remember that old bum, Bill Walters, who was found drunk and half-frozen on the edge of town two years ago. You took him to the hospital, visited him about every day for a month or more, paid the hospital's and the nurses' bills, pulled him through, and then got him a light job as watchman at your plant.

But don't misunderstand me. I am not comparing the people with old Bill Walters. I do not deny that they are as sick as you claim. For the sake of the argument I concede that they have all the faults you have set down on your list. But I maintain that, in spite of everything, the people composed of many nationalities have kept the Republic going for more than a hundred and fifty years, and that it has taken an immense amount of virtue to perform this single feat. I invite your attention to two facts: first, the men who tried to break up the Union in 1861 were, most of them, your noble Anglo-Saxons, or at least of British descent; and second, the Grand Army of the Republic was crowded with immigrants and the sons of immigrants from Ireland, Germany, and other parts of Europe.

If this seems recrimination, I will ask the jury to forget it, as judges sometimes say at trials. My point is that you should apply your medical realism to this business of the people. Here we are, about 135,000,000 of us, of many races and nationalities, varying degrees of intelligence and ignorance, characters good, bad and indifferent, many of us lazy and foolish, many more—most of us, I think—industrious and eager to accomplish something good for ourselves and our country.

The only issue I can see that has any sense in it is this: Where do we go from here? How are we going to get along together the best we can without fighting over every difference of national origins or personal opinion that divides us; maintain the Republic one and indivisible; keep alive and growing those sentiments of justice, decency, fair play and tolerance necessary to social living; increase knowledge; sharpen our intelligence; preserve and promote liberty; beat off all forces tending to despotism; stimulate co-operation in all matters of common interest; make the most of our opportunities where we are, as we are?

It was this question that led me to start this discussion-course with the words, We, the People of the United States, in the Preamble to the Constitution, not merely because they are in that instrument of self-government, but because they must stand at the beginning of all informed thought about the Republic. If you will not fling the word mysticism at me again, I will say it is interesting that the document which is to this day the pledge and symbol of our unity opens with We, the People of the United States . . . , that the people are still here, and that they come within the purview of the rights, liberties, and duties which the Constitution prescribes for our guidance. Furthermore, I am going to try to show that the Constitution is a living thing.

Dr. SMYTH, laughing: Very well. If you keep your feet on earth and don't fly off into the blue with the American dream, you may have the floor as long as you want it. Just remember that I do not care for Fourth of July sentimentality or poetic effusions that overlook divisions, sickness, poverty, degradation, stupidity, and folly right here among the people of the United States.

And please remember, said MRS. SMYTH, what you said about including women among the people.

BEARD: You are right, my friends, when you insist that we should keep our little boat close to the shore lines of reality. I shall try my utmost to do my part. Out of the various conflicting views of the Constitution, out of the conflicting interests that have claimed special privileges under it, out of the opposing opinions expressed about its meaning and the meaning of its clauses, out of this welter, I shall try to offer something substantial on which general agreement may be reached as to the very essentials of the Constitution—a written text, a body of practices, and a prophecy of the Republic for the ages. If I seem to be putting out to sea in a fog, tell me quickly. That will be a fine thing about the give-and-take of our fireside experiment.

II

Establish this Constitution . . .

THE second Friday night was stormy out of doors, and even by the fireside a tempest brewed as our discussion got under way. But having resolved to keep our arguments within the limits of conversation, we undertook to hold our minds to the subject of the Constitution as a plan of government and liberty for the Republic.

We, the people, I began, have a covenant to live together in a reasonable way, to govern ourselves in the civilian way, to adjust our conflicts of ideas and interests by civilian methods, all for the great purposes announced in the Preamble to the Constitution. This Constitution so established, this written document, is our covenant for these ends, and . . .

DR. SMYTH: Do you mean the Constitution just as it stands? The lawyers' document, never to be changed one jot or tittle? If so, we might as well adjourn right now. That would be like practicing medicine on a theory more than one hundred and fifty years old, tying ourselves down to the ideas of men long in their graves. Such a monstrous doctrine means that there is to be no progress in knowledge, no improvement in methods, a blind adherence to ancient history, a servile reliance on the fathers of the Republic instead of on ourselves. You talk like an old fundamentalist. Either that or there is an intractable opposition between science and what you call politics.

BEARD: Many people besides yourself have called me an old fundamentalist for my emphasis on historical experience and the writings of the fathers. Others have called me an anarchist for my insistence on individual liberty or on the necessity and often the desirability of change. And both types of critics have assumed that there is here a real contradiction of thought, as if there could be no change amid permanence and no permanence amid change, no interpenetration or reconciliation of the two at any point of time or place, or in any degree. Such critics bring the charge of inconsistency or weakness of mind against a person who at one time defends something old and at another time demands radical changes in existing practices.

Mrs. Smyth: Is a balance possible? Can the pendulum stop swinging?

Beard: Whether a balance is possible or not—that question we shall consider later—calling persons fundamentalists or progressives or radicals, without immediate and specific discriminations, seems to me to be unreal, just shadowboxing. And as to Dr. Smyth's demand for a science, we might as well understand right now that politics is not a natural science, like physics, or even medicine. That, too, we shall consider later. For the moment I shall merely give some simple illustrations of the relations between permanence and change and refrain from discussing the philosophy of a very complicated question.

Without some permanent habits, sentiments, and attitudes, any person would be a lunatic. Is any one so conservative that he will not accept a single change in anything he uses or in any of his habits, sentiments, or ideas? You, Dr. Smyth, do not call yourself an anachronism (a Tory, a dead one) because you brush your teeth regularly. You intend to keep up the custom, I assume, as long as you have teeth to brush. Another permanent habit, or principle, with you, is to treat your patients, and even strangers, courteously. Society would go to pieces, life would be a bedlam, if it were not for our fairly permanent habits as people. If you could not count on anybody's doing anything today the way he did it yesterday, your world would be a madhouse. And if nobody ever made any changes in things and habits, life would end for everyone.

Dr. Smyth: True enough. I see the point when you put it in kindergarten language. I yield the floor to hear your discourse on the nature of constitutional government which combines permanence with provisions for progress—something immortal like our hills amid our changing ways of life.

Mrs. Smyth: The theme of government by civilian as distinguished from military methods concerns me even more than this combination of permanence and progress. For I often wonder about the propensity of men to resort to violence in carrying on debates and trying to settle their differences. It seems to me that, by the nature of her functions in society, woman has been a conservator of life, given to making pacific adjustments such as the Constitution, as you explain it, evidently contemplates.

BEARD: Let me go into some detail. It will take me several minutes. If I become tedious, you may protest of course. I do not mean that we are bound to accept as permanent the very words of the Constitution as they are written on parchment or printed on paper. The document itself forbids that idea. Article V provides for changing the Constitution. Furthermore, the language of the Constitution on many matters is so broad that the people and their government may achieve almost any great ends of general welfare without altering a line in the document.

It is not as a lawyers' document, as you call it, Doctor, with every *t* crossed and every *i* dotted, that I regard our covenant. The bond of our covenant is the principle of constitutional government. That principle is a permanent principle even though constitutions as documents may be scrapped or burned, and the principle of tyranny, however phrased, set up in its place. The principle of constitutional government will always exist, we may assume, as an idea or ideal, to be contrasted with the authoritarian principle of despotism.

MRS. SMYTH: I am eager to have this immortal principle of constitutionalism succinctly stated!

BEARD: I will attempt to meet your challenge in this fashion. Constitutionalism embraces four necessary elements: (1) the great rules for governing ourselves shall be made by the process of proposal, discussion, and popular decision at the polls; (2) the powers of all officials shall be restrained by fundamental rights reserved to the people; (3) all officials exercising power shall be chosen by the voters, directly or indirectly; and (4) directly elected persons, having limited powers for a term of years, shall be automatically subjected to review at elections held periodically.

The principle of constitutionalism, composed of these four essential elements, is in eternal contradiction to the principle of authoritarian, totalitarian, dictatorial government. The principle of despotic government denies that the people are fit to govern themselves. It affirms that they are to be governed by the person or clique who can seize power by intrigue or open violence; that the people have no rights the despot is bound to respect; that dictatorship is to be limited, if at all, only by such rules as the dictator may choose in his whim to lay down.

There is more to constitutionalism than my brief definition indicates, but it may serve as an essential point for our discussion of the Republic. The principle of civilian supremacy which I have stated is a kind of beacon to light our way.

DR. SMYTH: Under your definition of constitutionalism, however, what becomes of the right of change by revolution? I am probably a bit sensitive on that point, for leaders of secession in my state, South Carolina, sometimes justified their action by appeals to the right of revolution as well as to the rights of states under the Constitution. It has always seemed to me that, even if the view of the Constitution that Lincoln expounded is accepted for the sake of argument, my ancestors were warranted in appealing to a right older than the Constitution—a right above or beyond the Constitution. The Declaration of Independence says something about the lofty right of revolution, if I remember my history.

BEARD: You do remember your history; and, since you raise an important point, Doctor, let us turn to that immortal Declaration and look at it line by line. It does not assert a miscellaneous or absolute right of revolution, without reference to reasons and ends. And it does not assert the right of an individual or a group to make a revolution for the mere purpose of seizing power and exercising power at their pleasure, for the accomplishment of their designs.

The section, so much talked about and so little read, runs:

We hold these truths to be self-evident: that all men are created equal; that they are endowed by their Creator with certain unalienable rights; that among these are life, liberty, and the pursuit of happiness. That, to secure these rights, governments are instituted among men, deriving their just powers from the consent of the governed; that, whenever any form of government becomes destructive of these ends, it is the right of the people to alter or to abolish it, and to institute a new government, laying its foundation on such principles, and organizing its powers in such form, as to them shall seem most likely to effect their safety and happiness. Prudence, indeed, will dictate, that governments long established should not be changed for light and transient causes; and accordingly all experience hath shown that mankind are more disposed to suffer while evils are sufferable, than to right themselves by abolishing the forms to which they are accustomed.

But when a long train of abuses and usurpations, pursuing invariably the same object, evinces a design to reduce them under absolute despotism, it is their right, it is their duty, to throw off such government and to provide new guards for their future security.

The Declaration of Independence, you see, does not proclaim the right of a tyrant and his gang to alter or abolish one government and institute another on the ground that they want power. It declares that the purpose of government is to secure the rights of life, liberty, and the pursuit of happiness for the people; that when any government becomes destructive of these ends, the people have the right to alter or abolish it and set up another.

But the new government is to carry out the purpose of government so defined; it is to be subordinate to the people's safety and happiness. Prudence, the Declaration of Independence says, suggests that a profound change in government, such as revolution, should not be made for light and transient causes. Note the language, 'when a long train of abuses and usurpations' reveals a determination to establish over the people an 'absolute despotism,' it is their right and duty to overthrow such a government and provide new guards for their security.

The Doctor suspects all talk about morals, and I share his suspicions in some ways, but the Declaration of Independence rests at bottom on moral grounds.

Dr. and Mrs. Smyth, in amazement: Moral grounds!

Dr. Smyth: I was taught to think of it as resting on rights given to us by nature and as directed to practical ends.

Beard: Well, it repudiates sheer force as a right and an end in itself. It was framed as a justification for the American Revolution against a foreign government and had practical ends in view. It approved revolution only as the last resort even against despotism and affirmed more than the right to revolt. It declared that revolution must be associated with the true ends of government—the moral objectives of life, liberty, and the pursuit of happiness.

Dr. Smyth: Yes, but isn't there also something in this Declaration of Independence about the right to life, liberty, and property?

Beard: No. You must be thinking about the French Declaration of the Rights of Man. That was proclaimed later—in 1789—thirteen years after the American Declaration. The French Declaration asserted that the rights of man are 'liberty, property, security, and resistance to oppression.' There was an immense difference in the two Declarations—the difference between European and American ideals at that time.

Gilbert Chinard, in his book on Thomas Jefferson who was mainly responsible for the language of the American proclamation, explains the difference. He says that the French philosophers were too pessimistic to think that man could ever be happy; they could only hope that man might be less unhappy. 'The whole Christian civilization,' Chinard adds, 'had been built on the idea that happiness is neither desirable nor obtainable in this vale of tears, but as compensation Christianity offered eternal life and bliss after death.'

Chinard goes on to say that he cannot conceive of anyone's proclaiming the pursuit of happiness anywhere in the world in the eighteenth century, except in the new world with its pioneering spirit. Lafayette, after his experience in America, drafted a declaration of rights for France in which he included the words *la recherche du bonheur,* the search for happiness, but his proposed declaration was rejected and the idea found its way into none of the three official Declarations of the French Revolution.

MRS. SMYTH: Then we were quite Greek, were we not? The Greeks freely used the word happiness, or their equivalent for it. The idea seemed to come naturally to them. Is that due to their paganism? Were they just heathen?

BEARD: The idea is as old as the Greeks, but the Greek philosophers associated it with the good life for a few, whereas to eighteenth-century Americans the idea of happiness represented a larger vision —the good of the many. Anyway, the Declaration of Independence made a bold departure from political tradition by omitting a mention of property and by making life, liberty, and the pursuit of happiness the great ends of government. Jefferson did not originate the idea of government as a guardian of happiness, but he stood for it. However, we are getting away from constitutionalism, I fear.

DR. SMYTH: Before you get back to your lawyers' document, Beard, I want to know more about this right of revolution in the Declaration. It seems to me that ever since Jefferson's day appeals have been made to it, and I think they are not to be so easily dismissed.

BEARD: True, Doctor, there has been a great amount of talk about the right of revolution, down to our own time. In fact, until near the close of the nineteenth century that right was openly proclaimed time and time again. It is only since we have acquired an army of witch-hunters, male and female, that it has become generally unconstitutional and subversive, in fact unlawful, to espouse the right of revolution in the United States. It makes Republicans angry to remind them of it now, but their saint, Abraham Lincoln, declared in his first inaugural address that:

. . . this country, with its institutions, belongs to the people who inhabit it. Whenever they shall grow weary of the existing Government, they can exercise their *constitutional* right of amending it, or their *revolutionary* right to dismember or overthrow it.

It is well that you called a halt for a further consideration of this matter, Doctor and Mrs. Smyth. I should not have said that we were getting far away from constitutionalism while we were dealing with the right of revolution. Whether any person will be able to bring it up in the future again in public—or in private either—will depend on what is done with freedom of press and speech. I am inclined to the opinion of Madison, the father of the Constitution, when he said, in effect, that the right of revolution exists, but that those who propose to exercise it should be prepared for the consequences of failure.

Mrs. Smyth: There is physical nature to reckon with and human nature, as well as right. Whether the right of revolution exists or not, whether it is recognized or not, some people will get together, talk about it, and plan revolution. You may insist that they have no right to do this, but saying it will not prevent their doing it if they are so minded.

Beard: Very true, of course. Individuals and groups have done it under every kind of government, in times of peace and in times of war. Under despotic systems, the state police will pounce upon revolutionaries as soon as news of their operations leaks out, or as soon as suspects can be located. Under federal law, as it now stands, loose talk about revolution is allowed; but, if men or women openly call for the overthrow of government by revolution or join organizations formed for that purpose, they are likely to suffer fine and imprisonment.

But let us not drift into the discussion of revolution itself and thus depart from the subject of tonight—the Constitution, the civilian way of governing ourselves. The theme of revolution we shall take up again later, under the head of the right of free speech and press.

DR. SMYTH, not quite ready for that postponement: Then you agree with the late Calvin Coolidge, that 'we have had our revolution' and don't propose to stand any more?

BEARD: No, I am saying that our system of government is constitutional, in the sense in which I have defined that term. It presents an eternal contradiction to despotic and irresponsible government, such as Caesar's or Napoleon's or Hitler's.

DR. SMYTH, thinking he had found an academic fixation in my mind: Of course our system presents that contradiction. We all know it. Why make it a point? There has never been any likelihood of a dictatorship here. With all their faults the American people have never been that kind of people, and they are not likely to stand for a despotism after all their centuries of freedom. There will be no excuse for such a coup d'état. We got through the eighteenth-century revolution without despotism and through the civil war also. We are not likely to become despotic now.

BEARD: Yes, we did get through the war against Britain without producing a Caesar or a Cromwell or a Napoleon. But it was a narrow squeak. Still the squeak gave distinction to the American Revolution—setting it off from other great upheavals in history. Leaders among the framers of the Constitution regarded the resort to constitutional government instead of a military dictatorship as their greatest triumph. In my opinion they were entitled to view their achievement in that way.

MRS. SMYTH: That is something else that was not in our history books or research assignments at college. I recall that Washington received dictatorial power during the war for independence and that there was some talk of setting up a monarchy afterward, but it is news to me that any Americans seriously thought of a wholesale military dictatorship. Why haven't we heard more of it, if it was a fact?

BEARD: I am unable to answer that Why. I stick to the fact. The power vested in Washington as commander in chief of the Revolutionary Army was given to him by the Continental Congress. He did not seize it himself, without civilian authorization. Twice, in 1776 and in 1777, Congress gave him almost plenary powers. At the conclusion of the war, if he had become drunk with power, he might have refused to surrender his sword. He might have tried to make himself a dictator in a time of peace.

But Washington was no Caesar or Cromwell at heart. That is to his everlasting credit. Though he had their actions as precedents, he spurned their examples as foreign to his spirit and his idea of the trust vested in him; as alien to the cause to which he had dedicated his life and fortunes. Nor am I laying too much stress on two attempts made in the Virginia Legislature to create a dictator, the first in 1776 and the second (which lacked only a few votes of passing) in 1781.

What I am referring to is a movement—one neglected by American historians—for a permanent military dictatorship, or rather a number of underground movements or demands looking in that direction, which took form during and after the war. These movements differed from the proposals to set up a monarchy, which have received more or less attention from historians. They were entirely apart from the action of the Congress in twice conferring upon Washington special powers. They represented a hang-over of historic despotism, a penchant for the crude way of dealing with social disturbances, a distrust of popular reason and discussion as means of government.

But those underground movements have not been dealt with in any systematic fashion in written histories of that revolution. In truth, little study of them seems to have been made. It was during my searches among the manuscripts and other papers of that period, extending over many years, that I came across references to demands or schemes for a thoroughgoing military dictatorship—that is for a seizure of power and the institution of a government resting on the sword instead of popular consent.

At first I paid scant attention to them, but eventually I had collected so many notes on this subject that I became impressed by the number and variety of such demands or schemes. Then I began more systematic researches into this matter. They are by no means complete, but I am now convinced that many men associated with the revolutionary cause expected, or wanted, the civil discord which attended and followed the American war against Britain to end in the establishment of a government dominated by military force.

This espousal of dictatorial methods by many Americans sets in fuller light the final decision in favor of constitutionalism, continuing the constitutionalism displayed by General Washington during the war. It gives a larger and truer background for appreciating the way in which the will to exalt civilian power above military force was ultimately asserted. It makes this eighteenth-century attempt to institute government by plan, proposal, discussion, and popular decision appear in its extraordinary historic significance, with all the lessons for us implicit therein. But you may think that I am lingering over dead history, as many of our fellow citizens do when I remind them again and again of the founding fathers.

The Doctor and Mrs. Smyth, with more than amiability, I felt sure, urged me to go on.

BEARD: Well, let me give you just a few illustrations of the kind of despotic temper the fathers confronted. In 1782 Col. Lewis Nicola, of Pennsylvania, a writer of military manuals, an officer in the Revolutionary Army, sent a letter to General Washington in which he said that he was no ardent admirer of the republican form of government, and that 'the war must have shown to all, but to military men in particular, the weakness of republics.' The Colonel then proposed that territory be set aside for soldiers and governed as military men might decide. To this letter Washington replied in a tempest of scorn and wrath that must have struck the Colonel speechless.

In the same year, 1782, General James M. Varnum, a Rhode Island lawyer, and soldier of the Revolution, wrote to Washington:

> The citizens at large are totally destitute of that love of equality which is absolutely requisite to support a democratic Republic. . . . Consequently, absolute monarchy or a military State, can alone rescue them from the horrors of subjugation.

Another officer of the Revolutionary Army informed Washington in 1787 that 'some principal men' of Massachusetts 'begin to talk of wishing one general *Head* to the Union, in the room of Congress.'

In fact, Washington's manuscripts in the Library of Congress and elsewhere contain many letters from his associates and acquaintances reporting or favoring movements for the erection of a government by arbitrary methods. Letters of this character were so numerous that he became thoroughly alarmed. Despite his longing for the peace of retirement to his plantation, he energetically sought to avert a renewed civil war by a resort to constitutional methods—

the creation of a new Constitution dedicated to government by proposal, discussion, and popular consent. If, as I believe, constitutionalism represents the highest type of government, then to Washington must be accorded the highest honors in the history of revolutionary leadership.

One more example, while we are on the theme of a possible dictatorship in America. In 1788 a constitutional convention was assembled in New York to reject or ratify the new Constitution proposed for the United States. On the floor of that convention, Governor George Clinton, one of the members, declared that in 1780-81 there

was a dangerous attempt to subvert our liberties by creating a supreme dictator. There are many gentlemen present who know how strongly I opposed it. . . . We were surrounded with difficulties and danger. The people when wearied with their distresses, will, in a moment of frenzy, be guilty of the most imprudent and desperate measures.

Alexander Hamilton, a member of the same convention, replied that he had known about 'this mad project,' that he had opposed it, and that it did not ripen into a 'deliberate and extensive design.'

My more recent studies of the times which saw the formation of the Constitution have given me a somewhat different view of the movement for the Constitution. One of the interpretations now generally held is that the Constitution was the outcome of a conflict between radical or agrarian forces on the one side and the forces of conservative or capitalistic reaction on the other. That conflict was undoubtedly raging, and the advocates of the Constitution were involved in it.

But I am of the opinion that there were three parties to the struggle. Besides the radicals and the conservatives there was an influential group on the extreme right of the conservatives—a group that was ripe and ready for a resort to the sword, especially after Daniel Shays and his followers in Massachusetts had taken up arms against the grinding creditors and the bigots who would yield nothing. Had the movement for forming a new Constitution by peaceful processes failed, there is no doubt in my mind that the men of the sword would have made a desperate effort to set up a dictatorship by arms. They would have tried to induce Washington to head up the struggle. But in vain, I believe.

Dr. Smyth: Why do you feel certain?

BEARD: Here are the reasons. A careful examination of all Washington's letters that are now available to students of history reveals that he strongly deplored all proposals looking to such high-handed actions. Judging by his letters, the dictatorial spirit in government was not in him. The examples of Caesar and Cromwell carried no appeal for him. He would have deemed an end in a military dictatorship as a demonstration that the Revolution was a complete failure, that all the labors and sacrifices of the war had been futile. I believe that the spirit reflected in his letters was genuine.

MRS. SMYTH: But just suppose he had been willing to lead the third party of extreme reaction; what then?

BEARD: I have more than my personal opinion to offer in reply. On that very point we have the testimony of James Madison, who knew Washington intimately. Madison took exception to the remark of one Henry Coleman in an oration on the fiftieth anniversary of the Declaration of Independence that it was a tribute to the virtue and valor of the Revolutionary army that the soldiers readily laid down their arms 'when they had the liberties of their Country within their grasp.' Madison said:

I cannot but regard [it] as at variance with reality. . . . Is it a fact that they had the liberties of their country within their grasp; that the troops then in command, even if led on by their illustrious chief, and backed by the apostates from the revolutionary cause, could have brought under the yoke the great body of their fellow Citizens. . . ?

In Madison's judgment it was not a fact. He had evidently thought of that contingency, terrible as it was, and he gave his matured views as follows:

I have always believed that if General Washington had yielded to a usurping ambition, he would have found an insuperable obstacle in the incorruptibility of a sufficient portion of those under his command, and that the exalted praise due to him and them was derived not from a forbearance to effect a revolution within their power, but from a love of liberty and of country which, there was abundant reason to believe, no facility of success could have seduced. I am not less sure that General Washington would have spurned a scepter if within his grasp, than I am that it was out of his reach if he had secretly sighed for it.

In short, Madison was convinced that the independent character of the overwhelming majority of the people was such as to make necessary the resort to peaceful and popular processes when the formation of the Constitution was attempted.

DR. SMYTH: In the light of this story, which is novel to me, are you just as certain that, in another civil crisis as great or greater, changes as momentous can be effected by constitutional processes?

BEARD: Of the future we cannot be certain. We can only speculate and hope. It was partly for this reason that your proposal to discuss the present crisis interested me. It is for this reason especially that, in my judgment, no other theme of national policy is so important for us as constitutionalism—the civilian way of living together in the Republic, the way of preserving our liberties and the decencies of social intercourse against the frenzies of the despotic and violent temper. How to preserve the idea of constitutional processes and keep it anchored firmly in the minds and affections of succeeding generations—that is the task of the present and future, a task of civilization, supreme over all others.

We closed there, with that question to mull over before our next session.

But Doctor Smyth turned back at the door to say: By the way, Beard, would it be taking advantage of your hospitality if we brought with us next Friday a dyed-in-the-wool Jeffersonian Democrat, William Robinson, who is coming to us for the week-end? We should appreciate it if you would let him sit in and chip in if he is so inclined.

BEARD, gratefully: That would no doubt be to my advantage.

As a Jeffersonian Democrat, doubtless your friend, Mr. Robinson, will want to lay emphasis on democracy and rights rather than on constitutionalism. If so, I shall have no objection to it. We shall examine the relations of the one to the other.

DR. SMYTH, waving his hand: Your remark suggests something that I had already begun to turn over in my mind.

III

Democracy and Rights
under the Constitution

THE Smyths arrived for the third Friday night, accompanied by their week-end guest, the Jeffersonian Democrat, William Robinson, who appeared to accept at once their peculiar way of entertaining him. He had neither the face of silence nor was he speechless. Indeed he proved to be a lively fourth member of our fireside seminar.

DR. SMYTH, opening the discussion: After we got home the last time, Sue and I, over our glasses of sherry, worked ourselves into confusion again and into some heat over three words or phrases which had been used here. One was democracy. Another was rights The third was constitutionalism. Perhaps we don't understand. Doesn't democracy include and cover both rights and constitutionalism? Or couldn't you define democracy in a way to embrace rights and constitutionalism? We do not want to trail off into a side path. To us this is sticking to the main line. So will you tell us just what is meant by democracy and rights, if they are two separate things. instead of inseparable?

When I replied that there is no main line in the subject of human government, their backs stiffened as if in resistance.

BEARD: Everybody who talks or writes about it makes his own. line. The more he knows and thinks the more certain he is to make his own line.

Then, to meet their question squarely—What is democracy?—I went to my files and brought out an armful of folders bulging with notes headed: *History and meaning of the word Democracy, from its origins in the English language to the year 1942.*

MRS. SMYTH: This reminds me of the way my professor, Lucy Salmon, at Vassar, used to treat our questions at college. No matter how simple a question was, she always had a ton of notes available and proceeded to make it complicated.

BEARD, joining in the laughter: Yet Lucy Salmon was sagacious as well as learned! I knew her well and respected her immensely as a first-rate thinker and a hard worker in the field of history. You asked me about democracy. You say you want to know what it means. Shall I try to answer you merely by guessing, by expressing an offhand opinion growing out of my own emotions or derived from reading the last edition of a newspaper, or from listening to the latest blast over the radio? Even the best of dictionaries, I have found by experience, are unsatisfactory for the meaning of the leading words used in the humanities. I know only one way to attempt to answer. That is to search for the origin of the word and explore its usage by persons of some intelligence up to our time.

Furthermore, I regard the minute exploration of the meanings of the primary words we use in discussing public affairs as an intellectual operation absolutely necessary to any fruitful and effective consideration of vital issues in our Republic. If there is not exactness in our terms, we talk *past* one another and up in the air, not *on* our subject.

The study of the history of ideas and their enclosing words as used in history is one of the most neglected types of inquiry in the United States. . . .

MRS. SMYTH: Oh, yes. I heard that you had once written a whole book on one idea—the idea of national interest in the United States.

BEARD: Was it really a waste of time on my part? Don't most Americans think that anyone who talks ought to know what he is talking about? Isn't that maxim a part of our folklore? Take democracy, liberty, freedoms, and all the other words that roll out in speeches, writings, and radio broadcasts. How few people who use them have ever spent a single hour studying their meanings, even in dictionaries! If we don't know what we are talking *with,* how can we know what we are talking *about?*

DR. SMYTH, grinning: Shoot. We are in for that and ready. In truth, that is why we are here—to get more than a hunch or a grouch or an opinion or a snap phrase on such an idea as democracy.

MRS. SMYTH: *We* really means *me* too. And you need not try to make your answer painless.

MR. ROBINSON: Like painless dentistry. Unless you can take the word of a Jeffersonian Democrat instead of many words from the mountain of notes in those files.

BEARD: Well, I shall not read them all to you, but just give you what I can as a clue to the problem of defining democracy. It is a problem, after all. We shall express mere prejudices if we go at the definition blindly.

MR. ROBINSON, almost shouting: Honestly now, Professor, have you worked up all those documents just hunting for that word?

BEARD, in turn emphatic: Yes, I have! How can we know what democracy has meant and means unless we explore the use of the term in our history? It is true, of course, that I have doubtless missed some important definitions of the word.

At any rate, here is what my research has discovered, in summary. The word democracy had come into the English language by the opening years of the sixteenth century, borrowed from a union of two Greek roots relative to people and authority or government. As it was early used by persons who wrote English it meant to them the kind of government which existed in Athens and other city states of antiquity; that is, direct government by enfranchised citizens, talking and voting in open-air meetings. At the outset the word democracy had no good or evil flavor in English usage.

But when the English started on the course of fierce quarreling that ended in the Cromwellian revolution of the seventeenth century, the word democracy took on the tone of the social war. Conservatives then employed it to signify government by the rabble, as they called the people at large. For them that was the worst possible form of government they could imagine—sheer disorder leading to the destruction of law, peace, and property. On the other hand, the radicals in the revolutionary upheaval took the side of the people at large and often went so far as to idealize the masses that conservatives called the rabble. Among the English radicals who adopted the word democracy there was a leveling tendency that ran in the direction of communism.

DR. SMYTH: And the radicals were called Levelers, were they not?

BEARD: Some were. From England, in that revolutionary seventeenth century, the idea and the word democracy were brought across the sea to our new world. For some of the English colonists in America it was a fighting word. Those dauntless radicals, followers of Roger Williams and Anne Hutchinson, at Rhode Island and Providence, called the system of government which they erected there, off in the wilderness, a democratie. But to the elders who had evicted them from Massachusetts and for the majority of writers, preachers, and ladies in all parts of America then, democracy was a fearful and hateful word and idea. In general it remained such until long after the American Revolution.

Our Revolution, like the earlier one in England, shook society from top to bottom. Tory preachers and writers on the eve of our Revolution warned the Whigs and patriots against the perils of democracy in their course. Democracy still carried such a dangerous or dubious flavor that it was not used at all in the Declaration of Independence or in any of the great state papers of the Revolution or in any of the first state constitutions. It did not appear in the Constitution of the United States.

During and after the Revolution more and more people took a lively part in political discussions. Free-lance writers, such as Tom Paine, the evangelist of the Revolution, and Mercy Warren, critical historian of the Revolution—note that the women were doing it too—joined preachers, lawyers, planters, and merchants in debates on government and social affairs. Here and there some became bold enough to call themselves democrats and face the music.

But a majority of the men who used the word in the convention that framed the Constitution continued to view democracy as something rather to be dreaded than encouraged. Until well into the nineteenth century, the word was repeatedly used by conservatives to smear opponents of all kinds, whatever the grounds of the differences in opinion.

Thomas Jefferson, unless my eyes failed me, never used the word in any of his public papers or publicly called himself a democrat.

Mr. Robinson definitely raised his eyebrows at that, but he delayed cross-questioning me.

Beard: Neither did James Madison, and, still more surprising, neither did Andrew Jackson.

Mrs. Smyth: But Jefferson was a great letter writer. Did he write something about democracy in his letters?

Beard: In his letters, Jefferson did occasionally use the word.

When he did, as a rule he applied it to direct government by voters in a small community only—as in the New England town meeting, so different from the Virginia system. On one occasion at least he made democracy identical with a republic.

While plain people were steadily adopting the name of democrats for themselves, politicians slowly fell into line. Clubs and local party groups began to take form in several states and style themselves democratic or democratic-republican. But Jefferson stuck to the name Republican for the party which finally lifted him to power. State and local organizations of that party took the name republican or democratic according to the degree of their radicalism or the nature of their sentiments.

As time passed, the word democratic seemed to gain on the word republican as the proper term for the party. But the party was still called by one or the other name or both hyphenated—the Democratic-Republican party. It was not, by any united action, called the Democratic party, for a long time. There was, indeed, no body empowered to give the party an official name until after the rise of the national convention in Jackson's day. And as late as 1840 the party of Jefferson and Jackson, in the resolutions of its convention, referred to 'the Democratic faith' and to 'their Republican fellow-citizens.' Not until 1844 did the Jefferson-Jackson party definitely and finally cut loose from the word Republican and call itself, by solemn resolution, in convention assembled, 'the American Democracy.'

MR. ROBINSON: Now you're telling us something! Now I see why you really felt it necessary to trace the use of that word in the historical records. I had not dreamed that it had such a bad odor in Jefferson's time, and that it was not more generally used to describe our system of government and our society at the time. Will you pardon me for asking a question at this moment? Was it actually the Democratic party that put the word democracy over on the country—making it first a party word and then a national word? Our great President, Woodrow Wilson, spoke of the war against Germany in 1917 as a war for democracy. Had he nothing more than a party sanction for calling America a democracy?

BEARD: Your question is pertinent, certainly, Mr. Robinson. If you will hold it for a few minutes, we shall go into that. Just a little more history first to make that matter clearer.

After the Jefferson-Jackson Republicans took the title 'the American Democracy' in 1844, that phrase, to the public, simply meant the Democratic party. It is true that many writers by that time spoke of the United States as a democracy, but that description was not universally accepted. Since the Democratic party had adopted the term for party purposes, its opponents could not very well call themselves democrats without becoming identified with the Democratic party.

Lincoln's party revived Jefferson's old title and called itself Republican. Though Lincoln himself occasionally used the word democracy and often expressed his faith in government of the people, the word does not appear in his great pronouncements, such as his First Inaugural or the Gettysburg Address. The word democracy was not for him the primary symbol that summed up the letter and spirit of the American system.

Nor did the Democratic party change that situation by its pressure on the Government. From the first election of Lincoln in 1860 to the election of Wilson in 1912, the Democratic party played a subordinate role in national politics. It carried only two presidential elections in all those years, in 1884 and 1892, with Cleveland as its leader.

If the indices to periodical literature are any basis of judgment, there was little general interest in democracy as the dominant characteristic, name, or symbol of American political and social faith between 1860 and 1917. Republican presidents still shrank from using the term in this broad sense. When James Bryce published his great treatise on the United States, in 1888, he entitled it *The American Commonwealth*. He did not use the title American Democracy, as Tocqueville, the French writer on America, had done fifty years before. Theodore Roosevelt, in his inaugural address of 1905, spoke of our 'democratic republic,' but the insertion of 'democratic' was exceptional for a President of the United States.

Mr. Robinson, in a tone of exultation: And so we come to my party's leader, President Wilson, now!

Beard: Nothing like official sanction was given to the idea that the United States is first and foremost a democracy until Woodrow Wilson, in making the war against the Central Powers a war for democracy, gave the stamp of wide popularity to the idea that the United States is, first and foremost, a democracy. In the circumstances, even Republicans could scarcely repudiate it without acquiring a subversive tinge.

Here endeth my historical review with this summary: Finally, by a long process, the idea of democracy, which had been spurned, if not despised, in the early days of our nation, by a majority of the people as well as by practically all high-born and conservative citizens, became generally, though not universally, recognized as the definition for the American way of life and our political system.

MRS. SMYTH: It's a strange and instructive story.

DR. SMYTH, in a philosophic mood: Well, it means that Americans have been borne along by an irresistible current to a goal they never set for themselves or for our nation.

MRS. SMYTH: All stories involve an ending, and the end of this story seems to be that there is nothing in our law or fixed tradition that commands us to call our country a democracy. In the course of events it has merely become popular to speak of the republic of the United States as a democracy. Am I warranted in seeing that end to the tale?

BEARD: But the word republic is not in the Constitution, either, Mrs. Smyth. In 1776 that word also had a bad odor. It does not appear in any of the first state constitutions. The federal Constitution does guarantee to each state a republican *form of government,* but what was meant by the term is nowhere explained in the Constitution. It early became a custom to refer to the United States as a Republic in some diplomatic and official papers, but the official title or style of our country is still The United States of America.

Speaking strictly, no law of the land officially declares us to be either a democracy or a republic. For a long time after the adoption of the Constitution, the word republic or republican was generally preferred in characterizing our system of government. Many conservatives still insist that it is only a republic, not a democracy. Democrats insist that it is a democracy, or a democratic republic. But there is no official warrant for either usage.

MRS. SMYTH: Well, I am surprised to hear that all Americans did not think of their country from the beginning of independence as a republic! You chose The Republic, as a center of gravity for our study course, as I remember, around which to keep our discussion revolving, in order to maintain a certain unity in it. Now you say that Americans have never officially entitled our system a Republic, that the word was not in the first state constitutions, and that the Constitution did not set up a republic.

BEARD: But I told you at our first session that the Constitution is a prophecy for the ages. The framers of the Constitution were, with perhaps two or three exceptions, all republicans in principle. The authors of *The Federalist* acknowledged that the axioms of republicanism were the accepted postulates of the Constitution. But if the framers of the Constitution had openly declared that 'We, the people, ordain and establish this Constitution for the Republic of the United States,' they would have frightened the advocates of states' rights with the specter of consolidation. By forming a stronger union, they forecast the consolidation to come and made it possible in the long course of time for the people to think of their country, one and indivisible, as a republic. Still there is nothing official about it. Some call it a democracy and others a republic. But the supreme law of the land does not establish either title as official.

MR. ROBINSON: That seems decidedly discouraging, unless my party can write the title of the party into the Constitution. If this is not done, somebody may come along and call our system a Socialist or Soviet Republic or a Communist Democracy, and there is apparently nothing in the supreme law to hinder them.

BEARD: But a name is not everything. While the intellectual and moral commitment of the people to the idea of democracy has progressed from repugnance or scant recognition to general acceptance, the actual law of the land has been moving in the democratic direction too. All presidential electors are now chosen, formally at least, by the voters of the several states instead of by the state legislatures, as the federal Constitution permits. Moreover, United States Senators, long elected by the state legislatures, are elected now by popular vote. There are other illustrations. For example, the Fourteenth and Fifteenth Amendments contemplate, though they do not force, the establishment of universal manhood suffrage. The Nineteenth Amendment declares that no citizen shall be denied the right to vote on account of sex, though it does not guarantee that every woman shall have the right to vote.

DR. SMYTH: Now we're getting to the constitutional aspect of democracy and rights, I see.

BEARD: As far as all important elections are concerned, the Fourteenth Amendment provides that if a state deprives adult male citizens of the right to vote, its representation in Congress shall be proportionately reduced. For practical or other purposes, however, the provision is a dead letter. States, North and South, actually deprive citizens, male and female, of the right to vote, by poll taxes, educational tests, and other devices. But Congress does not reduce their representation proportionately.

Mrs. SMYTH: So we are not out of the woods yet with respect to democracy and constitutionalism. I thought that the Constitution is the law of the land and that Congress and citizens are bound to obey it.

BEARD: They are bound theoretically. But as a matter of fact they sometimes ignore some of its provisions.

DR. SMYTH: I wonder if I could define democracy now, after this discussion?

He made several efforts and then tossed the ball back to me.

BEARD: How's this? As democracy has been conceived in the United States, it embraces certain elements.

First: People, not a legalized monarch or class, are the source of all political power. This does not necessarily mean all the people, but it has to mean a large proportion of them. How large a proportion is and perhaps always will be a matter of dispute. The voters directly choose the principal agents of government and, through their agents, indirectly, all other persons who have political power over life and property.

Second: Through agents chosen by the voters, all laws are made.

Third: At fixed periods all the chief agents of government, at least legislative and executive agents, must either retire or, if they seek continuance in power, must submit themselves and their actions to a popular review at the polls.

Fourth: In this process all voters are equal; that is, each one, without regard to intellectual, moral, or economic qualifications, has one vote and no more; and in elections, as a rule, the candidate who receives the highest number of votes, whether a majority or a plurality, is placed in office. All in all, democracy logically signifies equality in voting power, equality in the right to seek and hold office, and majority or plurality rule in elections.

This is a definition of democracy—that is political democracy—

in the United States. How fully and faithfully it is applied is a point outside the definition.

To this theory and its practice, however partial the practice may be, the people of the United States are now committed. Our system of theory and of practice stands in clear contradiction to all forms of fixed-class government, government by hereditary privilege, and tyrannical or dictatorial government. While there is a technical distinction between a tyranny and a dictatorship, the two have come to mean about the same thing in English. A tyrant or a dictator is the person who has seized political power by intrigue or force, who holds and exercises it absolutely at his own will or whim as long as he is physically or morally able, who is subject to no controls or restraints save fear, and who can be ousted only by revolution.

DR. SMYTH: Is there a sharp distinction between constitutionalism as you defined it at our second session and democracy as you are defining that tonight? If the voters, directly or through their agents, can, by a majority or plurality, decide on the form of government they wish, and, if they can make laws at will, can they not vote themselves a tyrant or a dictator and destroy all rights of persons and property at their pleasure?

MRS. SMYTH: Including life, liberty, and the pursuit of happiness?

DR. SMYTH: If my memory serves me, the first Napoleon was elected Emperor of the French by an overwhelming majority, and the third Napoleon was also elected by a huge majority. I do not see, in your mechanical democracy—one man, one vote; one woman, one vote; and majority rule—any guarantee whatever against tyrannical government, against the election of a demagogue or gang of demagogues who would end every human right in the country, especially all the rights of minorities. My father, who was a good old Cleveland Democrat, was always saying that a crowd could be as brutal as an individual tyrant, perhaps more brutal, and that he did not propose to prostrate himself before any majority if it trampled upon his rights.

BEARD: You are right, Doctor. Democracy, following the majority principle, does not guarantee the perpetuity of constitutional government. You have yourself answered the question you put at the very beginning of our session. I did not identify democracy with constitutional government. I did not make them one and the same thing.

Constitutional government necessarily implies a degree of democracy. But democracy, as majority or plurality rule, does not necessarily assure the supremacy of constitutional, that is civilian and limited, government under which provisions are made for the maintenance of human rights.

Under our system these human rights are defined and written down in the Constitution itself. They are thus put beyond the reach of ordinary majorities and pluralities; so that the voters cannot, as you suggested a moment ago they might, at ordinary elections vote themselves a tyrant and destroy all rights of person and property at their pleasure. If they were so moved, they could do this only by marshaling the extraordinary majority required to amend the Constitution.

Your father, Doctor, spoke not only like a Cleveland Democrat but also like a good old Jeffersonian Republican. Referring to the Virginia Legislature under the first state constitution, Jefferson exclaimed:

All the powers of government, legislative, executive, and judiciary, result to the legislative body. The concentrating these in the same hands is precisely the definition of despotic government. It will be no alleviation that these powers will be exercised by a plurality of hands, and not by a single one. One hundred and seventy-three despots would surely be as oppressive as one. Let those who doubt it turn their eyes on the republic of Venice. As little will it avail us that they are chosen by ourselves. An *elective despotism* was not the government we fought for, but one which should not only be founded on free principles, but in which the powers of government should be so divided and balanced among several bodies of magistracy, as that no one could transcend their legal limits, without being effectually checked and restrained by the others.

On this fundamental at least, I commented, Jefferson agreed with the stoutest Federalist.

Now, with what has just been said in mind, let us look again at constitutionalism. In my definition of it the other night I included the proposition that the powers of all officials are restrained by fundamental rights reserved to the people. Government is power.

But an essential to constitutional government is restraint on power, even the power of democracy. This restraint is expressed in constitutional provisions that can only be amended by extraordinary majorities; and it is also expressed in the organization of the government itself.

In our system the matured will of an undoubted and persistent majority large enough to amend the Constitution will prevail in the long run, unless checked by revolutionary resistance. According to this principle, the voters could vote themselves a despotism and perhaps force the acquiescence of the minority. This might be democracy under the mechanical theory, but it would certainly be a repudiation of constitutional government, and dangerous to individual rights, even if not utterly destructive. Most of what I have been saying bears on that distinction. Unquestionably we must link, in our thinking, constitutionalism with its guarantees of individual rights and democracy. But they are not synonymous. Indeed, they may be at war with each other.

MRS. SMYTH: This is where the issue of rights enters, I take it. You mean, I suppose, by restraints on governing officials, protection for our human rights. The Doctor and I were talking about them before we came here tonight. The suffragists always referred to woman's rights as natural rights and then often harked back to Tom Paine's *Rights of Man*. I have never examined that theory of natural rights. I have rather taken it for granted. And it never occurred to me that we might ever be facing the prospect of what Jefferson, you say, called an elective despotism. Still I do realize that there is much clamor even today about safeguarding rights, and it seems that I ought to be clear about them.

BEARD: It is true, Mrs. Smyth, that efforts have been made to give force to rights by calling them natural. That was an eighteenth-century custom. The clergy and monarchs claimed special rights as divine rights. The revolutionists resorted to nature. But let us go at this word analytically. The word natural does not mean that the forces of nature are all arrayed on the side of human rights. Natural, as so used, merely means, in effect, moral. A natural right is an asserted moral right, claimed by anybody who chooses to assert or claim. If enough people join in upholding the assertion or claim, such as the right to vote, for example—a thing nature did not provide—then that right has force and becomes a right respected by government and society.

In reality, no one possesses any real right or rights that he or she, in conjunction with others, cannot enforce against the community or government. All human rights rest on the moral standards of the community and the nation—on habits, sentiments, and practices favorable to the expression and enjoyment of such rights. But as such habits, sentiments, and practices change, concepts of natural rights also change.

DR. SMYTH: Humph! Then your political science is just a moral code. If so, we are sunk.

BEARD: It is not just a moral code or merely a moral code. There are many rules or principles in political science that are derived from hard human experience. They enable us to predict some results fairly well. Otherwise all government and administration would break down into chaos. Political science involves human beings, and human beings are moral beings. Note that I do not say righteous beings. If for decency, progress, order, and liberty in the community and the nation, we cannot rely upon the character, sentiments, allegiances, and moral habits of the people, upon what, in heaven's name, can we rely?

A long silence followed in the seminar. The fire crackled on the hearth. The clock ticked on the mantle. The Great Dane got up from his warm rug, stretched his legs, and walked out into the hall.

MR. ROBINSON: It's an awful thought to be deprived of Nature's sanction! But some communities or nations seem to have more political morality, as you call it, more capacity for self-government, for constitutional government, for self-restraint in the interest of general liberty, than other nations and communities. That is obvious. May not others develop that capacity? What I should like to know is how you account for the differences. And if a community or a nation is going down hill in political morality, what can be done about it, if anything? If workable answers cannot be found as to guarantees for human rights, are we not the sports of blind fate?

MRS. SMYTH: I don't believe that Mr. Beard's view or his political science is so deeply disheartening. In practical life we do not surrender to blind fate. Certainly rational people do not. They carry on. When our own little Johnny was desperately sick and the Doctor almost despaired of his life, we kept on fighting for it—fighting against fate with everything helpful that we could think of, and we kept on until he pulled through. There are many things that look like fate about which we seem helpless, which we feel we must endure, if we can, with all the courage we can summon. The Doctor often snorts about everything being fated and mechanistic. Yet he gets up every morning, early, and drives ahead at problems as if he could do something to solve them; and believe me, he does accomplish marvels.

BEARD: I am glad I have your support, Mrs. Smyth, for political morality. I know that the Doctor, one of the hardest-working and most moral men in this community, does not like to depend on morals for much of anything. I have heard him say that he suspects anybody who makes any public professions of virtue; that actions speak louder than words. I am chary about getting moral with him, but I have to stand by what I believe: namely, that rights rest at bottom on morals rather than on anything physical nature guarantees us.

The questions raised by Mr. Robinson about nations differing among themselves, and about improving the political morality of a nation that is decaying, call for answers which run deeply into the very character of all human history. I have no neat remedy to offer as a cure for degeneration. We ought to consider both questions, however. Let us come back to them later in our series of discussions, after we have covered some more concrete issues of government and rights.

A professor, you understand, even if unfrocked, simply has to be a bit systematic. Before I tackle the secret of the universe, which these questions have raised, I suggest that we go on searching for the essentials of constitutional government, of the civilian way in liberty and government.

If you survive this session, we shall examine next time examples in constitutional government set by three of our great Presidents—Washington, Jefferson, and Lincoln. I have said that the Constitution is a living instrument, a body of practices. You both complained that you hear so many abstractions over the radio, and certainly there is a tendency among speakers and writers to treat the Constitution as an abstraction, often to cover their own interests. It is for the purpose of giving a stronger basis of realism to our discussions that I intend to break our commentaries on the words of the Preamble and the provisions of the Constitution, by introducing these three great personalities and considering the ways in which they exemplified the terms of the written document.

MRS. SMYTH, as she drew on her coat: How different they were in experience, views, and times! We'll be back next Friday night, you can be sure.

IV

Washington and Jefferson Exemplify Constitutionalism

WHEN my interlocutors arrived, beaming, for our fourth session, I greeted them with the comment: You seem to be in high spirits tonight.

DR. SMYTH: Indeed we are! We have brought a Chinese puzzle, and we expect a good time watching you struggle with it. Here it is. How can you unite a planter-aristocrat, a slave-owning democrat, and a rail-splitting frontiersman—that is, Washington, Jefferson, and Lincoln—in a single picture of constitutionalism?

A long time ago I read a story about Washington that seemed to display in a flash his haughty attitude even toward his own associates, his lack of sympathy with plain people. As I recall the tale, Alexander Hamilton once declared that the closest of Washington's friends found him so reserved, so like an aristocrat, that none dared to address him in familiar terms. But a friend of Hamilton offered to bet that he was not afraid to slap the General on the back at his next public reception. The bet was taken. A few days later, when Washington was at a social gathering, Hamilton's friend went up to General Washington, shook his hand, and slapped him on the back, at the same time speaking to him as to a boon companion. Washington, amazed, retreated a few inches, drew up his shoulders, and froze the man in his tracks until he got strength enough to slink away in positive fright. There may be nothing in the yarn but that was a general feeling about Washington, was it not?

BEARD: The story seems to be true. At least its main features have been confirmed. The brash man who made the bet with Hamilton was Gouverneur Morris, a friend of Washington as well as of Hamilton, a distinguished gentleman himself. Certainly Washington was no democrat. His temper was aristocratic. The very word, democrat, seemed to represent in his mind the sum of political villainies.

And Martha, who stood beside him at his public receptions, was far from being a democrat. The two might have stood on a rather high platform to receive the public at official receptions if watchful radicals had not started a fierce debate on the propriety of such ceremonials, insisting that Washington and the First Lady must stand on a level with their fellows. A story about Martha's aristocratic feeling runs to the effect that one day, when she noticed a spot on the wall above a couch on which Nelly Custis, her niece, had been sitting with a caller, she exclaimed, 'None but a filthy democrat would mark a place with his good-for-nothing head in that manner.'

My friends, especially the Cleveland Democrat, Dr. Smyth, were surprised at Mrs. Washington's strong language about democrats, even though it seemed to match her husband's views on the subject.

Dr. Smyth: Furthermore, I have recently read some writings on Washington which argue that he was a much overrated military man, and that as President he was almost wax in Hamilton's hands. If so, are we not in danger of attaching too much significance to him as an exemplar of constitutional principles? Am I not right in thinking that Jefferson regarded Hamilton and his squadron of friends as masters of policies and measures during Washington's administration?

Beard: There is some relevance to our theme tonight in what you say. Not much, but some. It is true that we have contradictory judgments on Washington as a military man. I am not competent to pass upon them. One thing is certain, however. It is a fact beyond dispute that, whatever his faults, with unbreakable tenacity he clung to the task of fighting the war of the revolution for seven long, grueling years, through thick and thin, to the victorious end. That was a display of character, and the conduct of constitutional government calls for character.

As to his administrative policies, Washington was undoubtedly deeply influenced by Hamilton. Jefferson, who had opportunities to form his own opinion on this matter, believed that Hamilton was the dominant figure in matters of policies and actions. Yet I am convinced that Washington spoke truly when he said that he gave due consideration to the issues before him and rendered an independent judgment on them.

Washington's knowledge of constitutional law, political theories, and economics was, to put it mildly, decidedly limited. For the sake of the argument, let us assume that criticisms you have cited are valid and see how they stand up as we go along. Let us begin with your contention that Washington as an aristocrat had no sympathy with plain people, especially Jeffersonian democrats. Agreed? [Heads were nodded in assent.]

You say that Washington was an aristocrat. The word is vague but, however interpreted, what has the charge to do with constitutional government? Many features of limitation on power now associated with constitutional government were brought into being by persons you would call aristocrats. Magna Carta was forced on King John by members of the English aristocracy—by the barons and highest dignitaries of England. The people, as we use the term, had nothing to do with wresting Magna Carta from the King. Parliamentary government, freedom of press and speech, a high degree of religious toleration, the writ of habeas corpus—many leading doctrines incorporated in our American Constitution and Bill of Rights—were developed in England by members of the upper classes and forced on Crown and Church. There was nothing democratic about those rights in their origins and early applications, although in time they came to be applied generally to masses of people, even to people who could not vote.

Glances of astonishment came from our fireside assembly, seeming to ask: Where do Americans come into the making of constitutional history?

BEARD: Americans made many contributions of their own, in building their institutions on English experience, and they took special precautions in assuring civilian supremacy in government. Washington's deeds and public utterances exemplified the American doctrine of this supremacy. Consider his performances entirely apart from his so-called aristocratic sympathies. He did not sell out a nation in the bud. Twice Congress granted him dictatorial powers during the war. Twice he returned those powers unsullied. Again and again, during the war, while he was commander in chief, when officers and privates seemed on the point of mutiny or rebellion against the Congress, Washington was loyal to that body, despite all its faults, and they were many. His firm resistance to every proposal for the seizure of power showed his unfailing devotion to constitutional methods, even in a revolutionary war.

And when victory in arms came, Washington went before the Congress sitting at Annapolis, surrendered to it the great powers that had been entrusted to him, and retired to his plantation as a private citizen once more.

Would you like to hear what he said in his address to the Congress on that memorable occasion? Here are a few of his words:

> I now have the honor of presenting myself . . . to surrender into their hands the trust committed to me, and to claim the indulgence of retiring from the service of my country . . . . I resign with satisfaction the appointment I accepted with diffidence. . . . Having finished the work assigned to me, I retire from the great theater of action. . . . I here offer my commission and take my leave of all the employments of public life.

Thereupon the General walked to the chairman and delivered his commission to the president of the Congress. If he was an aristocrat, he displayed by this action the supreme qualities indispensable to constitutional government. After he had listened to the speech expressing the appreciation of the Congress for his services, he left the hall in silence and rode away to his home at Mount Vernon. If there is a more striking or important event than this in all the toilsome struggle of humanity for civil government, for self-government, I do not know where to find it. It illustrates constitutional government in its most significant and dramatic form.

MRS. SMYTH: That is really stunning! I mean moving.

BEARD: Moreover, amid the angry disputes that almost tore the young republic to shreds between his retirement from the Army and his election as first President of the United States, Washington steered his course in a constitutional line. As I have said, he spurned every suggestion that he become king or dictator of the new nation, and he urged the settlement of the nation-wide dispute over forms of government by plan, or proposal, discussion, and popular adoption.

Giving up the comparative ease of private life again, he accepted membership in the convention that drafted the Constitution, presided over its deliberations, and spent trying months in Philadelphia during the summer of 1787, laboring to prevent the dissolution of the convention in a conflict of interests and words. Passions ran high among the members. He acted as a moderating influence, seeking a resolution of the difficulties in a constitutional government. He seldom spoke from the floor. When he did, it was in an effort to draw the delegates together for some agreement—not to intensify their disagreements. At the end, he was dissatisfied with some features of the Constitution as finally drawn, but he signed it and aided in the campaign for ratification.

In two sentences in a letter written to a friend in the autumn of 1787, Washington revealed his own spirit, and the spirit of constitutional government:

> The Constitution that is submitted is not free from imperfections—but there are as few radical defects in it as could well be expected, considering the heterogeneous mass of which the Convention was composed, and the diversity of interests that are to be attended to. As a Constitutional door is opened for future amendments and alterations, I think it would be wise in the People to accept what is offered to them.

DR. SMYTH: I must admit that Washington was not too aristocratic in a political sense to go back to farming and private life after he had helped to draft the Constitution. I suppose there are two kinds of aristocrats: one that assumes the right to govern without the consent of the people; the other that assumes the privilege of an exclusive private life. I begin to get the meaning of your tenacious plea for us to cling firmly to the governing principle when we are discussing government.

BEARD: Good, Doctor! Then we can proceed faster. Remember that for eight years, as President of the United States, Washington strove to apply constitutional methods to all the problems that arose; to ground the Constitution in strong interests and loyalties. He tried to mediate between the hot disputants, Hamilton and Jefferson. With all the patience he could summon, he listened to their separate appeals and complaints and urged adjustments in their controversies. He combined strength and determination with the power to proceed in moderation when passions again seemed to threaten the future of the Union.

DR. SMYTH: He wasn't moderate in the Whiskey Rebellion.

BEARD: No, Doctor. Finally Washington was harsh and a bit high-handed there, but he did not rush to arms thoughtlessly like a sheer hothead. He tried conciliation before he used force. Furthermore, he did not consider himself indispensable in the office of President. He might have been re-elected indefinitely, but at the close of his second term he yielded the executive power to another, as he had earlier turned back to the Congress the power it had given him as military chieftain. This act, even if it represented his weariness at last, strengthened the constitutional government.

DR. SMYTH: Are you going to make a god of Washington? Are you going to defend all the measures and policies he adopted as President, and all his personal actions?

BEARD: By no means. I certainly do not claim that he was all-wise. The very idea of forming democratic societies was stench in his nostrils, and he said so. But he said it privately. To the end he was high-strung; yet he kept his temper well in leash in his official capacity. Privately he sometimes wrote bitter things about his associates, attributing evil and contemptible motives to his opponents. But his public utterances as President were conciliatory as a rule, if firm, and they betrayed none of the personal antipathies that shook his nerves. They were, in short, constitutional in conception and expression.

MRS. SMYTH: This seems to imply a tang of hypocrisy in our noble word constitutional, if a constitutional man does not say in public what he thinks and says privately. I understand the abomination of name-calling by a President. But the idea of hypocrisy disturbs me.

BEARD: In that sense every civilized person is more or less of a hypocrite, is he not? No person in his right mind gives vent in public to all the distempers and passions that fret him. Every rational person knows that restraint, control over passions, is necessary to civil intercourse. If there were no governors on emotions in family life, in public assemblies and official bodies, all communion would be in terms of fretfulness and quarrels, and become, in extreme cases, fights. A wise person knows that he has to get along with other people and work with certain realities, unless he makes up his mind to destroy persons and overcome facts by physical violence.

A public official under constitutional government is aware of the conflicting interests in society. He is familiar with the avarice, pride, and ambitions of individuals or blocs. His sympathies may be here or there, but he does not allow them to take exaggerated forms. He subordinates them to his larger objectives—in Washington's case the objective of creating a united and powerful nation.

Washington's public intercourse with his opponents was courteous. He confided his furies to himself or his intimate friends. His public utterances were well-considered and urbane, often to the point of irritating his own partisans. A constitutional statesman accepts defeat if it comes by constitutional methods. If he remains in office, he pursues conciliatory methods, knowing that the constitutional way of governing is a civilian way of reasoning together. This way is demonstrated in Washington's career and nowhere better than in his Farewell Address.

Dr. Smyth: Wasn't that mixed up in Hamilton's policies? Didn't Hamilton draft it with a view to sidetracking Jefferson and his partisans?

Beard: Yes, Doctor. Hamilton had a hand in drafting it. So did Madison. It was pleasing to partisan Federalists. It gave them aid and comfort. Nevertheless, the Farewell Address represented Washington's own matured views, and at bottom it was a plea for the continuance of the Union and constitutional government. Here is a copy of it. Take it home and read it line by line.

I shall not read it aloud now. I shall limit myself to a few points. First: the Address posits the Union as necessary to the security, the progress, and the true grandeur of the nation. In that sense it was above all partisanship. It was prophetic. It survived as prophecy the ordeal of the Civil War. It provides guidance for us as long as constitutional government endures.

Well, then, having adopted that postulate, Washington called attention to the fact that conflicting interests might disrupt the Union. He did not overlook their existence, but he insisted that, despite their validity and force, despite the factional divisions to which they gave rise, they should not be pushed to extremes—to the extreme of violence, to the breakup of the Union. He maintained that, however deep and real the social and economic divisions might be, there were common interests in society which transcended them in importance—common interests relative to the United States as a political unity, and relative to the life of the whole people. He warned his country against factionalism of the kind that subordinates the general interest to special interests, to personal ambitions, and to mere party advantages.

He advised the people to promote 'institutions for the general diffusion of knowledge,' declaring that 'in proportion as the structure of a government gives force to public opinion, it is essential that the public opinion be enlightened.' He warned the people about forming 'inveterate antipathies against particular nations and passionate attachments for others'; against becoming divided over, and involved in, European conflicts of interests remote from the primary interests of the United States. His predominant motive in shaping his administrative policies, he said at the close of his Farewell Address, had been to promote the progress of the nation to 'that degree of strength and consistency which is necessary to give it, humanly speaking, the command of its own fortunes.' All these principles are essential rules of constitutional government.

But we must not spend our whole evening on George Washington. Although amazingly different from Washington in many ways, Jefferson was equally constitutionalist in his principles and convictions.

MRS. SMYTH: How can you say that? My father was a soldier in the Union Army during the Civil War, and until his death he insisted that old Tom Jefferson, the nullifier, was the father of secession. If he was right, then old Tom Jefferson certainly does not belong in the same class with Washington as a constitutionalist. Besides if I am not mistaken, Jefferson played no part whatever in making the Constitution.

BEARD: Your point about nullification is well taken, Mrs. Smyth, and Jefferson had nothing to do with the actual making of the Constitution. He was serving as the American minister to France in 1787 when the convention met at Philadelphia. But he shared the wide opinion that the Union should be made stronger. At first he believed that a few amendments to the Articles of Confederation would suffice. When he received a copy of the new Constitution in the autumn of 1787, he was pleased with some of its provisions and dissatisfied with others. He was especially disappointed to find in it no bill of rights protecting civil liberties, for he did not want the government to be so powerful as to oppress the individual citizen. But after the Bill of Rights was added to the Constitution in 1791, Jefferson became a stanch defender of the Constitution.

I could see that my friends were both waiting for an answer to the charge that Jefferson was the father of secession but I kept them waiting a little longer, to point out meanwhile that Jefferson's defense of the Constitution was based on his own view of the document.

BEARD: In his opposition to Hamilton and Washington, Jefferson and his partisans claimed to be the true interpreters of the Constitution. According to their view of it, Hamilton and Washington, who had helped to make it, were distorting and betraying it, whereas in their opinion the Jeffersonians were restoring it to its pristine form. A large number of Jeffersonian Republicans, James Monroe for example, had opposed the ratification of the Constitution. Now, however, they proclaimed themselves the true-blue defenders of the Constitution as the people understood the document.

At the same time Federalists often denounced Jefferson as a foe of the Constitution; as the exponent of government by the rabble. In the campaign of 1800 a Boston critic of Jefferson—'Decius' in the *Columbian Centinel*—sneered at 'his rooted antipathy to the Federal Constitution and his fixed determination to overthrow it.' I am quoting the critic's words. But Hamilton gave a different version of Jefferson. Though he called Jefferson 'a contemptible hypocrite,' he declared that a 'true estimate of Mr. Jefferson's character warrants the expectation of a temporizing rather than a violent system.'

MRS. SMYTH: Here comes this charge of hypocrisy again. Politics seem to reek of it. Accusing an opponent of hypocrisy seems to be an ever-present temptation. But perhaps it is as hard to be sure of sincerity as to be sure of character, as you have said.

BEARD: If insincerity is to be the stamp on Jefferson, it should stamp Hamilton also. If we must engage in the great political sport of name-calling, we may turn the tables on Hamilton and assert that Jefferson was no more of a hypocrite than Hamilton. But Hamilton is not our subject tonight and Jefferson is. So we arrive now at the nullification business to which you referred, Mrs. Smyth.

Curious as it may seem, that business illustrates Hamilton's interpretation of Jefferson as a temporizing rather than a violent man.

Jefferson did draft the Kentucky Resolutions of 1798 in which the legislature of that state set forth the doctrine of nullification that so enraged your father. In that draft and in his letters written at the time, Jefferson treated the Constitution as a compact among states and declared that the states had a right to decide whether the Federal Government overstepped the bounds of the Constitution. He maintained that the states had the right to withdraw from the Union, if they thought the Federal Government guilty of 'repeated and enormous violations' of the compact. This is in fact the theory of secession. There is no denying it.

The provocations for Jefferson's actions were undoubtedly great. The Federalists had recently jammed through Congress the notorious Sedition Act, and the Federal Government was prosecuting and jailing Republicans of Jefferson's party for what now seems to us, with our practice of free speech, not seditious, but often vulgar, criticisms of President Adams and his administration. The Sedition Act certainly abridged the freedom of speech and press guaranteed in the First Amendment to the Constitution. John Marshall thought the Act bad law and opposed it, though he was a Federalist. But it looked as if the Federalists were determined to smash Jefferson's party by imprisoning critics and silencing the press.

There were grounds for alarm. One of Jefferson's friends, John Taylor, a distinguished political leader in Virginia, went so far as to propose a dissolution of the Union and the formation of a southern confederacy then and there; but Jefferson limited his own course to protesting and to formulating the doctrine of nullification. He did not formulate it openly. It was not known until long afterward that he had drafted the Kentucky Resolutions which embodied that doctrine.

Mrs. Smyth: Then my father was right. Jefferson *was* the father of secession. Not only that, it seems. If he framed the doctrine of secession secretly and privately, encouraged others to spread it, and then refused to stand by his own logic, Hamilton seems justified in calling him a contemptible hypocrite.

Beard: Suppose we look at the matter this way. If you rule out of your polite circle all statesmen who have privately encouraged radicals or conservatives to take dangerous or extreme steps, you will have few members of your group left, will you not? Let us consider Jefferson's situation a little more carefully. The Sedition Act was odious both to him and to a large number of people. As a political policy it was outrageous, oppressive, and defied constitutional principles. Jefferson helped to stir up opposition to it and privately declared that the states had the right to oppose its enforcement. He promoted that declaration in Kentucky by the state legislature. Yet he strongly opposed secession. He hoped, or thought, that opposition could remain political, that is constitutional.

DR. SMYTH, growing restive: If Jefferson had been alive in 1861, he might have favored dissolving the Union, whereas Washington might have been for the Union first and for Virginia second. Still both were planters. Maybe both would have been secessionists.

BEARD: We could speculate on that endlessly and get nowhere. All I have to go by, if we are to use positive knowledge, is the historical record respecting Jefferson. In practice and in his addresses to the country, Jefferson stood by the Constitution and voiced a conviction that constitutional principles should guide the nation. Inclined by sympathies to large personal liberty, he feared an excess of government. But he considered the formation of the Constitution and the resort to discussion instead of to the sword a shining achievement in the history of mankind. He had great faith in the people, in freedom of discussion, in education for citizenship, in 'the common reason of society,' to use his phrase.

If the voice of the people could be heard freely, considered freely and fairly, self-government, he was convinced, could be safely and happily conducted. He once said:

If this avenue be shut to the call of sufferance, it will make itself heard through that of force, and we shall go on, as other nations are going, in the endless circle of oppression, rebellion, reformation, and oppression, rebellion, reformation again; and so on forever.

In his First Inaugural Address, speaking openly to his country as a responsible statesman, Jefferson committed himself to every principle of constitutional government based on popular rule; and this document, I think, may be taken as a statement of his matured, deep-seated views. Let us make a list of the principles set forth in that great state paper:

The support of our State Governments in all their rights.

The preservation of the General Government in its whole constitutional vigor, as the sheet anchor of our peace at home and our safety abroad.

A jealous care of the right of election by the people—a mild and safe corrective of abuses which are lopped off by the sword of revolution where peaceable remedies are unprovided.

Absolute acquiescence in the decisions of the majority, the vital principle of republics, from which there is no appeal but to force, the vital principle and immediate parent of despotism.

The supremacy of the civil over the military authority.

The diffusion of information and the arraignment of all abuses at the bar of the public reason.

Freedom of religion; freedom of the press; freedom of person under the protection of *habeas corpus;* and trial by juries impartially selected.

'Such principles' (Jefferson continued) 'should be the creed of our political faith, the text of civic instruction, the touchstone by which to try the services of those we trust; and should we wander from them in moments of error or of alarm, let us hasten to retrace our steps, and to regain the road which alone leads to peace, liberty, and safety.'

DR. SMYTH: Those are all very fine words, but how does remembering them and reciting them help us in blocking politicians who try to put things over on us now?

BEARD: Your query is appropriate, and for the moment I shall meet it by turning your question around. If we want to block politicians who are trying to put things over on us, as you say, to what forces or sanctions in the minds of our fellow citizens are we going to appeal if not to historic principles widely accepted? Should we be stronger and wiser in resistance to political oppression if we knew no history, if we knew nothing about previous experiences with oppression and previous thought connected with such experiences?

DR. SMYTH: All right, we'll think that over. Let us pass that up for the present. Have you any more words from Jefferson on how to deal with victorious politicians and to preserve the constitutional rights of dissenters like myself?

BEARD: Yes, Doctor. Here they are. In 1801 the country had just passed through a savage political campaign marked by abuse, vituperation, and hatred. Referring to that sharp contest, Jefferson said:

This being now decided by the voice of the nation, announced according to the rules of the Constitution, all will, of course, arrange themselves under the will of the law, and unite in common efforts for the common good. . . . Let us restore to social intercourse that harmony and affection without which liberty and even life itself are but dreary things. And let us reflect that, having banished from our land that religious intolerance under which mankind so long bled and suffered, we have yet gained little if we countenance a political intolerance as despotic, as wicked, and capable of as bitter and bloody persecutions.

In demanding acquiescence in majority will according to the rules of the Constitution, Jefferson also recognized that minorities had rights and took them into account by saying: 'All, too, will bear in mind this sacred principle, that . . . will to be rightful must be reasonable; that the minority possess their equal rights, which equal law must protect, and to violate would be oppression.' Those were the constitutional doctrines expressed by Jefferson in his Inaugural Address.

Mrs. Smyth: The voice of the people was announced according to the rules of the Constitution in the election of 1860, and men professing Jefferson's doctrines refused to abide by the decision at the polls. They refused to rely on the peaceable remedies he advocated.

Beard: True enough. I am pleased that you brought that up. But thousands of people in the South were against secession. Thousands of people in the North, professing Jefferson's political faith, were as strongly for the Union. Many leaders of secession utterly repudiated Jefferson's fundamental doctrines of human rights. But Lincoln declared that 'the principles of Jefferson are the definitions and axioms of free society.'

Dr. Smyth, eager to be clear about my position: If I understand your argument, you are saying that there are many contradictions in Jefferson's private correspondence, but that we are to accept only his public utterances as representing his true and correct views; that he expressed bitter partisan sentiments confidentially to his friends; that he carried on most of his political agitations secretly; that he wore a different face in public—a constitutional face. If there had been presidential press conferences then, reporters would have unmasked him.

BEARD: There is some reason in this contention. But on that point, Doctor, Jefferson's public utterances represented his *matured* convictions, as distinguished from his more or less fleeting, often distempered, private views. Jefferson was not a facile public speaker. That fact enters into my judgment. He carried on his campaign against the Federalists largely by means of correspondence. When he made public statements, he gave them more careful thought.

As to wearing a mask in public, I am inclined to say, Let him who has never done it, stand up in public. However—and this may be taken as an aside—I believe that no sensible person blurts out everything that boils up in his emotions, and certainly a statesman should not do this thinking out loud in public, for he should make his public utterances under a sense of responsibility as grave as the occasion that elicits them. The license we allow ourselves in our irresponsible moods should be put aside when we become responsible. I am of the opinion that Jefferson realized the difference.

At any rate he left us in his public statements a body of constitutional principles still valid in our moments of error or of alarm.

I am probably as old-fashioned as Methuselah, but my notion of the office once held by Washington, Jefferson, and Lincoln is such that I believe no President should be encouraged or forced to speak offhand on any grave question of national policy. I would have every President follow the example set by Washington and Jefferson, mature his convictions for public declaration, express them carefully, weigh his words, under the sense of responsibility that ought always to be attached to his exalted position as executive head of our nation.

Does Lincoln come into line for our next meeting? the Doctor and his wife both inquired.

Yes, I promised. We, or rather I, had so much to say tonight that we did not cover as much ground as I had expected. I have not completed my treatment of your puzzle yet.

V

Lincoln Exemplifies Constitutionalism

A S if timed by fate for our fifth session, I had as my guest an old friend, Thomas Taylor, a Lincoln enthusiast, whom I took pleasure in introducing to the Smyths on their arrival.

This, I said in presenting him, is Mr. Taylor, a capitalist from Illinois—Tom, for short. He is a copper-riveted Mark Hanna Republican, the son of a radical Republican who was active in politics during Lincoln's administration. Tom tells me that he learned from his father all the history he wants to know. But he is willing to sit in with us tonight.

MRS. SMYTH: I confess that I have never heard of radical Republicans.

DR. SMYTH: It's a new one to me, too, although in my youth in South Carolina I heard a lot about Black Republicans.

MRS. SMYTH: I suppose, Mr. Taylor, that your father knew Lincoln personally and passed on to you a tendency to hero-worship?

MR. TAYLOR: Yes and no. Father had some acquaintance with Lincoln. They worked together organizing the Republican party in Illinois. But my father was not an admirer of Lincoln. He thought that Old Abe was a tricky politician in Illinois, and he never agreed with Lincoln's theories and methods as to the conduct of the war, or his attitude toward the Constitution. That is, as Beard said, my father was a radical Republican. But I am no lecturer on the subject and, besides, this is your party.

BEARD: Oh, it's nobody's party. Go ahead and tell the Smyths just what a radical Republican is, or rather was, for that will supply just the background we need for discussing Lincoln's constitutionalism.

MR. TAYLOR: In that case, I might tell my tale. According to my father's account, there were a lot of radicals among the Repub-

licans, especially after the firing on Fort Sumter, and they were
not little fellows either. The crowd included Lyman Trumbull of
Illinois, George W. Julian of Indiana, Thaddeus Stevens of Pennsylvania, Charles Sumner of Massachusetts, Joseph Medill, editor
of the *Chicago Tribune*—hundreds of men of that type, and most
of the fiery abolitionists, men and women. What they all agreed
upon I cannot claim to know, and I can only give you my father's
version of their case.

DR. SMYTH: You don't mean to say that the *Chicago Tribune*
was once radical, do you?

MR. TAYLOR: Revolutionary is a better word. A good old Tory
is often a fellow who has made his revolution and now wants the
business stopped once and for all. According to my father's account,
the radicals among the Republicans opposed Lincoln's policy of
temporizing with slave owners and moderate Southerners. They
opposed his conduct of the war, believing it to be half-hearted and
utterly inefficient. They deplored all his harping on the Constitution
and all his talk about trying to meet the rebellion by constitutional
means.

My father held that the Constitution was blown up when the
Confederates fired on Fort Sumter, that the country was then in
a revolutionary state, and that Lincoln should have seized dictatorial powers and used every weapon of war, revolution, and coercion. He believed that Lincoln should have proclaimed the emancipation of the slaves at the beginning of the war. He favored
confiscating the estates of Confederate planters and dividing them
up among the poor whites and emancipated Negroes. He opposed
all of Lincoln's mild policies for Reconstruction. All these things,
my father thought, should have been done without regard to the
Constitution or anything else. I do not know just how far my
father's views coincided with those of the other radicals, but such
they were in general. Beard has doubtless wasted his time reading
a thousand books on them but maybe he can tell us whether my
father was fairly representative.

BEARD: No, I have not read a thousand books on the subject,
but Mr. Taylor has fairly stated the position of many left-wingers
among the radical Republicans. And I could not want a better background for treating Lincoln's constitutionalism.

MRS. SMYTH: But there seems to be another side to the Constitution. We joined some friends for dinner this evening. In the course of the conversation it came out that we were running up here after coffee to discuss Lincoln's relation to constitutional government. Then from soup to coffee, we almost fought the Civil War over again.

I feel rather close to the Civil War because my father was in the Northern Army and he always claimed that he fought to save the Union and the Constitution. But my husband's Uncle Henry, who no doubt fought just as valiantly on the other side, insisted day in and day out that he fought for the constitutional right of his state to secede from the Union. When he came to see us a short time before his death, he went over all the old ground.

Uncle Henry was the soul of gentleness and courtesy, but he was rigid in his conviction that the Southern states had a constitutional right to withdraw peaceably from the Union. He held that Lincoln had no right to wage war on the Confederate States and that, by the harsh exercise of his executive powers, he violated the Constitution of the United States—was a tyrant, in short. This issue came up again tonight at dinner, because an angry Republican said that he thought the North ought now to secede from the South. But leaving that aside, since my father and Uncle Henry, holding opposite views of the Constitution, yet each fighting, he believed, to defend the true view, could not both be right, are you not up a tree in proposing to discuss Lincoln and the Constitution, making it *the* Constitution? I am eager to see how you get down out of it, if you do.

BEARD: I have had the same experience with relatives on both sides of that war and so can feel, as well as try to think, about the issue. I can well believe, Mrs. Smyth, that your father and the Doctor's Uncle Henry each regarded his cause as having a constitutional justification. It is hard for me to imagine men rushing to kill one another unless they have faith in the rightness of their action. . . .

DR. SMYTH, forgetting opinions he had expressed at earlier sessions: If the Constitution was more than an afterthought with the fighters in our Civil War, I have never been able to discover the fact. Men will fight just to be fighting, in my opinion. I see hundreds of half-frantic patients every year and I have watched the antics of the human species in general for a long time. If most people act on reasoned principles, I am incapable of discovering what their principles are. They seem to me to be about as reasonable as chickens with their heads off.

Take Sue's father, for instance. If he had been born and reared in South Carolina, the chances are that he would have rushed into the Confederate Army just like my Uncle Henry. And the same goes in reverse for Uncle Henry. And as for rights and wrongs, what's right in one place and time is wrong in another, Constitution or no Constitution. Historians have been publishing wrist-breaking books on constitutional principles for more than fifty years. I am willing to wager that Mason and Dixon's line still divides them as it did the fighting men, notwithstanding their tall talk about objectivity, science, scholarship, and all that and all that. Am I right?

BEARD: Not wholly right. Yet as a rule, Doctor, Southern historians do stand fast by Calhoun, Jefferson Davis, and Alexander Hamilton Stephens—that is, by their views of the Constitution. On the other hand, Northern historians, as a rule, are inclined to stand fast by Daniel Webster and Lincoln, in their views of the Constitution. [Tom Taylor, I noticed, looked pleased when the last names were mentioned.]

Some writers say that the South was 'historically' right about secession but 'practically' wrong in trying to stem what Woodrow Wilson called 'the great national drift.' But we are to have a session on the Union next Friday night. Then we shall go more fully into the nature of the Constitution in this respect. If we go into it now, we may wander far away from Lincoln's exemplification of the constitutional principle and get lost in a maze of fact and fancy, reality and rationalization.

MRS. SMYTH: Or not come out of that tree.

DR. SMYTH: Yes, I want to see you try to accomplish that feat.

BEARD: Since you insist, I shall now try to summarize the case for the Constitution as a binding covenant. I shall not state the case in the language of Webster or of Jefferson Davis, I . . .

DR. SMYTH: Shall engage in hairsplitting.

BEARD: Postpone that judgment, please. You have said that man is not a reasonable animal. Well, I do not pretend to know whether the people of the United States, or even a majority of them, ever indulged in reasoning about the right of states to secede from the Union while the Constitution was being framed and adopted in 1787-88. That question was certainly not debated in the convention that wrote the Constitution. Nor was it ever at any time submitted in that form to the people of the states for their decision. Many Northern men and many Southern men held that a state had a right to join the Union or withdraw from it. Out of my study of the papers and debates of the men who drafted the Constitution, I have come to the conclusion that the majority of them were more attached to the Union than to their individual states; that the majority intended to form a perpetual Union; and that they did not give any official recognition to the right of a state to withdraw from it after it had joined the Union. They were practical men, the crisis they faced was real to them, and they were convinced that disunion was already threatening the destruction of the existing states, as well as menacing the confederacy erected during the war against Britain.

MR. TAYLOR: What did Madison say, if anything, on the matter of a perpetual Union? He was the father of the Constitution and he was a President of the United States charged with defending or administering the Constitution. Did the nullification issue seem important to him?

BEARD: Madison expressed himself on the point in 1798, and again in 1833, a short time before his death. Though he protested with Jefferson in 1798 against the Alien and Sedition Acts, he opposed nullification when the issue was squarely raised by South Carolina after the Constitution had been long in effect. He regarded the Union as neither a consolidated nation nor a mere league of independent nations, and he looked upon an enemy of the perpetual Union as a deadly foe of his country's well-being. It has been claimed that Madison was not logical in this respect; not logical like Calhoun; not logical like Webster. But at least Madison helped to make the Constitution, and Calhoun and Webster *talked* about it.

However, we have Lincoln to consider tonight—Dr. Smyth's 'rail-splitting frontiersman.' Shall we not proceed to examine his position relative to the Constitution?

Not only silence gave consent. Consent was given in words.

BEARD: Despite his humble origins and his experience in rail-splitting, Lincoln's position was in many respects similar to that of Washington, the first President. Washington had accepted the supremacy of civil authority, as represented by the Congress during a war for independence. Though its delays, debates, and incompetence in numerous basic matters moved him to wrath, he acknowledged its authority and at the end of the Revolution surrendered his commission to that Congress. Washington did not have all the Americans with him, and not all the Americans were with the Continental Congress. Thus a civil war complicated the war for independence, but Washington stood fast on constitutional methods in his relations with the Congress.

Jefferson was more fortunate in his circumstances as an executive, for he had with him a majority of the people—a majority of the voters, and presumably a majority of all the people. While wars in Europe, with their repercussions in America, tried his soul, no armed conflict at home threatened the peace of the nation.

And now for Lincoln himself. Like Washington, Lincoln had a civil war to contend with—one that raged for years, in his case for four years. In front of him were the powerful armed forces of the Confederacy. At his back, in the North, were powerful divisions among the people of that section. Only a minority of the popular vote in 1860 had been cast for him and he was aware of his uncertain position as head of the divided nation. For the first time the war powers conferred upon a President of the United States by the Constitution were to be thoroughly explored and applied, with few precedents as guides. But from beginning to end, Lincoln tried to follow constitutional methods, at least in vital respects, as Washington had done in the Revolution.

He treated secession as an insurrection. . . .

DR. SMYTH: Ah, but that was just *his* idea! That was not the Southern idea.

BEARD: Was it just his idea? He held that the Constitution of the Union was in full effect. Had he been so inclined, he could have treated the conflict as a public war—between two countries. . . .

MR. TAYLOR: Yes, and he could have called the Union dissolved. And if the views of my father's radical colleagues had prevailed, he would have seized total power and followed the methods of a Caesar or a Cromwell. I have thought about that possibility a good deal. What a chance he had if he had wanted to be what we would now call a Fascist!

BEARD: Yet, let me remind you, he conducted his administration on the theory that the Union and the Constitution remained in full force and that it was his responsibility to keep the Constitution in force by suppressing a rebellion against the authority of the United States. As I shall emphasize later, he resorted to some measures of dubious constitutionality and was repeatedly accused even by some Northerners of acting like a dictator. But his violations of the Constitution, if such they were in fact, were trivial in comparison with his fidelity to the mandates imposed on him by the supreme law of the land.

Between his election in November, 1860, and his inauguration on March 4, 1861, he strove to allay, not augment, factional strife, as Mr. Taylor said. He asserted that his supreme purpose was to save the Union and the Constitution—not to intervene in Southern slavery. For that he was called a trimmer and a compromiser. Hotheads were not confined to the South.

DR. SMYTH: I suppose that was akin to the stand of Jackson in 1833. Jackson was a Southerner, and yet he was against nullification.

BEARD: The analogy is warranted. Shortly before Lincoln's inauguration, a combination of Democrats and Republicans in Congress passed a resolution of amendment to the Constitution which declared that Congress should never have the power to interfere with slavery in any state. Lincoln gave his approval to this resolution. If it had been adopted by the states, as the Thirteenth Amendment, it would have fastened slavery upon the country by supreme law. Lincoln was even willing to have that done to avoid war—to save the Constitution and the Union. But the leaders of the Confederacy would not have it.

MRS. SMYTH: Maybe the Northern states would not have taken it, either. The hatred of slavery was intense and the abolitionists were no compromisers.

BEARD: Anyway, the constitutional spirit that governed Lincoln he revealed in his First Inaugural Address. There he laid down his constitutional principles, which I shall quickly paraphrase. He said that he had no power, purpose, or inclination to interfere with slavery in the states where it existed; that he would maintain the rights of the states inviolate; that the Constitution provided for the return of fugitive slaves, and that Congress was bound to obey this mandate; that he would do no more than enforce the laws of the Union according to the obligation of his constitutional oath; that the rights of minorities and individuals declared by the Constitution would be respected, not denied; that, with regard to matters on which the Constitution is not explicit, the judgment of the majority must be accepted unless there is to be continual secession headed for anarchy; and that the issue of civil war lay in the hands of his dissatisfied countrymen, not in his hands.

Jefferson's theory of majority rule according to the Constitution Lincoln reiterated in his own language:

> The central idea of secession is the essence of anarchy. A majority held in restraint by constitutional checks and limitations, and always changing easily with deliberate changes of popular opinions and sentiments, is the only true sovereign of a free people. Whoever rejects it does of necessity fly to anarchy or despotism. Unanimity is impossible. The rule of a minority, as a permanent arrangement, is wholly inadmissible; so that, rejecting the majority principle, anarchy or despotism in some form is all that is left.

Having made his position clear, Lincoln closed with an appeal for that reasoned deliberation which is the very essence of constitutional government:

> My countrymen, one and all, think calmly and *well* upon this whole subject. Nothing valuable can be lost by taking time. . . . If it were admitted that you who are dissatisfied hold the right side in the dispute, there still is no single good reason for precipitate action. . . . In *your* hands, my dissatisfied fellow-countrymen, and not in *mine,* is the momentous issue of civil war. The Government will not assail *you.* You can have no conflict without being yourselves the aggressors. *You* have no oath registered in heaven to destroy the Government, while *I* shall have the most solemn one to 'preserve, protect, and defend' it. I am loath to close. We are not enemies, but friends. We must not be enemies. . . .

This appeal passed unheeded. The war came and . . .

DR. SMYTH: Then what about his actions which his critics called unconstitutional and high-handed?

BEARD: Far be it from me to minimize any of them. I have a long list of them here in my hand. It fills many pages. There on the shelf near you, Mrs. Smyth, is a faded old sheepskin volume by John A. Marshall, entitled *The American Bastille: A History of the Illegal Arrests and Imprisonment of American Citizens during the Late*

Civil War. If you and Robert want to take it home and read it, you can make a huge bill of indictment against Lincoln for yourselves.

Under Lincoln's administration many things were done which his critics called unconstitutional and high-handed. The screws were put on the Maryland Legislature to suppress the movement for secession in its midst. Many citizens were arbitrarily arrested in regions of the North far removed from the theater of war. Some editors and orators were seized for criticizing the Administration. Some newspapers were suppressed. Just how many persons were arrested it seems impossible to determine with any degree of accuracy, but certainly the number ran into the thousands.

Put all of Lincoln's so-called high-handed and unconstitutional actions together and multiply them by ten for good measure. Accept, for the sake of argument, everything critical that has been said against them. Charge them all up against Lincoln, even though he was not personally aware of or responsible for many things done in the name of the Government by civil and military officers and often overruled high-handed actions on their part. Forget the numerous pardons which Lincoln signed—even his parole of Roger Pryor who had been captured while in the Confederate service, his repeated refusals to permit executions, and his various proclamations of amnesty. Lay at Lincoln's door everything you can think of. Pile Ossa on Pelion.

Still most of these charges are debatable on good constitutional grounds. The business is highly complicated.

Mrs. Smyth: So complicated that you will wish to get an armful of your notes?

Beard: Correct. I should like to do that, but it would consume the rest of our time for the winter. So I shall have recourse to the simplest possible statements which, I think, will hold water.

The constitutional line between the powers of Congress and the powers of Lincoln as President and as commander in chief of the armed forces in time of civil war was and is difficult to draw. Students of the subject will debate over it, no matter how it is drawn. But I will lay down a few propositions about Lincoln.

The first is that Lincoln rejected the proposal of radical Republicans to set aside the Constitution and carry on the war for the suppression of the Confederacy as a war of sheer force, unhampered by any constitutional restraints. He might have done that. He did not do it. He refused to seize that dictatorial power. In the second place, Lincoln did not suppress Congress or try to purge it of opposition members, as Cromwell did with Parliament. His critics in Congress made constant trouble for him all along the line, but he sought with nerve-racking care to smooth out difficulties with Congress and to co-operate with it in the great work of carrying on the war and the regular processes of government.

Furthermore, Lincoln did not expel from his cabinet men who were intriguing against him, trying to undermine his authority, speaking bitterly of his intelligence and character. He was as nearly devoid of personal vindictiveness as any great figure in history with whose career I am familiar. He did not seriously interfere with freedom of press or speech, if we are to judge by the huge volume of abuse some newspapers indulged in. In fact, if we can believe John Hay, he seldom read the newspapers. Judging by the many newspaper files that I have personally examined, I am inclined to think that fifty volumes of abuse, condemnation, and savage criticisms could be compiled from the pages of Northern papers between 1861 and 1865. Outright suppressions of papers were relatively few.

To sum it up with reference to civil liberty, I agree with J. G. Randall, the great authority on Lincoln's administration and war powers, who said in his *Constitutional Problems under Lincoln,* in 1926, that, under Lincoln, the citizen was 'far more' free 'to speak his mind against the government' than he was 'during the World War.' Lincoln was in the midst of a raging civil war in which the capital of the country and the very existence of the national Government were in actual danger. Yet under his administration citizens had more liberty to criticize the Government and openly to denounce the war than they had under President Wilson at a time when the existence of the Government was never in jeopardy for an instant.

DR. SMYTH: The real test, as I see it, was at the elections. You remember that in 1941 there was talk about the suspension of the congressional elections for 1942. Nothing came of it. It seems to have been just rumor and newspaper excitement. Did Lincoln ever propose to stop elections for the duration of the war?

BEARD: If he did, I never heard of it. The presidential election of 1864 may indeed be taken as a supreme test of Lincoln's devotion to constitutional mandates. Was he to submit himself, the war, the

Union, and the Constitution to popular vote that year? According to the plain letter of the Constitution, the people had a right to review his conduct of public affairs and at the polls to approve his policies by re-electing him, or to reverse them by choosing an opponent. It was a grave hour in the course of the war. General Lee stood apparently invincible in the field. The Confederacy, though badly hammered, still presented a formidable front. War weariness was sapping the strength of the Northern drive. Powerful men in Lincoln's own party wanted to replace him.

Mr. Taylor: Indeed, his own Secretary of the Treasury, Salmon P. Chase, carried on an intrigue to wrest the Republican nomination from him. For a time it looked as if he might be rejected by his own party or, if nominated, rejected by the people of the North.

Beard: Moreover at the Democratic national convention at Chicago all the forces of opposition to Lincoln were represented, from War Democrats to pro-slavery extremists and peace-at-any-price men. August Belmont took the chair and publicly denounced Lincoln's administration as 'four years of misrule, by a sectional, fanatical, and corrupt party' that had brought the nation to 'the very verge of ruin.'

Among the Democrats at the convention was the outspoken C. L. Vallandigham, the states-rights Democrat of Ohio and leader of the peace Democrats called 'Copperheads', who had openly and repeatedly condemned the war and had done everything he could to break the Northern resolve to see it through. He had once been arrested by the military authorities, on charges of treasonable activities, and condemned to prison. Lincoln commuted the sentence and, with grim irony, banished him to the Confederacy where by sympathy he belonged. In a little while Vallandigham returned to the North and renewed his antiwar activities unmolested by Lincoln.

Mrs. Smyth: What sort of antiwar activities? How far did he go?

Beard: He went about as far as any agitator could go. He kept on making speeches in which he abused Lincoln in unmeasured terms, cursed the war, and demanded peace. He went about organizing an opposition to Lincoln, especially in the Democratic party, designed to put his obstructionist views into effect. At the Democratic national convention in 1864 he labored hard to commit the party to a straight-out antiwar program; and he was successful.

Here is the plank adopted by the Chicago convention as the solemn pronouncement of the Democratic party for the campaign:

This convention does explicitly declare, as the sense of the American people, that after four years of failure to restore the Union by the experiment of war, during which, under the pretence of a military necessity, or war power higher than the Constitution, the Constitution itself has been disregarded in every part, and public liberty and private right alike trodden down, and the material prosperity of the country essentially impaired—justice, humanity, liberty, and the public welfare demand that immediate efforts be made for a cessation of hostilities, with a view to an ultimate convention of the States, or other peaceable means, to the end that, at the earliest practicable moment, peace may be restored on the basis of the federal Union of the States.

After openly proclaiming this doctrine, while saying that every part of the Constitution had been disregarded and liberty trodden underfoot, the Democrats nominated as their candidate General George B. McClellan. Until ousted from his command, McClellan had been, in my opinion, a failure at war himself, and he had once been guilty of an insult to the President that only a saint could have forgiven. It is true that in his acceptance of the nomination McClellan refused to admit that the war had been a failure. He could hardly admit that. And he straddled a bit in other ways.

But, on this antiwar platform the Democratic campaign was waged against Lincoln. And it was a bitter campaign. Democrats complained that the liberties of the people had been suppressed by a despot in the White House. If there was any word in the whole vocabulary of abuse, denunciation, and damnation that they did not employ against Lincoln and his Administration, it would be hard to find it in the Oxford English Dictionary, supplemented by an American dictionary. Anybody who cares to have details can find plenty in the fifty-fifth chapter of Carl Sandburg's *Abraham Lincoln: the War Years*. Republican agitators, of course, paid the Democrats back in kind, with heaping measure. But Lincoln's course during the storm was dignified and reserved.

In August, 1864, while his prospects were gloomy, even before McClellan's nomination on an antiwar platform had been made by the Democrats, Lincoln wrote a note, sealed it, and asked members of his cabinet to endorse it on the cover. The note read:

This morning, as for some days past, it seems exceedingly probable that this Administration will not be reëlected. Then it will be my duty so to cooperate with the President-elect as to save the Union between the election and the inauguration, as he will have secured his election on such ground that he cannot possibly save it afterward.

A. Lincoln.

After the election was over, Lincoln opened the note and explained its meaning to his cabinet. He said that in case McClellan had been victorious, he had intended to call the General to him and say:

General, the election has demonstrated that you are stronger, have more influence with the American people, than I. Now let us together, you with your influence, and I with the executive power of the Government, try to save the country. You raise as many troops as you possibly can for this final trial, and I will devote all my energies to assisting and finishing the war.

This is not the language of a despot, a Caesar or a wrecker. It is the language of a man remarkably loyal to constitutional methods, ready to abide by the decision of the people lawfully made, prepared to dedicate all his powers to helping his successor to save the country between the election and the inauguration.

Mr. Taylor: But it was just the kind of pussyfooting and bowing to Democratic threats which irritated my radical Republican father so much! In father's opinion, Lincoln's conciliatory spirit and his toleration of obstructionist tactics prolonged the war and cost thousands upon thousands of lives. According to father's view, Lincoln could have crushed the rebellion in the first year of the war if he had clamped down on the appeasers and, in defiance of the Constitution, invoked the revolutionary spirit of the North in a total war on the slave-owning aristocracy.

Dr. Smyth: My God! How can you say that? I thought you were an admirer of Lincoln. Weren't you introduced to us as a Lincoln enthusiast?

Mr. Taylor: Oh, Beard didn't tell you that I no longer hold my father's views. Now I think that Lincoln was right and the radicals were all wrong—just crazy, in fact. You see, about thirty years ago I developed some large business interests in the South and for the first time came in contact with the kind of Southern people my father used to denounce. I found them just like my neighbors in

Illinois, eager to develop business enterprise in their region and to make a little money—just like the rest of us. In this way I came to see the Southern side of the case against Negroes and shiftless whites. If the radical Republicans had divided up the great estates among Negroes and whites, business wouldn't have had a ghost of a chance. The Tom Watson demagogues would have ruled the South —and maybe the country. What radical Republicans did in the South during Reconstruction until 1876 was bad enough.

DR. SMYTH: That is illuminating. I should like to go into it but I was on the verge of asking Beard another question. It is this. A few minutes ago you said that Lincoln filed a sealed note pledging himself to retire if defeated in 1864 and to co-operate with his successor in the presidency. As I understand it, the public knew nothing about that pledge. How do you know that Lincoln would have kept the pledge if he had been defeated in the election?

BEARD: We do not know, Doctor, that he would have been true to his vow. We must decide that according to our judgment of his whole course as President. However, I may add, for your benefit, that Lincoln made a similar pledge publicly during the political campaign. On October 19, 1864, less than three weeks before the decision at the polls, Lincoln told the people just what he intended to do. A short time before that day, the charge had been made that, if he was defeated at the polls, he would spend the time between the election and the inauguration doing his best to disrupt the Government of the United States.

It was in reply to this charge that he made the public pronouncement to which I have just referred, saying:

I am struggling to maintain the government, not to overthrow it. I am struggling especially to prevent others from overthrowing it. . . . Whoever shall be constitutionally elected in November shall be duly installed as President on the fourth of March. . . . In the interval I shall do my utmost that whoever is to hold the helm for the next voyage shall start with the best possible chance to save the ship. This is due to the people both on principle and under the Constitution. . . . If they should deliberately resolve to have immediate peace, even at the loss of their country and their liberty, I know not the power or the right to resist them. It is their business, and they must do as they please with their own.

There, as you see, Doctor, is a public pledge from Lincoln which is substantially the same as the secret vow which he filed under the signatures of his cabinet officers in the preceding August.

The constitutional philosophy that guided Lincoln he revealed even more fully and considerately in an address delivered from the North portico of the White House on the night of November 10, two days *after* the election. From the point of view of constitutional government and popular liberties, this speech, in my opinion, outranks the Gettysburg Address and the Second Inaugural. For the instruction of coming generations in such government and liberties, it should have precedence over those better-known appeals to the nation.

The November 10 address was written hurriedly, while a crowd of serenaders was gathering in the White House grounds to celebrate the recent victory at the polls. When he had finished it, Lincoln stepped out of the window opening on the portico. With John Hay by his side, holding a candle so that he could see his manuscript, Lincoln read it to the throng before him. The nation was waiting. Every word he spoke was freighted with meaning for the American way of self-government. Indeed it contained the whole philosophy of such government in peace and war:

It has long been a grave question whether any government, not too strong for the liberties of its people, can be strong enough to maintain its own existence in great emergencies. On this point the present rebellion brought our republic to a severe test, and a presidential election occurring in regular course during the rebellion added not a little to the strain. If the loyal people united were put to the utmost of their strength by the rebellion, must they not fail when divided and partially paralyzed by a political war among themselves?

But the election was a necessity. We cannot have free government without elections; and if the rebellion could force us to forego or postpone a national election, it might fairly claim to have already conquered and ruined us. The strife of the election is but human nature practically applied to the facts of the case. What has occurred in this case must ever recur in similar cases. Human nature will not change.

In any future great national trial, compared with the men of this, we shall have as weak and as strong, as silly and as wise, as bad and as good. Let us, therefore, study the incidents of this, as philosophy to learn wisdom from, and none of them as wrongs to be revenged.

But the election, along with its incidental and undesirable strife, has done good, too. It has demonstrated that a people's government can sustain a national election in the midst of a great civil war. Until now, it had not been known to the world that this was a possibility.

DR. SMYTH: Please read that last line again.

[I repeated it.] That is a startling sentence. In all history the world had not before learned that such a thing was possible. Pardon the interruption. Go ahead.

BEARD: I continue reading Lincoln's address of November 10, 1864:

It [the election] shows that even among candidates of the same party, he who is most devoted to the Union and most opposed to treason can receive most of the people's votes. . . .

But the rebellion continues; and, now that the election is over, may not all having a common interest reunite in a common effort to save our common country? For my own part, I have striven and shall strive to avoid placing any obstacle in the way. So long as I have been here, I have not willingly planted a thorn in any man's bosom. While I am deeply sensible to the high compliment of a reëlection, and duly grateful, as I trust, to Almighty God for having directed my countrymen to a right conclusion, as I think, for their own good, it adds nothing to my satisfaction that any other man may be disappointed or pained by the result. May I ask those who have not differed with me to join with me in this same spirit towards those who have? And now let me close by asking three hearty cheers for our brave soldiers and seamen, and their gallant and skilful commanders.

MRS. SMYTH: I heartily agree that the address you have read puts more meaning and warning into the idea of constitutional and popular government than the Gettysburg Address or the Second Inaugural, with which of course everybody is familiar. May we take a copy along so that we can study it line by line?

BEARD: Certainly. Here are two copies. Keep one of them. It is worth framing for your living room.

DR. SMYTH: Better for the den where we read and do less chattering. Good night!

VI

A More Perfect Union and Justice

W HEN he came into my study Dr. Smyth was limping slightly from an accident he had recently suffered while rushing along a country road to see a patient. After glancing at the chairs in the room, he chose a hard bench in the chimney corner. Mrs. Smyth paused for a moment at my big table, thumbed through the books and papers on it, and laughingly held up together a copy of Plato's *Republic* and the latest issue of *Time*. As the Doctor and I talked about his accident and exchanged neighborhood gossip, Mrs. Smyth became engrossed in A. D. Lindsay's introduction to the *Republic* and not until nearly half an hour had passed were we brought to order by a declaration from Dr. Smyth that he had a confession to make.

Dr. Smyth: Beard, you have seemed to understand my way of looking at things but I have been slow to grasp yours. In medicine, many if not most of the words used have a fairly precise meaning. A fibula is a fibula, for instance, and never a scapula. Quinine is quinine and never tincture of iodine. That is, for all practical purposes. Moreover, we assume in medicine that a hundred years ago quinine was substantially what it is today and will be the same a hundred years from now. With my training in such precise word-meanings as medicine affords, it has been hard for me to go with you in your kind of learning, if you don't object to my calling it learning.

You have apparently tried to define your words as medical scientists actually define theirs. That is, with exactness. And yet you have always left undefined fringes around the edges of your words and even shifted the centers of meanings as you have dealt with different periods of time.

At first I feared you had a screw loose in your mind and were just fumbling your way around this business of constitutionalism. I felt that I might get lost in a forest of meaningless words if I tried to follow you. But I have been endeavoring to analyze my suspicions of your learning and finally I have figured out your mental processes to some extent. In making this confession, I trust that it will help bring my mind closer to yours in the study which we are making together.

BEARD: I am used to attacks, Doctor, by men of science, and yours has been exceedingly gentle by comparison. A few years ago one of the most distinguished physicists in the United States, after hearing my lecture on 'The Idea of National Interest,' exploded during lunch in this fashion: 'If you fellows in history and the social sciences generally would only catch up with us in physics and discover the *laws* of human evolution, it would be possible for humanity to get some sensible control over humanity's fate.'

MRS. SMYTH: And what did you reply?

BEARD: My answer was: 'If you fellows in physics had to deal with the intangible and intractable data of human experiences, you would never be able to catch up even with Aristotle and you would lose your minds trying, unless you grappled with the methods of historical analysis.'

DR. SMYTH: This is the best possible introduction to the seminar of tonight. Since you now realize my problem, perhaps our minds can meet better somewhere along the line of discussion. Up to date you have dealt with the people ordaining and establishing a Constitution for the United States. You have illustrated, by the character, thought, and action of Washington, Jefferson, and Lincoln, the Constitution as forms or types of sentiment and practice. I am especially interested in the practice. As far as I am concerned, the Preamble to the Constitution calls for no battling over the words 'in order to form a more perfect Union, establish justice,' and so forth.

MRS. SMYTH: After all, the Preamble is really no part of the Constitution, is it? I am no lawyer, but my father was a lawyer and he warned me, in my youth, when he was coaching me on the Constitution for a high-school test, that the Preamble was just a pleasing introduction not binding on anybody in the government or outside.

BEARD: That is the lawyer's view of it, Mrs. Smyth. But in fact the Preamble is a declaration of purposes and the underlying spirit of the grand game, if such it may be called, of self-government and liberty to be played by the people of the United States. It is a commonsense statement of the game's objective, and an understanding of every game requires an understanding of its objective. Since the most serious game of all games—full self-government on an immense scale—was to be started for Americans in the late eighteenth century, the framers of the Constitution deemed it appropriate to make a declaration of the grand purposes of the play. Lawyers do say, repeatedly today, that the Preamble to the Constitution confers no powers upon Congress, the President, or the judiciary. In their sense of legalism, it does not. But in the sense that it fixes and expresses sentiments and aspirations cherished by multitudes of citizens, by the people, and since the business of self-government is the people's business, the Preamble helps to sustain the whole constitutional system.

So, I propose for our study tonight 'a more perfect Union and justice,' the first items set forth in the Preamble as objects of the new constitution-making—as aims to be fulfilled by the United States government. This bold yet cautious phrasing marked a decided break with the old Articles of Confederation which had been devised during the Revolution. It was a prophecy of a tendency toward a Union forever one and inseparable. The revolutionary confederation had been officially declared to be a 'perpetual union between the states' named. Its governing articles had explicitly announced that 'each state retains its sovereignty, freedom, and independence.' It had referred to their union as 'a firm league of friendship.'

On the face of things the new Constitution could be, and later was, interpreted in some quarters as merely strengthening the old league of sovereign states. But at the time the Constitution was adopted, it was widely understood to signify a revolution in the system proclaimed by the Articles of Confederation. All the members of the Convention of 1787 who had a hand in writing the Preamble were believers in strong government. None of them looked upon the more perfect Union as a mere league of sovereign and independent states. Running through articles, pamphlets, and speeches made against the Constitution, while its adoption pended, was the note that it actually meant, what it proved to mean, the establishment of a new and highly centralized form of government, an indissoluble Union, not a polishing up of the old league of friendship.

DR. SMYTH: Here is where I falter again in trying to go along with you. Aren't you relapsing into ancient history? Aren't you forgetting that it is the living issues of our own times with which we are primarily concerned, as we said when we first came up here to arrange for these discussions? Didn't some philosopher declare that the only thing we learn from history is that we learn nothing from it?

BEARD: Hegel asserted that, and it is false. We may not learn much from books on history. But what is it that most people have in their minds save their memories of past events or experiences arranged more or less in some scheme of thought? A rare few with creative minds, with strange prescience, foresee events and crises and divine what can, should, and will be done about them. They seem, in some fashion, to cut loose from the past and learn from— what shall we call it?—insight. Yet even they make use of history as knowledge and memories of past experiences.

The rest of us poor mortals, uninspired as we are, make use of little except what we have got out of history, out of the past, near or distant. You, Dr. Smyth, do not practice medicine on the science of the day after tomorrow. You practice *historical* medicine, at least mainly, that is, on the basis of medical experiences historically accumulated—theories and fragments of knowledge strung along from yesterday all the way back to Galen. So I need not apologize for going into ancient history.

Besides, when you came here to arrange for our disputes, you both agreed that, in addition to acquiring more knowledge about some contemporary issues, you wanted to train yourselves in methods of critical analysis with a view to arriving at more discriminating judgments on things done and said in our own times. You may remember that I laughed, and honestly too, at the idea of my serving you in that capacity. But can there be any better way of sharpening critical faculties than by exercising them on historical contests somewhat remote from our immediate passions and convictions—but not too remote for our knowledge and appreciation?

Furthermore, since judgments on contemporary policies are interpretations of history, of how the past is flowing into the future, then the knowledge of the past, I hold, is imperative in the formation of such judgments. History is the interplay of *ideas* and *inter-*

ests in the time-stream. That is an oversimplification, I admit, but it is a workable fiction in arriving at judgments and convictions.

And I know of no more instructive experience in the nature and influence of ideas than American experience with the idea of the more perfect Union, at first vague, long disputed, at last definite and triumphant. Furthermore the Union is the basis of our Republic —the central theme of our present interest. It was not without justification, therefore, that I began with the proposition that the Constitution was intended by its chief architects to mean what it finally came to mean in the course of history, a strong and indestructible union of states and people.

Mrs. Smyth: If I get the trend of your argument, you are saying that people do not know what they are doing half the time or more —at least people who do not possess rare special powers of discernment that are almost mysterious in nature. You are also saying that we can acquire some wisdom from history, from the study of what those who lived before our times have known or have thought they knew and have tried to do in producing results significant for the future. Why, that is what we are doing all the time, in things small and large. We think we know or have opinions about something going on or proposed, and we are trying to act on it as best we can to gain the end or ends set up. Others are battling against us. They tell us that we do not know what we are talking about, that our opinions are all wrong, and that we are fated to be defeated. From this point of view the old debate over the Union might have some instruction for us.

Beard, gratefully: Thanks for your help and your clear way of putting it.

Dr. Smyth: But we went into that matter in our seminar on Lincoln.

Beard: You will recall, however, that I sought to postpone it then and dwelt upon the theme, at your insistence, merely enough to show that the idea of the Union figured largely in Lincoln's conception of his constitutional duties. If you recall, Dr. Smyth, you then suggested that it was all a matter of rationalization by fighting men.

Dr. Smyth: Oh, I just expressed an ill-considered sentiment in an offhand fashion, although I believe that there was a great deal of rationalization in the whole business. Anyway, I was brought up to believe sincerely that the Union continued to be, after the Constitution as before, a league of states, that states were free to join it or not, and that states were free to leave it when they wanted to. If I am not mistaken, Woodrow Wilson, when he was a historian, before he became President of the United States, said somewhere that the Southern view of the Constitution was right; and here you are preaching up the old Northern fiction. Aren't you just rationalizing your old Republican predilections?

BEARD: Perhaps I am, a little, Doctor. Perhaps also your Southern ancestors were rationalizing their predilections.

DR. SMYTH: If I practiced medicine on my predilections, God help my patients! Don't historians pretend to know the truth about the nature of the more perfect union? Is there no agreement among you? Don't you claim to be sure of anything about it? Have you nothing more than opinions?

MRS. SMYTH: Don't be too hard on him, Robert. This very morning when we were talking about a case at the Hospital, you said: 'The best medical opinion is inclined to the treatment we are administering.' You yourself in your practice use informed opinion, knowledge, and, if I may say so, intuition.

DR. SMYTH: Yes but there are many cases where we either know what the facts are or we don't know. If we don't know, we try to find out.

BEARD: On this case of the Union, Doctor, we have a lot of facts. I have here Woodrow Wilson's *Division and Reunion,* written in 1892 to which you referred. On page 211 he says:

> The legal theory upon which [secession proceeded] was one which would hardly have been questioned in the early years of the government, whatever resistance might then have been offered to its practical execution. It was for long found difficult to deny that a State could withdraw from the federal arrangement, as she might have declined to enter it. But constitutions are not mere legal documents; they are the skeleton frame of a living organism; and in this case the course of events had nationalized the government once deemed confederate.

Mr. Wilson seems to be saying that the theory of the sovereign state and secession was so universally accepted by the people that it would hardly have been questioned in the early days of the government, and that it was for a long time found difficult to deny that a state could withdraw from the federal arrangement. Just stop and think for a moment how much one would have to know in order to prove that statement. There were millions of people in the United States in the early days of the government. Most of them are nameless and voiceless in history. Did the overwhelming majority so strongly hold to the idea of the sovereign state that the theory would or could hardly have been questioned? Perhaps they did, but we do not *know* and never can *know* that they did.

We do know, however, that the theory was many times questioned in the early days of the government by men of knowledge and competence. A number of state legislatures replied to the bold assertions made in the Kentucky Resolutions or the mild protests of Virginia or to both of them, in 1799—New Hampshire, Vermont, Massachusetts, Rhode Island, Connecticut, New York, Delaware, Pennsylvania, and Maryland. All of them rejected the cardinal doctrine of nullification. If any state legislature approved it, I am unable to discover the fact in our fragmentary records. Are we not bound to say then that the theory of the sovereign state and secession could have been questioned, was indeed actually questioned, by a large number of responsible men in the early days of the government? The legislatures of nine states are not to be lightly brushed aside as representing no considerable and respectable body of opinion.

In his sweeping statement, Mr. Wilson seems to be asserting that it was the intention of the framers of the Constitution to set up a system from which states, after joining the new Union, could withdraw at will. If so, my reply is that the proposition cannot be proved by exact reference to the writings of the framers which have come down to us.

What was the intention of a majority of the people who elected conventions to pass on the ratification of the Constitution? What did a majority of the delegates they elected actually intend? Did they believe that the Constitution left the states free to secede at will?

Given the papers that have been preserved, we cannot answer these questions. The secessionist theory of sovereignty was not raised in the Convention at Philadelphia. It was not discussed or passed upon there. The framers were practical men, not theorizers in politics. Years afterward, it is true, some Federalists, among them, Gouverneur Morris, who had been a member of the Convention, did hint strongly of secession, especially during the War of 1812, but they did not formulate the theory of secession as a constitutional doctrine. Or, at least, if any of them did, I am not acquainted with the fact. This we know: Madison was the only member of the Convention who lived to see the South Carolina doctrine of nullification and withdrawal proclaimed, and he wrote a blast against that view of the Constitution.

Let us look next at a few things that are clearly known. The old Articles of Confederation are characterized in the text itself as 'articles of Confederation and perpetual Union between the States.' Then the states were named. The Preamble of the Constitution, on the contrary, does not call the Constitution articles of agreement between states. It says that 'We, the people of the United States [taken as you will, collectively or by states], in order to form a more perfect Union . . . do ordain and establish this Constitution for the United States.'

To ordain and establish differs substantially from making a contract, compact, league, or articles of agreement between independent parties. If it does not, hope for any exactness of meaning in language is nonsensical. The old Articles speak of a confederacy and a league of friendship between states. The new Constitution says not a word about confederation or league between states. Near the top of the old Articles is the plain declaration that each state retains its sovereignty and independence. The Constitution is silent as death on these assertions respecting the sovereignty of states.

I do not want to split hairs, but I ask you to reckon with the facts I have cited. Judiciously examine the two historic documents side by side, and then say, if you can, that there is, in the language and plain intention of the words, no fundamental difference in letter and spirit between the Articles of Confederation and the Constitution.

MRS. SMYTH: There does seem to be a difference, but the Constitution did not declare that the sovereignty of the states proclaimed in the Articles of Confederation is at an end. Since it did not, what became of that sovereignty?

BEARD: My answer is that a proclamation does not make a thing true; that is it does not make a reality where there is none. Sovereignty is a word over which lawyers and scholastics wrangle endlessly. I shall not rehearse the quarrel here, but simply comment that if the states had possessed real independence and the power to enforce it, they would have possessed sovereignty in fact. A proclamation to that effect would have added little or nothing to the fact. The states did not possess the force to make good their claim to independence. A proclamation that they possessed what they did not have would not have given it to them.

The framers of the Constitution, as you can see by examining the records of the Convention, were bent on making a stronger union and on setting up a national government endowed with great powers. To them a discussion of sovereignty in the abstract would have smelt of the lamp and they were not disputatious monks in cells. They hoped so to constitute the Union that it would endure indefinitely.

Their practical spirit is reflected in a paper in the handwriting of Edmund Randolph, as amended by John Rutledge. Objecting to any 'display of theory' in the Preamble, the authors of the paper said:

> The object of our preamble ought to be briefly to declare, that the present federal government is insufficient to the general happiness; that the conviction of this fact gave birth to this convention; and that the only effectual means which they can devise, for curing this insufficiency, is the establishment of a supreme legislative, executive, and judiciary.

The framers were determined to form a union that would withstand the conflicts among the states, headed by ambitious politicians. Informed leaders among them knew the history of politics and government. They knew that, in the past, confederations of states had often been formed and then had fallen to pieces through the weaknesses of their governments. The history of Hellenic leagues and the fate of ancient Greece supplied them with solemn warnings.

They were well acquainted with the jealousies and quarrels that had rent the American states even while the British armies threatened their very existence. They knew that Great Britain, France, and Spain, with interests in the western hemisphere, would intrigue among the states if the states did not present a solid front to foreign powers. They envisaged new states rising in the West. They divined destiny—the rise of a great, forever united, power in America. Or, to put it in another way, they desired to effect that end. They saw forces working in that direction and also other forces pulling against it, toward dispersion and dissolution. They aided the process of unification and centralization. If it is not an Irish bull, I may say that they divined and aided destiny.

DR. SMYTH: In other words, they knew what they wanted—a strong union—tried to get it, and guessed right on the future.

BEARD: Splendid! If I had studied medicine, if I had not been compelled to read academic books and to study Supreme Court decisions, I might be able to say what I mean in such neat terms. The framers knew what they wanted, they tried to get it, and they guessed right on the long future. Of course by this I do not mean to say that the Union would have gone to pieces if the Articles of Confederation had been continued and the Constitution never adopted. The Union might have gone on; and it might not. It seems common sense to believe that the Constitution did form a more perfect Union, an enduring Union, and thus added insurance to such guarantees as already existed.

This discourse on a more perfect Union may sound like ancient history, I know. But I have dwelt on it for two practical reasons. The first is to deepen our sense of time, experience, history. A sense of history in a people is, in my opinion, necessary for continuity in institutional life and for adaptation to changes bound to come. My second purpose is to emphasize the blessings of Union, which we are likely to forget in our thoughtless acceptance of it. When you review attempts of the ancient Greeks to stop the almost endless wars among themselves by forming leagues and confederacies, when you study the break up of solidarity among Latin-American peoples and the wars among them, you will begin to see the immense significance of establishing a more perfect Union for the United States.

Without that Union, more perfect and enduring, we might have frittered away our energies in wars among ourselves and never have become a nation. In 1789 the elusive word union was generally acceptable to the people of all the states. It foreshadowed the coming of the nation. The framers of the Constitution were cautious enough to keep the words nation and national out of their document. In some of their early resolutions they used the term national as applied to the legislature, executive, and judiciary; but, knowing that it would alarm the people they struck it out.

DR. and MRS. SMYTH: Is that so?

BEARD: It is so.

DR. SMYTH, musing: Then there is realism in your method!

MRS. SMYTH: But internationalists tell us that this very unionism, this thing called nationalism, fostered by the Constitution, is positively vicious, is a source of wars among nations and must now be abandoned or severely modified in the interest of a new world order. Your review of the past makes it look like a great achievement, wrought in the interest of the American people and the Republic. In our time powerful efforts are made to discredit it and to supplant it by another sentiment—a sentiment of world solidarity.

It is not your ancient history that interests most people today or at least many people; it is what they call the peril of nationalism. Some of them, I know, speak in the same breath of America as a great power, with commensurate responsibilities to promote world welfare, when as a matter of fact if America had not achieved the national union of which we have spoken, it would have been no power at all.

I can see more rhyme and reason in your shuttling back and forth along the historical line. Still I confess to be in some confusion from looking backward so often and so much. To the living, it is the future that matters, and what is the relation to the future of all that you have said about the slow and almost mysterious unification of our Republic under the Constitution?

BEARD: Our twentieth session will be devoted to that general question. By that time, if our method has value, we shall be better prepared to handle it. For the moment I will merely say that those who condemn nationalism and announce a merging of the Republic in a world solidarity may well profit from a long and minute study of the way in which American solidarity came about, not overlooking the long civil war required to seal our Union.

The next item in the Preamble is 'to establish justice—'

DR. SMYTH, protesting: You mean Federalist justice. I remember some of my Democratic history—party tradition, at least. If I am not mistaken, a lot of men who voted early and often to establish justice later voted for the Sedition Act that sent Jeffersonians to jail for criticizing John Adams and his Federalist party administration.

BEARD: We might go on, while we are on this line and ask, with the Communists, what about bourgeois justice and proletarian justice? Or, with the fascists, what about capitalist justice?

But first let me make some comments on the Doctor's reference to

Federalist justice. Some of the men who favored the adoption of the Constitution certainly did vote for the Sedition Act of 1798. It was, no doubt, a Federalist measure. An uproarious Democrat, Mathew Lyon, a member of Congress from Vermont, was fined $1000 and sent to jail for four months on the ground that he had, among other things, written a letter ascribing to John Adams 'an unbounded thirst for ridiculous pomp, foolish adulation, and self avarice.' It is true also, Mrs. Smyth, that Abigail Adams and the women did not get their justice as soon as the Constitution and the Preamble went into effect.

DR. SMYTH: Then what is the use of talking about justice in the abstract?

BEARD: That is apparently what Randolph and Rutledge thought too, when they proposed to leave the words out of the Preamble. But the words to establish justice are there in our national covenant. I agree with both of you that discussing justice in the abstract is not much use. Discussing it, however, with reference to concrete practices affecting life, liberty, and property seems to me decidedly helpful in developing moral sentiments.

The human race would be meaner in character and poorer in spirit if such grand ideas as justice, mercy, truth, beauty, and goodness, and the sentiments associated with them, were banished from our lives. The ideals we profess are certainly inconvenient to us and make us look like hypocrites more often than we like. But suppose we have no ideal standards at all, suppose that every person were a law unto himself; then surely the right to rule would go to the persons who have the strength of the lion and the cunning of the fox. Power without ethical restraints is, in sum and substance, just what Mussolini and Hitler have taught and acted upon. So have some Communists, while deriding bourgeois justice.

This reminds me of a beautiful illustration of the point I am trying to make. Several years ago, Leon Trotsky, then living in Mexico, was charged by the Stalin government in Russia with a lot of crimes against the Soviet Republic. He cried aloud, with no little warrant I think, for justice. A committee of Americans, headed by John Dewey, was formed to examine into the charges and the evidence in the case.

Now Dewey was, in the communist lexicon, a bourgeois. Trotsky wanted me—another bourgeois, according to the canon—to serve on that committee. He wrote a letter to one of my friends in which he appealed to my interest in truth and justice. I did not join the committee, for various reasons. I had already studied the case enough to convince me that many of the charges against Trotsky were not only false but ridiculous, and I had said so publicly. Furthermore, I knew very well that such a committee could have no power to summon witnesses, demand papers, and hold a real trial. The point is that when Trotsky was in a jam with his old party, he wanted to be tried by standards of truth and justice possessing universal validity among civilized peoples—not merely by bourgeois or proletarian truth and justice—and, in my view of things, he was right.

Our knowledge and our practice of justice are seldom, if ever, perfect. Moreover the concept of justice grows with time and perhaps will never be perfect. Still, without standards of justice and a mental feeling for justice widely distributed among the people, society would go to pieces. Appeals for the realization of better things would lose much, if not all, of their force.

For example, Mrs. Smyth, when leaders among the women of America met at Seneca Falls in 1848 to frame their declaration of principles, they appealed to the grand abstractions of the Declaration of Independence—to the abstractions of 1776. That put many men to shame. I do not say that they got liberty and justice immediately. Neither do I say that their appeal to the principles of 1776 alone accounted for what they finally won. But in time they gained large installments of liberty and justice. By calling upon men to square their conduct by their noble professions they aided the progress of their cause.

And I should like to remind you, Doctor, of the Wilton case not far from our own community. Wilton was charged under an old statute of possessing and disseminating 'subversive and seditious literature.' Most respectable people were all worked up over the affair. The trial was held in an atmosphere of prejudice and vengeance. The judge and the jury were seized with the fever of Wilton's enemies. He was found guilty and sentenced to ten years in prison.

His lawyer took the case to the Supreme Court at Washington. There the charges and findings were reviewed by justices uninfluenced by local distempers. In the end Wilton was set free under the Constitution of the United States—if I may say so, under the justice of the United States. And you, Doctor, when the news of the Supreme Court decision came out, were happy, as you said to me, to see 'the old gang of witch-burners get what was coming to them.'

Of course, I am not claiming everything for these words in the Preamble, establish justice. Unquestionably, however, they gave some moral justification for establishing a federal judicial system. Under the Articles of Confederation there had been no scheme of national courts. If a citizen of one state got into legal difficulties in another state, he had to depend upon local courts and juries for justice and he was likely to be treated as a kind of foreigner. In any event, he got only such justice as the local judge and jury wanted to give him.

Furthermore, if a citizen of a state was defeated in a civil suit or convicted of a crime in local courts, he had no grounds for recourse to a national tribunal, remote from local heats, for a review of the justice or injustice meted out to him. In the circumstances there was also a sad lack of uniformity in the kind of justice administered and there were numerous conflicts among the states over the administration of justice.

In Number 22 of *The Federalist,* Hamilton, who had been a member of the committee that shaped up the Preamble at Philadelphia, laid great emphasis on the necessity of establishing a federal Supreme Court. Leaving matters to state courts, he said, would result in contradictions in decisions and there would be 'much to fear from the bias of local views and prejudices.'

DR. SMYTH: Oh, Hamilton again! Where was he when the Sedition Act was passed in 1798? With the Federalist crowd of oppressors, I suppose.

BEARD: The joke is on you, Doctor, for Hamilton declared that the sedition bill had provisions which were 'highly exceptionable. . . . I sincerely hope the thing may not be hurried through. Let us not establish a tyranny. Energy is a very different thing from violence.' To Hamilton justice meant more than Federalist party justice. And now after the lapse of more than one hundred and fifty years, as we shall see in detail later, grand rules of national justice are applied on a national scale. These rules are not perfect by any means, but, in hours when sheer force is proclaimed in Europe and Asia as the law of life, they are precious beyond measure.

Mrs. Smyth: Even so, the word justice is pretty vague.

Beard: I shall make it more specific when I come to speak of the human rights proclaimed in the Constitution and the amendments, and enforced by custom, law, and judicial processes.

Mrs. Smyth: But I suspect that it is still vague. While you and Robert were talking just after we came in, I glanced at the opening pages of the Introduction to A. D. Lindsay's translation of Plato's *Republic*. The participants in that great debate dealt with justice and they had a hard time with it. They tried to ground it, as Mr. Lindsay says, in such universal and ultimate facts of human experience that it must win the agreement of every man who will consent to use his reason. They worked out from the individual to the social and, if I remember right, came to a conclusion that perfect justice could only exist in a just or ideal society. Then they went on into metaphysics, the nature of reality and truth. In the end they were wrestling with eternity and the immortality of the soul. And there you are with justice!

Beard: Your account is in accord with what I understand to be the judgment of scholars in general on Plato's *Republic*. It was a grand piece of thought and speculation that haunted Western minds for more than two thousand years. But the Greek philosophers were never able to create even an approximately ideal society, at least in our sense of the word. And they never were able to found even an enduring league that would prevent the Greeks from slitting one another's throats in innumerable wars until the end came in dissolution—the death of thought and the arts.

The hard-headed framers of our Constitution were not as ingenious in speculation and in finespun definitions of ideas as Socrates and his companions. They spent little time trying to imagine what perfect justice and an ideal society would be like or look like. They refused to try by ideal standards the fruits of necessity and the frailties of human beings. They sought to institute a workable government and a workable society. They put justice into the Preamble of the Constitution; and, if I may make a rash assertion, they made it possible for the American people to have more justice, despite all the black spots on it, than any other people ever enjoyed over such an immense territory for so long a time—with splendid opportunities still ahead. I cannot prove that proposition. I merely leave it with you to think over at your leisure.

It is true that in this case, as in others before us, the framers did not foresee many of the vital consequences that were to flow from their provisions in the clauses of the Constitution for justice or for the establishment of a national judiciary. If John Marshall was right in his opinions under the clause of the Constitution which forbids states to impair the obligation of contract, some of them, no doubt, wished to write a system of natural justice into the very fabric of their text. Still, they left most of the domain of justice to the several states, subject to federal limitations, and dealt primarily with the restricted justice of federal affairs.

Nowhere in the original Constitution did they attempt to establish a complete system of national justice, that is, a national system of civil and criminal law covering the rights of persons and property. That would have been a revolution far beyond their powers, had they desired to make it. Nor do we have such a national system of civil and criminal law today.

But the Constitution that came from the convention in 1787, as we shall see in our tenth session on the rights of American citizens, did give to the Federal Government large powers over life and property and did place many restraints on the powers of the states to legislate in respect of life and property. John Marshall had scarcely been installed as Chief Justice in 1801 when he began to strike down one state law after another affecting property and personal rights, especially property rights.

Almost surreptitiously federal judges also began to develop a kind of federal jurisprudence respecting matters left to the states by the Constitution. This they did in dealing with suits beween citizens of different states. In such cases what law was to be applied? The law of the state in which the plaintiff lived, or the law of the state in which the defendant lived? Judges cut the knot by making some law of their own and kept at it until the Supreme Court, under the influence of Justice Brandeis, reversed the practice of a century and tried to put a stop to manufacturing federal justice of this type.

MRS. SMYTH: What was wrong with it? It seems reasonable enough to me. If the law of either one of the states was unjust to the plaintiff or the defendant, as the case might be, how could federal judges render justice without making their own rules for dealing with suits between citizens of the different states?

BEARD: I do not think that there was anything especially wrong with the practice, or that any good has or will come out of the action of the Supreme Court in reversing itself.

MRS. SMYTH: Then why did it reverse itself?

BEARD: I do not know. When he deemed it proper or desirable, Brandeis was an implacable foe of what he called bigness and a stanch supporter of states' rights. The reversal we are talking about diminished the power of national judges to make national law. It fitted into the theory of littleness.

There was another way in which federal judges made law under the original Constitution. That was by applying the common law to the interpretation of federal statutes and the Constitution. There was plenty of injustice in the old common law, but civilized judges could work wonders with it by a careful selection of cases and by a liberal use of independent reasoning.

However, I must say that the area of federal justice under the original Constitution was relatively small, in spite of its national significance. It was not until the adoption of the Fourteenth Amendment in 1868 that all state laws affecting life, liberty, and property were subjected to the control of the federal judiciary—gradually, as we shall see—and that a common and comprehensive scheme of national justice was developed.

I admit that the framers of the Constitution did not foresee this upshot. Hamilton doubtless would have rejoiced if he could have been sure that it was coming. Yet the original Constitution made provision for amendments, and by amendment and judicial interpretation this revolution in the nationalization of justice was affected.

MRS. SMYTH: But didn't Justice Brandeis often help to annul state statutes interfering with justice, with the civil liberty guaranteed by the Constitution?

BEARD: He did that and rendered opinions which will influence generations to come.

DR. SMYTH: I am still puzzled by your way of treating what seem to be plain propositions. The framers of the Constitution appear to have written certain definite views into the Constitution and to have surrounded them with intimations of other things that might occur in the course of things to come. Out of these definite provisions and intimations came extensions of their views and intimations they or anyone else never expected. According to your mode of thinking, human beings, even when they are sure that they know what they are doing, may gain some of their ends and yet set in train unexpected consequences far more important than their major designs.

I cannot say that your facts are wrong. On the contrary they impress me as well founded, but your mode of handling them introduces disturbing elements of uncertainty as to our own thinking and acting. It is decidedly unsettling. Justice, in your hands, has reality in it. This I admit. Still you make it always becoming something else, that is, more or less than it was, and hence ever shadowed by something that it is not at the moment. Perhaps I just like my dogmas straight and changeless. Yet really I do not, or I should never learn anything. I have been trying to figure out the element in your thinking which accounts for the uncertainty that accompanies the certainty of plain facts.

BEARD: The time element and its human content, Doctor.

As simple as that? he asked.

As simple and as complex, I answered and told him to fill his pipe before he braved the cold out of doors.

VII

Domestic Tranquility and Common Defense

W HEN I opened the door to my fellow students on the seventh Friday night, I was surprised to see with them a tall, ruddy-faced man about seventy years old, carrying a blackthorn as big as a bludgeon.

MRS. SMYTH: This is our old friend Colonel Blynn. He and Robert were schoolboys together, and the Colonel is spending a few days with us. We told him about our sessions with you on Friday nights and suggested that he could come along with us or, if he preferred, spend the evening in our library with a good detective story. The Colonel doesn't care much for books or professors, but to our surprise he said that he had heard about you and thought you might be not a 'bad guy.' In fact he said he had seen you in action at a hearing of the House Naval Affairs Committee in Washington in February, 1938. So here he is with us tonight.

Knowing that there are all kinds of army officers, I thought it prudent to sound the ground. After remarking that I was honored by his visit, I asked how it happened that an army man was at the Naval Affairs hearings.

COL. BLYNN: It happened this way. I am a South Carolinian like Dr. Smyth, and so I was interested in General Johnson Hagood of our state. I don't know him personally but I have great respect for him. You see, I was in the Spanish war. I did not get into the fray in time enough to be with Teddy on his famous charge up San Juan Hill, but I got a plenty in the Philippine war and managed to be marooned there for years. That February in 1938, I was in Washington looking up some old records and I read in the papers that General Hagood was going to testify before the Naval Affairs Committee. So I went up the Hill to see and hear the General and got so interested that I attended several sessions. Frankly I had never heard of you before, but I agreed so heartily with what you said that I came to the conclusion that you must be bright like me. When Robert and Sue told me about their sessions up here and said that you might take up national defense tonight, I decided to come along.

BEARD: I am delighted to have you, Colonel, and suspect that you really ought to take charge of our session on national defense.

COL. BLYNN: Not me. I served my country for about thirty years—in fact from my early manhood until I was retired on account of a wound received in France in 1918; but I am no expert on defense. The truth is that I have been like General Hagood all along. As you may recall, he said at those Naval hearings that he had been in the army for forty years and had never found out what all the fighting was about. The business of a good soldier is to fight and ask no questions, but at the age of seventy with one foot in the grave I can't help wondering occasionally what I have been doing on earth since I was a young man.

BEARD: I have the *Hearings* right at hand, Colonel. This is what General Hagood said in 1938, after telling of his long service in the Army: 'I have been trying for 44 years to find out what we were trying to do and have not been able to find out yet. The policy of the Navy is one thing. The policy of the Army is another thing, and as far as I have ever been able to learn the policy of the State Department is something else.'

COL. BLYNN: Yes. That's the cold truth and yet some smart fellow on the Committee tried to take the General for a ride because he told them cold truth.

BEARD: No, Colonel, if you will allow me, the Representative who directed a question to General Hagood at that point was Representative Melvin Maas. He was not trying to be smart. He was really astounded to hear that cold truth, as you call it, and he wanted to know more about it.

What was it in General Hagood's testimony that impressed you most?

COL. BLYNN, finding the place in the *Hearings:* See his remarks there about what it is that we ought to be defending, fighting and suffering for. General Hagood says (and mind you, he was a good fighter. I know):

We should give up all idea of regulating the affairs of the world at large. . . . We should devote our entire attention to the problem of giving adequate and complete protection to our interests lying within the continental limits of the United States.

That's what I think, after fighting forty years for something else.

COL. BLYNN: Aren't you a bit old-fashioned, Colonel?

COL. BLYNN: Yes, I guess I am. So let's get on with your business. I want to find out what you are up to.

BEARD: I am indulging, Colonel, in some historical reflections on America, her destiny, and obligations; and for the moment I am making these reflections turn on the Preamble to the Constitution. After much talking we have just got down to the words, 'insure domestic tranquility, provide for the common defense.' Though aware that this may seem professorial to you, while inviting you to interrupt as you please I shall proceed in the customary fashion.

Among the stern facts with which the framers of the Constitution sought to reckon was the probability of domestic discords to come—riots, insurrections, rebellions, and civil wars. They felt sure that the government they were setting up would have to deal with just such propensities of human nature in the coming years.

COL. BLYNN: My God, how right they were! I sometimes think that man would rather fight than eat—at least until he gets enough of it for a season. Excuse me. Go on.

BEARD: The framers had in memory the long story of civil turmoils. The conflicts of factions in Greek city states. The almost endless conflicts of patricians and plebeians in Rome. The slave revolts of antiquity. The servile insurrections of the Middle Ages. The conspiracies of more modern times. They knew about Catiline and Caesar. They were acquainted with the everlasting propensity of men to take up the sword in settling real or imaginary grievances, with the martyrdom of man, with the eternal struggle over the distribution of rights, privileges, and wealth. They, or some of them, had had recent experiences with the struggle between the radical left wing of the Revolutionary party in America and the radical right wing that was ready to take up the sword again. In 1786-87 they could hear alarms of Daniel Shays' rebellion in Massachusetts which frightened owners of property within an inch of their lives.

Mrs. Smyth: Tell us more about Shays. From my school books, I got the idea that he was a wicked trouble-maker, but afterwards I read Edward Bellamy's novel about that insurrection, *The Duke of Stockbridge*. It is in the town library. I confess that I felt some sympathy with Shays and his crowd. Who was he and what became of him?

Beard: It is a long story, Mrs. Smyth, and a sad one, in my judgment. Shays or Shay, as he was sometimes called, was of humble origin. It seems that his father was Patrick Shay and his mother Margaret Dempsey Shay, both Massachusetts colonials. Daniel rushed to arms on hearing of the battle at Lexington. He took part in the battle of Bunker Hill and was promoted for gallantry in action. He was at Ticonderoga, Saratoga, and Stony Point and served in the war until 1780. Apparently, he was a brave and competent soldier, for Lafayette gave him a handsome sword as a token of appreciation—a sword which in the midst of his poverty he sold to buy the necessities of life for his family and himself.

Col. Blynn: Ah, he had a bad streak in him or he wouldn't have done that.

Dr. Smyth: Claptrap! You don't know what you would do if you and your family were hungry. You have no family, never have been hungry, and hence are not entitled to throw any stones at Shays.

Beard: Well, Shays became involved in a movement of poverty-stricken debtors in Massachusetts, who were being hard pressed by their creditors, whose farms were being taken away from them on harsh terms. A clash of arms ensued. The insurrectionists were put down. Shays fled and was condemned to death by the supreme court. On petition he was pardoned. A broken man, he went over into New York and lived there from hand to mouth until his death in 1825. To most of the respectable people in Massachusetts, Shays was a horrible creature. His name became a bogey with which to terrify the public into supporting the Constitution. Jefferson thought that a rebellion now and then was a good thing, but not many of his class shared his opinion.

Col. Blynn: What I want to know is, Was Shays right or wrong?

Dr. Smyth: Let me answer that! Shays was neither right nor wrong. Anybody with any courage will fight for his family and his bread. Shays just happened to live at the wrong time. That's all.

If he and his crowd of farmers were alive today, Santa Claus in Washington would borrow money from the rich and lend it to them at low interest and give them fifty years to pay it back in. If Shays and his band were here now, they would be heroes instead of dirty rebels.

MRS. SMYTH: Now Robert, you and the Colonel are not getting anywhere with that line of talk. I am awakening to the fact that there is deep human interest in the history of the Constitution. I am moved by the story of this gallant but poor officer of the Revolution, who, by making trouble over poverty, helped to bring about the adoption of the Constitution. I suppose that we could spend the night discussing Shays. Yet I feel a little guilty in starting off on the Shays' business when we should be considering domestic tranquility.

BEARD: I am glad, Mrs. Smyth, that you asked for more information about Shays. There certainly is a lot of human interest in his revolt—and in the Constitution, too, if we but look for it. For a long time Shays was a hunted man. To the end of his days, he was a sad figure. What became of his first wife, Abigail Gilbert, historians have not yet reported. Doubtless she shared his sufferings and trials in Massachusetts. Long afterward, Daniel married again in Sparta, New York, a woman whose first name was Rhoda, but whose last name is unknown. When Daniel was buried at Conesus, New York, someone cared enough to put a small stone, bearing the inscription, 'Da. Shays,' at the head of his grave. The stone crumbled. The grave was neglected for nearly a hundred years. Then the County Historical Society repaired the neglect and had an appropriate marker erected. If you care to know more about the human interest of this affair, Mrs. Smyth, read the moving, if perhaps highly imaginative, story about Shays by Dorothy Canfield Fisher, in her book, *Raw Material*, published in 1923.

To return to the subject of domestic tranquility. To assure this tranquility, to provide for meeting such disturbances as Shays made, the framers of the Constitution put specific sections into the document. In the fourth Article they declared: 'The United States shall guarantee to every state in this Union a republican form of government, and shall protect each of them against invasion; and on the application of the legislature, or of the executive (when the legislature cannot be convened) against domestic violence.'

Under provisions of the Constitution, Congress can enact, and has enacted, legislation authorizing the use of the armed forces of the United States in executing federal law against persons engaged in insurrection or obstructing the enforcement of law by ordinary processes. The history of the numerous cases arising under these constitutional provisions is too long and involved for us to bring under review here.

Taking up the Doctor's comment on what Shays would get from Santa Claus in Washington if he were here today, I should like to add that the legislation of the New Deal, which has saved thousands of debtors from utter ruin, was enacted, ironically enough, under the very Constitution which owed its existence in some measure to Shays' insurrection. But we must leave domestic tranquility and turn to the subject of common defense.

COL. BLYNN: Before you do that, I want to say that I never liked the use of the United States Army in labor disputes. I don't doubt that strikers ought to have their heads broken at times. But I think that the local police should take care of such troubles unless they reach such scale as to threaten the country. My idea is that the Army's business is to defend the country against foreign foes, and not to intervene in quarrels between capital and labor. I have had some experience in dealing with such quarrels. I know that Army men are usually more level-headed and less free with shooting irons than the local police. Still I never did like it, and I don't like it now.

DR. SMYTH: Humph! You just have an exalted notion of your profession.

COL. BLYNN: Maybe so, maybe so. But I came this evening especially to hear about national defense, and I'd rather hear about that than wrangle with you civilians. You civilians do not seem to understand the point of view of Army men on anything. If I should cut loose, your beautiful fabric of political theory would look as if a Kansas cyclone had passed through it.

BEARD: Pray cut loose, Colonel. We are all here to learn something. There are no limits on free speech in our conferences. The only limit we recognize is that of sticking as closely to our subject as we can—conveniently.

DR. SMYTH: Tell us what is eating you, Colonel.

COL. BLYNN: First of all, I get mad as hell at the way civilians, especially politicians, go around blubbering about peace and treating the armed forces like poor relations and nuisances, until a war comes. After the First World War, when the officers of the Army and Navy were trying to prepare the country for the next row, which we all knew very well would come, we were told cock-and-bull stories by pacifists, politicians, and members of Congress. 'Oh,' we were instructed, 'there isn't going to be any more war. Look at the Washington conference on naval limits and the blessed Kellogg Pact solemnly binding all the great powers to settle disputes by peaceful means.' And all the rest of it. . . . You know the tune as well as I do.

We were sold the guff about war to end wars: one more big war and then war is all over forever. When Army men respectfully refused to believe it and asked for men and materials for the next war, they were called militarists. In time the next war came; and, so help me God, we weren't much better prepared for it than a Baptist Sunday-School picnic.

What gets my goat more than anything else is the long-haired men and the short-haired women running around peddling peace plans between wars and calling military men who refuse to believe their stuff militarists. Most of the fighting men I know in the Army and the Navy are nothing of the sort. I am talking about the fighting men, not the swivel-chair artists who lecture to women's clubs and peace societies. I was in the game for about forty years, and I know my buddies. They are for their country right or wrong, yes, damn it, right or wrong. They know very well that the peace-peddlers who condemn them as militarists will be around in a few days or years calling on them to fight and cheering the soldiers as heroes. Once in a while they ask themselves quietly, What are we fighting for, that is, for what advantage to our country and the people?

They don't want any highfalutin claptrap for an answer either, to make them fight when the job is put on their shoulders. I fought like the devil in the Philippines when I despised all the nonsense about civilizing our brown brothers that McKinley, Taft, Theodore Roosevelt, and Jeremiah Beveridge were putting out. If I had believed these dopesters, I would have thrown up my commission and hit for my home in South Carolina. The same was true with me when I was fighting in France in 1917 until I was knocked out. I believed the Germans had to have a licking. I didn't need a college professor to tell me that. And I did my bit to give it to them.

After I recovered from my smash in the shoulder and got home, nothing made me madder than to hear a smug civilian telling the world what 'we' fought for. It reminded me of a man who swore that he would never attend any Church except the Protestant Episcopal Church because he knew the prayers of that Church in advance. So he could go or stay away according to whether he wanted what was being prayed for. As for Methodists and Baptists, he would never go within gunshot of their services because, he said, they were always praying for a lot of things he didn't want and would make him sick if he got them. That is the way I feel about civilians who talk about war—what for?—and peace—what for?

Here the Colonel pulled out his watch and apologized for riding roughshod over our seminar. Though we told him to speak his mind freely, he refused to be budged and remarked very gently: Go ahead, Professor, with your line.

BEARD: With some reluctance, I take up my line. Four prime considerations weighed heavily with the framers in making the actual provisions of law authorizing an effective common defense.

The first was a realistic view of mankind which took account of war as a persistent phenomenon of history. To none of them was war an end in itself, a perfect good, the noblest profession for virile men; but all of them knew that war might be a means to a great end and anyway that it was to be expected in the economy of Providence. War had given them independence. It might be necessary, they thought, to preserve that independence.

Behind them was the history of war since the beginning of recorded time. The eighteenth century in Europe had been filled with wars—two of them, the War of the Spanish Succession and the Seven Years' War, extending into the American colonies and the far quarters of the earth. Other wars were brewing in Europe at the time. To men like Jefferson, then American minister to France, Europe was the home of eternal wars.

The second consideration with the framers was the fact that three great warlike powers—Britain, France, and Spain—possessed dominions in the neighborhood of the United States. They were likely at any time to become involved in another war on land and water in this hemisphere. In that case it would be necessary for the United States to have a care for its interests and perhaps defend them by arms. If they had overlooked war in general, they could not have failed to see the special dangers near at hand.

The third consideration was the fear of foreign intrigues in American affairs and the need of means to meet threat with threat. American leaders had had enough experience with diplomacy in Europe to put them on guard against childlike confidence in diplomatic exchanges as weapons of defense and instruments of power.

Yet, in the presence of these stark realities, the framers had a terrible fear of large military and naval establishments. Such establishments were expensive and consumed the substance of the people. They were themselves incitements to war, for men, like little children, are seldom content merely to play with their toys or watch them standing on a shelf. From Roman history, the framers learned that the civil government finally became a sport of the army, that the office of emperor was bought and sold at the pleasure of military chieftains.

On this point Madison doubtless expressed a general view when he said in the 41st Number of *The Federalist:*

The veteran legions of Rome were an overmatch for the undisciplined valor of all other nations, and rendered her mistress of the world. Not the less true is it, that the liberties of Rome proved the final victim to her military triumphs; and that the liberties of Europe, as far as they ever existed, have, with few exceptions, been the price of her military establishments. A standing force, therefore, is a dangerous, at the same time that it may be a necessary, provision. On the smallest scale it has its inconveniences. On an extensive scale its consequences may be fatal. On any scale it is an object of laudable circumspection and precaution. A wise nation will combine all of these considerations; and, whilst it does not rashly preclude itself from any resource which may become essential to its safety, will exert all prudence in diminishing both the necessity and the danger of resorting to one which may be inauspicious to its liberties.

How to institute armed powers great enough to defend the country and yet not too great to destroy its liberties—that was the supreme question which the framers faced in making arrangements for common defense.

Judging by the hot debates that occurred over the popular ratification of the Constitution, nothing was more feared by the American people at the time than a standing army.

Col. Blynn: That is strange. In fact it seems absurd to me. Nobody who is acquainted with the officers and men of the American Army could ever think of their wanting to seize the civil government of the United States and make a general an emperor or a dictator. It's ridiculous. It's true that recently one or two old officers played around with the Silver Shirts or some bunch of Shirts but they just made asses of themselves. To think of American soldiers drawn from homes all over the country trying to set themselves up as Caesars or Napoleons or Hitlers is simply comical. I think the fathers of the Constitution must have been looking under the bed for ghosts.

Mrs. Smyth: You should have been here the other evening, Colonel, when we were discussing underground efforts to set up a military dictatorship during and after the Revolutionary war—a move in which some military men had a hand.

Col. Blynn: I never heard of it. I don't believe that it is true. Anyhow, why pick on the Army? What about the Navy? They are the boys who are always talking about our sea power all around the world and they generally try to grab the lion's share of the money from Congress. One of their pedagogues by the name of Mahan got some of them drunk with big-power gin. They encouraged the country and many politicians high up to think that we could just tell other governments to obey our orders and make them obey the orders by sending big ships everywhere around in the seven seas. However that may be just an Army grouch. Why didn't the Americans of 1787 fear a Navy as much as an Army?

Beard: Some of them did, Colonel. Jefferson once said:

> I am not for a standing army in time of peace, which may overawe public sentiment; nor for a navy which, by its expenses and the eternal wars in which it will implicate us, will grind us with public burdens and sink us under them.

If you will allow a mere student of history to venture an opinion, I will say that you are hard on the Navy. Back in 1935, Admiral William S. Sims declared in a radio broadcast to the nation:

> Our country must remain at peace. Our trade as a neutral must be at the risk of the trader. Our army and navy must not be used to protect this trade. We cannot keep out of war and at the same

time enforce the freedom of the seas—that is, the freedom to make profits out of countries in a death struggle.

And after that broadcast, the World Peace Foundation took a secret poll of admirals and captains in the Navy on Admiral Sims' plan as a policy tending to keep us out of war. In their replies sixty-two naval officers were unqualifiedly in favor of it and thirty-nine were unqualifiedly against it. According to that poll, it does not appear that all your Navy boys have been heated up with big-power gin.

At all events, in the historical experience with which the framers of the Constitution were familiar, it had been armies, not navies, that had threatened the liberties of peoples. The struggle for civil liberties in England had been a struggle, in part, of civilians to wrest control over the army from the king and to subject it to Parliament. That victory the English had won in the seventeenth century. The framers of the Constitution were acquainted with that story, and they proposed to establish civilian control here, while at the same time making provision for common defense.

Let us first examine the powers conferred on Congress. The Constitution gives Congress an unlimited power to raise and support armies, to provide and maintain a navy, to make rules for the government of the land and naval forces, to provide for the organizing and arming of the militia, and to declare war. For practical purposes these powers are unlimited. Every man, every dollar, every bit of material resources can be drawn upon in building armed forces and waging war.

That certainly was necessary, for, as was said at the time, why limit the war powers of the United States when we are helpless to limit the powers of any country with which we are at war?

But the *exercise* of these powers is not to be wanton. It is limited in three fundamental respects:

According to the Constitution, Congress alone can declare war and it keeps control through the purse, for the Constitution declares that no appropriation of money for military purposes shall be for a longer term than two years. Thus Congress has a check on the armed forces which it creates.

In the next place, the Constitution vests control over the armed forces during peace and war in a civil officer of the Government. 'The President,' it specifies, 'shall be Commander in Chief of the

Army and Navy of the United States, and of the militia of the several states, when called into the actual service of the United States.' In other words, Congress cannot designate a military man as commander in chief; nor can the President shift responsibility for the supreme command to any officer of the Army or Navy. He may delegate powers to leaders of the armed forces, but he cannot escape the burden which the Constitution imposes upon him.

COL. BLYNN: I never thought of it before, but I wonder whether the President could put on a uniform, go to the field, and personally direct armed forces in combat. Did the framers of the Constitution discuss that point, and if so, how did they reason about it?

BEARD: The records of the Convention, as you doubtless know, Colonel, are far from complete. The subject you mention was raised in the Convention but was not thoroughly threshed out. References to it occupy only a few lines in the records we have and they are mere hints, just tantalizing hints. The opinions I offer you are my own but I will give you my grounds.

First, there is nothing in the Constitution or any of the records that precludes the idea of the President's putting on a uniform and taking personal command in the field. Of that I am certain. Did the framers expect or intend the President to do this? I am of the opinion that many of them did. Of this I am fairly sure. There is evidence worthy of respect that a majority of them may have intended to accord that right to the President as commander in chief.

What is the evidence for this? Luther Martin, a delegate from Maryland, in a report made to the legislature of that state in November, 1787, referred to the clause making the President commander in chief, and said, 'It was wished to be so far restrained, that he should not command in person; but this could not be obtained.' In a plan drawn up by Hamilton and known to several delegates, though not formally presented to the Convention, it was proposed that the President should have direction of war when it commenced but should not take the actual command in the field without the consent of both houses of Congress. The Paterson plan laid before the Convention provided that the Executive should direct all military operations but should not on any occasion command troops personally as a general or in any other capacity. This proposal was not adopted by the Convention.

On these and other grounds, I hold that the President could, under the Constitution, put on a uniform and take personal command in the field. What all the framers really thought, I cannot discover. I am inclined to the opinion that they left the question open, if they did not actually intend or expect the President to take charge of armed forces in the field. Anyway, nothing forbids the President to do this. No President has thus far assumed this power; but how on earth, Colonel, could he be restrained from doing it if he decided upon such a course? Ask the Supreme Court for a mandamus ordering him to take off his uniform and go back to the White House?

COL. BLYNN: Search me. But it seems queer business for the framers, as you call them, to put such unlimited powers in the hands of a civilian who might not know a thing about warfare, strategy, and tactics. When you come to think of it, it's the funniest thing on earth.

BEARD: Let me ask you in whom you would vest this power, Colonel, if you were making a constitution? Parenthetically, although I do not regard it as actually funny, I may agree that it does seem strange that a civilian should be commander in chief of the armed forces of a country. Now what about my question? Would you allow the President merely to appoint the commander in chief? If so, you would have to let him remove the man he appointed or else give the commander unlimited tenure. If the President could remove, then he would have to be the judge of the efficiency of any commander appointed and thus go into the actual conduct of war. Or would you allow Congress to elect the commander in chief? Or would you set up somehow a board of civilians or military men empowered to choose and remove the commander in chief? If so, what kind of a board?

COL. BLYNN: You professors can ask more theoretical questions than any other fellows I know. I confess that I am stumped. God knows, I don't, how to get commanders in chief who can win wars— which is the point. If anybody could solve that problem he would be a genius, and if every country solved it, wars would be all stalemates or victories for all parties.

I certainly would not want to have to fight under a commander in chief elected by Congress. As I recall, Congress set up a committee on the conduct of the Civil War, and it nearly drove Lincoln and the army officers crazy. It would never do to let the general staff or any army or navy organization choose the commander in chief. That would disrupt unity and give play to every ambition except that of winning the war, if I know my profession.

I confess that I am stumped. I guess that I shall have to agree with you that the framers did about as good a job as they could. So far it has worked fairly well or at least we have come out of wars with our skins left. But what power—the war power combined with all executive power—to put into the hands of one man! And besides the war power is more than merely power to command troops in the field. What is the war power anyway?

BEARD: You have reversed the tables, Colonel. I'm stumped on that question, and frankly do not know how to answer it.

COL. BLYNN: You mean to say that you have been studying the law and practice of the Constitution for forty years or more and cannot answer a plain question like that?

BEARD: Colonel, let me ask you to define war.

COL. BLYNN: I'll do it. War is the unlimited use of men and materials, all forces material and moral, for the purpose of destroying the forces of the enemy and rendering him powerless to offer any further resistance.

BEARD: That is good enough for me, Colonel. But if war is the *unlimited* use of men and materials to destroy the enemy, how are you going to define the war power of the President, for a definition is a limitation? Putting exercises in logic aside, the war powers of the President are in fact so great and so indefinite that their nature will not be fully known until our Republic has passed through all its trials and ceased to be. Then some historian will be able to tell you just what they *were*—not are—under the Constitution. The President's war power is the unexplored and dark continent of American government.

Still, it does have some legal and moral limits. The Constitution is in force in time of war as well as in time of peace. The President may do things in time of war that he cannot do in time of peace. For instance Lincoln in 1863 proclaimed the slaves free in places then in arms against the United States, although under the Constitution the whole Government of the United States could not touch slavery in any state. He did this under his war power as applied to the theater of war. But he left slavery intact in states to which the Constitution could apply in full force. In a large measure and in important respects, Lincoln scrupulously followed the mandates of the Constitution. For limitations on the war power, we must depend mainly upon the character of the President, the alertness and firmness of Congress, and the good sense of the people.

There is, in my opinion, no royal road to the successful and constitutional management of common defense or the successful conduct of war. We cannot leave everything to the technicians of warfare. They differ widely and often bitterly among themselves. Remember the long fight of the navy men for the battleship and against the air power. The technicians in the Army and the Navy thus unwittingly did harm to the country and were impervious to facts and reasoning, until they confronted the demonstrations of air power and of battleship vulnerability in the Second World War.

As Clemenceau said, 'War is much too important a business to be left to the soldiers.' Again and again in war, civilians have had to interfere with technicians to save their country from folly if not ruin. Now that war involves all men and all women, all industries, sciences, and arts, all management and all labor, common defense calls for a concentration of civilian and martial talents and for an intensity and wisdom of co-operation far beyond anything previously experienced in history. To this point we have come since 1787 under the Constitution of the United States.

One thing I feel sure of. It is that the war power of the greatest nation has material and moral limits and a failure on the part of the people and statesmen to recognize them will lead to disaster.

Well, said the COLONEL, as we were parting for the evening, I never realized that the Constitution is such an amazing war document; that the framers of it so squarely faced the business of war.

And a peace document too, rejoined MRS. SMYTH.

War and Peace, mused the COLONEL. What a story Tolstoy has given us! Wait a minute. Before I go, I want to unburden my mind of a matter which has long troubled me and which I mentioned earlier in the evening; that is, by whom and how is the question to be settled for what and where we are to fight? General Hagood said he never knew, and I have never been able to find out. There is a lot of good sense in what the framers of the Constitution said and in the provisions of the Constitution on war, but certainly we have got far away from the notion that our fighting business ought to be limited to national defense.

If what you read in the papers is so, we've been fighting to confer the blessings of civilization on our little brown brothers, to make the world safe for democracy, and a lot else besides defense. Congress can still theoretically declare war, but the President can conduct foreign affairs in such a way as to make war imperative on Congress and the armed forces. It seems to me that, with all due respect to you, Professor, your essay tonight smells a bit musty. Honestly, when it comes to war, nobody appears to give a damn about the Constitution or mere defense either. This talk-fest up here belongs to you and the Smyths, but I just want to leave that nut for you to break your teeth on.

With that shot, the Colonel brought his blackthorn down on the porch floor with a whack as he stamped out to the driveway.

VIII

Promote the General Welfare

I HAVE brought along a book which may interest you since it comes under the head of history, Mrs. Smyth said in greeting me, as I opened the door again to my fellow-searchers. It is Albert Deutsch's *The Mentally Ill in America: A History of Their Care and Treatment*. I also have another book by Deutsch, written in co-operation with David M. Schneider, called *The History of Public Welfare in New York State*. If you would like to look at it too, I should be happy to lend it to you. I thought that these histories might fit into our discussion of the general welfare tonight. Robert ridiculed the idea and said that the hard-boiled men who wrote the Constitution were not thinking of welfare in any such sense.

I had to agree with Robert. In preparation for this session we read the original Constitution again last night. When he had finished it, Robert said, 'It's a cold proposition. No God in it, nothing about the rights of man; not a word on suffering humanity; nothing human except omission of the word slavery, which they all knew existed under their very noses, even in Connecticut and New York. It is full of factual words and technical terms such as *ex post facto* and writ of *habeas corpus*.'

After we had gone all through it we both wondered how on earth the words general welfare got into the clammy document. We hope that you can help us out on this point.

Beard: I am glad to see that you are familiar with Deutsch's history of the mentally ill in America. I hope you have read the chapter on Dorothea Dix and her long struggle against benighted Americans to secure decent treatment for persons suffering from mental diseases, including her effort to educate the Congress of the United States. You may not know it, but I have always been interested in more than politics, economics, and law. When I read

Deutsch's chapter on Dorothea Dix I was ashamed of the noble males who fought her common sense and humanity.

DR. SMYTH: Aren't we getting off the track? I see nothing in the Constitution that has the slightest bearing on welfare as you and Sue seem to interpret it. And as for women, they did not get the right to an education until after the middle of the nineteenth century, and they did not have the national suffrage until 1920. The Constitution was written in 1787 and it is strange business to mix welfare and women with that undertaking.

MRS. SMYTH: Before we really start, I want to have one more word. Robert has confused education and schooling—which may be two different things. Women were educated before schools and colleges were opened to them. From early times in America thousands of influential women were well educated. We must not of course spend the evening talking about the way they got educated, but the fact should be stated so that we can keep our intellectual bearings. About as many women as men, in some regions more, could read and write as long ago as 1850. Furthermore the influence of women in history is not to be measured by the right to vote or any other mere legal privileges. Now, I am ready for the general welfare. We do want to know how the words got into the Constitution.

BEARD: Once more, I shall have to disappoint you. The history of how the words got there and what they were intended to mean is still somewhat obscure. As you know, from your reading of the document, they appear twice in the Constitution: first, in the Preamble; and second, in Section 8 of Article I: 'The Congress shall have power to lay and collect taxes, duties, imposts, and excises, to pay the debts and provide for the common defense and general welfare of the United States.'

The words general welfare were not in the Preamble of the draft referred by the Convention to the Committee of Style seven days before it adjourned. They were in the revised draft reported by the Committee of Style, two days later.

DR. SMYTH: That is the Committee of Style we were talking about a few nights ago—the committee that included Hamilton and a fine lot of other reactionaries? How do you explain that? Did they bring the words down out of the blue sky and put them into the Preamble?

BEARD: I cannot explain briefly and exactly how or why the words were inserted in the draft. The records available to us do not permit us to answer that question. But the committee did not have to go up into the sky for the words. They were in the old Articles of Confederation. That document declared that the states entered into a 'firm league of friendship with each other, for their common defense, the security of their liberties, and their mutual and general welfare.'

DR. SMYTH: That surprises me. If the words were in the old Articles, they surely did not mean a thing, for that was just a compact between independent states for limited purposes, and there was no such thing as general welfare. The United States consisted of sovereign states. To introduce general welfare was to introduce a contradiction in terms.

BEARD: At all events, Doctor, the words are in the Articles of Confederation and they are in the Preamble of the Constitution. They are also in the first Article of the Constitution itself—in the taxing clause. How they got there and what they originally meant— that is a confused story. Authorities differ violently over the truth of the story. If you want to go into details, here is a book of 378 pages of fine print on the subject: James F. Lawson's *The General Welfare Clause,* an important work printed as well as written by the author, in 1934. Chapter VIII deals with the proceedings in the Convention of 1787.

MRS. SMYTH: Do you mean to say that historians have big books on every word in the Constitution and have to be familiar with them all? If so, how are plain citizens ever to master the document?

BEARD: We do not have a big volume on every word, Mrs. Smyth, but we doubtless have as many volumes on the Constitution as there are words in it. My library is small but the wall behind your chair is covered with selected works. We even have a book on words that are not in the Constitution but *might* have been in it. Here it is, Jane Butzner's *Constitutional Chaff* (1941)—a treatise on suggestions and proposals brought up in the convention of 1787 and rejected. It is an important and entertaining book. Reading it makes one wonder what would have happened if this or that proposal finally rejected by the convention had been adopted; the election of the President by Congress, for example. Some of the proposals that were accepted got into the Constitution by a narrow margin; some of the proposals that were discarded were lost by a narrow margin.

DR. SMYTH: I should think that Miss Butzner's book ought to be suppressed by our local Society for Constitutional Vigilance. If some of the sacred words in the document got there by a narrow margin, what becomes of verbal inspiration—and the superlative wisdom of the fathers? But pardon my digression. At this rate we shall not finish general welfare before we die.

BEARD: That is no digression. It is difficult to imagine anything human that does not have a bearing on the Constitution, that is, on life, liberty, general welfare, and government in the United States.

As I was about to go on with general welfare, the bell rang. On answering the ring, I found standing at the door a young woman whom I had seen about town but did not know personally. As she asked for Doctor and Mrs. Smyth, the latter sprang up and said: 'Let me explain. This is Jean Robbins, in charge of our social work at the Hospital. I was telling her today about our session tonight on general welfare. Jean asked whether she might come in and I took the liberty of saying, Yes, counting on your hospitality. She is interested in the history of social work as well as being an efficient practitioner.'

BEARD: You are doubly welcome, Miss Robbins. You are likely to contribute more to our symposium than you get out of it.

MISS ROBBINS: I am sorry to be late. I was called far out on a hard case, just as I was preparing to start up here.

BEARD, after a brief review of what had been said: The words general welfare as they stand in the Preamble have not excited much attention, but oceans of ink have been spilt over the meaning of the phrase in the taxing clause of the Constitution.

Broadly speaking there have been two views of the general welfare phrase in the body of the Constitution.

One of them was expressed by James Madison.

DR. SMYTH: Then it ought to be sound, for, to say it again for the tenth time, he was the father of the Constitution.

BEARD: That is all right as to his being the father. But he did not express the opinion to which I refer—the starkest of his opinions on the subject—until he had joined Jefferson in wholesale opposition to Hamilton's program. When you deal with what one

of the framers said, you must take note of *just when* he said it—
before or after taking the political medicine of partisanship.

In helping Jeffersonians out in the party struggle, Madison declared that the general welfare phrase meant exactly nothing. He
said that Congress had the power to provide money for the common defense and the general welfare. But, he added, right under
these words is a list of the specific powers given to Congress; money
can be spent for the general welfare only in the form of an appropriation to a specific end among those enumerated. In other words,
according to Madison after he became the partisan, all purposes
coming under the head of the general welfare are listed in the
lines that follow these words in the Constitution; no other purposes
are contemplated by the words. This is the doctrine that the powers
of Congress are strictly defined within the narrowest possible limits
and that Congress cannot do a thing which it is not expressly empowered to do by a direct statement.

To illustrate the narrow way of looking at things, suppose I say,
'I authorize you, Mrs. Smyth, to collect money to provide for the
general welfare of the Hospital and then also specifically authorize
you to buy surgical instruments, tables, and chairs.' Suppose you
find the roof leaking badly and spend some of the money having
it repaired and thereupon I protest: 'My term, general welfare,
meant nothing. I only authorized you to buy instruments, tables,
and chairs.'

I submit that if our dispute were referred to any committee of
sensible persons they would say to me: 'If you intended to limit
Mrs. Smyth to buying the three kinds of objects, why on earth did
you put the words *general welfare* into your authorization? If they
convey no power whatever to Mrs. Smyth, putting them into your
authorization was senseless.'

That is my answer to Madison's narrow interpretation of the
general welfare clause. It has been the answer of other commentators on the Constitution for more than a hundred years.

It was the answer made by Alexander Hamilton soon after the
Federal Government was launched. Congress passed an act establishing the first United States Bank. There was nothing in the
Constitution about the power of Congress to charter such a corporation, partly public, mainly private. Jefferson and his friends, including Madison, attacked the law. Jefferson declared that the Con-

stitution should be strictly construed and that so construed it did not authorize Congress to create the Bank.

Hamilton insisted on a broad or liberal view of the Constitution. He called attention to the fact that the Constitution empowered Congress to make all laws 'necessary and proper' for carrying into effect the powers conferred upon it. The Bank, Hamilton urged, was useful and expedient in the management of federal finances— the collection of taxes, taking care of federal funds, and paying government bills. That was one prong of his argument. Then he turned to the general welfare clause for additional support. He said that, with regard to taxing and spending money, Congress was subject to only one limitation, namely, that it must be for the general welfare, as distinguished from local purposes. 'The constitutional *test* of a right application [of funds],' he maintained, 'must always be, whether it be for a purpose of *general* or *local* nature. If the former, there can be no want of constitutional power.'

This left open the important question, How do you decide whether an action is for the general welfare or for a local purpose? Hamilton answered: The question whether an action 'will really promote or not the welfare of the Union, must be a matter of conscientious discretion, and the arguments for or against a measure in this light, must be arguments concerning expediency or inexpediency, not of constitutional right.'

Hamilton took a broad view of the phrase general welfare. He remarked that it is 'as comprehensive as any that could have been used,' and that it embraced 'a vast variety of particulars, which are susceptible of neither specification nor definition,' including 'whatever concerns the general interest of learning, of agriculture, of manufactures, and of commerce.'

Hamilton's view was later confirmed by Justice Joseph Story in his commentaries on the Constitution. Story argued that the only limitation on the taxing power of Congress is that it is to be exercised for the common defense and general welfare, for national defense and national welfare, as contrasted with local or special purposes. A tax is unconstitutional, he added, if laid for objects 'wholly extraneous (as, for instance, for propagating Mahometanism among the Turks, or giving aids and subsidies to a foreign nation, to build palaces for its kings, or erect monuments to its heroes).'

Yet Story had to admit that Congress had even appropriated

money to aid distressed people in other countries. He called attention to the fact that Congress had voted relief to refugees of Santo
Domingo in 1794 and to citizens of Venezuela suffering from the
calamity of an earthquake in 1812. That was indeed stretching the
general welfare clause which was supposed to apply to the United
States; but Congress, under Democrats and Republicans alike, continued to make grants of money for general purposes in America
and in aid of suffering peoples in foreign countries.

DR. SMYTH: Is it true that, from the beginning of its history down
to the New Deal, Congress had been appropriating money for general purposes besides those specifically listed among the powers of
Congress?

BEARD: That is correct. The statute books from 1789 to 1933 are
crowded with appropriations for objects not mentioned in the
Constitution specifically.

DR. SMYTH: Then, why all the hullabaloo after 1933? How could
Congress vote money to feed suffering wretches in Venezuela in
1812 and not vote all the money it wanted to vote or could get its
hands on to feed the unemployed and hungry in the United States
in 1933, or in aid of commerce, agriculture, manufactures, learning,
and the general welfare?

BEARD: It is funny, positively funny, Doctor, for you to be asking
me this question in 1942. If my memory serves me right, you, as a
good Cleveland Democrat, joined our Liberty Leaguers in 1935 in
shouting that the whole New Deal was unconstitutional. You were
peeved at me for saying that, in my opinion, it was constitutional
all right and that the only question in my mind was whether and
how far the New Deal was useful or expedient.

DR. SMYTH: Yes. I remember all that and I remember also that
the Supreme Court declared most of the New Deal unconstitutional
as soon as it got a chance.

BEARD: But the same Court reversed itself or was set in reverse,
soon after President Roosevelt called upon Congress to reform that
venerable institution. At all events we may now regard it as settled
law that Congress may spend money in aid of the general welfare.
The proposition was clearly stated by Justice Cardozo, one of President Hoover's appointees, in Helvering *v.* Davis, a Social Security
case decided in 1937. I cannot do better than quote Justice Cardozo's
own words:

Congress may spend money in aid of the 'general welfare.' . . .
There have been great statesmen in our history who have stood for
other views. We will not resurrect the contest. It is now settled by
decision. . . . Yet difficulties are left when the power is conceded.
The line must be drawn between one welfare and another, between
particular and general. Where this shall be placed cannot be known
through a formula in advance of the event. There is a middle ground
or certainly a penumbra in which discretion is large. The discretion,
however, is not confided to the courts. The discretion belongs to
Congress, unless the choice is clearly wrong, a display of arbitrary
power, not an exercise of judgment. This is now familiar law. . . .
Nor is the concept of the general welfare static. Needs that were
narrow or parochial a century ago may be interwoven in our day
with the well-being of the Nation. What is critical or urgent changes
with the times.

The purge of the nation-wide calamity that began in 1929 has
taught us many lessons. Not the least, of the solidarity of interests
that may once have seemed to be divided. . . . Spreading from state
to state, unemployment is an ill not particular but general, which
may be checked, if Congress so determines, by the resources of the
Nation. If this can have been doubtful until now, our ruling today
. . . has set the doubt at rest. . . . The hope behind this statute is
to save men and women from the rigors of the poorhouse as well as
from the haunting fear that such a lot awaits them when the journey's
end is near. . . . The problem is mainly national in area and dimen-
sions. Moreover, laws of the separate states cannot deal with it
effectively. Congress, at least had a basis for that belief. . . . Only
a power that is national can serve the interests of all. . . . The issue
is a closed one. It was fought out long ago. When money is spent to
promote the general welfare, the concept of welfare or the opposite
is shaped by Congress, not the states. So the concept be not arbitrary,
the locality must yield.

Mrs. Smyth: All that is simply and beautifully stated. It is literature. I had always thought of Supreme Court opinions as dull,
heavy, forbidding, and beyond the grasp of persons not trained
in the law. What Justice Cardozo says seems to be just plain common sense clothed in living prose.

Beard: I agree with you, Mrs. Smyth. But Cardozo was a genius.
Many Supreme Court opinions are written in involved language.

I often think that I might have learned to write English if I had not read so many turgid judicial opinions. Justice Stone writes sinewy prose also, not as flowing as Holmes' or Cardozo's, but no less cogent. Long ago Chief Justice Marshall set a noble example. In fact some of the worst and some of the best English written in America can be found in Supreme Court opinions.

MISS ROBBINS: I should like to ask this question: Do you believe that the framers of the general welfare clause, if they were here today, would approve as constitutional all the federal legislation dealing with general welfare; that is, with old age security, maternal care, provisions for the unemployed, the defective, the delinquent, security of the home, the promotion of industry and agriculture so as to give employment and uphold the capacity of our economy to produce wealth enough for a high standard of living? I was brought up at home and in college to believe that all such government interference with economy and private affairs was contrary to the American way, as it is called, and to the Constitution besides.

BEARD: Miss Robbins, your inquiry is highly appropriate. The Supreme Court is constantly inquiring into the intention of the framers in putting certain words and clauses into the Constitution. It is constantly asking what the framers would think or do about new propositions, if they were still alive. I am tempted to answer your question by telling a story—which may be apocryphal. On the occasion of the celebration of Lincoln's birthday in 1933, a reporter for a newspaper called on Senator George W. Norris and asked him, 'What would Lincoln do if he were here today?' The Senator sat thoughtfully for a long time and then slowly and softly replied: 'What would Lincoln do if he were here? He would be just like me. He would not know what the hell to do.'

This yarn is not exactly apposite, but it illustrates the difficulty of answering your question. I do not pretend to know what leaders among the framers of the Constitution would have said and done under the head of the general welfare if they had been here, let us say, in 1933—or Jefferson either, for that matter.

But they certainly were men of vision and action. They set up a government endowed with large powers for action. They intended it to act in all matters of national or general interest, as such matters multiplied with the development of the country. They did, it is true, put limitations on the government, but they were concerned in their day with the efficient discharge of national obligations rather than with hampering and hobbling government. They were not committed to the doctrine of *laissez faire* and did not go around crying to government, Let us alone. What did they establish a government for? To do many things that had not been done and to interfere with a lot of things that the states and private citizens had been doing. In various respects the country was in a crisis in 1787, as later in 1933, and the framers, instead of lamenting, went into action.

DR. SMYTH: That is all right, but what about Miss Robbins' question? Would the framers have approved as constitutional all the Santa Claus legislation which she has listed as modern welfare work? Frankly I don't believe they would. I cannot imagine Hamilton worrying about child labor, poverty, or the employment of women fourteen hours a day in factories. Or Thomas Jefferson either, though he was not a framer.

BEARD: I just said, Doctor, that I do not know what they would have said and done about general welfare in 1933. But I am sure as fate that they intended to set up a government endowed with broad national powers and that they expected their posterity to use those powers in dealing with questions, crises, and disturbances arising from generation to generation. They cast important parts of the Constitution in general terms, and so coming generations could adapt it to their needs and interpret its general terms in accordance with their own understandings. They entrusted general welfare to the Federal Government and local welfare to states and communities, as welfare was then understood and practiced. When matters once local became, in the course of events, general, they were brought automatically under federal powers.

DR. SMYTH: Yet I insist that they did not include under welfare, whether general or local, government attention to the sick, the poverty-stricken, the unemployed, lame, blind, halt, and flat failures, such as you seem to be wanting us to provide for today in the name of welfare. Back in 1787 people had to hustle for themselves or take the consequences.

BEARD: I should like to leave that to Miss Robbins, Doctor. She was trained in welfare work at a neighboring institution which specialized in it, and I dare say had a course in the history of the subject. Besides, Doctor, I suggest that you take time to read the book on *The History of Public Welfare in New York State,* which your wife mentioned tonight.

MISS ROBBINS: I did spend two hours a week on the history of social legislation and welfare work from colonial times to 1925. I do not know what Dr. Smyth means by letting misfits, failures, the sick, and poverty-stricken take the consequences. At no time, from the very beginning of colonial settlements, did settlers, like the Spartans, put weaklings out to die or leave the poor and sick to perish uncared for in the streets or in their houses, if they had any.

There was from the very first a certain amount of neighborly and community charity. As soon as the colonists set up legislatures they began to pass laws dealing with Dr. Smyth's failures. Colonial statute books were filled with such laws, many of them cruel in their provisions. After independence, the state legislatures continued this line of crude law-making. For a long time the federal Congress left welfare work to the states and communities where it could be handled in those simple days. But many years before the New Deal, Congress had started a program of social legislation, touching hours and conditions of labor in certain employments.

A lot of the early welfare legislation, so-called, was brutal enough, unenlightened, even barbaric, according to the standards of today. Some of the colonial legislation was designed to oppress working people rather than help them. This you can see for yourself by examining H. W. Farnam's *Chapters in the History of Social Legislation in the United States to* 1860, published by the Carnegie Institution. After the rise of the factory system and great cities, thousands of laws and ordinances were made in the states and cities for the purpose of improving the condition of the workers, advancing public health, and taking care of men, women, and children hard hit by the adversities of fortune.

As if fearing that her recital might weary her auditors, Miss Robbins paused when Dr. Smyth took out his memorandum book to note down the title of Farnam's book. But the three of us, genuinely interested, urged her to pursue this history further.

MISS ROBBINS: All the while American ideas of welfare were changing. At first welfare work was associated with personal charity: the poor are always with us and we can improve our chances of salvation from hell by helping the poor. In time, organized philanthropy was widely substituted for personal charity. In time philanthropy acquired a bad odor. Then the phrase social work or welfare work was often substituted for philanthropy.

Oh, it's a long story that fills volumes! But at length, Americans evolved a theory of public welfare, which was not charity or philanthropy, at least entirely, but was as broad as human well-being in industry and in social living. Why, even under President Harding and President Coolidge, after Julia Lathrop, Florence Kelley, and Edith Abbott came East from the Hull House at Chicago, many kinds of welfare work were undertaken under the auspices of the Federal Government itself. It was inspired by a care for human beings, by distress at the sight of suffering and ill-health and slums and hideous surroundings generally. This development is esthetic as well as moral.

And welfare work is becoming a science about as exact as medicine, if I may say so. The practice of welfare calls for severe training, exact knowledge, and skills of many kinds. So that, whatever the word welfare may have meant in 1787, it now means, at least to people who study it instead of talking about or against it idly, the art and science of good working and living—individual and social, parts of the same thing—life worth living—American society civilized, from center to periphery. Under every form of government and economy, it is and will be necessary while the spirit of humanity lives. But I must spare you more. I am so full of it that when I get going I never know when to stop.

Dr. Smyth, looking at Miss Robbins in astonishment: I never heard anything like that from you before.

Mrs. Smyth: You never asked her anything about her training or her fundamental interests.

Miss Robbins: Why should he? At the hospital it is just one case after another—a blind baby, a tubercular mother, a man crippled at the factory in an accident, deserted children, old Mrs. Hensy suddenly losing her mind, and so on forever, every day, every hour. There's no time to talk about welfare under the Constitution. We are too busy practicing it.

Dr. Smyth: It wouldn't hurt to think a little about what we are doing. But I confess that it is a jar for me to hear that the Constitution can be stretched to cover the welfare of everybody in the United

States and that takes in our Hospital and about everything else.

BEARD: Pardon me, Doctor. The Constitution is not stretched to cover the general welfare. It does cover it. The interpretation has been made. The responsibility is ours.

DR. SMYTH: How long, oh Lord?

BEARD: If you were addressing me instead of the Supreme Being, I should say as long as we have moral sense and intelligence enough to discharge it.

DR. SMYTH: When you said early in our discussions that the Constitution is a document of prophecy, I thought you were playing an intellectual prank on us. The affair tonight seems to be the biggest prank of all.

You admit that you do not know how the phrase general welfare got into the Constitution. Madison, a father himself, said that it did not mean a thing; wasn't worth a pepper-corn. Joseph Story, who was appointed to the Supreme Court by this very same James Madison, declared that it gave Congress powers over all matters of broad national concern. Benjamin Cardozo, elevated to the Bench by that apostle of rugged individualism, Herbert Hoover, practically announced that, under general welfare, Congress can do about anything it wants to do for Tom, Dick, Harry, Will, Bridget, and Hannah, even save them from the haunting fear of poverty and the consequences of their own folly. Now comes Jean Robbins, who has been working under me for years quietly and efficiently, and blurts out things I never knew were in her head about the long history of social welfare. I guess I am stuck.

I thought that the New Deal was a passing distemper, until the Republicans in 1936 and again in 1940 promised to play the same Santa Claus role for the people and do it better. But I now realize that there is some reason in the business, although it is hard for a fellow born away back in Queen Victoria's reign to stand up and cheer this fulfilment of the Constitution as prophecy. My poor head is in a whirl. Please hand me my gloves. They are on your desk at the right.

MRS. SMYTH, with a glint of triumph in her eyes: Robert, I am driving with Jean to the Hospital for a moment. You had better have blackberry cordial tonight instead of sherry. I suspected as much and so put the carafe on the tabouret by your easy chair in the study before we left home.

IX

The Blessings of Liberty

THIS time we have brought Father Murphy along, DR. SMYTH announced as we settled down for the session on liberty. He was at the Hospital as I was leaving and asked me what was on for the night. I told him that we were booked for a long battle with you over liberty under the Constitution. 'That is interesting,' he remarked, 'for the Declaration of Independence and the Constitution were derived from Catholic sources and I wonder whether you are going to take account of that.' I replied that he had better come with us and see for himself—or rather, speak for himself—and help to enlighten the heathen. He hesitated but I assured him that we weren't running a secret conclave and that he would be welcome.

BEARD: Of course. Father Murphy and I are ancient friends. We often take walks along the sea and in the hills. He has his citadel of faith, the general boundaries of which I am acquainted with and never invade. But we have so many things human in common that we never lack topics to discuss agreeably. As a matter of fact, I made some searches for him into the profits of your company, Doctor, when he was helping to wring better wages for the employees during the strike two winters ago. In that affair Father Murphy made no distinction between Catholics and Protestants. Nor did I.

He and I have never had a session on liberty, however, and this is a good time to have it. The idea of liberty appears in the Declaration of Independence and in the Preamble of the Constitution. What do you mean, Father, when you say that these two documents were derived from Catholic sources?

FATHER MURPHY: Really, I came to learn, not to teach, and I should like to hear you discourse on liberty before I make any comments.

BEARD: The matter of the sources and sanctions of liberty is fundamental and I intend to deal with them. So, go ahead and set up something of your own for us to start with, as we often say.

FATHER MURPHY: Since you press me, I offer this first: the Declaration of Independence and the Constitution rest upon a number of fundamental ideas concerning nature, human nature, the ends of society and government, and the rights or liberties of human beings. You will all agree to that. In the next place, the most fundamental of all these ideas is the worth and dignity of the human being as such, not as an American or as a member of any other society. By this I mean the moral value of the human personality. In the third place, there is the principle of moral equality among human beings. You can give rights and liberties to classes. Members of Hitler's SS. have their liberties, all right. But unless you grant the moral equality of human beings, you will not accord liberty to all, as the Declaration of Independence and the Constitution profess to do.

Now the Church has taught, according to the Scriptures, that 'of one blood are all nations of men,' and that 'there is neither Jew nor Greek, neither bond nor free, neither male nor female; for ye are all one in Christ Jesus.' That is the universal humanity affirmed in the Declaration. Long before America was discovered, Catholic writers had developed doctrines of natural law. Thomas Aquinas taught the law of nature, or natural law, and treated that law as a body of rules discovered and formulated by the use of reason. He taught that the end of society is the good of its members. John Locke is one of the English philosophers upon whom Jefferson drew for the philosophy of the Declaration and Locke had drawn upon the ethical and political teachings of Thomas Aquinas, if not directly then indirectly through Thomas Hooker. Then the writings of Bellarmine must be considered. I am no expert in political philosophy but if we were down in my library I could put my hands on any number of old Catholic teachings foreshadowing the principles of the Declaration and the Constitution.

To sum up, in Catholic sources you will find every fundamental idea necessary to liberty and constitutional government: the idea of universal humanity, the unity of mankind; the idea that all members of mankind belong to this unity; that each individual, great and small, is a moral and rational being; that there is a natural law, related to divine law, underlying all civil law; that just civil law must correspond to this natural law; that each individual is entitled to moral rights and thus cannot be used for purposes alien to humanity. All these ideas are in Catholic sources.

DR. SMYTH: That is news to me and I do not get the bearing of it. The Church also taught that servants must obey their masters and that once meant in my state of South Carolina that slaves must accept their slavery. The Church also taught that we must render unto Caesar the things that belong to Caesar.

BEARD: What Father Murphy has said is certainly borne out by quotations from Catholic writers. But if I were so inclined, I could cite other selections from Catholic sources, as Dr. Smith started to do, which support absolute government by princes subject to the prerogatives of the Church. But I prefer to avoid this type of controversy. I agree that the ideas included in Father Murphy's summary are all in Catholic sources, and that undoubtedly Catholic teachings have had a profound influence on Western thought. How to measure that influence is beyond my powers.

But practically all those ideas appeared in Mediterranean countries long before the birth of Christ, long before the founding of the Catholic Church. We know that some early Catholic fathers resorted to the ancient Greeks, especially Plato, for ideas respecting economic and social affairs. We know also that medieval Catholic writers, such as Thomas Aquinas, relied heavily upon Aristotle for sociology and economics. We know that the Stoics, Greek and Roman, held beliefs respecting mankind which were substantially identical with the ideas Father Murphy has drawn from Catholic sources—ideas far in advance of those expounded by Plato and Aristotle, that is, more advanced in the direction of modern thought.

Let me sum up the Stoics' views. They believed in the universality of humanity. They cut across all divisions of race, nationality, country, class, state, and conventions. They broke down the division between Greek and barbarian, proclaimed the brotherhood of mankind, and a cosmopolitan citizenship of the world. Each human being has a portion of reason. God and reason rule the universe, through the law of virtue. The justice which follows from this fact is natural, not merely a body of rules made by particular peoples for their convenience. In obedience to natural law so conceived, the individual has both liberty and responsibility. While the individual as a rational being enjoys liberty, as a member of universal humanity he owes obligations to other members and must serve the ends and needs of the good life in society. Zeno, for instance, looked forward to a world society in which all differences would be merged in the brotherhood of mankind.

Those ideas came into Roman law—another powerful influence on Catholic thinkers in the middle ages. Many of the greatest Roman statesmen and jurists were Stoics in philosophy, more or less. Governing many races and nationalities, with diverse religions and customs, they sought principles common to the varieties of humanity under their jurisdiction. In administration they developed a *jus gentium,* a body of the principles generally accepted among mankind, a kind of common law or law common to all peoples. The *jus gentium* certain Roman thinkers gradually fused with the natural law of the Stoics. In that way Roman jurists came to look upon the law of nature as a force behind particular laws and an ideal of justice to guide judges and lawmakers in shaping particular laws. 'In every matter,' said Cicero, 'the consent of all peoples is to be considered as the law of nature.' The voice of nature he found in 'universal consent.'

Here is Matheson's translation of *The Discourses and Manual of Epictetus,* the Greek slave-philosopher, born in the first century of the Christian era. What view of mankind did he hold? He regarded every human being as a member of his own community and of the universal community of God and mankind. He said the will of God is the law of nature. All human beings are children of God, have a portion of reason, can learn justice or the law of nature, have rights, can realize their rights only in contributing to the common welfare, and are under obligations to make divine and natural law prevail throughout the earth.

What am I saying? I am saying that the Catholic sources cited by Father Murphy either confirmed or stemmed from older teachings; that many of the ideas he cites were not created *de novo* by the Catholic writers but were, often with modifications, taken from so-called pagan works. It was at first only through Catholic mediation that these ideas, many of them derived from Greek and Roman writings, came into the Western world as the Roman Empire declined.

Moreover, many Protestant writers used the writings of the Church fathers, especially in dealing with civil polity. From the development and spreading of these ideas we cannot exclude Protestants. The stream of thought has never been broken absolutely. When modern writers try to make Protestantism the source of democracy and liberty, I dissent, as I dissent from the bare proposition that the Declaration of Independence and the Constitution derive from Catholic sources.

I have no idea what the Western world would look like if there had been no Catholic Church between the first and the sixteenth centuries. It is idle to speculate on that. The Church certainly was the great mediator between antiquity and the modern age. Nor do I pretend to know what the Western world would look like had there been no Protestant revolt. That also is a subject of idle speculation. Protestantism has likewise entered into the making of our age. And after the Renaissance, ideas of the ancient world were brought directly into the stream of Western thought by the recovery of ancient learning—the original writings of Greeks and Romans that had long been lost.

FATHER MURPHY: Some day, when we take another walk in the mountains, Beard, we can argue out some counter-points that I should like to make, but I really came to hear what you were going to say about liberty under the Constitution. Let us get back on the main theme.

BEARD: Just how the word liberty got into the Preamble of the Constitution and just exactly what the framers meant by it is debatable. But we know some things about the business. Liberty was in the Declaration of Independence. It was a powerful word in the American revolt against Great Britain. It was especially cherished by the left wing of the revolutionary party. Because the framers knew that they had to overcome a powerful opposition on the left in order to secure the adoption of the Constitution, they made concessions to the libertarian sentiments of the left wing. They put the word liberty into the Preamble but not into the main body of the Constitution. And they did not add a bill of rights specifying the liberties they intended to include under the liberty which appears in the Preamble. I suspect that tactics had something to do with putting 'the blessings of liberty' into the Preamble of the Constitution. Yet I do not stress the point. There were many liberties which the framers wanted to see well established in the law of the land.

DR. SMYTH: Yes. I saw a letter in a newspaper the other day to the effect that they intended to incorporate all the liberties of free enterprise and *laissez faire* in the Constitution.

BEARD: That, Doctor, just introduces fog and hiss into history. The doctrine of *laissez faire,* as we understand it with all the trimmings added by Ricardo, Herbert Spencer, William Graham Sumner and company, had not been fully developed in 1787. True, Adam Smith's *Wealth of Nations* had been published in 1776, but Adam Smith put severe qualifications on his main dogmas, which vitiated them as the pure milk of the word. As to the French authors of the creed, they were better known to Jefferson and his fellow thinkers than to Hamilton, Washington, Madison, and other members of the Constitutional Convention, except Franklin.

The majority of the men in the convention leaned to the mercantilism that Adam Smith criticized rather than to his *laissez faire* and free trade. And soon after the Constitution was adopted, Hamilton and company went in for protective tariffs, subsidies, and bounties for the promotion of American industry and trade. That was not *laissez faire* in the correct sense. One of the prime objects of the Constitution, as Daniel Webster said, was to provide for the regulation of commerce, not for free trade.

Certainly the framers did not intend to establish universal *laissez faire,* to let everybody alone. They intended to interfere vigorously with a lot of things that state legislatures, farmers, and individuals were doing in the United States. They intended to interfere with commerce, industry, exchange, banking, and many other things as previously carried on. On the other hand, they wanted to stimulate private enterprise by government actions and to stop a lot of practices recently followed by private enterprise, as we now use the phrase. Their idea of liberty was not identical with the idea of *laissez faire*—far from it.

As I started to say, they doubtless intended to incorporate many particular liberties in the Constitution. They wanted to maintain national independence, national freedom from dominance or interference by any foreign power or powers. No doubt about that. They wanted to establish a certain liberty of commerce throughout the American Union, subject, however, to federal regulations. They intended to establish liberty of movement for citizens throughout the Union. They wrote this principle into the Constitution.

If you will bear with me while I do it, I shall develop the issue as concisely as I can. It has become the fashion recently to exalt the Bill of Rights, the first amendments to the Constitution, as if no rights were proclaimed or taken into account by the original instrument itself. I do not wish to underestimate in any respect the significance of the Bill of Rights as a salutary influence in American thinking about liberty and justice. Of that we shall hear more in other sessions here. But the exaltation of that list of liberties tends to obscure facts that are equally, if not more, fundamental.

Rights are not established or imposed by proclamation. Proclamations and institutions merely help to define, enlarge, and sustain them. Yet, if these rights are not deeply rooted in the theories, customs, sentiments, and practices of the people, paper assertions are like chaff in the wind. Moreover the very form of government itself has a distinct bearing on liberty, as we shall see when we come to our seminar on Power and the Control of Power. It was with reference to liberty that the framers of the Constitution sought to prevent the concentration of too much authority in the hands of any department of government. That works for liberty. To minimize the bearing of the separation of powers, as instituted by the Constitution, in favor of a paper bill of rights is, I think, to miss the chief secret of liberty under government.

Besides all this, certain important blessings of liberty are incorporated in provisions of the Constitution as it was completed in 1787. Without calling these safeguards against arbitrary power a bill of rights, the original draftsmen distinctly specified a number of liberties in the Constitution—liberties included in the general phrase 'the blessings of liberty' as long understood in the English-speaking world.

In Hamilton's famous argument designed to show that a bill of rights was not, as Jefferson contended, necessary to protect the rights of the people, he listed in Number 84 of *The Federalist* specific provisions of the Constitution that made for liberty of person and property. It is important for our purposes to consider some of them at length under the head of the blessings of liberty.

First of all, 'the privilege of the writ of *habeas corpus* shall not be suspended, unless when in cases of rebellion or invasion the public safety may require it.'

Why is this a precious liberty? Most Americans never think of it. It would be interesting to know how many Americans are aware that it is in the Constitution or what it means.

What does it mean? It means that, as long as we keep this liberty, the Government of the United States cannot secretly, or openly for that matter, arrest persons as individuals or groups, throw them into prisons or concentration camps, hold them there indefinitely, and do what it pleases to them. This was a practice tyrannical governments had once followed in England, were following in Europe in 1787, and have in recent years revived in Germany, Italy, and other parts of Europe.

A year or so ago, two refugees from fascist despotism in Europe, during a discussion at my house of things in general, asked me, 'What has the dull lumbering Anglo-Saxon ever done for civilization?' I shot back that at least the Anglo-Saxon had originated and developed the writ of *habeas corpus*. As they were literary men, I had to explain its meaning to them, and after I had explained it, they admitted that this was something to be set down in favor of the Anglo-Saxon.

Now I am not saying that American criminal procedure is ideal, that the third degree is unknown to the police, or that other abuses do not exist in it. I am merely contending that this restraint on federal officials in the name of personal rights is a liberty precious to all citizens as well as to those who may be charged with crime.

As I contemplate these simple words in the Constitution, a vision of the horrors of dungeon, torture, and punishments in the long history of governmental tyranny rises before me like an image of hell. If the writ of *habeas corpus* were introduced in any modern despotism and administered by judges enjoying a high degree of independence, it alone could make a revolution in that despotism.

A second liberty in the original Constitution guarantees that no bill of attainder shall be passed. What does that mean? It means that no legislature, no law-making body, can pass a bill singling out one person or a group of persons by name and condemning them to death or imprisonment, without granting them a hearing or public trial of any kind. The long and bloody story of the bill of attainder was vivid in the history of that tyranny with which the framers of the Constitution were familiar. They were resolved that it should not be repeated in the United States.

MRS. SMYTH: Were they actually afraid that American legislatures elected by Americans might adopt such a cruel practice?

BEARD: They were. For that reason they incorporated the rule in the Constitution. And it ought to be advertised that Thomas Jefferson, with all his confidence in the people, had a similar fear of legislatures, even those popularly elected. Let me repeat a quotation from Jefferson. Speaking of the Virginia legislature in his *Notes on Virginia,* he said:

> One hundred and seventy-three despots would surely be as oppressive as one. Let those who doubt it turn their eyes on the republic of Venice. As little will it avail us that they are chosen by ourselves. An *elective despotism* was not the government we fought for.

A third liberty to be found in the original Constitution provides that no *ex post facto* law shall be passed. More dull and ponderous words! But what a history of terror lay behind *ex post facto* laws in 1787. And in our time a large part of fascist despotism in Germany and Italy has been based upon *ex post facto* legislation—some of it approved by the so-called legislatures of those countries.

What does this provision mean? It means that in our daily living and thinking we can enjoy the liberty of doing and saying all that the existing law permits. After we have done and said certain things, no law-maker can, after the fact, *ex post facto,* brand our sayings and doings as crimes and have us condemned to fine, prison, or death for our lawful deeds and words. Hamilton was right when he said:

> The creation of crimes after the commission of the fact, or, in other words, the subjection of men to punishments for things which, when they were done, were breaches of no law, and the practice of arbitrary imprisonments, have been, in all ages, the favorite and most formidable instruments of tyranny.

Only those who have been cruelly punished by the despots of our time for acts innocent in the eyes of the law can appreciate, with appropriate gratitude of spirit, the significance of these few words in the Constitution of the United States. We do not appreciate them, for we have never suffered under *ex post facto* laws and have not ourselves been compelled to struggle for such rights against brutal force.

A fourth liberty guaranteed by the Constitution provides that the trial of all federal crimes, except in cases of impeachment, shall be by jury and in the state in which said crimes are committed.

FATHER MURPHY: But trial by jury is no guarantee of liberty, unless you have a jury composed of men (now, women also) who believe in those doctrines of humanity that lie at the base of all just law.

BEARD: I heartily agree with you in that. I am not sure that even the profession of such beliefs is a guarantee of liberty and justice. One of my friends, who happened to be in Vermont during the First World War, attended the trial of a local clergyman who was charged with giving to a few neighbors a pamphlet in which he argued that the servants of Christ must not fight. The clergyman said other things of the same nature, but that sentence stuck in my mind. The jury that tried him was composed of good citizens in the community who professed beliefs in doctrines of humanity. He was found guilty of encouraging insubordination in the army and interfering with recruiting and was sentenced to fifteen years in prison—fifteen years—for doing that. The jury and the judge were excited, and his liberty of speech was treated with scant respect.

DR. SMYTH: I would never submit anything which calls for sense, knowledge, or understanding to the kind of jury that our sheriff picks up at the court house. I saw a jury at work on the case of Bill Hunks not long ago. Bill, as you know, Father Murphy, liked his bottle. He is not a member of your church, but I know that you personally have often helped his family in time of need when Bill has been drunk. He is a good workman at our factory when he is sober, but one day he got his hand in a machine and it was badly crushed. I fixed him up and he drew his compensation pay while he recuperated, which took a long time.

Then a lawyer inveigled him into suing our company for heavy damages, due to special negligence on its part, they charged. The company's lawyer answered that Bill was under the influence of liquor when he was hurt. I honestly testified that I smelt it when I operated on his hand. A crowd of witnesses was heard on both sides. There was plenty of evidence to show that Bill had often come to the mill drunk and had been sent home. The company's engineer showed that the machine in question was well protected and that a man with his wits about him was not apt to get hurt while working with it. Everybody with any sense who heard the testimony felt that Bill himself was responsible for his troubles. But, to my utter astonishment, the jury found for Bill against the company and gave him all the damages he claimed. There is jury trial for you.

I certainly should not want to rely on any jury for my liberty or liberties.

FATHER MURPHY: On the other hand, judges as such cannot always be relied upon to do justice with insight and moderation. When the big strike occurred across the border in our neighboring state not long ago, the federal judge there issued a blanket injunction which was so broad that I could not make out what it forbade strikers to do—or rather what it did not forbid them to do. The leader of the strike gave out a statement that the injunction deprived labor of all its rights, and he criticized the judge for making his own law in favor of the employers. For this he was haled into court before the judge who issued the injunction. Fearing that there might be trouble, I went over and accompanied Father Martinello to the court room. The judge gave the strike leader a browbeating, screamed at his lawyer, and sentenced the accused to six months in jail for contempt of court. A jury could not have been worse. It might have been better.

BEARD: You are both trying a human institution by an ideal standard. That is all right, if you do not expect too much from mankind, in too great a hurry. It does not take a profound knowledge of history to make one aware that mankind has as much, or more, to fear from judicial tyranny as from the tyranny of juries. Look at the perversions of justice by judges in the long history of the law. I do not want to run too far off into a discussion of that subject. As to myself, I agree with Hamilton that, historically, jury trial is to be regarded as among the institutions that make for the liberty of persons in a world in which perfection is seldom if ever found.

Let us go on with liberty under the Constitution. Hamilton's fifth item among the liberties guaranteed by the original Constitution is the clause respecting treason. It reads:

> Treason against the United States shall consist only in levying war against them, or in adhering to their enemies, giving them aid and comfort. No person shall be convicted of treason unless on the testimony of two witnesses to the same overt act, or on confession in open court.

Treason is a terrifying word in the history of tyranny. In community consciousness it is worse than cold-blooded murder. It is an offense against the power of the State and, if the tyrannical State is allowed to define treason, it may brand as treason the lightest criticism, make trials for treason secret, and give victims no opportunity to confront witnesses. Under our Constitution, treason is strictly defined, and the prosecution must produce witnesses to the overt act and give the accused his day in open court. Here in the quiet of our chamber, the very idea of treason seems remote; but to ears attuned to history it sounds like thunder.

Among his items of liberty, Hamilton also included the clause by which the United States is forbidden to grant any titles of nobility—a clear prohibition against the establishment of a legalized class of privilege (Article I, Section 9). 'This,' he said, 'may truly be denominated the corner-stone of republican government; for so long as they are excluded, there can never be serious danger that the government will be other than that of the people.' Hamilton was unduly optimistic, but great popular struggles of his age were directed against privileged orders—for liberty against privilege. And this clause of the Constitution was undoubtedly popular at that moment in the United States.

But substantial as were these and other liberties set forth in the original Constitution, the document was severely criticized because it contained no long bill of rights, giving an extended list of liberties. A bill of rights was a great favorite among the left-wingers of the American Revolution. It would have been expedient for the framers to have prefaced the Constitution with a bill of rights. But there were not many left-wingers among the members of the Philadelphia Convention in 1787. The overwhelming majority, from start to finish, were bent on setting up federal agencies endowed with large powers while preventing them from running away with power, and they did not favor adding a bill of rights.

FATHER MURPHY: Pardon me, but not long ago we celebrated the Bill of Rights Day here in town, and a speaker declared that the convention was equally divided on that subject. He had a book with him to prove the point. The name of the author I remember as Elliot. What about that?

BEARD: Here I shall have to introduce some hair-splitting pedantry, as you, Father Murphy, called it one day when we were discussing Tom Paine's *Rights of Man*. The book cited at the celebration must have been Elliot's *Debates in the Federal Convention*. Here it is. In Volume V, on page 538, Elliot reports, as Madison's notation, that on a motion for a committee to prepare a bill of rights for the Constitution, the states divided equally, five Northern states for it, five Southern states against it, and Massachusetts absent, September 12. But Elliot is in error. If you will examine the Journal of the Convention printed in Elliot's first volume, page 306, you will see that there he correctly reports that the motion to appoint such a committee was 'passed unanimously in the negative.' That is misleading too, for New York was not represented on the floor that day, and Massachusetts was recorded as absent.

MRS. SMYTH: So, you can't trust your own authorities!

BEARD: No, nor my own eyes. I can look all through a haystack for a needle, miss it completely, and then find it sticking in my forefinger the day after I have declared that the needle was not there. Henry Adams said somewhere, in effect, that his own books were full of errors, despite his labors. That made him ashamed of himself, but he took some consolation in the thought that other books also were full of errors.

As the facts now seem to stand, the question of a bill of rights was not brought up in the Convention until late in its proceedings. George Mason, of Virginia, on September 12, five days before adjournment, expressed the wish for a bill of rights. Elbridge Gerry made a motion that a committee be appointed to draw up such a bill. Mason seconded the motion. There was no debate, although Roger Sherman of Connecticut and Mason each made a comment. The vote on the motion was taken as usual by states, and every state represented on the floor voted against it. This is confirmed by Farrand, *Records of the Federal Convention,* Volume II, p. 588.

In *The Federalist* Hamilton took the position that the Federal Government was merely intended to 'regulate the general political interests of the nation,' and not 'every species of personal and private concerns.' Hence, he argued, a detail of particular rights was less applicable than in the case of state constitutions.

He went further and affirmed that, in respect of the Constitution, such a bill of specifications would be dangerous. It would contain references and exceptions to powers not granted at all and thus afford pretexts for claiming more than was granted. For instance, the Constitution gave Congress no express power to regulate the press and, if a clause had been added proclaiming freedom of the press, it might be assumed that Congress had power to regulate the press *except* in matters touching its freedom.

Addressing himself immediately to freedom of the press, Hamilton asserted that declarations on this subject in state constitutions amounted to nothing. 'Who can give any definition which would not leave the utmost latitude for evasion?' he asked. Then he concluded, very logically, I think: 'Its security, whatever fine declarations may be inserted in any constitution respecting it, must altogether depend on public opinion, and on the general spirit of the people and of the government. And here, after all . . . must we seek for the only solid base of all our rights.'

MRS. SMYTH: Are you contending that things would not have been different if no bill of rights had been added to the Constitution? That it is useless verbiage?

BEARD: Not at all, Mrs. Smyth. I am glad, of course, that the Bill of Rights was added. I merely hold with Hamilton that, whatever fine declaration of rights you may have, liberty in final analysis actually depends on the spirit of the people and the government. There is no way of *proving* that things would have been better or worse if no bill of rights had been added to the Constitution. History is not an exact science. We cannot repeat our history without a bill of rights and thus find out by experiment the answer to your question. But the Bill of Rights gives the courts principles to act upon; it has an educative effect; it makes many people think about liberty; it provides them with statements of great doctrines to learn and ponder. In other words, it helps to make the opinion and spirit of the people and the government—on which, as Hamilton insisted, the blessings of liberty depend. Later, with your permission, I shall consider some of the meanings given to what Hamilton called the fine declarations to be found in the Bill of Rights and other items of the Constitution.

FATHER MURPHY: Doesn't it all go back to natural law, the eternal law which teaches us our moral rights and duties?

BEARD: Well, Father, the liberties the American people enjoy and believe in enough to uphold them differ in many respects from the liberties cherished by other peoples in the world, even in Christendom. Whether Americans continue to enjoy and uphold them will depend in part, in large part, on their character. As to that natural law which is called eternal law, Thomas Aquinas said of it that man could know it in some reflection but that it can be fully known only by God Himself and by the blessed who see God in His essence.

Ultimates are beyond me. I know that leaders among the framers of the Constitution feared and opposed political tyranny, official arrogance, a press censorship, a union of State and Church, and the suppression of individual rights by political agencies and popular tumults. I know that they sought to provide safeguards against arbitrary power while establishing a government endowed with immense powers. That is, if I know anything, I know this much.

I am convinced that various clauses in the Constitution and the amendments aid us in securing the blessings of liberty. They provide for checks on the exercise of power by officials, for certain definite processes of law in the conduct of government, and for keeping in the hands of the people a large domain of civil liberty. I am convinced also that the more the people study this system of government and liberty and the more they understand and cherish it, the more likely it will be that civil liberty will be upheld and developed in the United States—kept alive and creatively applied amid changing circumstances.

DR. SMYTH: Before we go home I wish to ask whether you believe that men who want to destroy civil liberty, who proclaim it a sham and delusion, should be allowed to carry on propaganda advocating the destruction of liberty in favor of an absolute system of some kind?

BEARD: It is midnight, Doctor. Your question is important but not easy to answer in a word. Ideally, I should say that those who would deny liberty to others should not enjoy the liberty to carry on destructive propaganda against it. Practically speaking, it would be difficult to draw a law to that effect which in administration would not open the door to persecution. Since we have a session on freedom of the press and speech coming, let us postpone the problem until we take up the rule of 'clear and present danger.'

DR. SMYTH: That is all right with me. I never knew a professor who could answer a plain question with a yes or no in half a second.

I have known some who could answer cosmic questions in less time, MRS. SMYTH jested as she gave the signal for adjournment.

X

Rights of American Citizens

OUR tenth colloquium was enlivened by a participant from abroad, Dr. Norbert Braun, formerly of Munich, a visitor in the home of the Smyths. Introducing him, DR. SMYTH declared emphatically: Dr. Braun is, if I may say so, the most competent specialist in surgery of the eye in the world.

Oh, no, protested DR. BRAUN as I welcomed him. Dr. Smyth is too generous. I had good luck, amazing luck in an operation I performed at his Hospital last week and in his enthusiasm he attributes miracles to me. In fact, I am a very ordinary eye doctor! But that has nothing to do with my coming tonight. Mrs. Smyth told me at the dinner table that you were discussing American citizenship and I wanted to learn more about it. I have had some experience in citizenship recently. Though I am an *ernsthafte Bestie* of the blond persuasion, I married a Jewess in Munich, and because I refused to give her up I was harried out of Germany. Yet, I did not come to talk about myself. I came to hear more about citizenship in the United States—which, thank God, I now hold!

BEARD: If you will let me ask you some questions, Doctor Braun, I can develop the fundamental nature of American citizenship better than in any other way. For instance, were you arrested at the beginning of your trouble?

DR. BRAUN: I was seized by the State Secret Police.

BEARD: Were you allowed to consult your lawyer?

DR. BRAUN: No, I was just taken to an underground room at the police station and held there for two weeks while I was subjected to questioning.

BEARD: Were members of your family notified?

DR. BRAUN: No. I was seized at my office. None of my family or friends was notified. They were in fact almost frantic and feared the worst.

BEARD: Were you subjected to torture?

DR. BRAUN: Not exactly physical torture. It was a kind of third degree as you call it in the United States—refined mental torture. But I do not want to think of that horror again.

BEARD: Were any charges lodged against you?

DR. BRAUN: None except that I had a Jewish wife. Oh, yes, the police tried to make me confess that I had secret connections with politics but as I had been nonpolitical I had nothing to confess, and that enraged them.

BEARD: How did you finally get out of the clutches of the police?

DR. BRAUN: As far as I know, it was pure luck. A man whom I had known for a long time, a member of the Elite Guard of Hitler, had an eye badly damaged in a street brawl, and when he was taken to the hospital, he insisted that I be called at once to treat him. He then discovered that I was missing. Suspecting the cause of my disappearance, he had a search started; and, to make a long story short, I was found in the police station and released, with a curse, to perform the operation. A police officer went with me.

When they learned it would take me several days to make sure that the injured man was out of danger, they agreed that I should stay in the hospital. As soon as I had finished my preliminary work on the patient and made him comfortable for the night, I got a friend in the hospital to take a note to my wife telling her to pack a few things in a light bag, including all the jewels we had, and slip out the back way with the children to a dark corner of a certain park. When a call came for an ambulance, I followed it with a second ambulance, driving it myself, ringing my bell like a madman. With my heart in my throat I drove into the park.

There, thank God, were my wife and children. To shorten the tale, that night we got over the Swiss border and found lodging with a Swiss friend, an oculist, with whom I had often worked on special cases. A few days later he went into Germany for me and by bribery got my passports fixed up by a high Nazi. In time I secured the visa for admission to the United States. Here we are. It is like going from hell to heaven. As soon as I could, I applied for first citizenship papers. Before I could complete my naturalization, I learned that the German government had deprived all of us by name of our German citizenship.

BEARD: In other words, Doctor Braun, by a mere official decree, you, your wife, and children, were deprived of your citizenship and all the rights attached to citizenship?

DR. BRAUN: It was the other way around. We had been deprived of every decent human right before we got out of Germany, and then an official decree took away from us a meaningless thing, a hollow, empty thing—German citizenship. It is all a terrible nightmare, but we are safe now in possession of our American citizenship, which we intend to cherish and honor as much as we can.

BEARD: Your story makes a background for considering all the rights of humanity attached to citizenship in the United States.

These rights are the product of a long development. The original Constitution as framed in 1787 dealt with some of them, not all. Indeed the Constitution recognized two kinds of citizenship. It spoke of citizens of the state and citizens of the United States, and it said, 'the citizens of each state shall be entitled to all privileges and immunities of citizens in the several states.' This provision meant that when a citizen of one state went into another, he was entitled to the privileges and immunities enjoyed by citizens in the second state. The original Constitution did not expressly deprive states of the power to naturalize aliens, to make citizens out of foreigners, but it gave Congress the superior power to 'establish an uniform rule of naturalization.' Under that provision Congress has acted, and states can no longer make laws for the naturalization of aliens.

Until the Civil War, many questions of citizenship were left unsettled, especially whether free Negroes and children born to them were citizens of the United States. To settle some of these questions, the Fourteenth Amendment adopted in 1868 provided that:

All persons born or naturalized in the United States, and subject to the jurisdiction thereof, are citizens of the United States and of the state wherein they reside. No state shall make or enforce any law which shall abridge the privileges or immunities of citizens of the United States. . . .

Certain exceptions are made in practice. For instance, children of foreign ambassadors born in the United States are not automatically citizens. Children born of American parents residing abroad are American citizens, if they fulfil certain conditions. The important point for native Americans is that, with few exceptions, all persons born in the United States are citizens of the United States until by some act of their own they renounce that citizenship. This rule is written down in the Constitution and cannot be changed by Act of Congress.

MRS. SMYTH: As I understand you, it would take an amendment to the Constitution to deprive a native-born citizen of the rights of citizenship. But certain classes of persons, certain Asiatics, cannot become naturalized under the law, and the other day I saw a letter in a newspaper calling upon Congress to deprive Japanese actually born in the United States of their American citizenship.

BEARD: That remark is pertinent. The right of citizenship is a constitutional right by birth. Congress cannot deprive anyone of that right. Nor can any executive official, by mere decree, deprive any American citizen, even a naturalized citizen, of citizenship. Persons who hold that right by birth in the United States cannot be deprived of it by any action short of a constitutional amendment.

DR. SMYTH: Now that is strange. I know a case of a young Swede, born in New York City, who was held in a local court not to be an American citizen, although his brothers and sisters born in America were declared to be citizens.

BEARD: Oh, I know that case, Doctor. It is one of the many curiosities of the law. That Swede was born in New York City, of Swedish parents, but not on land. He was born on board a Swedish ship in the harbor of New York. It has long been a uniform rule that children born on the public ships of a foreign country, though in the territorial waters of the United States, are, in effect, born on foreign soil, that is, within the jurisdiction of the country to which the ship belongs. The parents of this boy had never been naturalized. They are not citizens, but their other children born in the United States are all American citizens. There are more curious quirks like that, but the general rule is that persons born in the United States and subject to its jurisdiction are citizens of the United States and of the state wherein they reside.

MRS. SMYTH: I think that there is another curiosity, as you call it, that ought not to be overlooked: the case of an American-born woman who marries an alien. Until a few years ago, she lost her citizenship simply by marrying a man of foreign nationality.

Women had to campaign for a long time—and against prejudices and conventions—to get the law changed. I was in it and know something about it.

I regarded it all along as an injustice for the government of the United States to hold that, merely because an American woman married a foreigner, she lost her citizenship, no matter how much she wanted to keep it. I would have called it unconstitutional if I had not heard men argue by the hour and week over what they called constitutional or unconstitutional. Long ago there was the ridiculous case of Nellie Grant, daughter of General U. S. Grant, who lost her citizenship by marrying a British subject. After her husband died and she returned to the United States, Congress passed a special Act in 1898 restoring her citizenship—her birthright. The whole business was unfair. Because she was the daughter of General Grant and a woman of influence, she got a special favor, but other women had to suffer the loss of their citizenship and take it.

Of course things have been different since Congress was forced to take steps to correct this violation of personal liberty. It had to be driven step by step, in 1922, 1930, and 1934, to make amends. Even now there are injustices remaining. But I shall not go into them.

BEARD: On all that I agree with you, Mrs. Smyth. It properly belongs at this stage in our discussion. There were other important cases of women restored to their American citizenship by special acts of Congress even while their husbands were still living in their foreign homes. It was unjust, a matter of pull; in fact, shameful. That is the trouble with the subject matter of our colloquium. There are so many exceptions to general rules, and there is so much pride and prejudice mixed up with it that I have often been tempted to give up the study of government for some definite subject like medicine or engineering.

DR. BRAUN: Oh! general rules are just the beginning of medicine, too. After I began to practice, I soon found out that no two cases are ever exactly alike in details and circumstances. And there is a lot of guesswork in handling every case, except the very simplest, perhaps. Some of my colleagues like to call it trained insight. There may be something in that, but what it is I have never been able to discern. Often I have to act so quickly on it, in an unusual case, that I cannot discover just what mental processes I am using in the operation. So, if you get out of constitutional law into medicine, you may find yourself out of the frying pan in the fire. What interests me especially, if you will pardon a digression, is the rights of citizens as such. Does the naturalized citizen have the same rights as a natural-born citizen, perhaps I ought to say, as a general rule?

BEARD: No, Dr. Braun. A natural-born citizen cannot be deprived of citizenship and expelled from the country, but a naturalized citizen may be, in certain circumstances.

DR. BRAUN: That is startling!

BEARD: You need not worry, Doctor. Your attachment to the Constitution and America is too warm and too unreserved to put you in any peril; and in any case a naturalized citizen whose citizenship is challenged has the protection of the courts: the right to be heard in open court, to have counsel, to call witnesses, and to have a fair and impartial trial. A naturalized citizen may be deprived of his citizenship only on the ground that it was procured illegally or through fraud or misrepresentation of some kind.

DR. BRAUN: Have there been actual cases of naturalized citizens who have been deprived of their citizenship?

BEARD: A number of them, Doctor. You will find types of cases summarized admirably in Luella Gettys' *The Law of Citizenship in the United States* (1936 edition), which I have used extensively in my own studies. Of course, false oaths made for the purpose of securing naturalization papers are proper grounds for canceling certificates of citizenship. Everybody agrees that this is a just and proper rule of law.

In order to be admitted to citizenship, an applicant must be, under the law of naturalization, a person of good moral character. Good moral character is not easy to define, and witnesses who support the application of an alien may not know all about the person or have rather crude notions respecting good moral character.

Miss Gettys gives cases under this head. For example, before and after a certain alien in the West was admitted to citizenship, he operated a house of prostitution in connection with a saloon in San Francisco. This fact was discovered afterward, and the man was deprived of his citizenship. In another case, a man concealed the fact that he was a bigamist at the time of his naturalization. If this had been known then, a certificate would not have been given him. When it was later discovered, his certificate was canceled.

Again, an alien, to be naturalized, must take an oath of allegiance to the United States and must be 'attached to the principles of the Constitution.' Here is room for a good deal of discretion on the part of judges. In one case it was discovered that a naturalized citizen had described himself privately as 'a pure, red Communist,' opposed to representative government, before and after naturalization. On this ground his certificate of citizenship was taken away from him.

However, judging by another case, if he had acquired these radical ideas *after* his naturalization, at least a few years afterward, that would not have been ground for cancellation. In one such case, the judge said that it would be too conjectural to hold that a man who was discovered to have joined a radical organization five years after his naturalization was in that 'state of mind' at the time of his naturalization.

In another case, a naturalized citizen was charged with having been active in agitating for a resumption of trade relations with Soviet Russia while the United States Government refused to recognize the Russian Government, and with thus being opposed to the policy of the Administration in power at Washington. On this charge an effort was made to deprive him of his American citizenship. The judge in the case rebuffed the attempt. The following passage from the judge's opinion is, in my view, the proper ruling:

Among the privileges of American citizenship is the right of every citizen to differ with these other citizens on whom has been imposed the responsibility of public office, with respect to the policies to be followed in the administration of the affairs of the republic, and this, of course, includes the right to make all lawful efforts to arouse, and direct toward the official representatives of the people, the force of public opinion in regard to such policies. This, surely, is of the very essence of the principles of our Constitution, and in the application of such principles I see no reason for discrimination as between citizens and aliens. Nor can I follow the government [the prosecution] in its contention that belief by an alien that changes should be made in our form of government indicates lack of attachment to the principles of our Constitution. . . . The Constitution itself, providing as it does for its own amendment in any respect deemed desirable by the people, seems to me to unanswerably refute any notion of the sort.

MRS. SMYTH: If we follow that chain of reasoning, it seems, does it not, that a naturalized alien has about all the rights of a natural-born citizen? Or do you have exceptions to that general rule?

BEARD: There are exceptions. First of all, only a natural-born citizen is eligible to the office of President.

DR. BRAUN: That does not interfere with my ambitions!

BEARD: A second exception seems to be that a naturalized alien would scarcely dare to become a conscientious objector in time of war.

DR. BRAUN: That does not affect me either. But I should like to know how that distinction came to be made.

MRS. SMYTH: It arose in connection with the case of Madame Rosika Schwimmer many years ago, did it not? I should like to know more of the details of the case.

BEARD: The case is fairly simple. Rosika Schwimmer applied for American citizenship in due form. At the hearing on her petition, she was asked whether she would be willing to bear arms. She answered that she was a pacifist in principle and would not be willing to bear arms. There was nothing in the naturalization law about bearing arms. The question was merely put to her by the examiner in the course of the hearings.

When the case came before the District Court, the judge denied her petition on the ground that her negative reply to the question meant that she really was not attached to the principles of the Constitution. On appeal, the Circuit Court reversed the decision of the lower Court and declared that the question about bearing arms bore no necessary relation to the law respecting naturalization.

Then the case went to the Supreme Court of the United States, and in 1929 the Court denied citizenship to Madame Schwimmer. Justice Pierce Butler rendered the opinion. He said that the fact that Mrs. Schwimmer was an uncompromising pacifist, 'with no sense of nationalism but only a cosmic sense of belonging to the human family, justifies the belief that she may be opposed to the use of military force as contemplated by our Constitution and laws. . . . Such persons are liable to be incapable of the attachment for and devotion to the principles of our Constitution that is required of aliens seeking naturalization.' Justice Holmes dissented.

MRS. SMYTH: I recall that Justice Holmes in his dissent made some perfectly delicious remarks. Do you have his opinion handy? If so, read some of them to us.

BEARD, finding the opinion: Here is one:

The whole examination [of Mrs. Schwimmer] . . . shows that she holds none of the now dreaded creeds but thoroughly believes in organized government and prefers that of the United States to any other in the world. Surely it cannot show lack of attachment to the principles of the Constitution that she thinks that it can be improved. I suppose that the most intelligent people think that it might be. Her particular improvement looking to the abolition of war seems to me not materially different in its bearing on this case from a wish to establish cabinet government as in England, or a single house, or one term of seven years for the President.

Is that the passage you wanted?

MRS. SMYTH: That is good, but the passage I was thinking of had something about the Sermon on the Mount.

BEARD: Here is the one you mean:

I would suggest that the Quakers have done their share to make the country what it is, that many citizens share the applicant's [Mrs. Schwimmer's] belief and that I had not supposed hitherto that we regretted our inability to expel them because they believe more than some of us do in the teachings of the Sermon on the Mount.

MRS. SMYTH: That's it. That was a good dig by Holmes, the skeptic, at Justice Butler, who took pride in being a devout Christian. But all that has to do with naturalization, not the rights of a naturalized citizen. After an alien has been lawfully naturalized, can he or she believe anything that other citizens believe?

BEARD: Of course, a naturalized citizen can believe what he pleases, but he must be careful what he says or does. I suppose that if within a short time after naturalization he should proclaim himself a conscientious objector in time of war or a revolutionary communist, he might be prosecuted and lose his citizenship. Of course it would all depend on the prosecuting officers, the judge, and the jury, and to a considerable extent on the state of public sentiment at the moment. I am not sure but I suspect that, if public excitement ran high, such a naturalized citizen would lose his citizenship in a pinch unless the Supreme Court, on appeal, saved him.*

---

* Desiring to help the Smyths in "keeping up to date" on the business of "denaturalizing" aliens who have become citizens, I wrote them the following letter:

Hosannah Hill, June 29, 1943.

Dear Dr. and Mrs. Smyth,

Enclosed you will find a pamphlet of sixty-eight pages, dealing with the decision and

Dr. Smyth: Of all the clotted nonsense in the world! The naturalization and citizenship business seems to be run in such a fashion by the Government that even you, after studying it with some care at least, can't be sure of a naturalized citizen's rights. We should be in a frightful state at the Hospital and the factory if we never could tell how anything would turn out, but had to consider the whims or tempers of prosecutors, judges, juries, and excited citizens.

And look at my friend Dr. Braun, a naturalized citizen. He wants to be a good citizen according to American principles. He is busy day and night with the most difficult cases of eye surgery. He has no time to study constitutional law—law, did I say? Law? It looks more like Saint Vitus' dance than any law that I am acquainted with in physiology or biology. If I had to work with such law as the kind you are talking about, I should go crazy and have to shut up shop.

We ask you a plain question. You give us a general rule. Then you make a lot of exceptions in particular cases. Then you immediately say that in other or similar cases, prosecutors, judges, juries, and the excited public might decide one way or the other, for or against a bewildered naturalized citizen. He might be deprived of his citizenship for some perfectly innocent remark or action, because he could not tell in advance which way the cat would jump in a prosecutor's office or a courtroom or in the town square. And you fellows call your subject political science. It seems to me more like astrology or necromancy than science. If I operated at the Hospital on such a science, the Board would send me to the State Hospital for the Insane.

Mrs. Smyth: Now, Robert, let us be fair all around. You are not always as sure of your own business as you seem to be now. Not long ago, you walked the floor half the night, wondering whether to operate in a difficult and dangerous case. You decided first one

---

opinions of the Supreme Court in the case of William Schneiderman *vs.* the United States, rendered June 21, 1943. Here you will see that belonging to and being active in a revolutionary party prior to naturalization and concealing the facts at the time of naturalization do not, at the moment, afford grounds for depriving him of his citizenship. This supplements the views I expressed at our fire-side seminar on the subject. If you see Dr. Braun, please let him read the pamphlet. He will be interested in it. There are two or three pages in it which will remind him of his mother tongue.

Sincerely yours,

Charles Beard.

way and then the other. You decided one way and then woke me up to ask my opinion. I told you honestly that I did not *know* what was best and that you must make up your own mind. Soon you decided the other way and asked me about that and received the same reply. You even seemed to think that I was to blame because I did not know the right answer.

Finally you wore yourself out and went to sleep on the divan before the fireplace. You woke up early, went over to the Hospital, consulted three colleagues, and the four of you decided on an operation. It failed. The patient died. And you have been stewing about it off and on ever since. The last I heard of it, you suspected that the patient would have died, operation or no operation.

You blast at government for being unscientific. It seems to me that it is just intensely human. Ordinarily human beings act according to certain customs, and you can tell fairly well what most of them are going to do from day to day, at least in normal circumstances. But you never can be sure how specific individuals are going to act. Nor can we be sure how we ourselves will act under stresses and strains we have never before encountered.

Dr. Smyth: I sit corrected, Susan. I must try harder to apply my own experiences as a medical practitioner to other types of human experiences. I shall be glad if Beard can be definite, but I shall do my best to keep calm while he discusses the privileges and immunities of citizens of the United States, even if the said privileges and immunities are not very definite.

Beard: They are not definite in all respects but I shall strive for the utmost exactness in my statements. In our coming sessions on freedom of press, speech, and religious worship, we shall go into the subject at greater length. For the present, I shall make some distinctions with reference to privileges and immunities guaranteed to American citizens.

There is a distinction in law, somewhat shadowy it is true, between the privileges and immunities belonging to citizens of the United States and those belonging to citizens of states. There are some privileges or immunities that a person enjoys as a citizen of the United States, and states are forbidden by the Fourteenth Amendment to abridge these rights. Other rights or privileges a citizen enjoys as a resident or citizen in a particular state, and these rights the Federal Government cannot abridge. Finally come the rights and privileges all persons enjoy, and these cannot be taken away from them by a state or by the Federal Government. There is a strong tendency now to regard certain fundamental rights and privileges to be observed by both the states and the Federal Government as identical and as in force throughout the Union.

DR. BRAUN: That is rather hard for me to grasp.

DR. SMYTH: Never mind, Braun. It doesn't mean a thing to me either, and I was born, reared, and educated here. In fact when the biggest newspaper in town (for circulating purposes) took a poll a month ago as to who were the ten first citizens of the town, I was included in the list. I wasn't too proud of the list, though.

Turning to me, DR. SMYTH said, Can't you give us some ABC's?

BEARD: Here is a copy of the Constitution for each of you. It is, by the way, from the original parchment and has the old spelling and capitalization which are not found in copies now printed unofficially for general use. The first eight pages contain the original Constitution. Then come the Amendments to the Constitution. The first ten Amendments were adopted as a group in 1791. They are often called the Bill of Rights. Now look down the list and you will see the Fourteenth Amendment. There is the reference to 'the privileges *or* immunities of citizens of the United States.' Now look back to Article IV. There is the section which declares that 'the citizens of the United States shall be entitled to all privileges *and* immunities of citizens in the several states.' Note the word *and,* as distinguished from the *or* in the Fourteenth Amendment.

(Here Dr. Smyth squirmed in his chair but said nothing.)

BEARD, again: It was early contended, and cogently, I believe, that the privileges *or* immunities mentioned in the Fourteenth Amendment included all the rights, privileges, and/or immunities named in the Bill of Rights, which were and are restraints on the Federal Government, not on the states. According to this interpretation, in order to find out most of the privileges and immunities of American citizens you merely had to read the Bill of Rights. That is, as a general rule, leaving out of account for the moment the rights guaranteed to citizens in the original Constitution, with which we dealt at our ninth session.

In 1873 when the Supreme Court passed upon the Fourteenth Amendment in the so-called Slaughter House Cases, the majority opinion declared that there are two classes of privileges and immunities. In the first class are all the privileges and immunities that belong to a citizen as a citizen of a state as such. In the second class are all those privileges and immunities belonging to a citizen of the United States as such. Thus the Court denied the contention that those words in the Fourteenth Amendment forbade states to abridge any of the liberties declared in the Bill of Rights.

Under this narrow view, the rights of citizens as citizens of the United States *as such* include only a few rights: for example, the right to petition the Federal Government for a redress of grievances, to transact business with federal officers, to share the offices of the Federal Government, to use the navigable waters, to have the privilege of the writ of habeas corpus, and a few others. Other rights of citizens, the Court said in this case, are still under the control of the states, as they were before the Fourteenth Amendment was adopted. Thus there could be as many sets of privileges and immunities as there were states in the Union, subject to the provisions of the original Constitution and the Thirteenth Amendment abolishing slavery.

As things stood then in 1873, therefore, a state could, if it saw fit, establish a state church, compel all its citizens to pay taxes to support this church, and compel them to attend its services. To give another example, as things stood under that Supreme Court decision, a state could, if it saw fit, create a press censorship or indeed abolish freedom of press entirely.

Dr. Smyth: Do you mean that any state ever could set up a state church of any kind?

Beard: Yes. In each of nine of the thirteen English colonies there was an established church of some kind. During the revolutionary period, the Church of England was disestablished in each of the six colonies where it had special privileges. But the Congregational Church retained its privileges as an establishment in New Hampshire until 1817, in Connecticut until 1818, and in Massachusetts until 1833. During the slavery controversy several Southern states put strict limitations on freedom of the press. So, to repeat, under the decision of the Supreme Court in 1873, states were apparently free to establish churches, censor newspapers, and otherwise interfere with liberties enumerated in the Bill of Rights.

But during the past twenty-five years, as I said before, the

Supreme Court has been showing a tendency, a strong tendency, to reverse the rule of 1873. It has been including under the Fourteenth Amendment many of the privileges specifically named in the Bill of Rights. We shall discuss them more fully in our next two sessions. Meanwhile, to make these generalities more concrete. I will express the opinion that the Court would not now allow a state to establish a church or set up an official press censor.

Such freedom of religious worship and such freedom of the press as a citizen or person enjoys as against the Federal Government, under the Bill of Rights he now also enjoys as against the state, under recent decisions of the Supreme Court applying the Fourteenth Amendment. In this way the Bill of Rights and the rights guaranteed by the Fourteenth Amendment tend to become identical. It would ease my pains as a student and relieve Dr. Smyth's mind if they were identical.

But they are not entirely identical—as yet. For instance, in all cases of serious crimes against federal law, federal officers must leave the right to indict in the hands of a grand jury, according to historic forms. But on their part states may, if they choose, dispense with the grand jury even in cases of serious crimes and allow a single prosecutor to indict and force the accused to trial.

Dr. Braun: Would it not be simple to have a uniform system throughout the United States?

Dr. Smyth: It certainly would spare us a lot of confusion and uncertainty. Beard, don't you favor uniformity of civil and criminal law?

Beard: Honestly, simplicity may be the essence of tyranny. It is usually in complexity that we find liberty. I do not favor forcing uniform civil and criminal law upon the Union. A determination to force it upon all the states would make a huge disturbance, if not a revolt. But I rejoice in the tendency of the Supreme Court to develop a system of justice that assures to all citizens, indeed to all persons in the United States, a large number of common or uniform rights.

Dr. Smyth: I noticed that now and then during the evening, you have slipped in the word persons. Just this moment you referred to all persons. There seems to be a distinction between the rights of citizens and the rights of persons, and you have not made that distinction clear.

BEARD: There are some rights that belong to all persons in the United States, including citizens. There are other rights that belong only to citizens. You will find illustrations in the first ten Amendments, and in the Fourteenth Amendment. But if I should go into exceptions, distinctions, and discriminations, you would probably say that the fog is the biggest you have yet encountered here on my hill.

MRS. SMYTH: According to the views you have expressed tonight, managing a government is like managing a household. There must be certain rules, or the household would go to pieces. Good sense makes exceptions and condones infractions of the rules in many cases. So the fewer rigid rules, the better. Success in household management depends upon constant modifications and adjustments. Dominance by a patriarch or a matriarch might be easily established in some cases, all right, but it would be likely to keep the household in a bad temper.

BEARD: That is akin to the art of government applied on a large scale. Economy, as used in political economy, is just a Greek word for household management. While politics is not as exact as the multiplication table, it is not all moonshine.

After we have reviewed the uncertainties we might discuss the art of government.

Anyhow, dear old Tom, the city engineer, the most popular official in town, is on the job as usual, I remarked as we stepped out on the porch and looked at the city spread out in every direction with its street lights all ablaze.

Yes, said DR. SMYTH as he waved good night, old Tom is as reliable at the city electric light plant as the stars are in heaven.

XI

Freedom of Speech and Press

AFTER the usual preliminaries of gossip about the weather and local events, DR. SMYTH opened our eleventh session by saying: Before we get down to cases on civil liberties, I should like to have some light on two questions that have arisen in my mind. First, why is it that, except in some small countries such as Switzerland and Sweden, civil liberties are largely confined to the English-speaking nations? Second, why is it that even in English-speaking countries civil liberties are nearly always in jeopardy or at least in controversy?

BEARD: You are asking for more of your regular law-of-gravitation answers. I wish that I could give them. I can only submit to you types of explanations. The prevalence of civil liberties among English-speaking peoples has been explained on the ground of race, in the following terms: Anglo-Saxons are Teutons; from the earliest times, Teutons, as contrasted with Latins, have displayed a spirit of independence and liberty—

DR. SMYTH: But what about the Germans? Aren't they Teutons? They have been notorious for their acceptance of despotic governments. Certainly Germany has never been the home of revolutionary uprisings in favor of liberty—successful uprisings, I mean.

BEARD: It is for such reasons that I am unable to agree with the racial or Teutonic explanation of the emphasis on civil liberties among the English-speaking peoples. There is power in the character of peoples, but I am more inclined to account for this emphasis with reference to geographic and economic conditions. The English Channel cut Great Britain off from the Continent, and for nearly a thousand years Britain was free from the threat of an armed invasion from the Continent. This enabled a transfer of energies from the arts of war to the arts of peace.

In protecting herself Britain could use the navy, which in its impact on the people differs essentially from the army. An open and dangerous frontier and an immense permanent army mean domination by an army class and an iron solidarity in a nation, that gives little leeway to liberty of person and property. In the United States the English-speaking people and their fellow citizens from other countries have had an immense continent, with huge elbowroom. The two oceans long protected Americans as the Channel protected the British.

This allowed the development of diversity in economics, politics, religion, and the arts—a diversity that hampered the seizure of all power by any single group. Diversity also helped to educate Americans in toleration. Again, in these circumstances, through concern with practical affairs and a good living, Americans developed a sense of diversity and toleration, a sort of American philosophy. For me there is more meaning in this explanation than in any other.

DR. SMYTH: But if devotion to civil liberty is not innate, if it depends on external circumstances, then we are sunk. Our continental elbowroom is all gone. We are going to have to build an immense protective army, no matter how this war comes out. The oceans are narrowed by the bombing plane. Hence, according to the circumstances theory, civil liberties are on the way out for good.

BEARD: There is reason in your argument, but you overlook one consideration. Americans have been well educated in the knowledge and the defense of civil liberty through the long centuries. They have institutionalized it, and their education in this respect may prevail against hostile outward conditions. Our heritage, experience, and institutions should help us to keep a large amount of liberty intact, despite the changes you have recited.

DR. SMYTH: That is true, but the long drumming of adverse pressures is likely in time to de-educate us into the spirit of submission. Isn't that so?

BEARD: I concede that it is possible. I hope that it does not come to pass.

MRS. SMYTH: Then you have no absolute guarantee for civil liberties in any natural law or innate racial qualities?

BEARD: Unhappily, no. Now suppose we take up the Doctor's second question, Why are civil liberties nearly always in jeopardy? I cannot answer that question either. There seems to be in the human spirit an eternal conflict between the passion for liberty and the passion for authority. Too much of the one seems to induce a reaction to too much of the other. Those who advocate liberty are often mere negationists, extremists without a sense of responsibility for maintaining the liberty they enjoy. The same may be said of those who swing to extremes of authority. As human beings are highly dynamic in action, a settled equilibrium seems impossible. It would be a dead center. The problem is one of enforcing a sense of responsibility on those who assert rights or powers and of holding the dynamic swinging within some median parallel lines. Both liberty and authority are always likely to be in jeopardy through the conflict of forces.

DR. SMYTH: What you have said at least helps me to get my bearings, and I am ready for a plunge into specific questions of liberty.

BEARD: We have dealt with certain principles of liberty and the rights of citizens as developed under the Constitution as it stood in its original form. We have touched upon general principles of justice, liberty, and security of person. Now we come to the consideration of two groups of specific rights: freedom of speech and press, and religious liberty. The first of these we have before us tonight: liberty of speech and press.

Once more, however, I must emphasize a distinction. The Bill of Rights, so-called, the first ten Amendments, constitutes limitations on the power of the Federal Government to interfere with the liberties named in the Bill. It leaves to the states *all powers* except those conferred on the national authorities by the Constitution and those denied to the states by the Constitution. We must constantly keep in mind that, as far as these ten Amendments were concerned, the states were for a long time and in important respects free to define or abolish civil liberties. The states could establish a church by law, create a censorship of the press, destroy freedom of speech and religious liberty. In other words, for about seventy-five years, the states enjoyed numerous powers over civil liberty almost as despotic as those enjoyed by an absolute monarch or dictator.

At the close of the Civil War, three new Amendments were adopted—the Thirteenth, the Fourteenth, and the Fifteenth. Adopted, did I say? In a way, adopted. In fact, they were forced upon the Southern states, then prostrate before Northern armies or administrative agencies. These three Amendments impose restrictions on the power of states to interfere with liberty, and recently the Supreme Court of the United States has been interpreting the Fourteenth broadly. Subject to a number of exceptions, generally formal, the Fourteenth Amendment, as now interpreted, imposes on the states limitations substantially the same as those imposed on the Federal Government by the first nine Amendments in the Bill of Rights.

Hence we now have a body of restraints on behalf of civil liberty, in vital respects identical, imposed on both the states and the Federal Government. Only by clearly grasping these facts are we in a position to deal with civil liberty in the United States. So, we can now say that freedom of speech and press is a limitation on the states as well as on federal authorities.

Mrs. Smyth: If I understand your proposition, liberty of speech and press, as against state authorities, does not rest on specific clauses of the federal Constitution. As to the states, it rests merely upon interpretations which the Supreme Court has made of the Fourteenth Amendment. To put it in another way, there are no words in the federal Constitution which expressly forbid states to interfere with freedom of press, freedom of speech, and freedom of religious worship. The courts have simply read these liberties into certain words in the Fourteenth Amendment.

Beard: That is my proposition exactly.

Dr. Smyth: Then the Supreme Court, having read them into the Constitution against the states, can read them out again. The Court has often reversed itself, I have learned. Freedom of speech, press, and religious worship, as against state authorities, is not in the Constitution but in the minds of Supreme Court Justices. Therefore it is precarious.

Beard: As I should rather phrase it, this freedom is in the decisions and opinions of the federal courts. These decisions and opinions will doubtless influence future decisions and opinions of the courts. States must obey the decisions of the Supreme Court.

Mrs. Smyth: Still, Robert is right, is he not, when he says that liberty of speech, press, and religious worship, as against the states, is not in the Constitution? Judges put it there. Judges can take it out.

Beard: I agree with that, but much is involved in your statement. So, with your permission, I shall pass over its implications and go directly to my main theme. Liberty of speech and liberty of press are substantially identical. They are freedom to utter words orally and freedom to write, print, and circulate words. There are some distinctions, but I leave them out of account. Neither federal nor state authorities can abridge this freedom or these liberties. The language of the first amendment runs: 'Congress shall make no law . . . abridging the freedom of speech, or of the press.' And, under Supreme Court decisions: 'No state shall make any law abridging the freedom of speech, or of the press.'

This freedom is not absolute; nor is it very definite in all respects.

DR. SMYTH: I could have guessed that those words were coming.

BEARD: Here are some of the definite respects. Neither Congress nor the states can legally establish in time of peace a board of censorship to which speakers and publishers must submit their utterances before making them public. Whether in time of war a state can create such a censorship, I am not sure; but certainly in time of war Congress or the President can do that.

There is another definite thing: Liberty of press and speech is subject to the law of slander and libel. Neither speakers nor publishers can make statements deliberately designed to injure the character or good name of any person without laying themselves open to actions at law. Furthermore, obscene language may not be used by public writers or speakers with impunity.

There is a third very definite rule of law, now binding throughout the country. It is that no person can, with disloyal intent, advocate the overthrow of government by revolution, that is, by violence. And what is more significant, perhaps, no person can be a member of an organization which, with disloyal intent, indulges in such advocacy or has such advocacy as a part of its program. This positive limitation on freedom of speech and press is to be found in statutes enacted by many states, extending over the years, but especially numerous since the First World War. In 1940, the Congress of the United States wrote this limitation into the Alien Registration Act of that year and made it the law of the land. Lists of federal and state statutes affecting freedom of speech are to be found in Zechariah Chafee's *Free Speech in the United States* (edition of 1942), Appendix II and Appendix III.

We have a fairly definite idea of what that type of legislation means in the states where it has long been in force. Experience with it, as handled by judges and juries, gives us a foretaste of what the federal Act of 1940 may mean as applied in coming years. From this experience it is reasonably certain that as administered it is a drastic limitation on freedom of speech and press.

MRS. SMYTH: This raises again the question of the right of revolution which we had before us early in our sessions. Judging by what you have just said, a state can forbid the public advocacy of political changes by violent methods. Many states have done this and the Federal Government has joined them. Could you illustrate specifically the prohibition that states have imposed or may impose on such freedom of speech and press?

BEARD: A good example is an old California statute (now modified) penalizing criminal syndicalism. The definition of criminal syndicalism in it was as follows:

. . . any doctrine or precept advocating, teaching or aiding and abetting the commission of crime, sabotage . . . or unlawful acts of force and violence or unlawful methods of terrorism as a means of accomplishing a change in industrial ownership or control, or effecting any political change.

The California act also made it a crime to be a member of any organization, group, society, or assemblage of persons organized or assembled to advocate or abet criminal syndicalism.

MRS. SMYTH: And has the Supreme Court of the United States upheld state legislation making the peacetime advocacy of change by revolutionary methods a crime?

BEARD: It has, in a number of decisions.

MRS. SMYTH: Then, in those states which have these laws any person who makes a speech in public or who prints an article to the effect that he favors exercising the right of revolution, the right to overthrow or dismember government, which Lincoln set forth in his First Inaugural, is liable to fine and imprisonment?

BEARD: Yes. That is now the established law of the land for those states and in effect for the United States.

Now let us consider the kind of restrictions Congress, under settled decisions of the Supreme Court, may impose on speech and press in time of war or emergency, for wars and emergencies seem to be common these days. During the First World War, Congress passed two stringent statutes. The first, the Espionage Act, made it a crime to speak, print, or act in any way that was likely to interfere with the recruitment of forces and the conduct of the war. The second, called the Sedition Act, strengthened the Espionage Act and, among other things, made it a crime to utter, print, write or publish any disloyal or abusive language about the form of government of the United States or the Constitution. This second law was certainly as strict as the Sedition Act of 1798 which stirred Jeffersonian Democrats to wrath.

DR. SMYTH: Were these acts upheld by the Supreme Court? As I recall, there was a struggle over them and Holmes and Brandeis at least battled against them.

BEARD: For this once, your memory does not serve you well, Doctor. The Espionage Act was sustained unanimously by the Supreme Court and Justice Holmes wrote the three great opinions of the Court defending the constitutionality of the Act—in the Schenck case, the Frohwerk case, and the Debs case. The Sedition Act was also upheld by the Supreme Court. Holmes wrote a memorable dissenting opinion in one case and Brandeis in another. But their dissents bore on particular points of application under the Sedition Act, not on the validity of the whole act. Neither Holmes nor Brandeis attacked the terms of the law as a whole on constitutional grounds.

DR. SMYTH: But didn't they do something to mitigate the harshness of the law?

BEARD: As dissenters they were unable to *do* anything to mitigate the penalties imposed on persons convicted under the Sedition Act. But they spoke with great force for interpretations of the Act, which, if adopted, would have limited the rigors of the law in its enforcement. Yet, as I have said, Holmes wrote three opinions sustaining the Espionage Act. Respecting two of them, Zechariah Chafee, in the book I have cited, holds that Holmes made a harsh application of the law—one that went beyond his own theory of 'clear and present danger.' These were the Frohwerk and Debs cases.

DR. SMYTH: 'Clear and present danger'—that is the phrase I was trying to remember. It is my understanding that Holmes and Brandeis established that doctrine, though I could scarcely define it if I had to. How would you define it?

BEARD: In general terms as follows: In regulating freedom of speech and press, Congress can only proscribe speeches, publications, and kindred acts that produce or are immediately likely to produce a clear and present danger that substantive evils will happen—evils such as an armed uprising, desertion from the army, or acts of revolutionary violence. Once it was widely held by American judges that anything which *tends* to produce a disorder or insurrection, which any government has the right and duty to suppress, can be forbidden by limitations on speech, publication, and assembly. That is of course a doctrine dangerous to liberty. If a person objects publicly to a tax on whiskey or tobacco, that may *tend* to set his neighbors off on a riot to smash liquor or tobacco shops.

Holmes and Brandeis insisted that there must be a distinction between loose and general talk about revolution and words uttered or published in times and circumstances which make them likely to set off a social explosion at once. Utterances so formulated and so made as to create a clear and present danger of disorder, riot, revolution, or armed resistance may be forbidden under this theory. Loose and general talk about revolution cannot be forbidden under it.

DR. SMYTH: Here is a case, Beard, where your emphasis on distinctions seems to me to be helpful. The distinction you have just made is a good one. Otherwise a person could be sent to jail for uttering almost any severe criticism of any government officials or any politicians. That would be too bad. I either read somewhere or was told by a friend that the Holmes-Brandeis theory of clear or present danger is now the dominant theory on freedom of speech and press, that is, the theory recognized by our courts.

BEARD: People who ought to know better, I think, are constantly making the statement that the clear and present danger theory is accepted doctrine for the federal courts at least. Personally I believe that the theory is a good working proposition, but, to speak summarily, it is not the dominant theory—the law of the land. I could cite numerous examples, some from Holmes himself, showing departures from the theory in concrete applications. And it all boils down to concrete applications: A person is or is not sent to prison for given utterances at given times and places. The theory of the clear and present danger is not the controlling principle in respect of free speech and free press.

Mrs. Smyth: Then, pray tell us what is.

Beard: I do not know exactly what it is, if there is one. The clear and present danger rule is, I think, an excellent principle. It is now fairly well established in the *thought* of the Supreme Court of the United States, especially on account of the fact that the present justices are in general sympathy with the doctrines of Brandeis and Holmes. But the principle is not the law of the land. Though familiar with this principle, the Supreme Court has been and is split wide open on concrete applications of laws relative to civil liberty. Besides, the business is complicated by the question of what circumstances permit legislatures to justify drastic laws on grounds of emergency. Take, for example, the Whitney case in California about twenty-five years ago.

Mrs. Smyth: I know something about that affair. It involved Anita Whitney, a woman of wealth and sensitive social sympathies, who became tangled up with communists or radicals. I remember when she was convicted; but, unless I am misinformed, Justice Brandeis, with Holmes, dissented and wrote a grand declaration of human rights in this case.

Beard: You are partly misinformed, Mrs. Smyth. Miss Whitney was charged with crime under the California syndicalism law. She was not charged with having said or printed a word 'tending to show that she ever advocated a violation of any law.' The burden of the charge against her was that she was a member of the Communist Labor Party. She was also accused of having attended two or three meetings of the party or its committees in California. Convicted in a California court, she was sentenced to prison for a term of from one to fourteen years. The case went up to the Supreme Court in Washington, and the Court unanimously upheld the validity of the syndicalist law as applied to Miss Whitney and confirmed her sentence. On this both Brandeis and Holmes agreed with all the other Justices.

Mrs. Smyth: Then how did Brandeis' declaration of human rights come into the case, if he agreed to uphold the California law and the conviction of Miss Whitney? That seems like a serious contradiction on its face.

Beard: You must remember the technology of the law. A judge may agree, and often does, with the other judges on the decision, but disagree as to the reasoning on which the decision rests or by which it is justified. In the Whitney case, Brandeis agreed to the decision but did not agree to the reasoning of Justice Sanford's opinion supporting the decision.

Brandeis did not dissent. His opinion was not dissenting opinion but concurring. He concurred in the decision but adduced other reasons to support it, and Holmes joined him in this. He took the ground that Miss Whitney had not furnished satisfactory evidence or proof that the California law was arbitrary or unwarranted—at least proof sufficient to permit the Supreme Court to determine whether it was or was not arbitrary or unwarranted. It was in his concurring opinion upholding the conviction of Miss Whitney that Brandeis laid down what has justly been called 'the great principles and the fundamentals of human nature upon which freedom of speech rests.'

DR. SMYTH: Let me get this straight. Brandeis and Holmes voted to send this Miss Whitney to jail and then handed her an essay full of noble principles. I never heard of Anita Whitney until you and my wife mentioned her name just now. I never heard of the case before. But it seems to me like the case of a physician who kills a patient and then preaches a fine sermon at the funeral. Jurisprudence appears to be a labyrinth indeed. I am getting on to your curves, Beard, bit by bit.

BEARD: Your analogy, Doctor is not exact, and you are unjust to Brandeis. I think that his grand statement of principles in the Whitney case has helped to advance the cause of civil liberty in the United States.

DR. SMYTH: That may be. I know nothing about it. But please answer this question, Under the decision to which Brandeis and Holmes agreed, if Congress or a state legislature declares that an emergency exists, can it suppress free speech and free press almost at will, constitution or no constitution? If so, there is no sense on earth in having a constitution or limited government. All a gang of despots in a legislature has to do is to declare an emergency and make itself as supreme as Adolf Hitler and his crowd in Germany.

BEARD: My answer to your question is No. A mere declaration of an emergency is not enough in itself to justify any act that Congress or a state legislature may decide to pass. Such a declaration will carry weight with the Supreme Court, but an accused person has a chance to prove to the court that the alleged dangers of the emergency were not sufficient to sustain the declaration. If the accused does present such proof, the Supreme Court will presumably give it weight in determining whether the law in question is constitutional or not. It is not likely that the Courts would sustain drastic legislation by what you call a gang of despots, on the mere ground that it had declared an emergency.

DR. SMYTH: Well, answer another question. Has the Supreme Court ever actually declared unconstitutional any of these statutes which forbid openly teaching the right of revolution—the right asserted in the Declaration of Independence and by Abraham Lincoln? Yes or No?

BEARD: To the best of my knowledge and belief, the answer again is No. In a Kansas case it set aside such a state law *as applied* in that case, but it has never squarely declared an entire statute of that kind null and void.

DR. SMYTH: All right. Then answer this question. Suppose a person should read in public the words from Lincoln's First Inaugural asserting the right of revolution, organize a Lincoln society for teaching that doctrine, and engage in teaching it. Could he be sent to prison under these antisyndicalist laws? Yes or No?

BEARD: He could be. Yes.

DR. SMYTH: Would he be?

BEARD: Probably, but it would doubtless depend upon circumstances. I cannot answer that question with a single Yes or No.

DR. SMYTH: I do not know either history or law; but, despite all the palaver about civil liberty in recent years, there isn't as much real liberty now as there was in 1861. You know I have no sympathy for any of the infernal radicals. I have respect for the best American traditions. I know that liberty is not absolute. But there may come a time when the conservatives of the country who want to uphold fundamental rights of person and property against politicians in power will have to preserve the spirit of liberty by—

MRS. SMYTH: Wait a moment, Robert. Weigh your words.

DR. SMYTH: I will do that. Politicians may lawfully get possession of the forms of our government and crucify its spirit. It may be necessary then to rescue the spirit by violating the forms which have become empty shells. That is the right I am talking about. And now Beard tells me that under the so-called progressives the right has been destroyed or at least made so uncertain that mere talking about it in public will put even a simon-pure American, a lover of his country, into the penitentiary for years. Then, as regards civil liberty, we are in a worse condition now than ever before in our history. All the legal hairsplitting by your enlightened and progressive judges just adds up to that amount of degradation. Beard can say anything he likes about my statement. In view of the judicial decisions he has cited, my conclusion is true. But let's get on. What I want to know now is this. What kind of sedition law has Congress passed for this present World War? Any?

BEARD: You may not care about what I am going to say. Still, I cannot help saying that your statement is too sweeping. In some respects, there has been a decline in civil liberty. In other respects, there have been gains. How the conflicting tendencies will work out in coming years, I do not claim to foresee. The battle between liberty and authority apparently, is eternal, and the upshot just ahead of us, I feel sure, will depend upon the character of the American people and their intellectual and moral leaders.

Mrs. Smyth made an obvious gesture in the direction of peace, and Dr. Smyth leaned back in his armchair as a shadow of conviction spread slowly over his face.

BEARD, tackling Dr. Smyth's last question: Doctor, we have what amounts to a new Sedition Act. As I have already indicated, in 1940 Congress added to the old Espionage Act of the last war, still in force, a new sedition law. This law—

DR. SMYTH: But in 1940, the United States was not at war, and we were told by politicians that there was to be no war.

BEARD: The new law was passed in anticipation of war. This sedition law was hooked onto the Alien Registration Act of 1940. At the time there was a genuine concern over the possibility of sabotage and other disturbances by aliens. It was generally agreed that all aliens should be registered, so that their names and addresses could be known to the public authorities. While this registration bill was up in Congress, advocates of a new sedition act attached their project to the registration bill. Probably they could not have got it through Congress as a separate measure. Owing to the sentiment against aliens, however, they were able to push it through as an attachment to the alien registration bill.

DR. SMYTH: Then that was a contemptible political trick. I suppose no member of Congress dared to protest against it.

BEARD: It was in keeping with a practice that is quite common. There was, however, some protest against the sedition section. A member of the House of Representatives, in a spirit of whimsical objection, moved to amend the bill to provide that 'it shall be unlawful for any person connected in any capacity with the Army, Navy, or Coast Guard of the United States, to read any newspaper, book, magazine, or other publication, including the Bible and the Congressional Record, while in said service.' His motion was defeated by a vote of 117 to 1.

DR. SMYTH: Good for him! It would have been still better to provide that nobody in the armed services or outside shall read anything except documents supplied by the Army and Navy or hear anybody except the anointed politicians. What did the new sedition part of the bill actually provide? I suppose that it is another one of your complicated measures.

BEARD: The new sedition law is not simple. Perhaps I can best sum it up in the language of Arthur Garfield Hays, a lawyer who is an expert in such matters:

The Act of 1940 makes it a crime, when made with proper disloyal intent, (1) to advise, counsel or urge, or in any manner to cause insubordination, disloyalty, mutiny, or refusal of duty by any member of the military or naval forces of the United States, (2) to distribute written or printed matter which does this, (3) to knowingly advocate, advise, or teach the desirability of overthrowing government by force and violence, (4) to organize or help organize, or (5) to knowingly become a member of, any group which has this as its purpose.

My fellow students sat a long time in contemplation.

DR. SMYTH, with some signs of impatience: You can't object to that! It is in line with all you have been saying about constitutionalism, the conduct of government by proposition, discussion, and popular adoption in the civilian way. That law permits anyone to advocate any changes he likes in our society or form of government and merely forbids him to advocate making these changes by violence. It is obvious to common sense that it abridges freedom of speech and press, but you ought to cheer it as a sign of progress. It merely upholds the constitutional way of transacting public business. I have my opinion of it and the obscure men who made it. But you have no right to grumble about it.

Mrs. SMYTH, coming to my rescue: On its face, this section of the Alien Registration Act looks like support for constitutionalism, although it may abridge the freedom of speech and press guaranteed by the Constitution. But in view of what has been said here about the Whitney case and other cases on the enforcement of such laws, the catch is clear. As administered by prosecutors, judges, and juries, the law will encourage and permit witch-burners to persecute and imprison persons who talk loosely about revolution or merely criticize bitterly the politicians who happen to be in office at the moment. More than this, it will permit the persecution and imprisonment of persons who happen to be associated with any group that may adopt a platform or program of violent words. The danger lies not so much in the words of the Act as in the administration of it by prosecutors, judges, and juries, goaded on by people who love to hound any objectionable neighbors. To my way of thinking, the Whitney case illustrates what may or will happen under this Act. What is wrong with this statement of the business?

DR. SMYTH: There is nothing wrong with it, Sue. You have framed a good objection to the Act, but it is worthy of a legal casuist. I wish to God that there were a Thomas Jefferson among us now capable of going after this Act as he did the Sedition Act of 1798, on grounds of liberty, with no ifs, ands, or howevers. But there is no Jefferson among us, and I take that as a sign of what has happened to our national character in a hundred and fifty years of Beard's progress. Away with it all! I must go. I have to stop in at the Hospital to see a patient on the way home. What is on the carpet for our next session? Religious Liberty, I believe. Will you give me the name of a good book to read about civil rights?

BEARD: The book I have already cited, Zechariah Chafee's *Free Speech in the United States,* published by the Harvard Press in 1942.

Mrs. SMYTH: One more question, What became of Miss Whitney? Did she serve her ten years?

BEARD: No. She was pardoned by Governor Young of California who relied heavily on Justice Brandeis' opinion as justification for clemency.

Dr. Smyth, at the door, snorting: What's that? After your blessed lawmakers, judges, and juries got through with sending a mild-mannered woman to prison for perhaps ten years, a politician in the governor's chair gave her justice! It's a world turned upside down, when we have to depend on executive pardons to get justice. Any more cases of that kind?

Beard: Many. Governor Alfred E. Smith made some notable pardons in that class. Presidents Harding and Coolidge pardoned war prisoners who had not yet finished their terms. President Harding, with the aid of Mr. Harry Daugherty, Attorney General of the United States, pardoned Eugene V. Debs and let him out of prison, after President Wilson had sternly refused to grant clemency to Debs.

With an unearthly chuckle, Doctor Smyth returned to his car, crying out: Harding, Daugherty, Coolidge, and Al Smith, our salvation from the administration of justice! What next? See you next Friday to find out.

XII

Religious Liberty

WHY the broad smile tonight? I inquired as my guests came in for our conference on religious liberty.

DR. SMYTH: Well, you have managed to make simple mundane affairs so complicated and indefinite that we wondered all the way from our house just what you would do when you had heaven and earth to wander over.

BEARD, trying to surprise them: We are fortunate in having a definition of religion at law given to us by the Supreme Court of the United States. In passing upon a statute prohibiting polygamy, Justice Field speaking for the Court said, 'The term religion has reference to one's views of his relations to his creator, and to the obligations they impose of reverence for his being and character, and of obedience to his will.' In other words, he meant that religion has to do with views respecting the relations of the individual to a supreme and extramundane being.

MRS. SMYTH: If that is from the Supreme Court there must be a joker in it somewhere. What if, in obedience to God's will as privately interpreted, an individual goes about making disorders like some of Jehovah's Witnesses? Several of them were arrested in our city in 1940 for denouncing the American Legion, war, the Catholic hierarchy, and the Daughters of the American Revolution. Then not long ago a few children were put out of the public schools somewhere for refusing to salute the flag as the state law required. They claimed that their highest allegiance was to God, not the flag. Didn't the Supreme Court uphold the right of the state government to compel all children to salute the flag, even if their views of religion forbade them to do it?

DR. SMYTH: Before you take up that catch, I should like to ask a question about the definition of religion you just recited. What if a person has no views on his relations with a supermundane being, or is a positive atheist? Would a law prohibiting atheism, in effect forcing all persons to profess a religion of some kind, violate the rule of religious liberty? To put it in another way, does religious liberty include the right to profess no religion?

BEARD: In practice it does. The point has never been tested by the Supreme Court. If Congress should pass such an act, I am fairly sure that the Supreme Court would declare it unconstitutional. If a state should adopt such a law, I am inclined to the opinion that it would now be deemed unconstitutional, under the Fourteenth Amendment rather than under the head of religious liberty.

To return to Mrs. Smyth's joker and renew the method of discrimination which the Doctor accepts grudgingly, there is a qualification on religious liberty in the Supreme Court opinion to which I referred, as follows:

> However free the exercise of religion may be, it must be subordinate to the criminal laws of the country, passed with reference to actions regarded by general consent as properly the subjects of punitive legislation.

That is, no person can, in the name of religious worship or God's will, resort to rites and practices which violate the ordinary laws for the protection of life and property. Nor can any person in the name of religion, as the Supreme Court once said, commit 'other open offenses against the enlightened sentiment of mankind.' It was on that ground that polygamy was abolished.

DR. SMYTH: At last the cat is out of the bag. Religious liberty is just as definite as the enlightened sentiment of mankind.

BEARD: But there are some definite propositions coming under the head of religious liberty. I shall state a few of them. Congress can make no law respecting an establishment of religion. This means that Congress cannot adopt any form of religion as the national religion. It cannot set up one church as the national church, establish its creed, lay taxes generally to support it, compel people to attend it, and punish them for nonattendance. Nor can Congress any more vote money for the support of all churches than it can establish one of them as a national church. That would be a form of establishment.

DR. SMYTH: But it votes money to support chaplains and rabbis in the armed forces of the United States and for a chaplain to say prayers for Congress. I have no objection, for soldiers, sailors, and members of Congress need prayers.

BEARD: That has nothing to do with an establishment of religion. My next proposition under the head of religious liberty is this: The Constitution is a purely secular document. The promotion of religion is not among the declared purposes set forth in the Preamble. No religious qualifications whatever are required to hold any office or place in the Government of the United States. A person of any religious faith or none at all may hold any office or place in that Government. This is a long step away from the practices that prevailed for centuries in Europe, in the American colonies, and formerly in many states. In short, the Constitution treats religion as a private matter, extraneous to the interests of the Federal Government.

DR. SMYTH: But it requires all officeholders to take an oath to support the Constitution and nobody who denies religion can take an oath on the Bible, that is, honestly.

BEARD: You are speaking of a section in Article VI, but you are wrong about the oath. After listing certain classes of public functionaries, the section provides that they 'shall be bound by oath *or affirmation* to support this Constitution; but no religious test shall ever be required as a qualification to any office or public trust under the United States.' Thus any person assuming such an office or public trust may affirm on his conscience instead of taking an oath on the Bible.

Here's my next proposition: The Constitution does not confer upon the Federal Government any power whatever to deal with religion in any form or manner.

MRS. SMYTH: How do you account for the severe aloofness of the Constitution from religion? You have said that some states had established churches at the time and that many states had religious qualifications on voters and officeholders for a long time after the adoption of the Constitution. I suppose that the number of sects and churches in different parts of the country had something to do with the fact that the framers left religion entirely out of the Constitution, even the name of God? I looked for it there in preparation for tonight and did not find it.

BEARD: No doubt the diversity of sects and churches partly accounted for the exclusion of religious considerations from the Constitution. No sect had a majority. The imposition of any sectarian system was out of the question as a matter of practical politics. The framers could have introduced the name of God in the Preamble. None of them seems to have been an atheist, though several were certainly skeptics or Deists who did not accept trinitarian Christianity. But they were not proclaiming a Constitution. They were forming a union of the states and people. In view of the strong sentiment in favor of states' rights, it was dangerous enough to introduce 'the people' into the Preamble. To have ordained and established the Constitution in the name of God would have been alarming and inexpedient, if not inappropriate. On practical grounds, the framers thought it best not to meddle with religion at all, had they been so inclined, and most of them were not so inclined.

MRS. SMYTH: The section allowing an affirmation instead of an oath for holders of offices and places of trust may have been due partly to a recognition of the Quakers. They are opposed to taking an oath, though they are Christians.

BEARD: That is true. There were Jews also, and one of them, Jonas Phillips, petitioned the Constitutional Convention in 1787 against any form of oath that required belief in the inspiration of the New Testament. Phillips said in his petition:

> To swear and believe that the new testament was given by devine inspiration is absolutely against the Religious principle of a Jew, and it is against his Conscience to take any such oath. . . . I solecet this favour for my self, my childreen and posterity and for the benefit of all Israeletes through the 13 united States of America.

What influence Phillips' petition had, I know not, but it expressed a sentiment as to religious liberty that was not confined to Jews.

DR. SMYTH: Do the recorded debates in the Convention throw no light whatever on its opinions as to introducing any references to religion into the Constitution? Please note that I am getting wise as to the search for evidence. Surely, when they discussed qualifications for office, they must have considered religious tests for office, at least in relation to good character. The religious tests then in state constitutions had a bearing on character as well as faith.

BEARD: You must be thinking of the first constitution of your home state, South Carolina. I mean the one written in 1776 during the transition from colony to state.

DR. SMYTH: I never saw a copy of it.

BEARD: It required officeholders to take an oath, and provided that 'all persons and religious societies who acknowledge that there is one God, and a future state of rewards and punishments, and that God is to be publicly worshipped, shall be freely tolerated.'

DR. SMYTH: I am not familiar with the history of my state, but I know many people today who think that an officeholder is not to be trusted unless he believes in hell and heaven, a future state of punishments and rewards. I sometimes wish that all officeholders, and voters too, really did so believe. It might help things.

MRS. SMYTH: Anybody elected to office in our city must at least pretend that he does. That is irrelevant, however. I should like to hear an answer to Robert's question about the debates in the Convention on religion.

BEARD: According to the records, which are not full, there was no debate on religion. Something was said about it in connection with qualifications for offices and public trusts, but very little. In a statement published after the Convention adjourned, Luther Martin, delegate from Maryland, gave an account of what had happened at Philadelphia on this point:

> That part of the system which provides, that *no religious test* shall ever be required as a qualification to any office or public trust under the United States, was adopted by a great majority of the convention, and without much debate; however, there were some members *so unfashionable* as to think, that a *belief of the existence of a Deity,* and of a *state of future rewards and punishments* would be some security for the good conduct of our rulers, and that, in a Christian country, it would be *at least decent* to hold out some distinction between the professors of Christianity and downright infidelity or paganism.

DR. SMYTH: What kind of point was this Luther Martin making? Was he very pious?

BEARD: Martin was against the Constitution and tried to defeat its ratification in Maryland and afterward became a fierce Federalist. He was not pious in the Puritan sense. He was a brilliant lawyer, witty, ingenious, and generous. A biographer has said of him that his 'chief faults were his intemperance and his improvidence in financial affairs.'

Doubtless another consideration weighed heavily with the framers in their insistence on the widest possible religious liberty as far as the Constitution was concerned. All of them, I feel sure, had religious beliefs of some kind. Several were Deists and others were Christians. But whatever their personal religious faiths, they bent their minds to the main business of strengthening the Union and many of them feared the introduction of passionate sectarian controversies into that business. Although James Madison was brought up a good Episcopalian, he was so distressed by the religious controversies which raged around him that he developed almost a mania against every form of religious or sectarian quarreling.

George Washington also was brought up in the Episcopal Church. While living in New York and Philadelphia, he attended services regularly; at home in Mount Vernon, his attendance was less regular. As to his religious beliefs there is much dispute. There is dispute also as to whether he ever declared himself publicly to be a Christian. But one thing is certain, he was a man of broad tolerance and heartily disliked sectarian quarrels. He once said:

Of all the animosities which have existed among mankind, those which are caused by difference of sentiments in religion appear to be the most inveterate and distressing, and ought most to be deprecated. I was in hopes, that the lightened and liberal policy, which has marked the present age, would at least have reconciled *Christians* of every denomination so far, that we should never again see their religious disputes carried to such a pitch as to endanger the peace of society.

In a letter to Lafayette, he wrote: 'Being no bigot myself, I am disposed to indulge the professors of Christianity in the church with that road to heaven, which to them shall seem the most direct, plainest, easiest, and least liable to exception.'

In practical matters Washington showed indifference to theological opinions. Once, when he was seeking employees of skill and competence, he declared that 'if they are good workmen, they may be from Asia, Africa, or Europe; they may be Mohammedans, Jews, or Christians of any sect, or they may be Atheists.' So, between his fear of raising unnecessary strife and his liberality of views, Wash-

ington, as president of the convention which drafted the Constitution, must have favored keeping religion out of the Constitution
and treating full religious liberty as highly desirable for the new
Republic.

Given the attitudes toward religion taken by leaders among the
framers of the Constitution and the plain letter of the original document, we are bound to say that the Constitution contemplates non-
interference with churches and religions by the Federal Government. The First Amendment merely confirms the intentions of the
framers. As far as that Government is concerned, it cannot make
any law respecting the establishment of religion. Neither can it
make any law prohibiting the free exercise of religion, except when,
in the guise of religious exercise, a cult adopts rites or practices
which offend the moral sense of the nation or transgress the ordinary civil and criminal law.

Now we come to guarantees of religious liberty against interference by the authorities of the states—by state governments. There
is not a line in the original Constitution or in any amendment touching this subject expressly. The protection of religious liberty against
the states rests upon a recent development of certain provisions in
the Fourteenth Amendment, especially the following: 'No state
shall make or enforce any law which shall abridge the privileges
or immunities of citizens of the United States; nor shall any state
deprive any person of life, liberty, or property without due process
of law; nor deny to any person within its jurisdiction the equal
protection of the laws.'

Dr. Smyth: I suppose that you are going to twist the words,
privileges, immunities, liberty, and equal protection, to cover
churches and religions.

Beard: Twist is slightly invidious. I merely propose to consider
interpretations of these words by the Supreme Court. You must
add one more word to your list. That is property.

Before the Fourteenth Amendment was adopted in 1868, any state
was constitutionally free to establish a church, impose religious tests
on voters and officeholders, turn education over to parsons or priests,
require everybody to attend church, and in fact set up a religious
monopoly about as strict as that which obtained in western Europe
during the Middle Ages. That is, as far as the federal Constitution
was concerned, a state could do all this. How far a state can now

go in that direction, under the Fourteenth Amendment, remains uncertain.

MRS. SMYTH: But our states are so liberal that none of them would venture to violate religious liberty, I should think. So I do not see how any violations of religious liberty could arise for the Supreme Court to settle. The disturbance by Jehovah's Witnesses which I mentioned a while ago was a case of plain disorder. It had nothing to do with religious liberty as I understand such liberty.

BEARD: You have just forgotten some of your history. Entangled in the story of evangelizing religions are agitations, oppressions, wars, and punishments—all of these being disorders, in short. Still that is not the whole history of religious liberty. How did violations of religious liberty arise? Out of attempts of states to legislate on religion directly or indirectly—attempts which went beyond bounds set by the Supreme Court. There is an immense volume of state legislation touching religion, and some of it bears marks of definite discrimination.

But in 1922 the state of Oregon went too far in this line. At least so the Supreme Court thought. In 1922 the voters of Oregon approved, on a referendum, a law requiring all children, with few exceptions, to attend public elementary schools. In effect they abolished private schools. The law was to go into force in 1926.

This law was challenged in the case of Pierce *v.* Society of the Sisters of the Holy Names of Jesus and Mary. The Supreme Court of the United States held the Oregon Act invalid under the Fourteenth Amendment. It declared (1) that the Act 'unreasonably interferes with the liberty of parents and guardians to direct the upbringing and education of children under their control,' and (2) that it violates *due process of law* in depriving private schools of 'business and property for which they claim protection.'

DR. SMYTH: But the Oregon law did not interfere with religion or religious worship. Does religious liberty include the right of a sect to control absolutely the education of its children? Education is not religion. Can a sect teach young citizens anything that it pleases even about citizenship?

BEARD: Those are broad questions difficult to answer in terms of law. How far a sect can go in teaching its children is uncertain. It could not teach criminal syndicalism or the right of revolution, I feel certain, in the light of various judicial decisions.

DR. SMYTH: But according to your statement, a sect could so neglect instruction in the fundamentals of American citizenship as to bring up children entirely out of harmony with, if not dangerous to, American liberties.

BEARD: It might all depend upon the phraseology and ingenuity of the instruction carried on by the sect.

MRS. SMYTH: Does what you are saying amount to this: If anybody is clever enough in undermining American institutions he cannot be touched by the law; but if he is raw, awkward, and brazen, he goes to jail? In my opinion the brazen person may be the less dangerous. He can be understood and caught easily. The clever person can get away with subtleties that are far more insidious, and escape the law's hand.

BEARD: I concede all you say, but how could it be otherwise?

MRS. SMYTH: Frankly, I do not know. That is another fog bank. Suppose we make a detour around it and hear about Jehovah's Witnesses. When did that troublesome sect get started? What does it believe?

BEARD: It seems to stem from a religious society incorporated in Pennsylvania in 1884, later known as the Watchtower Bible and Tract Society. In connection with this society, other associations were formed, one called the International Bible Students' Association, all under one direction. For a long time, the leader or director was Pastor Charles T. Russell, who preached the second coming of the Lord and commanded his missionaries to go from door to door distributing tracts. Later Judge Joseph F. Rutherford was the leader, until his death in 1942. It was under Rutherford's management that the name Jehovah's Witnesses was adopted. Since I am no theologian, I hesitate to define their religious beliefs. As I understand their teachings, they regard the making of modern history as a terrific battle between Satan on one side and Jesus on the other, with the Witnesses as the agents commissioned of God to overthrow Satan and usher in the Kingdom.

DR. SMYTH: That belief in the struggle between God and Satan does not seem much out of line with Christian tradition. Anyhow it looks harmless enough. Why spend so much time with the Witnesses?

MRS. SMYTH: They may be harmless enough, but when they push into your house with piles of pamphlets, when they set up a phonograph and start playing a record on 'Is Hell Hot?' you find them troublesome enough. I almost had to call the police to get them out of our house.

DR. SMYTH: That just seems an excess of zeal on their part. They evidently believe their religion and work hard to convert sinners. Why so much fuss about them? They don't amount to anything.

BEARD: You haven't kept up to date in your religious history. The Witnesses' Society owns an enormous printing plant in Brooklyn and much property elsewhere; it distributed 309,000,000 pieces of its literature in 1939; its speakers and phonograph records reached 19,000,000 people that year; before it was ousted from the radio it was reported to be spending $50,000 a week on broadcasts; it then had about 45,000 working Witnesses and perhaps a million members scattered over the world.

DR. SMYTH: If we believe in religious liberty, why not let them alone? As long as they stick to preaching their religion, they have a right to go about trying to gain converts.

BEARD: The trouble is that they do not stick to religion pure and simple. Their religious convictions lead them to denounce Satan's workers, as they call them—bankers, war-makers, the American Legion, the Daughters of the American Revolution, and the Catholic hierarchy, for example. And in so doing they stir up mobs, the local police, and infuriated citizens.

DR. SMYTH: Isn't that what Anne Hutchinson and the Quakers did in colonial Massachusetts? They were either driven out or put to death for their uproars. Anyhow, what has this to do with the law of religious liberty?

BEARD: In attempts to stop the agitations stirred up by the Witnesses, local laws have been passed or old laws applied, and police officials have broken up meetings, made arrests, and on some occasions broken heads. Whatever may be said about the Witnesses, they have the courage of martyrs. And they have money to hire lawyers and fight cases through the courts. As a result in recent days they have made more contributions to the development of the constitutional law of religious liberty than any other cult or group. Believe me, they are making it fast. Sometimes they win and sometimes they lose.

DR. SMYTH: That sounds exciting, something like an old-fashioned Yale-Harvard football game at Thanksgiving. How's the score now? It is unfortunate that Henry Mencken no longer runs *The American Mercury* to keep the score.

BEARD: Some of the incidents may be funny enough, but the law that is being made may not turn out to be so funny. In one case, seventy-five Witnesses were indicted under the Indiana criminal syndicalism law and held under a bail of $225,000.

DR. SMYTH: Whew! Why arrest preachers of religion under an act to catch labor leaders, and why the big bail?

BEARD: They were accused of advocating doctrines that worked for the overthrow of government. All the other cases involving the Witnesses likewise brought into question their attitude toward government, not merely religion; scarcely religion at all, although religion formed the basis of their claims to immunity. Although several are now pending, three cases will serve to indicate the ramifications of religious liberty at law.

The first is the Cantwell case in Connecticut. The state had a law forbidding persons to solicit money for religious or charitable purposes without securing the permission of a designated local official. Jehovah's Witnesses insisted that if they bowed in this manner before an earthly power in carrying on their work, it would be a violation of God's commandments. They refused to apply for permits and kept on preaching and collecting money for their work. Some of them were arrested and found guilty.

But the Witnesses refused to take the verdict calmly. They fought the case up to the Supreme Court of the United States and got a decision in their favor. The Court declared that the law requiring official permits ran counter to the freedom of speech and religion guaranteed by the Fourteenth Amendment. Thus the Witnesses won this bout and added a chapter to the subject of religious liberty.

DR. SMYTH: Then in the name of religious liberty, members of all sects can go around spreading their literature and collecting money for their cause?

BEARD: Unless they make too much disturbance by their literature and by word of mouth. We are not through with the Witnesses yet. On two other counts, claims they made in the name of God under the Constitution, they were defeated. One was the now famous Gobitis case of 1940. This involved the validity of a state law requiring children in the public schools to salute the flag—a ceremony regarded by legislators as inspiring loyalty to the United States.

Some of Jehovah's Witnesses protested against this law on the ground that the salutation was idolatrous, contrary to the teachings of the Bible and to the idea of God's supremacy over all earthly powers. The Supreme Court, Justice Frankfurter rendering the opinion, upheld the state law and sent the Witnesses reeling to the ropes.

MRS. SMYTH: No dissent in that case?

BEARD: Yes, one, by Chief Justice Stone. He agreed that the government had all powers necessary to assure its own survival, and maintain good order, health, and safety, not expressly denied by the Constitution. But the Chief Justice insisted that compelling children to violate the teachings of their sect by saluting the flag was not among the necessities of State.

DR. SMYTH: Good for the Chief Justice! He has some sense of discrimination for the relative importance of things. If the United States is in such a sad plight that it is afraid of a few little children taught by their parents to believe that saluting the flag is idolatrous, we might as well proclaim the great experiment in liberty a flat failure.

I see now why you were inclined to doubt whether the clear and present danger rule is a part of our constitutional law. Did Justice Frankfurter and the justices who agreed with him believe that a bunch of little school kids born of Jehovah's Witnesses were such a clear and present danger to public safety that they must be excluded from the opportunity to get an education? I am inclined to the opinion now that the clear and present danger rule is all tosh. But I must watch my step, for I am adding to uncertainty myself. Anyway, Justice Frankfurter's law is the law, in spite of the dissent by the Chief Justice.

BEARD: Perhaps not.

MRS. SMYTH: What are you saying? Isn't it the law? Isn't it settled?

BEARD: Not yet. In January, 1943, the Federal Circuit Court at Charleston, West Virginia, in another case involving the refusal of Jehovah's Witnesses to salute the flag, in effect reversed Justice Frankfurter and his brethren of the Court. Speaking for the Circuit Court, Judge John J. Parker declared that forcing the flag salute 'upon one who has conscientious scruples against giving it is petty tyranny unworthy of this Republic.'

MRS. SMYTH: How on earth could Judge Parker do that when he

had Justice Frankfurter's opinion and the decision of the Supreme Court before him? I thought that lower courts are bound by the decisions of the Supreme Court.

BEARD: Generally, the lower courts are, but often they follow their own ideas, especially in cases which cannot be appealed. Judge Parker noted in his opinion that changes had taken place in the Supreme Court since the Gobitis case of 1940. He was aware of the dissent by Chief Justice Stone. He was aware of the fact that Justices Black, Douglas, and Murphy, who voted with Justice Frankfurter in 1940, had since changed their minds and had dissented in another Jehovah's Witnesses case. To shorten the story, Judge Parker decided to put the flag salute up to the Supreme Court again, and the Supreme Court agreed to review it once more.*

You may think the flag business simple, but street disorders connected with the gospel meetings conducted by Jehovah's Witnesses are certainly troublesome to police officials. In another case, Jehovah's Witnesses took issue with a New Hampshire law making it a crime to use offensive, derisive, or abusive words in the streets against any person lawfully there. Some Witnesses made a street disturbance in a New Hampshire town. One of them was arrested, and on the way to the police station he cursed the city marshal and the town government as Fascists or agents of Fascists. For the use of offensive language, the Witness was indicted and found guilty. The Supreme Court of the United States sustained the conviction and the law of New Hampshire.

To summarize, in the United States preaching and teaching in respect of religion, the conduct of religious rites and practices, and

---

* Thinking that my friends, the Smyths, might miss the full significance of West Virginia's case on saluting the flag, I wrote them the following letter respecting it:

Hosannah Hill, July 4, 1943.

Dear Dr. and Mrs. Smyth

For your information, I enclose a pamphlet of thirty-six pages giving the decision and opinions of the Supreme Court in the case of The West Virginia State Board of Education, etc., et al., Appellants, *vs.* Walter Barnette, Paul Stull, and Lucy McClure, On appeal etc., June 14, 1943, reversing the Gobitis decision. I thought that you might like to study the "reasoning" of the several Justices for yourselves. I also enclose an article by my old friend, Professor Thomas Reed Powell, of the Harvard Law School, on the case, clipped from *The New Republic* of to-morrow, July 5. If you will read these enclosures carefully, you will see why it is so hard for mere laymen, such as we are, to discover how and why we are governed in the Republic. Hoping that you are no worse for our winter sessions, I am,

Yours faithfully,

Charles A. Beard.

P. S. You will note that Jehovah's Witnesses do not have to salute the flag now.

verbal demonstrations against religion or any religious sect are in general free. Yet they are all subject to certain limitations of law. Government can enact any legislation necessary, or deemed necessary, to its survival. It can make war, establish compulsory military training and service, and compel religionists to obey or submit to punishment. It may, to use the words of Chief Justice Stone, suppress 'religious practices dangerous to morals, and presumably those also which are inimical to public safety, health, and good order.' What degree of tolerance exists and will exist depends upon restraints observed by religious propagandists themselves and upon the sentiments and attitudes of communities and the nation.

Mrs. SMYTH: In matters of religious conscience, sectarians often claim that their words and practices are in obedience to the will of God. Does the Supreme Court have to pass on that claim?

BEARD: It does not have to pass on the validity of any such claims. It merely asserts the supremacy of the law over such claims. But in one case of religious conscience, the opinion of the Court declared that unqualified allegiance to the nation and obedience to the laws of the land 'are not inconsistent with the will of God.'

As DR. SMYTH started out to his car, he said over his shoulder: I suppose that this judicial dictum also comes under the head of political science.

XIII

Power and the Control of Power

ON the morning after our session on Religious Liberty, I met the Smyths on the street in town. They asked me whether I had slept well after leading them on a merry chase through the labyrinth of theological speculations. I told them that I had slept well after reading Plutarch *On the Delay of the Divine Justice*. Mrs. Smyth wondered whether it would not be a good idea to have a colloquium on that subject also.

DR. SMYTH demurred: Beard could doubtless make out a case that it is relevant to our consideration of the Republic but, frankly, I think it is about time to explore more fully the subject of our *government,* under which the civil liberties we have talked about are enjoyed more or less. The constitutionalism of which we spoke in the beginning seems to be a method of adjusting the perennial and confused relations of government authority and private freedom. For several sessions we have discussed it from the angle of liberty or liberties. I want to know more about the nature of authority and how it works in the United States. As we cannot meet every night for a hundred years, I propose that we take up this matter for a while.

MRS. SMYTH: Perhaps I incline to the side of liberty instead of power, but I do recognize the limits on our time.

So I suggested that we branch out into Power and the Control of Power. The Smyths concurred and, as we were about to part, the Doctor, glancing at his watch, said: Come along and have lunch with us. You are like old Diogenes in that you have no official duties anywhere and can't plead a previous engagement.

Where are you going for lunch? I asked. Home?

Not if we can help it, MRS. SMYTH replied. There is a telephone at home. Let's go to the Blue Bottle Tavern. It has a little back‹ room on which we have a kind of lease. Jerry who runs the place holds it for us on Saturdays.

Off we went and had baked beans and apple pie and a decanter of Jerry's best red ink, as the Smyths called it. After the lunch was over Dr. Smyth drew designs on the table cloth with a big black pencil until he felt moved to begin a quiz.

DR. SMYTH: Just what do you fellows mean when you talk about power in politics or human affairs generally? The word is always buzzing over the radio or staring at me in print. I hear or read about the power of the President, the power of organized labor, the power of public opinion, the power of big business, the power of women, the power of Congress, the war power, the power of the United States, America as a world power, decisive power, the division of power, the power of propaganda, the power of the press, and so forth and so forth, words without end. Jumbles, contradictions, confusions, claims, assertions, pretensions, threats, praises, damnations, and so on—all hooked up with something called power. Now you come along Main Street and begin to talk about Power and the Control of Power.

I get so impatient with editors, radio commentators, book writers, columnists, book reviewers, and the whole tribe of word artists who talk about power that I could clear all the books, newspapers, magazine, and radios out of the house. But you have put your head into my noose, and I don't intend to let you off until I have wrung some kind of understandable definition out of you or sent you home in an ambulance.

I have an idea of what is meant by power in physics, that is, measurable power—horse power, foot-pound power, and even muscle power. I suspect with Carlyle that the human animal is run by the same cosmic energy that flames from the sun. Is this power in human affairs that you are talking about anything more than cosmic energy on a rampage? Some people and some nations seem lazy and others active. Isn't that due to a difference in the energy with which they are endowed? If so, all the various kinds of power or alleged powers are just one power—cosmic energy, measurable energy; and when the cosmic show runs all the way down, the human show blows out too.

BEARD: Ultimately there is physical power in government. If you refuse long enough to make out a correct income-tax return and refuse to obey an order to appear in court, you will get a touch of government power. Three or four husky fellows will take you by the scruff of the neck and the seat of the pants and hustle you into a police van motored by the power of internal combustion. The ultimate test of a government's existence is whether it has enough of this kind of power to compel obedience to its laws and decrees, either actually or through fear of consequences.

Indeed, government over a large geographical area seems to have begun when a band of warriors headed by a leader or chieftain conquered an established agricultural population, settled down upon it, and derived the means of subsistence from its labor. From the earliest days of government to the latest moment, physical power to compel action or obedience has been a prominent feature of government.

But this physical power has not been and is not the sole characteristic of government. Now the power of government is a highly complex affiliation of powers, although the physical power to compel is the ultimate test of a government's capacity to survive. To physical power is added the power of what we call human will, which is not identical with muscular force. A person of slight physical build may have more strength of action and endurance than a big person with huge biceps. And I am told that you doctors of medicine have no way of measuring physical power apart from the power of will— the power of tenacity and purpose.

To this power of will in governing persons are added other psychological propensities of human nature, besides fear, which unite the governing and the governed; for instance, ambition, avarice, loyalties, gratitude, and affections. They are all imponderables, but we can scarcely doubt their existence. Then there is in the history of government something which I call, for want of a better name, fate. I cannot define it, but I can illustrate it. We are fated in the United States to use the English language, with all its meanings and psychological intimations, in the conduct of our private and public affairs. Our whole historical past upon which we draw for knowledge, guidance, and inspiration is for us fated, that is, the past is beyond our power to change.

One more point for this moment. This composite power which

we call political may be concentrated in the hands of one person and his clique, or it may be widely diffused among many persons. If the dispersion is wide enough, you have a democracy. Too much concentration is despotism. Too much diffusion approaches anarchy and dissolution. Despotism and anarchy are both mortal foes of human liberty. They are triumphs of physical force.

But I must stop this unpremeditated rattle. Otherwise I shall not have time to collect my wits for our session on Power and the Control of Power.

You mean, Dr. Smyth laughed, no time to lay traps for the unwary.

To my surprise and somewhat to my chagrin, the Smyths brought along with them to our session on power, Arthur Harton, a smooth lawyer, perhaps the smoothest in our community.

Dr. Smyth, half apologetic: You know Harton. He is the attorney for the rich widow whom we declared incompetent today and sent to a private asylum. I was telling him about our fireside seminar and mentioned that you were going to raise the question of power in government. He expressed a desire to take part. I knew that he would add to the gaiety of our festivities. So here he is.

I gave my approval with as much grace as I could command. Mr. Harton wore a morning coat every day in the week and had a better bedside manner than any undertaker in town. I suspected that he had many good retainers from major interests in the region, for he seemed to have no petty court business. He apparently loved to speak on ceremonial occasions when the noblest sentiments were appropriate. It was hardly possible to have a Fourth of July celebration within a hundred miles without the aid of his mellifluous voice. Yet I realized that he had the same right that I had to be on earth and could not change his nature any more than I could change mine. So I welcomed him.

Taking the center before the fireplace and warming his hands behind his back, Mr. Harton said: Yes, indeed, I am glad to be here. The separation of powers is my favorite subject. I gave a talk on it to the high school boys and girls last week in the auditorium. I told them that the greatest thing the framers of the Constitution did was to divide the powers of government, as they are in fact divided by nature, into three kinds—legislative, executive, and judicial—and then to vest each kind of power in the hands of distinct, separate, and independent agencies—Congress, the President and the Judiciary. I told them also that whenever this rule of good government is violated, the safety of the Republic is in danger.

And what do you think? A young whippersnapper of a woman who teaches civics at the school tried to tell me that I had oversimplified the facts in the case! If that is the kind of teaching we are to have, I am going to run for the School Board and clean house. Teachers have got into the habit of thinking that the schools belong to them.

MRS. SMYTH, with a devastating smile: To whom do the schools belong?

And after she had demonstrated that they did not belong to Mr. Harton, she apologized for the delay and suggested that I open up the subject of power and the control of power.

BEARD: I shrink from starting on a note of discord, Mr. Harton, but the teacher of civics was right, emphatically right. I do not know what the framers of the Constitution thought on the subject, that is, all of them, but Hamilton and Madison do not agree with you at all. They did not believe that the powers of government are strictly divided by nature into legislative, executive, and judicial. They did not believe that these powers could or should be kept entirely separate. And they recognized the fact that there is an indivisible power of government which is the prize of ambitious men.

In Number 41 of *The Federalist,* Madison expressed this idea as follows:

The Constitution . . . may be considered under two general points of view. The FIRST relates to the sum or quantity of power which it vests in the government, including the restraints imposed on the states. The SECOND, to the particular structure of the government, and the distribution of this power among its several branches.

Hamilton and Madison realized that there were certain distinctions between legislative, executive, and judicial activities but no sharp dividing lines. They were especially concerned to see that the indivisible power of government did not fall into the hands of ambitious men bent on dominating society through government.

They were resolved that no such power should be conferred on any-body, not even the very best men.

MR. HARTON: Well, Hamilton believed that the rich and wellborn should govern. And, just between us, Hamilton was right.

BEARD: Did you say that to the high-school boys and girls?

MR. HARTON: Of course not. That would stir up class feeling, just the thing we do not want in this country, where there are no classes. Anyway, I do not believe that Hamilton distrusted the very best people. It was the masses he distrusted.

BEARD: I should say that Hamilton *feared* both the classes and the masses. He distrusted all human beings when it came to the question of power in government. We are not sure whether Hamilton or Madison wrote Number 51 of *The Federalist,* and our uncertainty is partly due to the fact that its sentiments were in line with the sentiments of both men.

Anyway, the following passage from this Number shows positive distrust of human beings in general as the reason for not allowing too great a concentration of the power to govern:

The great security against a gradual concentration of the several powers in the same department, consists in giving to those who administer each department the necessary constitutional means and personal motives to resist the encroachments of the others. . . . Ambition must be made to counteract ambition. The interest of the man must be connected with the constitutional rights of the place. It may be a reflection on human nature, that such devices should be necessary to control the abuses of government. But what is government itself, but the greatest of all reflections on human nature? If men were angels, no government would be necessary.

Then the author of this Number of *The Federalist* stated the central problem of power in government:

In framing a government which is to be administered by men over men, the great difficulty lies in this: you must first enable the government to control the governed; and in the next place oblige it to control itself. A dependence on the people is, no doubt, the primary control on the government; but experience has taught mankind the necessity of auxiliary precautions. This policy of supplying, by opposite and rival interests, the defect of better motives, might be traced through the whole system of human affairs, private as well as public. We see it particularly displayed in all the subordinate distributions of power, where the constant aim is to divide and arrange the several offices in such a manner as that each may be a check on the other—that the private interest of every individual may be a sentinel over the public rights.

Mr. Harton, forgetting his trust of the very best people: There is my whole theory of the separation of powers! Of checks and balances.

Mrs. Smyth: Not quite. The statement just read distinctly does not say that the powers of government are divisible into three kinds and that each kind must be given to a separate and independent agency.

Beard: Not only that. Neither critics nor friends of the Constitution in 1787—1788 agreed that it recognized the three kinds of powers as sharply divided and that it vested each kind in an independent agency.

Madison wrote in Number 47 of *The Federalist:*

One of the principal objections inculcated by the more respectable adversaries to the Constitution, is its supposed violation of the political maxim, that the legislative, executive, and judiciary departments ought to be separate and distinct. In the structure of the federal government, no regard, it is said, seems to have been paid to this essential precaution in favor of liberty. The several departments of power are distributed and blended in such a manner as at once to destroy all symmetry and beauty of form.

This was a criticism brought against the Constitution by its foes while adoption was pending. Did Madison reply by saying that the criticism was unwarranted? No. He said that the criticism was based on a misunderstanding of the celebrated theory of the separation of powers. He maintained that only a *degree* of separation was required by the maxim, and that this degree could be secured only by connecting and blending the departments.

He conceded that in theory the three classes of power might be discriminated. But he said clearly that all the maxim means is:

The accumulation of all powers, legislative, executive, and judiciary, in the same hands, whether of one, a few, or many, and whether hereditary, self-appointed, or elective, may be justly pronounced the very definition of tyranny.

This statement by Madison is quite different from the proposition that the three powers can or should be sharply divided and each kind placed in the hands of an independent agency. Theoretical boundaries could be drawn around each of the three kinds of power, he admitted, but he knew that the boundaries thus drawn must be to some extent arbitrary.

And he was emphatic in declaring against the complete separation and independence of the agencies to which the several kinds of power were to be confided. He went further, saying:

> I shall undertake to show . . . that unless these departments be so far connected and blended as to give to each a constitutional control over the others, the degree of separation which the maxim requires, as essential to a free government, can never in practice be duly maintained.

In short, Madison declared that complete independence of the departments is undesirable; and that to prevent any one from seizing dominant power, the departments must be tied together in such a way as to give each some control over the others. It would not be going too far to assert that Madison believed in the interdependence, not the independence, of the three departments.

Mr. HARTON: But the judicial power is definitely vested by the express words of the Constitution in the judiciary, and nowhere else.

BEARD: So the words stand written. Still the highest judicial power of all is vested in Congress.

Mr. HARTON: Pray tell us what that is.

BEARD: The House of Representatives may impeach, and the Senate may act as a court to try, all civil officers of the United States from the President and the Chief Justice of the United States down, for treason, bribery, or other high crimes and misdemeanors.

Mr. HARTON: I had overlooked that. In a way it is a judicial power. Yet it is not very important.

BEARD: In a sense it has not appeared to be important, for the power has seldom been exercised, but it is there. By the impeachment process Congress can remove the President, the Supreme Court Justices, and any other Federal officer. It is a sleeping power. How much influence it has had as a potential, no one can exactly estimate.

To return: the Constitution did not create independent departments. It created blended or interconnected departments.

Mrs. SMYTH: Then I cannot understand why we have all been

taught, what Mr. Harton has said, that the powers of the government are separated, that the three departments are separate and independent. Didn't the framers of the Constitution intend to effect a complete separation? The theory of the division of powers was certainly in the air at the time.

BEARD: Just what the framers, that is, all of them, intended on that point when they met at Philadelphia in the spring of 1787, I have no way of knowing. But it is known that not all of them convened with the intention of setting up independent departments, each deriving its strength from an independent source of power. The first plan presented to the Convention, that of the Virginia group, which Madison led, provided that the chief executive and the judges of the national judiciary should be elected by the national legislature. Furthermore, the convention at least twice voted in favor of having the President elected by Congress. It was relatively late in their proceedings that they adopted election of the President by the electoral process now in force—a process which the party system has reduced to a mere form. If there is any institution that violates the spirit of the Constitution, it is the party, for the party seeks control over the whole government.

MR. HARTON: How can you say that? It is the two-party system that makes our plan of government workable and preserves liberty in the United States.

BEARD: That may be, Mr. Harton, but many signers of the Constitution certainly intended that the presidential electors assigned to each state should be freely chosen, that the electors so chosen should canvass the field for eligible persons and exercise an independent judgment in selecting the President. By providing that the candidate next to the top of the electoral vote should be Vice President, they in effect gave both major parties a share in the Executive. The party system has reduced these electors to rubber stamps who have to vote for the man nominated by a political assembly—the national convention—unknown to the Constitution. So I contend that in this respect the party system runs counter to the spirit of the Constitution. To other aspects of the political party we shall devote a whole session.

Let me now set up a little table showing how the framers of the Constitution blended and interconnected the three departments in such a way as to make them checks on one another:

Under the original Constitution, members of the House of Representatives elected directly by the voters were to be checked by Senators elected by the state legislatures. This remained in force until the adoption of the Seventeenth Amendment in 1913. Still the Senators, though elected now directly by the voters, in a way represent states as political entities and act as checks on the membership of the House.

The President, elected by a theoretically independent process, can be impeached by the House and removed by judgment of the Senate.

All of the executive offices under the President are creations of Congress. Congress creates them and can abolish them at will. In addition Congress could, if it saw fit, compel members of the President's cabinet to report to it, and could compel them, individually or collectively, to appear on the floor of either house of Congress or Congress in joint session, to account for their conduct, to answer questions. It cannot remove cabinet officers, save by impeachment, but it can make them responsible to the national legislature and thus strip them of their independent status.

Federal judges are not independently elected, like the President. All federal judges are nominated by the President and must have the approval of the Senate. More than once the Senate has rejected a presidential nominee. After their appointment, judges may be removed by impeachment.

There is the blending and interconnection of the three departments as far as choice and removal are concerned. Now let us look at the blending or interconnection of the three departments as far as the legislative, executive, and judicial powers are concerned:

Congress has no executive power as such. As someone has said, it merely administers two restaurants and a waste paper office. That is, it cannot appoint officers and direct their actions by administrative orders. But it creates every executive office under the President, prescribes the duties as minutely as it desires, and can in one way direct them—by resolutions interpreting the laws to be enforced by officers. If it does not like the way an executive officer under the President conducts his office, Congress can abolish the office or perhaps cut off his salary. Nominally all legislative powers are vested in Congress.

But the President has legislative powers by law and practice. The Constitution gives him the veto power and it requires a two-thirds vote in both houses to overcome an executive veto. And do not forget that after Congress has enacted a law, with presidential approval, it cannot repeal that law without the President's consent, save by a two-thirds vote, unless it has reserved that right in the law itself—a new and dubious practice. By writing laws in loose or general terms, Congress has conferred on the President or executive agencies immense legislative powers in fact; that is, powers to fill out the detailed prescriptions of statutes. Our guest, Mr. Harton, knows that it is true, whatever the theory, for I once heard him deliver a blast against the practice in a speech at the city auditorium.

Finally, numerous boards and commissions in the executive department exercise judicial powers of deep and intense significance for life, liberty, and property; they are called "quasi-judicial" powers but they are none the less judicial in fact and procedure; and a high judicial function is vested in the President: that of reviewing the decisions of federal courts in criminal cases and correcting injustice by pardoning persons convicted of offenses against federal law.

The federal courts have legislative powers in fact. They can expand or contract statutes by interpretation. I could cite cases in which the Supreme Court has interpreted statutes to mean the opposite of what Congress intended them to mean. Then the courts exercise the power to declare acts of Congress null and void. That is in effect a legislative power—one not explicitly conferred upon the courts by the Constitution.

MR. HARTON: I protest. You are reiterating the old complaint of laymen that the judges 'make law by interpretation,' and you are insinuating that the Constitution does not confer on the national judiciary the power to declare acts of Congress unconstitutional—mark my word, unconstitutional. You are adopting popular fallacies, heresies which are dangerous to the good order of society. I object to both.

DR. SMYTH: Now, Harton, you can't get away with all that. You were the attorney for our Company in the big damage case arising out of an explosion. I was a witness for the Company. I heard you conduct the case, and I remember well your concluding argument, especially on a number of points on which the judge ruled against you. You and the lawyer for the other side argued these points before the judge, who was, if I may speak of the judiciary in such language in your presence, a bit of a demagogue.

At all events I thought he was bent on soaking our Company. Again and again you told that judge that his interpretation of the statute in question was contrary to the express terms of the Act and the rulings of the highest court of the state on that language. What is more, when you lost your temper, you distinctly said to the judge, 'It is the business of the courts to apply the law as it is written in the statutes, not to make law.' If a judge cannot or does not make law, why on earth did you feel it necessary to warn that judge against doing it? Making law, as I see things, is legislation.

Mr. Harton: Oh, well, Smyth, that was all said in the heat of an argument. There are exceptions to the rule, minor exceptions, but it is dangerous business for people to get the idea that judges can make law, can legislate.

A little gasp escaped Mrs. Smyth, but she evidently thought that silence was best, as Henry Adams once said, or more tactful. So she allowed Mr. Harton to go on without interruption.

Mr. Harton: What I especially object to is the statement we just heard that when the Supreme Court sets aside an act of Congress it exercises a legislative power akin to the President's veto; and the further statement that the Constitution does not confer on the courts the power to declare laws unconstitutional. What the courts do is to enforce the Constitution as the supreme law of the land. When a court declares an act of Congress invalid, it merely says that it conflicts with the Constitution and is hence of itself invalid. The court does not make the fact. It proclaims the fact.

Dr. Smyth, before Mrs. Smyth could speak: I am no lawyer but I have ears. First, what Beard said was that the Constitution does not *explicitly* confer upon the federal courts the power to declare acts of Congress null and void. Explicitly means distinctly, so as to leave nothing implied, unequivocally, positively, precisely. At least that is what it means to common sense, if not in the lawyers' vocabulary. Here is a copy of the Constitution. Can you put your finger on any provision which gives the federal courts positively and unequivocally the power to declare acts of Congress null and void? Second, Beard did not say that the courts do not or ought not to have the power under the Constitution.

Mr. Harton: I am not going to quibble. There is no clause in the Constitution that states in so many words that the courts shall have the power to declare acts of Congress unconstitutional. But the

Constitution does declare that it is the supreme law of the land and all legislative, executive, and judicial authorities in the country must take an oath to obey it. If Congress does not obey that supreme law, if Congress passes an act contrary to that supreme law, the courts, in a case properly arising, are bound by their very oath of office to declare that act null and void as unconstitutional.

BEARD: We are to have a session on that subject, Mr. Harton, and we should be glad to have you take part in it. For the moment I want to keep our discussion to my main propositions: The Constitution contemplates *power* as well as *powers;* it does not create three independent departments of government; it creates blended and interconnected departments; it does not give *all* legislative powers to one, *all* executive powers to another, and *all* judicial powers to the third. In other words, the separation of powers is a fiction, partly true, but essentially false, or at least misleading. The framers understood that government in action is power. They tried to pit the ambitions, interests, and forces of human beings in the three departments against one another in such a way as to prevent any one set of agents from seizing all power, from becoming dangerously powerful.

MRS. SMYTH: It looks as if they intended to create a perpetual deadlock.

BEARD: I think not, Mrs. Smyth. They strove to set up a government capable of great and powerful action, but still a limited government, one under effective restraints within itself.

MRS. SMYTH: You mean a kind of dynamic symmetry or equilibrium.

MR. HARTON: Now, Mrs. Smyth, that is a bit poetical. A dynamic equilibrium is a contradiction in terms. That is like saying a noisy quietude, or an unbalanced balance, a moving immovability.

BEARD: I beg to differ, Mr. Harton. I think Mrs. Smyth's term 'dynamic equilibrium' is fairly descriptive when applied to the Government of the United States as contemplated by framers of the Constitution. The compass in a Sperry gyroscope, as Elmer Sperry once told me, maintains a perfect balance (practically perfect) while an airplane or ship is rushing at tremendous speed, rolling, swaying, and dipping. Balance and movement are compatible. As I understand the thought of the men who made the Constitution, they intended to establish a government of action; they knew that in action the departments would at times display tendencies to extremes of power; and they sought to keep these eccentricities within the bounds of limited action, a moving parallelogram of force.

A smile of courteous finality came over Mr. Harton's face. As he looked at the pictures on my four walls: Thomas Jefferson, Abraham Lincoln, John Ruskin, and a scroll of Chinese sages, he pointed to the Chinese characters down the side of the scroll, and asked: What do those characters say?

I replied: A Chinese scholar whom I trust once translated it freely as follows: 'After summer, autumn.'

Well, inquired MR. HARTON, what has that to do with the sages?

Symbolically, many things, I suggested.

At that juncture Dr. Smyth joined Mr. Harton in a hurried exit. Only Mrs. Smyth was inclined to linger and study the faces of the sages.

XIV

Congress as Power

MRS. SMYTH, as she drew off her glove: Our Representative in Congress dropped in at the Hospital today to see our town boss who has been ill since the election in November, 1942. I thought of asking him to join us but I refrained. He is busy in the new Congress and is cross with our League of Women Voters because he thinks that the League knifed him in the election.

BEARD, with raised eyebrows: I thought the League was non-partisan.

MRS. SMYTH: Officially it is supposed to be nonpartisan, but our leaders in the local League took the position that it was nonpartisan to support the Democratic candidate as against the Republican candidate in the election and they lost. However, I do not want to go into that. I really refrained from inviting our Representative for the reason that I feared he might be quarrelsome. Everybody who reads newspapers knows that dictators everywhere have risen on the ruins of legislatures and also that criticism of Congress is rife throughout the United States. I have been anxious about this tendency for a long time and have looked forward eagerly from our first session to our seminar on this subject.

Our Representative seems to be a very capable and industrious man, but when he talks about Congress he goes into petty details and never touches anything important. He spoke recently before our League of Women Voters and spent all his time on the Speaker of the House, the committee system, and rules of procedure.

When he was asked what place he believed Congress should hold in our system of government, he either had not thought about that subject or was purposely vague. Someone wanted him to explain why it was that Congress after 1933 had surrendered to the Executive the initiative in all great matters of legislation; and he merely went into a tirade against President Roosevelt, as if Congress had no responsibility for what had happened.

One of our members reminded him that he had voted for all the New Deal bills in the famous hundred days after March 4, 1933, and he lamely replied that then the country seemed to be behind the President. So I decided not to invite him here tonight. I want to know more than the technical rules of congressional procedure. They may be repealed or modified any day. My ideas are not very clear in my own mind, but, since I have heard you read so many great passages from *The Federalist,* I wish to learn something about the philosophy of Congress, if that is not too big a word for my ideas.

Dr. Smyth: I share my wife's opinion that this business of Congress is important in all efforts to maintain liberty and self-government in America. I do not think that our members of Congress are as bad a lot as several of our columnist oracles insist, but it seems to me that public affairs have become too complicated for a body of over five hundred members to manage. It is like our Hospital Board of twenty-five members. If they tried to run the Hospital, instead of electing the Director, they would make a mess of things. The illustration is poor but it shows what I mean.

Sue and I have been talking it over and have decided to ask you to begin with the role the framers of the Constitution expected Congress to play in our Government. The passages you have quoted from their writings convince me that they were wise persons for their day, in fact for all times. I am beginning to share your wholesome respect for their judgments. When I compare their utterances with some of the drivel I hear on all sides today, I am still more inclined to the view that the fathers, as you call them, were far ahead of the bright boys and girls who are now filling the newspapers with their essays on Congress. So get your notes and books together and tell us something about the way the fathers thought Congress was to serve the country.

Beard: I am sorry that you did not bring our Congressman so that we could have some ballast from a practitioner. Having that in mind I invited ex-Senator Tessell to supply it. He and I have been friends for some time—a friendship dating back to the days when he was in the Senate of the United States—years ago. He was one of the big guns of the party and regularly in the headlines. In the landslide of 1930, his constituents sent him back to private life, failing to appreciate his talents for public service in that financial crash.

We had become friends in connection with a bill or two before the Senate when a mutual friend urged me to furnish to the Senator some information he thought I possessed. One of the bills was the proposed censorship of literature, coming into the country, for the sake of national purity. I could name a few books, ancient and modern, that Americans had been accustomed to read, though of foreign composition; and equipped with such a list, the Senator was able to shape up one of his great speeches, as the papers acclaimed it, on the subject of literary censorship.

He took the position that Americans could read those books without moral injury. In a long editorial, a metropolitan paper praised the Senator for his discrimination and knowledge and declared him gifted with immense learning and a profound understanding of public questions. Before that he had always poked fun at learning, but he relished the tributes to his own immense learning when they came. Senator Tessell is now practicing law in New York.

Bringing the Senator in from his coffee, over which he loved to linger, I introduced him to the Smyths: Senator Tessell has been kind enough to accept my invitation and give us the benefit of his long experience in the Senate of the United States. I thought my theoretical knowledge, if it is even knowledge, should be checked up or offset by practical knowledge. None of my friends can do this better than the Senator.

After the Smyths had expressed their pleasure at meeting him and given the Senator the impression that they had followed his career in the Senate (reminding me of our discussion of hypocrisy among statesmen), the Senator, in a jovial mood, remonstrated gently.

SENATOR TESSELL: It is a privilege to be with you, I assure you. When Beard told me about your sessions this winter and invited me to attend this one I saw a chance to do some missionary work. High-brows like him can talk about the history and theory of Congress but they lack a feeling for the real things in Congress, the feeling and understanding that come from long experience there. High-brows are occasionally useful, at formal dinners, for instance, if you have some *femmes savantes* present, but on the whole they make a lot of trouble for the country by spreading untested ideas among the people. It was for doing this that old Socrates got the hemlock. There was more than a touch of justice in it, but of course we are more enlightened and tolerant than the ancient Greeks.

BEARD: Senator, just what do you mean by a high-brow? You have often applied the term to me and now I should like to know what you mean by it.

SENATOR TESSELL: A high-brow? Well, there are two kinds of high-brows. First and worst, there is the New-Deal high-brow who thinks he knows just how to run the government and goes to Washington to try his hand at public expense. He reminds me of Bob Burdette's immortal lines:

> I love the man who knows it all,
>> From east to west, from north to south,
> Who knows all things, both great and small,
>> And tells it with his tiresome mouth.

Then there is the high-brow who sits and sits and reads and reads, and travels around all over the earth taking notes and collecting books to be read and read, but can never make up his mind on anything for sure. You ask such a high-brow for the truth about any matter and he does one of two things—gives you what he calls an opinion, or replies: This is to be said on the one side and that is to be said on the other.

[I refrained from glancing at Dr. Smyth.]

Somewhere in the mountain of books and papers in Beard's house is a collection of the platforms of all the political parties in the United States since the beginning. I have seen it. Alongside of it, in Beard's handwriting, is a lot of notes about the planks of the parties on specific issues, all in parallel columns. Beard has read all the platforms of all the parties and digested them, but he doesn't believe in any of the platforms or any of the parties. There's a true high-brow for you! I am willing to wager that, although he was brought up, as he should have been, a good sound Republican, he has voted around all over the lot, half the time in mere squawking protest. I simply can't understand how anybody could get that way or why the country manages to develop so many high-brows of this kind.

MRS. SMYTH: Don't you think, Senator, that our educational system is largely responsible for it? When I studied history at college years ago, I was told that I must be objective, that is, put aside my biases, examine both sides of every question up for discussion, and see the whole as it actually was. My husband tells me that at the medical school his professors kept warning him to study conflicting theories about diseases, to avoid being the slave to any theory, and to test all theories by observation and experiment. The scientific spirit, as I have encountered it, is one that tries to see all around a subject and all the way through it, and that spirit too is partly responsible for many high-brows. On the whole it is our educational system that is mainly responsible for the development of so many skeptics, as you call them.

But I cannot say that it is entirely evil. Where you have liberty, there is bound to be difference of views among people of all classes. Only a monolithic education, such as Hitler gave the Germans, can prevent the creation of independent investigators and make everybody believe the same things with fervor enough to want to kill everybody who believes other things.

Senator Tessell: I think you are dead right about our educational system. I am a trustee of my old college and I have seen it at work. Not long ago we had before the board the question of appointing a professor of political science. The President nominated a man whom I had never heard of, and he said that he was a scholar and a gentleman; but, to save his life, the President could not tell whether this fellow was a good sound Republican or a good sound Democrat.

Though I was broad-minded enough to stand for either one, I wasn't willing to stand for anybody who thinks there might be something in collectivism, New Dealism, communism, and anarchy. And, believe me, we could not find out from the President of the college whether this nominee did or did not think that there might be something in these terrible intellectual diseases of our times. After wrangling for hours, the trustees knuckled under and approved the nomination. According to my impression, college presidents are about as bad as their professors, and our educational system is manufacturing high-brows wholesale. But I thought you were proposing to discuss Congress.

Beard: Suppose, Senator, you start us off by giving us your view of Congress in summary form, laying emphasis on the Senate, with which you are especially familiar. I assume that you have read

Professor George H. Haynes' great work, *The Senate of the United States: Its History and Practice,* published in 1938, in two volumes.

SENATOR TESSELL: Never heard of it. So that's it? My God, it weighs two or three pounds and has more than 1100 pages! You see, I haven't kept up with the Senate since I left it. But, apart from the fool laws it has been passing recently at presidential dictation, Congress is still the same old body. The quality of the members is not as high as it used to be in my day, but it still operates in its historic style, subject, as it must be, to the controlling provisions of the Constitution. Since you ask for my view of Congress, I will give it to you. My view ought to be everybody's view, for the matter is as plain as the nose on a face. I can recite my regular lecture to women's clubs. I know it by heart.

The Government of the United States consists of three separate and distinct departments. The President executes the laws, the judiciary applies the laws in specific cases, and, as the Constitution says, the Congress exercises all the legislative powers. There you are, as clean as a whistle. Now Congress, as you all know, is divided into two bodies, the Senate and the House. Their legislative powers are substantially equal. But to the Senate is given the power of ratifying or rejecting treaties and presidential nominations to important federal offices. The House alone originates money bills, but the Senate may amend them. Any Senator or member of the House may introduce any bill he wishes to have passed. The bill is referred to the appropriate standing committee, according to the subject matter of the bill. Each body has twenty-five or thirty standing committees. Each committee is bipartisan in make-up. If a committee to which a bill has been referred thinks the proposal worthy of consideration, it may hold hearings on it, approve it, and report it, with or without changes, for debate and action.

When reported, it is placed on a calendar; and when it is reached in due time, it is debated. In the matter of debate, the two chambers differ. In the House each member is limited, as a general rule, to one hour. In the Senate, there is no time limit on the Senators' speeches. While the Senate may, it is true, cut off long-winded orators by adopting a rule of cloture, that takes an extraordinary majority and is seldom done.

If a bill passed by one body is amended by the other and a disagreement arises, the differences are smoothed out by a conference committee composed of designated members from the two chambers. When a bill has been duly passed, it goes to the President for his signature or veto. If he vetoes it, a two-thirds vote in each house is necessary to pass it over his objection. That is the business in a nutshell, all according to the provisions of the Constitution.

BEARD: What do you mean by your words according to the provisions of the Constitution? Do you mean as prescribed by the Constitution, or as allowed by it?

SENATOR TESSELL: Both. The Constitution lays down some rules as to the election of the Speaker of the House, the quorum, and so forth; but in general both chambers are free to adopt any rules of procedure that do not violate the Constitution.

BEARD: That is what I wanted to bring out. The methods of organizing each house, the committee system, the limitations on debate, the party machinery behind the scenes, the procedure for the introduction and discussion of measures, the methods of committee hearings, the practices of committees charged with investigating public questions, the staffs of experts employed to assist the houses, the details or the generalities of laws passed, the relations between the two houses, the relations of the houses, separately or together, with the President—all these and other matters of vital importance to responsible government are not fixed in fact by the Constitution but are determined by laws and rules of the chambers. If I am right, Congress could scrap all the rules, procedures, laws, and methods of procedure built up during the past hundred and fifty years. It could give a fresh consideration to the matters I have listed, and it could then provide new organizing rules and methods better adapted to the complexities and difficulties of our modern age.

SENATOR TESSELL: Come to think of it, of course it could. But why on earth should anybody want to do that? The present system may not be perfect, yet it has stood for decades and there is nothing fundamentally wrong with it. I know that Congress is under a fire of criticism by the smart columnists and others. The trouble is not with Congress but the kind of men and women the people insist on sending there. If there is any fault with Congress, it is the people's fault. I am not fond of quoting Woodrow Wilson, but here in Haynes' book, where you have a marker, is a correct statement of the whole business:

The Senate of the United States has been both extravagantly praised and unreasonably disparaged. . . . The truth is, the Senate is just what the mode of election and the conditions of public life in this country make it.'

BEARD: I dissent from that.

SENATOR TESSELL: You would dissent from the Ten Commandments.

BEARD: I regard Mr. Wilson's statement as lacking in exactness, as largely rhetorical. The methods by which members of Congress are elected certainly have a considerable, if immeasurable, influence on the quality of the persons chosen. The same may be said of 'the conditions of public life in this country.' Neither the Senate nor the House is *just what* the methods of election and the conditions of public life make it. Taken in its plain sense, if it has any, Wilson's statement means that Senators and Representatives are automata, jumping jacks, going through performances mechanically determined by the methods of election and the conditions of public life.

If Senators and Representatives are dominated by methods of election and conditions of public life, then they have no free will to shape their own conduct and procedure. They have no backbone, no power over their course. They are compelled by something not themselves to split each house up into thirty or forty tyrannical committees. They are forced by an outside power to waste time day by day, week after week, month after month, over petty bills, claims, and disputes. An overriding necessity dictates that they must divide and diffuse their intelligence, instead of concentrating it on the great business before them. It drives them into supine dependence on executive will. It paralyzes their own capacity for constructive thinking and action. They can develop no leadership in national affairs. They must continue to abide by the mass of precedents their forerunners have built up since 1789. They must be as confused, trivial, or tumultuous as the methods of election and conditions of public life that are supposed to have lifted them into power and to dominate them while they are in power.

This idea of Congress I regard as false to fact and to the Constitution of the United States. If members of Congress believe in it, they are misled and thus help to reduce their own stature; they avoid their opportunities for creative work and their responsibilities to the nation besides. If millions of intelligent citizens believe that this must be the situation, if makers of public opinion keep hammering this idea into the heads of voters everywhere, if Senators and Representatives bow to this measure of their stature, then the national legislature will decline in its own esteem and in the esteem of the public.

In my opinion, individuals and groups rise in stature and power in some relation to their conception of their responsibilities and opportunities. There is no duty of legislators so humble that it does not symbolize some greatness of quality. And the duty of Congress as contemplated by the framers of the Constitution is as great as the greatness of our nation and of all that this nation may be and may accomplish in the coming years.

The framers of the Constitution expected, if some among them did not intend, that Congress should be the dominant branch of the Federal Government. They sought to establish a strong Executive, but, reasoning from past experience in America, they assumed the supremacy of the legislature. They put it first in order in the Constitution, the Executive second, and the judiciary third. They vested in Congress immense legislative powers. They gave it the power of the purse and the power of the sword—the two mighty engines of government. They authorized Congress to determine the structure of the executive department, the powers of all administrative officers, the number of justices in the Supreme Court, the appellate jurisdiction of that Court, and the form and jurisdiction of inferior Federal courts.

And, what is highly important though usually forgotten, they left Congress free to determine the nature and form of its relations to the President and his subordinates. If Congress has largely failed to develop this phase of its responsibility and has allowed the President to assume a dominant position, the fault lies with Congress, not with the Constitution.

The framers of the Constitution intended that Congress should represent the varied and effective interests of the country. The Senate was to represent the states in their corporate capacities; and the House, the multitudinous interests of the people in general— agricultural, commercial, industrial, moral, and intellectual. That the Federal Government might be kept in constant touch with the sentiments and desires of the voters, biennial elections were provided for members of the House.

Senators and Representatives were expected to be mediators between the National Government and the people; they were to be possessors of power and defenders of liberty; they were to legislate for the nation and to serve as educators among the people, instructing them by addresses and by campaign speeches in matters of public policy. They were to represent economic interests but they were to be more: the constant adjusters of conflicting interests under a conception of their duty, within the Constitution, for the nation committed to their keeping.

DR. SMYTH: Another tribute to the framers' wisdom! More proof that they took a realistic view of human beings and their interests— economic and moral. But surely they did not foresee the rise of lobbies, blocs of special interests, and all the corruption that has accompanied the recent appearance of these domineering bodies, outside of Congress and inside. If, as you seem to be insisting, Beard, they understood the nature and power of economic interests, why did they not make provision for the direct representation of these interests as such? Perhaps the idea of representing interests instead of heads is a new one.

BEARD: Your term 'representation of interests' is not new; neither are the ideas and the realities for which it stands. They were well known to the framers of the Constitution. What we call lobbies, that is, groups speaking for particular interests, appeared at the opening of the first Congress at New York City in the spring of 1789, and every Congress organized since then has been acquainted with them. The word bloc is relatively new; there were actual blocs, however, in the first Congress. No Congress has ever been without them. If you wish glimpses of early blocs, you can find them in my *Economic Origins of Jeffersonian Democracy*.

DR. SMYTH: Well, what about corruption? Were the fathers acquainted with that also?

BEARD: The word corruption is carelessly used and when so used tends to create confusion in the public mind.

SENATOR TESSELL: I can clarify this. In an exact sense, it means taking or receiving money in the form of bribes. An official is corrupt if, in return for a gift or payment of money, he does something he would not have done otherwise, if he votes for or grants a special privilege or refrains from some action merely because he is paid for it. It is not corrupt for a Senator or a Representative to vote for a measure favoring some particular interest, such as agriculture or commerce or manufacturing, if he takes no bribes from that interest. Lobbies and blocs are not necessarily corrupting in this sense. I doubt whether many of them are in fact.

BEARD: In general, Senator, I accept your definitions, but there are qualifications. In your opinion, is it corrupt for a member of Congress to vote for the measures of a special interest and then, on retiring, to accept a retainer from that interest as its lawyer in Washington or before the courts?

SENATOR TESSELL: It is corrupt, if he agrees to the retainer while in Congress. It is not corrupt if the retainer comes to him in due course after he retires.

BEARD: Suppose he follows a certain policy in Congress with full expectancy that the retainer will come from that special interest?

SENATOR TESSELL: Now you are getting into what Dr. Smyth calls metaphysics, as you tell me. I am not going to chop logic. Out of long experience, I maintain that there has been, relatively speaking, little corruption in Congress in the true sense of the word.

BEARD: My studies of American history incline me to confirm that opinion. The average American, if there is such a person, appears to think that when anybody, except himself, follows a special interest, the operation is corrupt. The notion is false and the public is led astray by this conception of business and politics.

With few exceptions, the great political scandals in connection with the Federal Government, whether accompanied by corruption or not, have appeared in the Executive Department, not in the Legislative Department. There were some deals bordering on corruption in the first Congress. Later Congresses were occasionally plagued by them. The Crédit Mobilier scandal of the Civil War and reconstruction period was a congressional scandal.

But consider the long list of scandals in the Executive Department, especially since 1865—the Star Route Fraud, the Whiskey Ring, the bare-faced stealing of national resources through the Federal Land Office, Teapot Dome, and the Harding scandals. They were all in the Executive Department. We have grounds for believing that the Presidents, from Grant to Harding, knew little, if anything, about the scandals going on under their respective administrations; nevertheless, if they did not know, they were derelict in their duty. If their official burdens were so heavy that they could not keep track of such actions by their high subordinates, then our presidential system is in so far sadly defective. As a rule it has been owing to congressional vigilance that scandals in the Executive Department have been unearthed, investigated, and stamped out. One more argument for Congress.

MRS. SMYTH: I have followed this discussion with deep interest. I had been inclined, for some reason, to regard the connection of special economic interests with politics as corrupt. I see now that it is not necessarily or generally corrupt. Obviously the existence of all kinds of economic and sectional interests is a fact. How could they fail to exist? They have arisen with the economic and political growth of the country. Our ways of working and earning a living create these interests. We cannot abolish them without abolishing the business of getting a living and living. Still I am puzzled by one of Robert's questions that is unanswered. Why didn't the framers of the Constitution provide for the frank representation of economic interests in Congress?

BEARD: First let me say that framers of the Constitution were familiar with the idea of class representation which has been talked about recently as if it were an original discovery of modern minds. The parliaments of Europe which arose during the Middle Ages were class parliaments. They were composed of representatives of the great estates, or classes—aristocratic, clerical, burgher, and small landed classes. I have discussed this briefly in my *Economic Basis of Politics*. Framers of the Constitution were familiar with such representation of interests.

Furthermore, the subject was up for consideration at the time the Constitution was adopted. Hamilton, in Number 35 of *The Federalist,* discussed the problem of representing landed, mercantile, and other economic interests directly in Congress. You can quickly read that Number for yourselves and discover the reasons he assigned for opposing any such system for the Congress of the United States.

Meanwhile, I can state that the idea of class representation in Congress was dismissed on four broad grounds:

First, the scheme of congressional elections made possible any representation of economic interests the voters might desire or deem feasible. Certainly agriculture, manufacturing, commerce, and labor have had representation and could have more of it as far as the Constitution is concerned.

Second, men like Madison thought that there was likely to be too much crass representation of powerful economic interests and that unless checked it might easily tear the government and the country apart.

Third, except for slavery, the laws of the United States did not draw legal lines between classes. The fluid nature of social conditions did not make possible a rigid stratification into fixed classes. In old Europe, before 1787, there had been relatively little movement of people across class lines. In the United States such a movement has been one of the striking characteristics of our civilization.

Fourth, framers of the Constitution looked upon human beings as *political* as well as *economic* creatures. They knew that the country confronted problems other than those economic in character—problems of Union, of ambitious leaders, of national defense, of liberty, of justice, of education. They knew that some men were more desirous of sheer power than of riches. They sought, as it were, to have represented in Congress the dawning consciousness of national unity and responsibility, as well as potent economic interests.

I do not say that the two types of human interest are sharply separated in fact, but the political animal may differ substantially from the pecuniary animal in ambitions and talents. How to get a fair working balance among interests so necessary to national life is a continuing problem in the grand strategy of statesmanship. On the whole, I think, the framers of the Constitution were amazingly successful in handling the problem. At least their Constitution has survived hundreds of constitutions drafted since their day by persons presumably more modern and more expert in the problems of the modern age.

DR. SMYTH: Then you are defending the whole rotten borough system of the Senate—the system which gives two Senators to each state, large and small. You favor letting Nevada, with 110,000 inhabitants, have the same weight in the Senate as New York with 13,500,000 inhabitants. I do not see how you can lend any countenance to it. It is simply preposterous.

SENATOR TESSELL: The senatorial rotten boroughs, as you call them, Doctor, are not much worse than the Southern rotten boroughs overrepresented in the House. Some Southern Representatives speak for eight or ten thousand voters, while many Northern representatives speak for more than two hundred thousand voters.

If you propose to clean house, the representation of the South will be reduced along with that of the grasshopper states with a handful of inhabitants. And what is more, if the Constitution as it now stands were enforced by the Senators and Representatives bound by oath to support it, the representation of the Southern states would be reduced.

BEARD: Moreover, the representation of those Northern states which impose literacy, poll taxes, and other qualifications on voters would also be reduced.

DR. SMYTH: I do not quite understand that.

BEARD: The Fourteenth Amendment provides that when a state deprives any adult male citizens of the right to vote in the major elections, its representation in Congress shall be proportionately reduced. The general position of the rule has been altered by the adoption of woman suffrage, but the rule is still in the Constitution. It is, however, academic now. Congress never has enforced it and is not likely to enforce it.

Leaving that aside, I should like to go back to your quarrel with the equal representation of the states in the Senate as preposterous. I also want to couple with it Senator Tessell's quarrel with the over-representation of Southern states in Congress. Why, Doctor Smyth, is unequal representation in the Senate preposterous? I take it that you regard it as absurd because it conflicts with the democratic idea that all heads are equal and that every representative in a legislature should represent the same number of heads. Or if you do not make it a matter of democratic logic, I suppose that you think the country would be better off in important respects if Senators were apportioned according to population. Have I caught the drift of your thinking?

DR. SMYTH: You have on both counts, but I begin to scent trouble. The states with small populations are not likely to surrender their equality in the Senate. It cannot be taken away from them without their consent. Nothing short of a revolution would ever get rid of their unfair power in the Senate, and people do not seem inclined to make more revolutions on the logic of democratic theories—one head, one vote, and an equal number of heads in every legislative district. There is not much use in pursuing that further. Would the country be better off if small states were deprived of their equal representation in the Senate? You are going to ask me to prove that it would be; and, to save my soul, I should not know how to go about it.

BEARD: One way to go about proving it would be to examine the Senate votes on bills you favor or condemn. Either way, you would find that the states with small populations—Rhode Island, Vermont, Delaware, Nevada, Idaho, and so forth—do not vote solidly together for or against bills demanded by the most populous states. According to studies that have been made, the line-up in the Senate on important bills is never strictly one of small states against large states. Similarity of interests, economic and intellectual, principally economic, seems to be more influential than equal numbers of heads in determining the kind of laws the country receives from the Senate.

As to Senator Tessell's proposal for reducing Southern representation in Congress, I am of the opinion that nothing short of a bitter sectional fight could ever effect that change, even though Congress may succeed in abolishing poll taxes by ordinary legislation. What may come we do not know. But it would take a great crisis in national affairs to make that an issue and in a great crisis more will be involved than such tinkering with our legislative machine.

DR. SMYTH, with a gesture indicating that our long session must close: Well, with all due apologies, I am not satisfied. You have let Congress off too easily. Our congressional government or presidential government or whatever you call it is under fire. It is charged by many responsible critics with being incompetent and inefficient in our mechanical and scientific age when government must be competent and efficient or perish. Unequal representation in the Senate and House opens the way for minority dictation. There is something awry somewhere, but I suspect that patching up Congress or the Executive Department is not enough. So I propose that, after we have discussed the Executive and the judiciary, we add a new session to our program—a critique of the congressional-presidential system. What about it?

Your idea is excellent, I replied, as my guests made their way out into the snowstorm.

XV

The Executive as Power

DR. SMYTH, making another dig at my method of analysis: Since, at our last session, you seemed unable to draw a clear line between legislative, executive, and judicial powers, I am prepared to hear you say tonight that since 1933 President Franklin Roosevelt has constitutional warrant for seizing all the power he can get his hands on. The line cannot be drawn; hence he can draw it to suit himself. Furthermore, according to your theory, or whatever you may call it, the opinions of the Supreme Court vary, so that we cannot rely on that body to define and hold positive limits on the executive power. In short, all talk about the division of powers which we heard in grade school and have heard ever after is worse than deceptive; it is nonsense. If I am to take your views at face value, political power is a dark continent that has no external boundary of its own, physical or intellectual; and within this dark continent covered with mist there are no boundaries either—at least no boundaries that we can be sure of. Before we begin I wish that you would tell me in simple words, just what the President of the United States is.

BEARD, slowly: I shall begin by making statements under the head of what the President is. If you hear one you do not like, you may protest against it. First of all, the President is a person chosen indirectly by a majority or a minority of the voters.

MRS. SMYTH: A minority of the voters?

BEARD: Yes, by a minority. Thousands of people entitled to vote do not take the trouble to vote. Sometimes a third or nearly half of them stay away from the polls. But we can rule them out. More than once a President has been elected by a minority of the voters who took the trouble to vote. For example, in 1860 the combined votes against Lincoln amounted to about a million more than his total. Wilson's vote in 1912 was more than a million short of the vote for all the candidates against him. And stranger still, two Presidents, Rutherford Hayes in 1876 and Benjamin Harrison in 1888, did not even get a popular plurality; that is, they stood lower in the scale of votes than their defeated rivals. So all we can truly say is that the President is a person elected according to the rules of the game provided by the Constitution, the laws, and party practices.

MRS. SMYTH: I was aware that our electoral system is complicated, but I had not realized that a President could be elected by a minority.

DR. SMYTH: Don't mention it or Beard will go to his filing case and show that *no* President has been the choice of a majority of the people. That is more quicksand and I want to get on with what the President *is*.

BEARD: What the President *is* depends in part upon the size and character of the vote cast for him, especially the character of the vote and intensity of the popular resolve behind it.

Now my next statement in reply to your question: The President is not a fixed quantity or quality. As a personality, he may be avid of power or more or less indifferent to it. Like Coolidge he may not want to be great; or like some other Presidents he may be hungry for dominion over others, even suffer from delusions of grandeur.

He is in part his own view of his office. He may believe, with Theodore Roosevelt, that he can do anything that the Constitution and laws do not forbid him to do. Or, Doctor, like your hero, Grover Cleveland, he may take a limited view of his powers, especially respecting matters on which he does not wish to act.

The power of the Executive varies not only according to the personality of the President. It varies according to circumstances. In times of crisis, as during the Civil War, the First World War, the panic of 1933, or the Second World War, executive power is about as great as the President can make it or cares to make it, within physical limits and subject to the restraints imposed by Congress, the Supreme Court, and the temper of the people.

DR. SMYTH: Why don't you say that the power of the President is what he can get away with and let it go at that?

BEARD: For the reason that your statement lacks exactness. You see that I do strive for exactness in political science, as you do, Doctor, in medical science. You wanted to know what the President *is* and I am trying to indicate by making relevant statements. The President is, again in part, all the activities he carries on, under powers conferred upon him by the Constitution and the acts of Congress as understood and contemplated by Congress and the people—or rather as understood and contemplated by his supporters in Congress and among the people. There are a multitude of things he cannot get away with.

DR. SMYTH: Yes. Roosevelt could not get away with his court packing plan in 1937, but he got away with enough, at that. Go ahead with your statements.

BEARD: The President is head of his political party, and has great powers as the dispenser of patronage, jobs, contracts, and other perquisites of his office. He has the prestige of his high office, the office occupied by Washington, Jefferson, and Lincoln. He possesses all the imponderable powers conferred upon him by the traditions of the office, as cherished by the people, even by his opponents. If he possessed only ponderable powers, we could easily dispose of the subject tonight by listing them precisely. But we must, if we are realistic, recognize the imponderables. The President is, in one way, a symbol of national unity and authority; or he is so regarded, or so regards himself, especially when he speaks on foreign affairs to other nations in time of peace and in time of war.

MRS. SMYTH: But what happened to President Wilson when he appeared as the symbol of national unity? He spoke for the nation during the First World War, and nobly, I believed. He presented a plan for putting an end to war. Robert seldom gets enthusiastic over anything political. But we threshed out the question of the Fourteen Points and the League of Nations at home, and we both came to the conclusion that President Wilson did speak for the nation, was right, and ought to be supported by the nation.

Then along came that awful Henry Cabot Lodge, Borah, and Harding—and Theodore Roosevelt, too—and proclaimed from the housetops that President Wilson did not speak for the nation. If it had not been for the rule requiring a two-thirds vote for the ratification of treaties, the Senate would have approved the League of Nations. A minority of the Senators defeated it. A majority of them favored it, and I think that the majority, like President Wilson, really represented the sentiments of the country on the subject. One could almost say that President Wilson, while using his power to speak for the nation in foreign affairs, was destroyed politically and shattered physically, by a minority of obstructionist politicians.

During the First World War, President Wilson seemed to be the most powerful man in the whole world and the man most highly respected. Remember how the masses of England, France, and Italy were thrilled by his ideas and looked upon him as a savior! Then all his power was destroyed by a petulant minority. Remember the spiteful things Lodge and Theodore Roosevelt wrote about Wilson in their letters. Their malice was worse than catty. It was deadly.

Dr. SMYTH: I know now what Beard will say to that. He will say that the President is partly times and circumstances; politics is a fight; Wilson had his day and lost the power he had accumulated. In other words, as I should put the case, Wilson simply could not get away with it. I also know Beard's reply to that remark. He will agree that there is something in what I have just said.

BEARD: Let all that you have both just said stand. It will illustrate what I have asserted about the immeasurable powers of the President and the limits imposed on them by his opponents and by that vague thing called public sentiment. There is only one of Mrs. Smyth's remarks that I shall question now. It is her comment that the majority of the Senators who favored approving the League of Nations represented the sentiments of the country. That may be true, but I do not know that it is true.

Only one-third of the Senators who passed upon the League had been elected in November, 1918, that is, *after* President Wilson's general foreign policies respecting a new world order had been announced; and even then the specific terms of a league of nations were not before the country. Two-thirds of the Senators had been elected *before* those specific policies had been proclaimed, even before the United States had entered the war against the Central Powers.

Would President Wilson and Senators in favor of the League of Nations actually have been elected in 1916 if they had presented to the people a program of war and the League of Nations as framed at Versailles in that campaign? I doubt it, although both parties favored some kind of international association against war during the campaign. One of the Democratic slogans in the campaign was that President Wilson had kept us out of war. The Democrats lost in the congressional election of 1916, and at the first congressional election after 1916 they were badly defeated. In 1920, when the country had the first chance to pass on the League of Nations, it swept the Democrats out as if in a fury.

Mrs. Smyth: Then you think that President Wilson was a visionary, not a prophet?

Beard: He was a visionary in the sense that he was utterly mistaken in his belief or expectation that he could induce the Senate and people of the United States to enter the League of Nations as designed at Paris in 1919 by the Peace Conference. What do you mean by calling Wilson a prophet?

Mrs. Smyth: He prophesied that if the United States did not join the League, another big war would come soon. Well, it came. Was he not a prophet in that?

Beard: How do you know that if we had joined the League, another big war would not have come anyway, and sooner?

Mrs. Smyth: Of course, I do not *know* it, but I am convinced of it. If after this war the United States does enter a world league or federation and lasting peace comes, then President Wilson will be vindicated as a prophet.

Beard: How long will your new peace have to last in order to make President Wilson a prophet? A thousand years?

Mrs. Smyth: I see your point and do not wish to press mine any longer just now, for our theme tonight is not the League of Nations.

Beard: Aside from the hazardous business of prophecy, the struggle over the League illustrates my contention that what the President *is* depends in part, in large part, upon his personality—his qualities of mind, his psychological propensities. He is not omnipotent. His power is limited. What he is or can get away with often depends upon his capacity to judge the limits of his own powers. That involves insight, knowledge, and a sense of the possible.

President Wilson evidently thought that he had the power to force the ratification of the Treaty, with perhaps minor reservations respecting the League of Nations, and that the country would support him. His chief opponents in the Senate were belligerent. He chose to make it an open struggle—political battle instead of conciliatory negotiation. Had he made concessions on reservations, the

United States might have entered the League of Nations. President Wilson overestimated his power and was broken in the contest of power. The President *is* power, but limited power. And marvellous is the eye that can discern its strength and its limitations.

DR. SMYTH: But the Constitution intrusts the conduct of foreign affairs to the President, does it not?

BEARD: Before I take up that question, let me ask you a few simple questions by way of preliminary so that we may know what we are talking about when we say foreign affairs. I shall ask you questions and you can give your answers. My first question is, What do you mean by foreign affairs?

DR. SMYTH: I should say, travel, intercourse, and commerce between the people of the United States and the people of other countries and transactions between their governments; making treaties; regulating commerce; declaring the policies of the United States in relation to other nations; exchanging ministers, ambassadors, and consuls; controlling immigration and emigration; deciding upon the size and nature of our armaments; exchanging notes and carrying on negotiations with other governments; declaring war and making peace. There may be other things, but these are the most important that I can recall.

BEARD: They suffice. Now let me put some yes or no questions to you, the kind you like to put to me. Can the President alone regulate intercourse with other countries at his pleasure—that is, tariffs, tonnage duties, financial exchanges, and travel?

No. Congress has that power.

Can the President at his pleasure regulate immigration and emigration?

No. Congress passes immigration acts.

Can the President determine the conditions of naturalization and the rights of aliens in the United States?

No.

Can the President fix the size and nature of our army, navy, and other armed forces?

No.

Can the President alone set up ministries and consulates in other countries and pick his own ministers and consuls?

No. Since Congress must provide the money for them, it could control this branch of foreign business, if it wanted to do so. Besides, the Senate must approve the persons named by the President as ministers or ambassadors.

Can the President make treaties with other countries?

No. A treaty must have the approval of two-thirds of the Senate. But the President can make minor agreements without asking the consent of the Senate.

Can the President declare war?

No. That power is supposed to be in the hands of Congress.

Can the President make peace?

If it takes a treaty, the Senate must approve.

Can the President declare the foreign policy of the United States and impose it upon the country by his own will?

There are two questions. Certainly the President can declare the foreign policy of the United States. But he cannot impose it upon the country by mere declaration. If President Wilson had enjoyed that power, the United States would have been in the League of Nations and the Second World War would not have broken out.

BEARD, in conclusion: Excellent, Doctor. I have only one possible exception to your answers. How do you know that the Second World War would not have occurred, if the United States had joined the League of Nations?

DR. SMYTH, after a long pause: I don't exactly know it. But I believe it. With a strong League, no country would have dared to go to war.

BEARD: What we can say, then, in response to the question raised by the Doctor, may be put this way: The President is power. He has power of knowledge, will, and decision. His decisions, applied through all the agents and material instruments at his command as the Executive, can set in motion actions that deeply affect every aspect of life, liberty, and property, even the very basis of the Republic. But this power is limited by Congress and the Courts; by his own capacities or incapacities; by the amount of popular support he can marshal and maintain; by his own sense of self-restraint —by time and circumstances, by the contingencies and requirements of peace and war.

DR. SMYTH: Your words are plain enough, but the substance covered by them eludes me. At least some of it does. As I comprehend your language, the President may be more powerful in some ways than in others. That is to say, the contingencies or necessities at a given time may be in some branch of domestic affairs like the banking crisis of 1933, and at another time in foreign affairs. Furthermore he can make contingencies himself, bring on crises himself and then take advantage of his own disturbances to enhance his power. This is especially true in foreign affairs. Still, I am under the impression, from things I have read, that the President's power in foreign affairs, to conduct foreign affairs, is for practical purposes unlimited. Is that not true, according to the Constitution?

BEARD: Let me ask you whether you think the Constitution confers upon the President unlimited powers over foreign affairs?

MRS. SMYTH: Since you say that Robert's answers to your questions are correct, it is evident that the President does not have unlimited powers.

DR. SMYTH: Anyway, that follows logically from your constitutional principle that all our agents of government, from the President down, have limited powers. I see that. But this system makes a mess for us, keeps us in an eternal wrangle among the agents of government so that we are seldom sure of anything. It helps to paralyze us for action when action is absolutely necessary. In foreign affairs, at least, the President ought to have a free hand, it seems to me.

The Doctor knitted his brow, as if his own declaration was boiling in his mind. A puzzled look came over his wife's face.

MRS. SMYTH: No, that will not do. According to the definition of foreign affairs or relations we accepted a few minutes ago, there is no positive line between domestic and foreign affairs. If you gave the President the absolute power to fix foreign policy, any policy he adopted would need money for enforcement. Unless he could lay taxes himself, he would have to go to Congress for the money, and that would give Congress supremacy over him. I do not think that the country would want him to have full power to regulate all commerce and immigration, to declare war, to make peace, to fix tariff rates. When you come to think of it, almost anything the President can do in foreign affairs may slash right into our own industry, commerce, life, liberty, property, oh, everything we call domestic! I give it up. There seems to be no easy way to run either domestic or foreign affairs. It is clear that the President has large powers over foreign affairs, and I cannot see why the framers of the Constitution did not intrust him with more powers. Surely they had confidence in the Executive office for which they made provision?

DR. SMYTH: From what we have heard here, I can throw light on that. They didn't trust anybody—too much, at least. I am surprised that they trusted one another enough to sign their own document! However, I suppose that none of them went so far as to fear that the President of a republic might betray his country in dealing with other countries.

BEARD: Your supposition is naïve, Doctor, but don't take offense at the word. In Number 22 of *The Federalist,* Alexander Hamilton said:

One of the weak sides of republics, among their numerous advantages, is that they afford too easy inlet to foreign corruption. An hereditary monarch, though often disposed to sacrifice his subjects to his ambition, has so great a personal interest in the government and in the external glory of the nation, that it is not easy for a foreign power to give him the equivalent for what he would sacrifice by treachery to the state. . . . In republics, persons elevated from the mass of the community, by the suffrages of their fellow-citizens, to great stations of pre-eminence and power, may find compensations for betraying their trust. . . . Hence it is that history furnishes us with so many mortifying examples of the prevalency of foreign corruption in republican government.

MRS. SMYTH: Was Hamilton mean enough to say that about republics, when the United States was a republic? Still he was talking in general terms. He couldn't have been mean enough to think that of any man chosen to head our Republic.

DR. SMYTH, sardonically: He was mean enough to think it, but not mean enough to say it publicly.

BEARD: You are both hasty in your surmises. I do not concede that Hamilton was mean in taking this view of republics. He was speaking of actual experiences with republics in the past and had evidence to support his contention that there had been foreign corruption in republics. There had been foreign corruption in monarchies also. But let that pass. Hamilton thought and publicly said that the Constitution was so designed as to guard against improper foreign influences in the executive department.

DR. SMYTH, as Mrs. Smyth gasped: Where did Hamilton say that?

BEARD: In Number 75 of *The Federalist* on the treaty-making power. This is what Hamilton wrote:

However proper and safe it may be in governments where the executive magistrate is an hereditary monarch, to commit to him the entire power of making treaties, it would be utterly unsafe and improper to intrust that power to an elective magistrate of four years' duration. . . . A man raised from the station of a private citizen to the rank of chief magistrate, possessed of a moderate or slender fortune, and looking forward to a period not very remote when he may probably be obliged to return to the station from which he was taken, might sometimes be under temptations to sacrifice his duty to his interest, which it would require superlative virtue to withstand. . . . An ambitious man might make his own aggrandizement, by the aid of a foreign power, the price of his treachery to his constituents. The history of human conduct does not warrant that exalted opinion of human virtue which would make it wise in a nation to commit interests of so delicate and momentous a kind, as those which concern its intercourse with the rest of the world, to the sole disposal of a magistrate created and circumstanced as would be a President of the United States.

DR. SMYTH: That is the worst thing I ever heard. It is as bad as anything old Machiavelli ever wrote. It is an insult to the American people. Surely Hamilton did not spread that around widely as his opinion. If he had, he would have been driven out of politics.

BEARD: You are mistaken again, Doctor. Hamilton's statement was published in *The Federalist*. Let me repeat: This volume is a collection of articles written by Jay, Madison, and Hamilton for newspapers as arguments in favor of the ratification of the Constitution. These articles were published and then widely reprinted for the purpose of inducing the people to support ratification. They are regarded by lawyers and the Supreme Court, and not only by teachers of history and political science, as commentaries of the highest value in discovering the intentions of the men who framed the Constitution and in ascertaining the nature of our national government.

Mark well my words—and his! Hamilton did not say that any President under the Constitution would ever betray our country. He said that an ambitious executive of a republic, *unless restrained in power over foreign affairs as our Constitution provides,* might come under foreign influences and betray his country. He was arguing against conferring upon the President unlimited power over foreign affairs.

DR. SMYTH: Your comments do not help very much. Hamilton's very idea smirches the character of the American people and tends to destroy our confidence in the President as our national leader and the symbol of our national unity, especially in foreign affairs. I am not now defending any President in particular. I am referring to the high office of chief executive and to any person who may be elected by the people to that office.

BEARD: It is my turn now, Doctor, to take you to task. You have objected to my use of symbolism in any form, and at this late hour you speak of the President as the symbol of our national unity. You recognize him as our national leader. Let me ask, What do you mean by symbol of our national unity?

DR. SMYTH: It seems clear to me. When the President speaks as Chief Executive, as head of the nation, all other countries in the world are bound to recognize his voice as the voice of the nation, and we are also bound to regard it as such. In this respect the President is the leader of the nation.

BEARD: You sound like the Justice of the Supreme Court who declared, in the Curtiss-Wright case of 1934: 'In this vast external realm [of foreign affairs], with its important, complicated, delicate, and manifold problems, the President alone has the power to speak or listen as a representative of the nation.'

What law of the land, what provision of the Constitution or any statute, what axiom of our political tradition states that the President's voice is the voice of the nation which all citizens are bound to accept as such? I can answer for you. The answer is, None, absolutely None. The Constitution does not use the term foreign affairs. It does not declare the President to be the symbol of national unity or his voice to be the voice of the nation.

It is true that under custom accepted by Congress and the courts, the official communications of the Government of the United States with foreign governments must be through the President's office or the creature of Congress—the State Department. But it is through an Act of Congress and custom, not through any mandate of the Constitution, that this rule has come into force. When the Department of State was originally instituted, Congress provided that the

Secretary shall perform such duties as the President may intrust to him relative to correspondence and other business connected with our foreign relations. Congress could have required the Secretary of State to report to the legislative department as well as the executive department or to it alone. In the case of the Treasury Department, it did require the Secretary to report to Congress. But in making the Secretary of State the special minister of the President, Congress did not enact that the President's voice in foreign affairs must be regarded as the voice of the nation. Such a law would have been futile, had it been made.

And as a matter of fact, Doctor, you are also in error, when you think that foreign governments must accept anything the President says in the way of foreign policy as binding on the nation. Perhaps it should be so, but it is not so. Foreign *peoples* have been misled by thinking that the President alone can make commitments which the nation must fulfil; but foreign *governments* know that there are constitutional limitations on the power of the President to make treaties and do other things in the way of regulating and controlling our commerce and intercourse with other countries. Other governments have known this since the adoption of our Constitution.

MRS. SMYTH: Why, of course, on second thought, that must be a fact. I know nothing about the law, but I do remember how President Wilson was treated. He prepared and announced a foreign program for us during the First World War. I believe that it was a right program. Still, Clemenceau and Lloyd George and other men at the Paris conference must have known that the President had to get the approval of the Senate for the treaty he signed, including the League of Nations. Anyway, President Wilson's voice was not accepted as the voice of the nation in this important business. I think it should have been, but it was not. So, Robert, that much of your theory goes overboard.

BEARD: Two more questions: Would you be willing to give the President an absolute power to commit the nation to any foreign policy he might deem desirable for any reason? And, since it might take all the economic and armed force of the nation to implement his policy, what would become of the power of Congress over domestic affairs?

DR. SMYTH: No, in a pinch, I should not be willing to give the

President an absolute power to bind the nation to a foreign policy. And I get the idea there is no sharp line between foreign affairs and domestic affairs. If the President is absolute in one, he must be absolute in the other also, or at least strong enough in money and arms to make good on any of his foreign commitments. Once more you have got us into a kind of intellectual jam. Power must be limited but there is no way of fixing the limits definitely, once and for all. Like a magician, you fall back on that elusive thing called the exercise of judgment.

Mrs. Smyth: We use judgment every day, or should, and we do not know exactly what it is, except, perhaps, that when we have collected a lot of facts in a given situation and are puzzled about how to act on them, we finally make up our minds, reach a decision in a jump, using our own judgment. Still there is something in the idea that the President is our national leader. Let us explore that.

Beard: The question then becomes, What and how much is in the idea of presidential leadership? To bring this problem to a focus, let me read you the following propositions taken from Woodrow Wilson's *Constitutional Government:*

[The President is] the political leader of the nation, or has it in his choice to be.

The nation as a whole has chosen him and is conscious that it has no other political spokesman.

Let him once win the admiration and confidence of the Country, and no other single force can withstand him, no combination of forces will easily overpower him.

His position takes the imagination of the Country.

He is the representative of no constituency, but of the whole people. When he speaks in his true character, he speaks for no special interest.

If he rightly interprets the national thought and boldly insists upon it, he is irresistible; and the country never feels the zest of action so much as when its President is of such insight and calibre. Its instinct is for united action, and it craves a single leader. It is for this reason that it will often prefer to choose a man rather than a party.

A President whom it [the country] trusts cannot only lead it, but form it to his views. . . . If he lead the nation, his party can hardly resist him. *His office is anything he has the sagacity and force to make it* (emphasis mine).

DR. SMYTH: The President certainly has it in his choice to be the political leader of the nation, *if he can be.* It is not true that the nation as a whole has chosen him. As you reminded us a few minutes ago, he is in fact chosen by only a portion of the voters, perhaps even less than a plurality. I am not sure that the country is conscious that it has no other political spokesman. It is conscious that it has no other President at the moment. His position certainly may or may not 'take the imagination of the country,' or even his own party. Look at the way the Democrats utterly repudiated Grover Cleveland during his second term—or rather the Bryan mobster-wing of the Democrats. The President speaks for no special interest, Wilson says. While I wish to God that was always true, I realize it is not always true. A long line of Republican Presidents certainly spoke for the special interests of big business, and Wilson himself said so, somewhere, didn't he?

BEARD: I hesitate to break into your commentary on Wilson's propositions relative to presidential leadership, but I will answer your question by quoting these sentences from *The New Freedom,* a collection of his speeches made during the campaign of 1912: 'Our government has been for the past few years under the control of heads of great corporations. . . . The government of the United States is a foster child of the special interests.'

I may add that if, as Wilson said, the whole government was controlled by the special interests during the period in question, then the President at that time was no leader; he was a kind of office boy. But let us go on with the propositions from Wilson's *Constitutional Government* published in 1908.

DR. SMYTH: Really, I am through. I want to modify my previous reckless statement that the President is our national leader to run as follows: the President may be an accepted leader of such a large majority of the people that neither Congress nor the courts nor the minority can withstand him and he may have his own way—up to a certain point. I suppose it is another case of great but limited power, on which you are constantly harping. Yes, it must be limited power or the President would have or could have the power of a Hitler or a Stalin. Wasn't it William James who said that it is almost impossible to have any good thing without having too much of it? This political science is beginning to get on my nerves.

I should like to get back to my medicine but, horrible thought, I have to testify tomorrow in a lunacy case. I have to decide whether a man who has been my patient is or is not crazy enough to be deprived of control over his own property and put under a conservator. I have been trying to make up my mind for two weeks utterly in vain, but at 10:30 in the morning it must be made up and I must swear to the truth of the make-up.

The Doctor sighed as if he were through with everything.

MRS. SMYTH, with flashing eyes: I do not like Wilson's statement that the nation craves a single leader and that the President's office is anything he has the sagacity and force to make of it. Craving for a single leadership sounds to me a lot like Hitler's doctrine. Too much single leadership and too much force add up to totalitarianism. Of course, President Wilson did not mean to put this meaning into his words, but they can be so interpreted.

There is danger in such talk. Perhaps that is just suspicion on my part. People, all of us, do have a tendency to run from responsibility, to crave some authority able to settle tangled problems once and for all. On the other hand we all have a tendency to resent authority when it is established, and to do as we please in spite of it. It is hard to be uncertain about things, to be always making adjustments among conflicting interests and wills, to be tolerant, to take half a loaf instead of a whole loaf. It almost seems as if running politics is in some ways like running a nursery where every child is determined to have its own complete way but never, or seldom, can be allowed to have it. I am just rambling on and must stop it. You can both ignore what I have said if you like. I am no authority on political science.

BEARD: You are more of an authority than you imagine. I do not want to ignore what you have said, for I think it is true. One of the greatest rulers of human beings in all times, one of the thinkers most experienced in the art and science of politics, Marcus Aurelius, soldier, administrator, head of the Roman empire, philosopher—a fascinating and tragic figure—once exclaimed that people are like 'little children quarreling, crying, and then straightaway laughing.' The business of government was for him the business of ruling and getting along with such people and, as things go, he was ingenious at least, if not a genius. The nursery, the family, the community is a microcosm of universal politics.

Dr. Smyth, giving me a hard glance that softened into a smile: The Judiciary as Power, according to Marcus Aurelius, is next, isn't it?

XVI

The Judiciary as Power

D R. SMYTH, drawing a piece of paper out of his pocket: I was in Judge Ranyin's chambers this afternoon on some Hospital business and happened to tell him that we were coming here this evening to discuss with you the Judiciary as Power, particularly the Supreme Court of the United States. The Judge broke out in wrath and declared that you didn't know a thing about the Judiciary or the Constitution either, and he cited as authority Justice Holmes' contemptuous disposal of you in the *Holmes-Pollock Letters*. He got still madder when I asked him to come along and hold up his end of the argument. He had no time to waste, he went on; he had given a lifetime to legal business and did not intend to fritter away an evening talking with a man who knew nothing whatever about it

But he sat down and wrote the following proposition, which he asked me to put up to you the first thing on my arrival:

The Supreme Court of the United States exercises no power of its own. Its highest function is to apply knowledge of the Constitution to acts of legislatures and to determine whether those acts square with the Constitution, the supreme law made by all the people. The presumption of the Court is always in favor of the validity of an act of Congress or any legislature, and it sets aside an act only when the act violates the Constitution beyond all reasonable doubt. The Court is not a political department of the Government, and exercises no political power. It does not exercise power at all. It merely gives effect to the superior power of the Constitution.

What do you think of that? It is what I was brought up to believe.

MRS. SMYTH: I can guess your answer. It is that the proposition is a view held in certain quarters but does not wholly conform to various relevant facts in the case. You see I am getting on to your constitutional angles myself.

BEARD: Your statement suits me, though I was not intending to put it that way exactly. I was about to remark that the Judge's memorandum from on high reminded me of the editorials of the *New York Times* written against the appointment of Louis Brandeis to the Supreme Court in 1916. When President Wilson nominated Brandeis, the *Times* was shocked and made a long protest. It said that Brandeis had been an advocate of reforms, a pleader of causes, and had no place on the bench. 'The Supreme Court,' the editor expostulated, 'sits not to expound or advance theories or doctrines, but to judge of the constitutionality of the enactments which Congress may decree. . . . The court needs no advocate [of social justice], can never put itself in the position of pleading for any cause.'

After the Senate committee by a purely party division recommended the confirmation of Brandeis by the Senate, the *Times* continued to deplore the very idea of appointing Brandeis. He was all right, perhaps, in politics, but never in that high tribunal, it said. 'The Supreme Court, by its very nature,' the editor asserted, 'must be a conservative body; it is the conservator of our institutions, it protects the people against the errors of their legislative servants, it is the defender of the Constitution itself.' And more—a whole column in the same vein.

MRS. SMYTH: That is curious. How the *Times* must have reversed itself! When Brandeis resigned from the Court full of honors and praise, the *Times* paid a great tribute to him; or, perhaps, it was when he died. Did it never occur to the editor that the Supreme Court, as well as Congress, could err? Or isn't it really human?

DR. SMYTH: Besides, what was the matter with the editor? Did not he know that many advocates of reforms and pleaders of causes, politicians I mean, have been appointed to the Supreme Court? I am no scholar in history, but am I not right in thinking that many such advocates had been elevated to the Court before Brandeis came on the scene?

BEARD: Suppose we take Judge Ranyin's proposition, Mrs. Smyth's question, and your question as our starting points. The Judge says that the Supreme Court exercises no power of its own and that its highest function is to apply *knowledge* of the Constitution to acts of legislatures and to determine whether those acts square with the Constitution. That is a theory widely held among lawyers. Does it square with the facts? It does not.

Parts of the Constitution are matters of fact and of knowledge about which there can be no difference of opinion. The Constitution fixes the term of the President at four years, not two or six or any other number. In a case involving the issue of the President's term, the Court would apply *knowledge*. It has no power on that issue.

DR. SMYTH: What would it do if in the midst of great emergency, a social revolution, or war, the President as Commander in Chief should just extend his term? I imagine that the Supreme Court would have small chance to exercise even its knowledge.

BEARD: In such a case the Constitution would be either dead or suspended. But we are speaking of times called normal. There are other parts of the Constitution that are not mere matters of knowledge, parts as to the meaning of which the wisest and best informed judges may and do disagree. For instance, 'No person shall . . . be deprived of life, liberty, or property without due process of law'; and 'Congress shall make no law . . . abridging the freedom of speech, or of the press.' In fact many of the most important clauses of the Constitution are vague and open to various interpretations. The great political controversies that have shaken the country have turned upon or involved these general clauses on which the wisest and best informed have differed, may and do differ. It is right here that the Supreme Court has power. As Justice Stone said somewhere, in effect, in such cases the only restraint on the Justices of the Court is their self-restraint.

MRS. SMYTH: Then it does have power, that is, a power of negation—to declare laws null and void.

BEARD: A negative power is also positive: its exercise may set in train national emotions and forces which will produce the most extraordinary results. Mere opposition often makes us think carefully and formulate our ideas clearly. Even when the Court declares a law void, the opinions of the Justices may be so framed as to offer an absolute bar to such legislation or so formulated as to indicate other ways by which legislatures may accomplish the same or similar ends under the Constitution. It is within the power of the Justice who holds a law invalid to determine whether his opinion is to be wholly negative or largely constructive in thought. Thought is power. Then, in many cases of high national significance, there are dissenting opinions in which Justices may differ from their brethren and set forth reasons for sustaining the validity of legislative acts; in the Dred Scott case of 1857 or the income tax case of 1895, for example.

Dr. Smyth: The business of dissenting opinions has always troubled me. Of course medical doctors in consultation often disagree but they do not write opinions about their disagreements.

Mrs. Smyth: It might be a good thing if they did. It might make them stop and think if they had to go on record and, besides, it might help to educate the public and the profession.

Dr. Smyth: Not a bad idea, perhaps. However I see that it is risky to bring up medicine again. So I'll bring up Judge Ranyin again. He says in his memorandum that the Supreme Court does not set a piece of legislation aside as invalid unless it violates the Constitution 'beyond all reasonable doubt.' Yet right along the Supreme Court has split three to six or four to five on the validity of acts of Congress. As a casual reader of newspaper headlines, I know that. How on earth can anybody say there is no reasonable doubt, when four out of nine men, all supposed to *know* the law, insist that there is a doubt? As I understand it, the opinion of the Court may hold that an act of Congress is invalid and four dissenters may assert that the exact opposite is true. It seems to me that if lawyers had any sense of humor or of propriety, they would quit talking that way.

Beard: I think the rule that the Court should assume that a law is valid unless it is invalid beyond a reasonable doubt is a good rule. It runs against hasty and ill-considered action by judges. Still, an excellent rule may be made to savor of hypocrisy if too much talked about by persons lacking in discrimination. I think that lawyers and judges ought to remember, also, Justice Stone's dictum that 'Congress and the courts both unhappily may falter or be mistaken in the performance of their constitutional duty.'

At all events, the mere opinions of the Court are a form of power. They help to educate the lawyers and the country at large in matters of constitutional government and public policy . . .

Dr. Smyth: But isn't the opinion of the Court in a case the law of the case, and the dissenting opinions just dead-letter fulminations?

Beard: No, the opinion of the Court is not the law or the decision in the case. The decision is a very definite thing; for instance, in its *decision* in a constitutional case the majority of the Justices agree that an act of government is or is not valid under the Constitution. That is definite. The *opinion* of the Court is the argument or reasoning of the Justice who writes it, designed to show *why* the decision should be as it is. But, of course, all the Justices in the majority group may not agree on this opinion. While agreeing on the decision, they may differ violently as to *why* it should be so decided. Sometimes, the opinion of the Court, as distinct from the decision, is the opinion of only two or three Justices, and two or three other Justices may each write a separate opinion intended to show why the decision is right—an opinion called concurring, which rips into the opinion of the Court and purports to show that its reasoning is bad.

Then there may be one or more dissenting opinions designed to show that the decision and opinion of the Court are both wrong and that the case should have been decided the other way. Moreover, dissenting opinions are not, as you suggest, just dead-letter fulminations. The doctrines of law set forth in dissenting opinions may in time become the law of the land. The Court may reverse itself later and take the view of dissenters at a previous time. This has been true of many great dissenting opinions by Justice Holmes and Justice Brandeis. And don't forget Chief Justice Stone's dissent in the Gobitis case.

In my view, the great decisions and opinions of the ablest Justices are power, a creative or a destructive power, and the Supreme Court Justices should have this power on their own account and exercise it. Not many people read these opinions unless their interests are involved in the litigation. But lawyers often do, even when they have no immediate stake in the cases; and lawyers are very influential in the affairs of the nation. They constitute a kind of governing élite —the aristocracy of the robe, as my old professor, John W. Burgess, used to call them.

In my view, the great decisions and opinions of Chief Justice Marshall between 1801 and 1835 were primary contributions to stabilizing and perpetuating the Republic. Able lawyers everywhere read his opinions and got from them ideas and convictions respecting the nature of the Union. Probably, more people read the speeches of Daniel Webster, but the views of Webster coincided with those of Chief Justice Marshall. As I am given to see things, Marshall was a godsend to the country.

DR. SMYTH: Coming, as you have said, from a long line of Federalists, Whigs, and Republicans, you would think so.

BEARD: Perhaps. Yet if you believe that the establishment of our Republic as indivisible was a good thing for us, then you must think likewise. If you think it would have been better for all of us that the Republic should have been broken to pieces in 1861—1865, then you may conclude that Marshall was not a godsend to America. It all turns on an *if,* not on brute facts.

At this stage in our discussion, Dr. Smyth drew another slip of paper out of his pocket, with the comment that Judge Ranyin had given it to him with instructions to ask me what I had to say about it. The note was copied from Charles Warren's *Congress, the Constitution and the Supreme Court,* and ran as follows:

> It is a solemn fact that, even in times of comparative freedom from emergency or excitement, Congress, or one of its branches, has violated the provisions of the Bill of Rights at least ten times since the year 1867; and at least ten times has the Supreme Court saved the individual against Congressional usurpation of power.

DR. SMYTH, commenting: This looks like a pretty serious indictment of Congress and a strong case for the Supreme Court. Judge Ranyin asks, What is your reply to that? I suppose that when Warren holds that the Court has saved the citizens' rights ten times, he cites ten judicial cases to support or prove his contention?

BEARD: I wish Judge Ranyin had come up with you. Since he would not, here is a copy of Warren's book and here are my notes on the ten cases. You are right. He does cite them. But it would take a week for us to go through all the cases. However, here is a copy of an article on the very passage Judge Ranyin cites from Warren—an article by a competent lawyer, Professor Henry W. Edgerton, now a federal judge in the District of Columbia, printed in the *Cornell Law Quarterly* in 1937. Edgerton analyzes Warren's ten cases. Two of the cases involved only action by one branch of Congress, not congressional legislation. The other eight cases boil down to very little liberty saved by the Court, if any. Edgerton, in my judgment, shows that Warren's sweeping statement amounts to a misrepresentation of the situation; that his solemn fact is not a fact, is on a fair estimate less than half a fact.

Judge Ranyin need not get excited on any such score. I am as much in favor of decisions by the Supreme Court upholding the citizens' liberties as he is. Indeed, I regret that the Court has not set aside many acts of Congress which do, in my view, violate the Constitution and yet have received judicial approval. Though Warren is very much excited about the alleged infringements he cites, he apparently is not much disturbed by a long line of Supreme Court decisions upholding state and federal legislation *against* freedom of press, speech, and civil rights generally.

DR. SMYTH: What about Judge Ranyin's statement that Supreme Court Justices are above partisanship? I presume he meant that they ought to be above partisanship, for he has been vociferous in contending that President Franklin D. Roosevelt's Judges are just New Deal judges. Perhaps he thinks that until the New Deal all Justices were above partisanship. If so, that is a question of historical fact which a study of history can answer.

BEARD: If partisanship is taken in the narrow sense to mean that Judges of the Supreme Court have perverted the Constitution and the law to serve some low interests of party managers, I think it would be true to historical facts to maintain that the Supreme Court has been remarkably free from partisanship. There have been a few cases in which traces of political jobbery have appeared, but they are so few that they may be discarded and the Supreme Court acquitted of partisanship in this sense.

But in the larger sense of grand public policies espoused by political parties, the Supreme Court has not been above and indifferent to the great conflicting interests of parties. On the contrary, the Justices on that bench have reflected those interests in the momentous cases of American history—such as the Dred Scott case of 1857, the Legal Tender cases of 1872, the income tax case of 1895, the Insular cases after the Spanish war, and some of the New Deal cases. This is not to say that the Justices of the Court in such cases always divide according to their party labels. They do not. Nor indeed do hot partisans in general divide sharply over such issues. There are Republicans sympathetic to the New Deal, and there are Democrats who have fought it from the beginning.

MRS. SMYTH: I should think that one test would be whether, in selecting Supreme Court Justices, Presidents have been indifferent to party considerations and chosen freely or equally from both parties. If it is just a matter of getting a competent lawyer who knows the Constitution, then Presidents might choose men outside their party about as often as they do men inside. For instance President Roosevelt appointed Harlan Stone Chief Justice after the resignation of Mr. Hughes and Mr. Stone is a Republican. How many such cases of such nonpartisanship have there been in our history?

BEARD: Not many. I recall only two offhand. Let us look at the roll:

President Washington nominated three Chief Justices in his time —Jay, Rutledge, and Ellsworth. All Federalists. Not a Jeffersonian Republican among them.

President Adams nominated John Marshall, an ardent Federalist politician, to succeed Ellsworth; and Marshall held on until his death in 1835, handing down decisions reflecting the great policies of the Federalist party.

The next Chief Justice was Roger B. Taney, a Democratic officeholder chosen by Andrew Jackson. Taney held on to the place until his death in 1864. In none of his great opinions did Taney get far off the Democratic line of policy.

It was Lincoln's lot to select Taney's successor, and he chose Salmon P. Chase, a former Democrat, who had been head of the Treasury Department under Lincoln and wanted the Republican nomination in 1864. A zealous politician if there ever was one.

After Chase came, first, Morrison R. Waite and then Melville Fuller. Waite was a good, sound, though not fierce, Republican, picked by President Grant. Fuller was a good, sound, active Democrat, nominated by President Cleveland.

Then came the first political break in the historic rule. President Taft elevated Edward D. White, of Louisiana, a Democrat, to the place of Chief Justice. White was a good, sound, conservative like Taft, but a party Democrat, no Bryan Democrat.

The next Chief Justice was William H. Taft, nominated by President Harding. As to their party politics, no comment is necessary.

After Taft's resignation, President Hoover selected Charles E. Hughes. No comment on party politics is needed here.

With the elevation of Justice Harlan Stone to the Chief Justiceship by President Roosevelt came the second break. It would seem then that, unless we count Chase as a Democrat, there have been only two departures from the political rule as to Chief Justices since the organization of the Supreme Court under the Constitution.

DR. SMYTH: But all of President Roosevelt's other appointees to the Court were good, sound New-Deal Democrats—Black, Reed, Murphy, Douglas, Frankfurter, Jackson, Byrnes, and Rutledge. Stone had often been favorable to the New Deal in his opinions. President Roosevelt did not make Owen Roberts Chief Justice, for Roberts had been what you call a good, sound Republican. He would scarcely have dared to make Murphy or any of his other appointees Chief Justice. Besides, he needed some age and dignity in the Court. Give me that list of Chief Justices. I want to show it to Judge Ranyin and ask him whether he still thinks that the Supreme Court is above partisanship. As a doctor of medicine I do not know a thing about jurisprudence, but I need only common sense to see through a hole in a millstone.

BEARD: Here is the list and also a list of all the other Supreme Court Justices since the creation of the Court under President Washington, with annotations relative to their politics and their appointments. Look it over.

DR. SMYTH, dryly, after running through the list: This very string of facts indicates to me that there has been a lot of partisanship in the narrow sense of the term.

BEARD: In some appointments, perhaps so, but my rule still holds good, namely, that even partisan judges have seldom, if ever, sunk to the level of petty politics, although they have often sustained or struck at actions involving grand national politics. It is right here that they have displayed their power, for good or ill. Yet I would warn you that the work of the Court is not all on dramatic cases. What it does by decisions and opinions relative to routine matters, in the aggregate may well outweigh in terms of national interest and welfare its actions in highly controversial cases.

As a recognized center of power, places in the Supreme Court have been the objects of ambitious men and a concern of party managers since the early days of the Constitution. It is true that John Jay, first Chief Justice, thought that the Court was of relatively little importance and esteemed more highly the governorship of New York, to which he was elected after serving as minister extraordinary to Great Britain. And in 1801 he refused re-appointment as Chief Justice. That, however, was a temporary and exceptional view. Washington and John Adams, by their appointments, committed the Court to trusted Federalists. But certainly from Marshall's day onward, many ambitious men have looked upon membership in the Court as an opportunity for the exercise of power, as well as a place of honor and dignity, and have sought to attain it by various methods of political maneuvering.

MRS. SMYTH: Innocently no doubt, I have always thought of that membership as an honor which went to great lawyers, with no seeking or political maneuvering on their part.

BEARD: There are of course a number of cases in which the honor has apparently gone to men who have not sought it or perhaps even permitted their friends to seek it for them. But John P. Frank recently published in the Wisconsin *Law Review* articles on "The Appointment of Supreme Court Justices: Prestige, Principles, and Politics," and he conclusively explodes the idea that great lawyers and politicians always wait quietly, without expectancy, until a discerning President, after surveying the geniuses of the country, finds them to be just the right men for the Supreme Court.

Beveridge in his *Life of John Marshall* says that John Adams nominated Marshall as Chief Justice 'without previous notification even to himself.' That may be so but it is the kind of statement that no historian can prove. Marshall was then (and for several weeks after) Adams' Secretary of State, and they were intimately associated in office. It may be that Adams nominated Marshall without asking him whether he would accept.

For many of the later Justices the records are ample and convincing. They permit us to say that ambitious men, usually though not always active politicians, have zealously sought membership on the Court and employed great ingenuity in their own behalf. William Howard Taft's early ambition was to be a Justice of the Supreme Court. After the election of Harding in 1920, as Pringle shows in his *Life and Times of William Howard Taft,* Mr. Taft made a point of visiting Harding, enlisted the interest of Harry Daugherty in his behalf, and, with great trepidation of spirit, pulled wires to secure the Chief Justiceship. His labors were successful, thanks partly to Daugherty's sympathetic co-operation. And no man in the United States was more concerned than Taft with getting the right kind of justices for the Court—that is, good, sound conservatives who held his own views respecting the powers and functions of the Court. From Washington to Franklin D. Roosevelt, Presidents have recognized the fact that the Supreme Court is a center of great power and have tried to select justices in general sympathy with their policies. This rule applies to Republicans and Democrats alike.

And why not? The Supreme Court is not a group of disembodied spirits operating in a vacuum on logical premises that express or affect none of the powerful interests over which party conflicts rage. In a refined but none the less real way, its members express these conflicts of interest. It would be preposterous for a President who believes that his policies are sound and constitutional to nominate judges who hold opposite views—judges who would declare his policies unconstitutional. Presidents are sometimes disappointed in details but in the general run they get what they expect.

DR. SMYTH: I remember hearing that Theodore Roosevelt was disappointed—yes, angry—because Justice Holmes did not decide some cases to suit him.

BEARD: That is true. But one of the reasons Theodore Roosevelt assigned for nominating Holmes was the progressive views on labor and social legislation Holmes had expounded as judge in Massachusetts. These views Holmes continued to expound as a Justice of the Supreme Court throughout his entire career in that tribunal. As we have learned in our sessions, there are few rules in politics without exceptions. If there were no rules, however, there would be chaos in government and society.

DR. SMYTH: But Justices of the Supreme Court abstain from politics after they are appointed, however active they have been previously?

BEARD: Though in general they abstain from active participation in party politics, here again there have been exceptions. A number of Justices during the past hundred years have actively, if quietly, carried on underground campaigns to get the nomination for the presidency. I know of no evidence that Justice Charles E. Hughes worked to get the Republican nomination in 1916; still he got it and resigned from the Court to run for President. Many Justices while in service on the bench have maintained intimate relations with their party brother in the White House, and have advised him in law, tactics, and strategy. There is some popular resentment at this, but the practice has been common to the latest hour.

MRS. SMYTH: At least they do not make political speeches for their party brother in the White House.

BEARD: Campaign speeches, no. At all events I never heard of any case under that head, although Justices have occasionally been accused of injecting campaign speeches into their opinions, sometimes with an eye to their own political prospects. Yet Justices of the Supreme Court have gone around making speeches in support of presidential policies. Speaking more politely, we should perhaps call them addresses. They are usually delivered on ceremonial occasions, such as the Fourth of July, or at commencements when Justices receive honorary degrees from colleges and universities.

Going to my files I brought out an armful of speeches by Supreme Court Justices and judicial opinions savoring of the stump, and spread them out on a table.

Mrs. Smyth: I see a reason for classifying these papers by presidential administrations but what are all these curious underscores and check-marks?

Beard: The lines underscore the passages in addresses and opinions by Supreme Court Justices that correspond to pertinent presidential or party policies. The check-marks indicate the precise presidential or party statements which correspond to the judicial utterances *seriatim*. Here is a good one. This is an address delivered by a Supreme Court Justice at a college commencement. In parallel columns you see, on one side, this Justice's declaration of American faith and, on the other side, his President's declaration of 'my policies' to which the Justice's beliefs correspond.

Evidently fascinated by these exhibits, the Smyths examined many of them, folder by folder, commenting with amusement and astonishment as they came across distinguished names with which they were especially familiar.

Mrs. Smyth, taking up one clipping: Why, I heard that address when I went to a college class reunion. I was deeply moved by it. I thought it was magnificent. The Justice looked so grand in his robes and spoke with great fervor. Now I fear that he was merely dishing out White House policies. Here is another one in which the Justice makes a subtle attack on Wilson's New Freedom policies. Here is another one, in which the Justice seems to think that things have not been right since Grover Cleveland's time. This is positively the most entertaining collection of orations I have ever seen.

DR. SMYTH: They may be entertaining, but I think the whole business is a shame. Supreme Court Justices should not be traveling around the country making addresses that are ill-disguised political speeches. I almost think that it is a shame for you to have collected and annotated these papers.

BEARD: In other words, you hold it disgraceful for anyone who is studying a subject to try to find out all he can about it. I do not call it a shame for Justices of the Supreme Court to be running in and out of the White House or making addresses upholding or criticizing presidential policies. I really believe that it is dangerous to the country, in that it impairs the dignity and influence of the Court which gives it power in protecting civil liberties against arbitrary or tyrannical action on the part of Congress and the President.

MRS. SMYTH: It also shows that some of the Justices have been men of small minds or men capable of subordinating their duties as Justices to the policies of other men. They should not be making speeches at all, in my opinion. They ought to attend to their judicial business.

BEARD: Justices are human beings. Some of them have been small men. I have no objection to their being decorated with honorary degrees if they want such baubles, or to their making addresses if they get any satisfaction out of that. I merely think that they should be careful. They do not have the power of the purse or the sword but they have a power of the spirit, not an unlimited power, but an undoubted power associated with their high office. In my judgment they can easily impair that power by indiscretions in public addresses and in judicial opinions. For the sake of civil liberties and self-government throughout the country, they should be everlastingly on guard against every form of utterance that might diminish the respect of the nation for them—for the power of their spirit in matters of liberty, public welfare, and self-government.

DR. SMYTH: That seems sound to me, but, in your care for civil liberties, you are laying stress on the negative power of the Supreme Court—the power to declare legislative and executive acts void. That is power, I admit, yet negative power.

BEARD: But it is not wholly negative. Sometimes the Court holds a state law unconstitutional only as interpreted and applied in the particular case. By its opinion in this instance, it may guide state officials to proper ways of enforcing the act. When the Court does declare a law void as written, it does not necessarily close the door on all legislation of the kind. If it blocks the actions of police officials in a case involving civil liberty, it does by implication, and may often by direct statements of its opinion, tell those police officials how to observe the provisions of the Constitution on human rights.

Negation, as I have said before, may be a form of constructive or creative proposal or suggestion. Whenever the Court deals with the validity of a legislative or executive act, it deals with questions of public policy and private rights, of governmental power and freedom. And we must not forget that in cases properly brought before it the Court influences, if it does not absolutely control, the actions of all inferior judges and courts, federal and state, involving public policies and civil liberties.

It is a tribunal to which the humblest private citizen may appeal through counsel with full confidence that, if the Court finds his plea lawful, he will be decently and respectfully heard, without scorn, browbeating, and contempt.

Dr. SMYTH: That reminds me of a case in one of our local courts in which the judge, instead of acting as an impartial arbiter, lectured witnesses and poured both ridicule and contempt on the defendant, right before the jury. He overruled every objection to such abuse that the lawyer for the defendant made. He ordered that lawyer to sit down when he was making what seemed to me to be a fair attempt to dissipate the air of prejudice the judge himself had created.

Mrs. SMYTH: I suppose you have a bushel of notes on such incidents.

BEARD: I have a load of them that I could bring in. I'll just show you a copy of an address by Charles E. Hughes to the Harvard Law Alumni in 1920. In this address, Hughes expressed alarm over the way judges, prosecuting attorneys, and juries went to excesses in condemning persons tried under various sedition acts during the First World War; and he wondered whether, in view of the terrible precedents, the Constitution could survive another great war, even if victoriously waged.

The gruesome story is told with quiet eloquence by Zechariah Chafee in his *Free Speech in the United States* (new edition, 1942). In this survey Chafee shows that one of the grave dangers inherent in vaguely phrased sedition laws is the loose and vindictive way judges of the lower courts can interpret and enforce them, with the aid of loud-mouthed prosecutors, often engaged in trying to advance themselves in politics by pandering to the temporary passions of overwrought citizens. It is necessary for us to remember, therefore, the power the Supreme Court has in reviewing and overriding judges, prosecutors, and juries in the lower courts. If, by its own ineptitude and folly, the Court loses its spiritual appeal to the nation, then the last safeguard for civil liberties is shattered. Then the private citizen will be deprived of the one tribunal to which he can now go for relief.

DR. SMYTH: But he always can appeal to his member of Congress and perhaps get a hearing, if not redress, before a congressional committee.

BEARD: A citizen in jail charged with criticizing the Government has a small chance of getting a hearing before a congressional committee. Judging by the experience of the past twenty-five years with congressional committees in charge of bills pertaining to civil liberties, the citizen, even if not accused of any crime, stands a better chance of being browbeaten and ridiculed by one or more committee members than he does of getting a quiet judicial hearing. Some of the worst and most ignorant enemies of constitutional rights have been and are members of Congress. In no case is a citizen who protests against sedition bills likely to obtain from a congressional committee as a whole the kind of solemn, dignified, and even-tempered hearing that the Supreme Court provides.

MRS. SMYTH: You mean, if he can afford a competent lawyer and the expense of getting there to be heard. One evening, not long ago, you referred somewhat caustically off the record to a recent decision of the Supreme Court holding that the right of a man accused of a serious crime to have a counsel assigned to him by the trial court is not a right guaranteed by the Constitution. I remember also your surprise at finding Justices Stone and Frankfurter voting to uphold this inhuman doctrine, as you called it.

BEARD: I was a bit hot about that decision and hotter still about the black-letter sophistry employed by Justice Roberts in the opinion of the Court. I gave thanks that Justices Black, Douglas, and Murphy dissented and fairly blistered their brethren of the majority. Undoubtedly there is a deficiency in this respect. As a general rule federal and state courts do assign counsel to persons unable to employ counsel, but there are exceptions in state courts. In some state and local courts, only poor persons accused of the graver crimes are allowed free counsel.

Lawyers point out, and so did the Supreme Court in the Maryland case, that if free counsel were allowed to paupers in every case, then persons accused of petty violations of the traffic laws should have lawyers assigned to defend them.

But common sense tells us that a distinction may be made between trivial crimes and grave crimes. In the Maryland case, in which the Supreme Court denied the right of counsel, the accused had been condemned to prison for eight years on conviction for robbery. In my view there ought to be a public defender connected even with petty courts for the purpose of affording defense to persons charged with petty crimes and unable to pay for counsel. Great criminals are sometimes made by the mistreatment of petty criminals or of innocent persons. Here is a field for constructive work, and there already are public defenders in a few jurisdictions.

This illustrates the point I have often made, namely, that by its decisions and opinions the Supreme Court of the United States may operate with tremendous effect in the development of grand justice in the United States, filling it with the concreteness of daily and hourly practice. My phrase grand justice acquires real meaning from the action and language of Justice Hugo Black in the case of Chambers et al. *v.* Florida.

MRS. SMYTH: Oh, tell us about Justice Black. We know only the bitter words exchanged over his nomination to the Court. Do you know him? Have you ever met him personally?

BEARD: I cannot say that I *know* him—or myself either. But I had the curious experience of passing a completely impersonal judgment on him. It happened, in 1934, as I recall the year, that I was invited to speak at a little dinner in Washington attended by several Senators, Representatives, government officials and their wives. I had never met Mr. Black, had never seen him. In the seating arrangement at the dinner, I was placed on the left of a gentleman whose name I did not get when I was introduced to him.

During the dinner, we talked casually about many subjects. My neighbor was evidently interested deeply in history and well versed in it. He asked me a number of questions about land tenure in ancient Rome, in Europe, and in the United States. Out of my slight knowledge of the subject I made the best answers I could and named a number of important books on it. My unknown neighbor's discussion of my answers and of the books I mentioned showed that he had made scholarly searches on his own account. His information and his discernment, the gravity of his spirit, his eagerness to get at the bottom of things, his judicial temper in weighing my objections to some of his views, all awakened in me an extraordinary interest in the nameless personality on my right. In our give and take over hot contemporary questions, about which we differed squarely as to various points, he displayed the same high qualities. As soon as the affair was over, I drew the chairman of the meeting into a corner and asked him to write on my card the name of the man who had sat on my right at the table. Then I learned that this unknown man, on whom I had passed an impersonal judgment, was Senator Hugo Black!

Mrs. Smyth: That *is* a story. It must be a good thing to be deaf sometimes and not know to whom you are talking. It makes your judgment more objective. I am glad to hear this story. Until this moment, I had mere impressions as to Mr. Black's qualities, some rather bad impressions gathered from reading critical editorials during the fight against his confirmation by the Senate. Please tell us now about the Chambers case.

Beard: The Chambers case was decided in 1940. Justice Black wrote the opinion that sustained the decision. It was a case of four Negroes accused of murder in Florida, arrested, subjected to a third-degree treatment, which wrung vague confessions of guilt from them, and finally condemned to death. They claimed that they had been cruelly treated by Florida officials and that they were about to be deprived of life and liberty without the due process of law guaranteed to all by the Constitution of the United States. Through counsel they applied to the Supreme Court for relief, *in forma pauperum,* as paupers; and the Court, reversing the decision of the Supreme Court of Florida against the Negroes, saved their lives and released them from prison.

In his opinion, which will ring with power as long as liberty and justice are cherished in our country, Justice Black reviewed the third-degree treatment meted out to the Negroes by Florida officials, and asserted, with moderated eloquence, great American principles

of civil liberty. The whole document ought to be read by all citizens
who care for the perpetuity of the Republic, but we have time for
only a few passages:

As assurance against ancient evils, our country, in order to preserve
'the blessings of liberty,' wrote into its basic law the requirement,
among others, that the forfeiture of the lives, liberties or property
of people accused of crime can only follow if procedural safeguards
of due process have been obeyed.

The determination to preserve an accused's right to procedural due
process sprang in large part from knowledge of the historical truth
that the rights and liberties of people accused of crime could not be
safely entrusted to secret inquisitorial processes. The testimony of
centuries, in governments of varying kinds over populations of different races and beliefs, stood as proof that physical and mental torture
and coercion had brought about the tragically unjust sacrifices of
some who were the noblest and most useful of their generations. The
rack, the thumbscrew, the wheel, solitary confinement, protracted
questioning and cross questioning, and other ingenious forms of
entrapment of the helpless or unpopular had left their wake of
mutilated bodies and shattered minds along the way to the cross,
the guillotine, the stake and the hangman's noose. And they who have
suffered most from secret and dictatorial proceedings have almost
always been the poor, the ignorant, the numerically weak, the friend-
less, and the powerless. . . .

For five days petitioners were subjected to interrogations culminat-
ing in Saturday's (May 20th) all-night examination. Over a period
of five days they steadily refused to confess and disclaimed any
guilt. The very circumstances surrounding their confinement and
their questioning without any formal charges having been brought,
were such as to fill petitioners with terror and frightful misgivings.
Some were practical strangers in the community; three were arrested
in a one-room farm tenant house which was their home; the haunting
fear of mob violence was around them in an atmosphere charged with
excitement and public indignation. From virtually the moment of
their arrest until their eventual confessions, they never knew just
when any one would be called back to the fourth-floor room, and
there, surrounded by his accusers and others, interrogated by men
who held their very lives—so far as these ignorant petitioners could
know—in the balance. The rejection of petitioner Woodward's first

'confession,' given in the early hours of Sunday morning, because it was found wanting, demonstrates the relentless tenacity which 'broke' petitioners' will and rendered them helpless to resist their accusers further. To permit human lives to be forfeited upon confessions thus obtained would make of the constitutional requirement of due process of law a meaningless symbol.

We are not impressed by the argument that law enforcement methods such as those under review are necessary to uphold our laws. The Constitution proscribes such lawless means irrespective of the end. And this argument flouts the basic principle that all people must stand on an equality before the bar of justice in every American Court. Today, as in ages past, we are not without tragic proof that the exalted power of some governments to punish manufactured crime dictatorially is the handmaid of tyranny. Under our constitutional system, courts stand against any winds that blow as havens of refuge for those who might otherwise suffer because they are helpless, weak, outnumbered, or because they are non-conforming victims of prejudice and public excitement. Due process of law, preserved for all by our Constitution, commands that no such practice as that disclosed by this record shall send any accused to his death. No higher duty, no more solemn responsibility, rests upon this Court, than that of translating into living law and maintaining this constitutional shield deliberately planned and inscribed for the benefit of every human being subject to our Constitution—of whatever race, creed or persuasion.

MRS. SMYTH: That is a fitting climax to our study tonight. Now I understand your feeling—may I call it *mental feeling?*—about the Supreme Court, what it is and may be in our national life. I had always thought of it as a mysterious arcanum for lawyers, far beyond comprehension by ordinary mortals like myself. Yet it is really power; it may be grandly human power! I should think that the Justices of the Court would be overwhelmed by the sense of their responsibility. Surely all the people of the United States should know and appreciate its role in the maintenance of our Republic. Vibrating through Justice Black's clear and simple English appears that personality which you have just described to us.

Dr. Smyth himself seemed deeply moved and, as we parted, expressed his feelings in a handgrip tighter than usual.

XVII

Critique of the Federal System

WE were a long time in getting to the agenda for our seven-teenth meeting, for a tragic death in our community that morning had stirred the whole town. We found it hard to shake off the pall of private grief and turn our minds to what seemed to be remote—public affairs. After exchanging views on the sad occurrence and wondering over and over again how it happened, we managed to shift our thought to the theme of the evening. In fact, catching myself up short, I realized the futility of dwelling on an incident about which we knew little and could discover no more by exchanging idle guesses. So I deliberately diverted attention from the subject.

BEARD: At our seminar on Congress you expressed the desire to devote a session to what you called a critique of our federal system. It would be helpful to have before us at the outset your ideas on the subject. That would prevent us from just shooting in the dark.

DR. SMYTH: I have tried to conjure up a little competence for this meeting by putting on my thinking cap. You know and I know that 'we, the people' as newspaper readers have gathered from news columns and editorials a number of criticisms, sometimes definite, sometimes vague, to the effect that our federal system is out of date, is not fitted for the times in which we live. Not long ago, while the New Deal battle was on, the Supreme Court was attacked for block-ing the will of the people. The President was criticized with equal severity for trying to override the Court rough-shod.

Now Congress is assailed for blocking grand projects proposed by the President, again as a crowd of rubber stamps, or as plain dunder-heads and nincompoops. Years ago President Harding was de-nounced as a weak President who always yielded to the politicians in Congress. Afterward Coolidge was ridiculed as a do-nothing

President and Hoover as a bewildered President. From time to time we have a crop of political scandals which certainly add nothing to the credit of our system of government.

Perhaps the major part of the criticism comes under the caption that our political machinery, made for a small country mainly rural in economy, is not fitted for our industrial age, for managing and regulating an economy that is technological and national in scope. This impression I have gathered from reading and talking with men of affairs. For instance, down at the Union Club not long ago, several of us had a confab with John Shuttleford, a big man in the manufacturing field. Shuttleford is a considerate fellow who refused to join the hate-Roosevelt crowd. He tried to go along with the Roosevelt administration as best he could, and his relations with labor are known to be steady and friendly. So he is no common grouser.

Shuttleford told us that, much to his regret, he doubted whether our eighteenth-century political machine could much longer stand the strain of dealing with complex economic matters, even to the minimum amount necessary to public safety. And he questioned whether it was capable of administering the measures absolutely required to prevent periodical depressions from producing revolutionary discontent. He was of the opinion that many government functions, such as boondoggling, should and could be lopped off, but that it was foolish to expect a return to the few and simple government functions that existed when as a young man he first entered business.

One of our group asked him a question about the tyrannical bureaucracy, and Shuttleford astonished his business companions by saying that there is a great deal of plain bunk in such talk. A lawyer present retorted that it would be all right if Congress would make laws in detail and not enact blanket statutes for bureaucrats to fill in by their harebrained decrees. The lawyer argued that there should be easy appeals to the Courts against all orders and decrees of the bureaucrats. Shuttleford replied that this was all theoretical; that in practice any such reform would hamstring business, at least a lot of manufacturing concerns.

He then gave an example out of his experiences. His concern manufactures machinery for steamships. In the interest of safety at sea there are federal laws regulating construction, he went on to say. Everybody knows that this is absolutely necessary to prevent the use of unseaworthy vessels by owners greedy for profits at all risks. The federal laws in this case occupy only a few printed pages. The details are worked out by engineers who know the shipbuilding business.

Turning to the lawyer, Shuttleford remarked very quietly: 'The orders and regulations issued by what you call the bureaucrats under these few pages of law fill a book of two or three hundred pages of fine print. If Congress enacted all the engineers' specifications into law, the statute would be out of date in a few weeks owing to rapid changes in ship machinery and construction. In this case the law simply *must* be general with the details left to federal administrators.

'In all my years, I have tried to be reasonable and have never had any trouble with the federal steamboat inspectors. Often we have forty or fifty cases in a year to be settled with the inspectors. I should go crazy if I had to prove every technical case in engineering to a committee of Congress. Besides I should be bankrupt if I had to wait on Congress for necessary modifications in legislation.'

Keeping his eyes on the lawyer, Shuttleford continued: 'Now as to your idea of appealing to the Courts every time I have an objection to a ruling by the Steamboat Inspection Service. I did appeal once, on good legal advice. I had to spend precious days in court with my engineers. The lawyers did not know a thing about engineering. The engineers knew nothing about law. The judges knew nothing about engineering. At no time during the trial of the case could I discover whether the wordy disputes were over law or over the type of construction necessary for installing a given type of pumping machinery. What a headache! I won the case at the end of two years and, so help me God, by that time a change in construction and installation made the devices we were disputing about as obsolete as oxcarts. Courts are all right for some things, but henceforward I am going to deal with bureaucrats.'

BEARD, as Dr. Smyth paused: Please go on with Shuttleford. It is like a breath of fresh air from the world of reality. I have always liked him. His exterior is cold but he is always courteous in an even way. Let us hear more from him.

DR. SMYTH: There is not much more to tell. Shuttleford, modestly declaring that he is no statesman, called for reforms in our system of government along the following lines: Congress ought to be smaller; the number of Senators from what he called grasshopper states ought to be reduced; the hullabaloo national party conventions ought to be abolished and the President be elected by Congress; and there ought to be a small legislative council composed of members from both houses, in constant session, working with the President and his administrators in interpreting and enforcing laws. Shuttleford admitted that the chances of effecting these reforms were slight. He closed with the words: 'I am worried. I fear that people will not see the necessity of revamping our old political machinery to fit modern industrial conditions or that such reforms may be delayed until we run into a smash which will make the breakdown of 1933 look like a tea party.'

BEARD: Well, Mrs. Smyth, your husband seems to have gathered in a lot of ideas for a critique of our federal system. Have you other suggestions?

MRS. SMYTH: After the question of a session on criticism came up, I wrote out at home on this sheet of paper a few topics, which I shall 'read into the record':

What about the scandals that constantly rise in our great cities from the operations of bosses and political machines, such as Hague's in Jersey City or the Kelly-Nash crowd in Chicago?

Since the Federal Government is spending so much money in our local cities and communities and building up armies of officeholders and recipients of federal funds, aren't our states and local governments in danger of losing their independence?

If this local independence, this local practice in self-government, is destroyed, what will happen to the spirit of the citizens and to the country at large?

Supposing that this increasing centralization continues, will the states and local units become mere shells and perhaps be abolished?

I realize that our communities depend on industries large and small, which in turn depend on the national and international market. I feel that Mr. Shuttleford is right in insisting upon the necessity of a big federal regulating machine to make constant adjustments in business and finance. So I am wondering, with shuddering horror, whether there is something in fascism or communism. I do not mean in the fantastic and cruel notions associated with these systems, but in the acceptance of strong, centralized, almost dictatorial government. To subject our whole economic life to the changing winds and storms of party politics may well become dangerous—impossible. I hear people who dislike fascism and communism, as heartily as I do, talk this way. How much of our liberty and self-government, how much of constitutionalism can we retain and at the same time keep our national economy going in a way to provide the people with the conditions needed for a decent community and nation?

BEARD: You have given me a large order composed of many specific items, some of them widely scattered from any center I can easily visualize. The best way for me to proceed, I think, is to concentrate your related items under the best formula I can devise, and to consider this covering formula first, leaving the odds and ends of criticisms for separate treatment.

The most exact formula I can hit upon is: *Our federal political machinery, devised for a simple agricultural society, is not competent to resolve efficiently the issues forced upon government by the needs of our great industrial nation.*

That, I take it, is also the substance of the complaint by Mr. Shuttleford.

What is the nature of this inefficiency?

Congress seems powerless to initiate important legislation. There are constant conflicts between Congress and the President and within the branches of the executive department. Hence endless delays and endless bickerings.

If the President and Congress are deadlocked over a vital question, there is no way of compelling them to reach a rational adjustment or of appealing to the voters at a general election; that is, allowing the people to settle the dispute in a short time.

The two Houses of Congress are so organized, with committees and special privileges for senior members, that it often takes months, even years, to get a desirable bill through Congress—if the President does not drive it through.

Perhaps worst of all, or a part of it all, is the utter irresponsibility of executive officials and members of Congress. They can dodge, intrigue underground, or emit clouds of ink like cuttlefish, to obscure the issues and confuse the public.

DR. SMYTH: That is a pretty neat way of putting most of the case in a nutshell.

BEARD: I am not quite through yet. In this criticism it is generally assumed that legal responsibility to the people makes for efficiency.

MRS. SMYTH: I should say that it makes for democracy but not necessarily for efficiency. Many of our corrupt and wasteful political machines in cities are elected by the people, stand in well with the people, and are kept in power for years by the people. In the days when we had prohibition, thousands of Americans were willing to accept the waste of municipal money by politicians as long as they could buy their beer and whisky under the noses of police officials. In other words, they preferred liberty to honesty and efficiency.

BEARD: Your statement is all right, but it is a common assumption that responsibility or accountability to the people works for competence and efficiency in government as well as for democracy. To put it the other way around: democracy is weighted on the side of efficiency, directness, and the exercise of intelligence in the conduct of government. It is on this basis that able critics of our federal system have demanded the abolition of our presidential-congressional system and the adoption of parliamentary government instead. Henry Hazlitt has recently argued persuasively for such a reconstruction of our system in his book *A New Constitution Now* and in special articles on the subject. His book I regard as a clear and effective criticism of our system of checks and balances and, within the logic of his theory, a cogent argument for a parliamentary scheme of government.

Mrs. Smyth wrote the title of Mr. Hazlitt's book on a library card and engaged the Doctor in a conversation as to the best procedure to be followed during the rest of the evening. At the conclusion of their colloquy, MRS. SMYTH reported the upshot:

Our theme tonight is above all a critique of our own system of government, to which the parliamentary form presents certain contrasts. Just what are the features of the parliamentary form which are marked departures from our system—features which critics propose to substitute for specific features of our own type? Suppose that you dwell at length upon this question, taking your time, without interruption from us until we have a fairly complete picture before us.

BEARD: Thus instructed, I list the following essentials of parliamentary government, especially as operated in Great Britain, to be contrasted with the presidential-congressional-judicial system:

1. The chief executive or premier is chosen, not independently by the voters, but by a conference of the majority party in the legislature, thus informally by the legislature. In practice the actual selection of the premier is more devious. There is a higgling among the members of the majority. The choice is usually narrowed to the two or more members of that majority who by long service and talents are marked for the office by a kind of natural selection.

2. The cabinet officers who serve under the premier as a rule come from the same party as the premier and are selected, with his consent, by the same method of higgling within the party conference.

3. A true parliamentary system requires a legislature of one chamber or a legislature in which one chamber, like the House of Commons in Great Britain, is supreme for practical, operating purposes. If there were two chambers of equal powers, deadlocks between them could arise, and thus what are called the evils of the check and balance system would prevent the smooth working of the parliamentary machine.

4. Parliamentary government is a kind of hair-trigger government. The political party which wins a majority in the legislature by that fact wins the indisputable right to choose the premier and all cabinet officers. The executive is in theory a servant of the legislature. The majority in the legislature can resolve to turn the executive out of office at any time by an adverse vote on an important issue. On the other hand the executive in such a cabinet crisis has a certain degree of independence. The whole cabinet may refuse to obey the legislature, resign, and allow the legislature to choose its successor. Or it may advise the Crown to dissolve the legislature, call a new election, appeal to the people. If it wins a majority in the new legislature, it continues to hold office. If it loses, it automatically goes out of power and is supplanted by a cabinet presumed to represent the latest expression of popular will.

Under this system members of the legislature and the executive do not hold office for any fixed term of years as in the case of our Representatives, Senators, and President. According to the theory, the cabinet and the parliament retain power as long as they correctly reflect the most up-to-date sentiment of the country. There may be a law requiring an election at least every five or seven years, but the parliament may repeal that law and extend terms indefinitely. If there are clashes between the cabinet and the legislature, two or more elections may be held in the same year. If no clashes occur, there is supposed to be no need for an election.

The hair-trigger feature of the system lies in this: at any moment the political gun may go off. If, at any moment, on any issue of weight, the legislature breaks with the executive, it may force a resignation of the cabinet or a new election. Or if the executive, in conflict with the legislature, believes that the legislature does not have the confidence of the country, the executive can force a dissolution of that body.

Thus there can be no long deadlocks between the executive and the legislature, such as produce delays, inaction, and confusion under the American system of divided powers. The will of the majority in the election of the legislature immediately prevails, and that will can be discovered at a new election at any time.

5. Under the parliamentary system, the executive is directly and constantly responsible to the legislature and can be held to responsibility by threats of an adverse vote. The executive has the power of initiating the budget—the program of expenditures and taxes. It also has the power of initiating all important measures on legislation. Private members of the legislature have certain rights of initiating legislation, even measures involving expenditures and taxes, but these rights are very limited.

6. The premier and other members of the cabinet in the parliamentary system are as a rule members of the legislature, chosen in the regular course of legislative elections. They have seats in the legislature; they may be heard there at will in support of their measures; they may be questioned there as to matters of administration— law enforcement—large and small. They may force a concentration of the able minds in the legislature on great measures of public interest. Thus they are able to prevent prolix and irrelevant discussions and to bring debates to a focus at any moment on matters of high significance to the nation.

In this way the best minds of the executive serve the legislature in preparing projects of legislation and members of the legislature may constantly scrutinize all acts of the administration.

7. To complete the *logic* of the parliamentary system, the courts

of law have no power to set aside statutes as unconstitutional, for that would introduce deadlocks between the courts on the one side and the executive and the legislature on the other side.

This in brief is my formulation of the parliamentary theory of government. In practice there are many variations of detail. The system works best where there are only two great political parties, fairly equal in popular support. Where there are many political parties, as in France before 1940 or Germany during the Weimar Republic, the hair-trigger system produces almost constant clashes between cabinet and legislature and is likely in any case to paralyze government rather than strengthen it.

The theory of parliamentary government as I have formulated it rests upon certain fundamental assumptions. According to the theory, the legislature fresh from the people is sovereign, that is it can exercise practically all powers over the life, liberty, and property of the people. It is to be immediately and constantly responsive to the sentiments of the people as revealed in legislative elections. The will of the popular majority so disclosed is to be almost instantaneously expressed in the legislation and administration of the government. The responsibility of the executive to the legislature and to the country is clear and definite. The control the legislature has over the administration works for efficiency in administration. The power of the executive over legislation works for a concentration of talents on the business of legislating. In short, as the theory goes, parliamentary government is best adapted to eliminate deadlocks and confusion in government, to meet the needs of government in a complex industrial society, and to assure efficiency in administration.

MRS. SMYTH: So far you have spoken of the theory of parliamentary government. I can see that in fundamental points it is opposed to the features of our constitutional government as we have discussed them in our previous sessions. But what about practice in the long run?

BEARD: Ah, practice is another matter, even in Great Britain where the system is supposed to be in effect in its purest form. To go into practice would take months of our time. But I can declare with confidence that the introduction of parliamentary government in many other countries has not automatically worked according to the theory. The present state of France, Italy, Germany, and Yugoslavia, for instance, indicates that it may break down or may be incompetent to meet the needs of complex societies.

Parliamentary government is not like a good watch which runs regularly in all sorts of conditions. Its actual operation depends on the traditions of the country, on the experience of the people in self-government, on the number and character of the political parties or factions, and on obvious and subtle variations in civilization. Mark well, I do not say that parliamentary government was the cause of Hitler's rise to power in Germany or of France's collapse in 1940. That would be a ridiculous simplification. Nor do I say that our system of constitutional government would have worked as well or any better in Germany or France.

In the eighteenth century, radical political philosophers in Europe had a childlike faith in constitutions. Many believed that it was merely necessary to draw up the right kind of paper constitution in order to establish popular government and assure its success. More than a century's bitter experience has taught the portion of mankind capable of learning that this belief is utopian. No constitution works perfectly. To be workable, even in a limited sense, any form of government must be adapted to the traditions, political experience and habits, the prevailing economic interests, and the intellectual and moral values of the people for whom it is devised.

It is customary to speak of the common bonds of all humanity, of the natural rights all human beings enjoy, of the similarities among nations and peoples. Universal traits of mankind I have no desire to minimize or underestimate. But anybody who has studied the histories of the various nations and has traveled widely and observed closely cannot fail to be struck by fundamental divergences in the experiences, temper, economies, and social institutions of the various nations of the earth.

Civilization in the United States is by no means identical with civilization in Great Britain or any other country, despite similarities in specific features. Our history, our experience, have been in many ways unique. Our form of government has been adapted to our character and circumstances. Latin-American constitutions more or less modeled on our plan have not worked in the same way or encountered similar successes. To expect a common form of government for all nations of the earth is, in my view, a fantasy. To expect that the British parliamentary system, if adopted here, would work as it does in Great Britain, or indeed accomplish here the wonders attributed to it, is in my view also a fantasy.

Dr. Smyth: That is more gloom. You allow validity to many criticisms brought against our system. You picture the theory of parliamentary government as if it would introduce into government competency for dealing with the needs of a complex society, responsibility with reference to all official acts, and efficiency in administration. Then you straightaway declare that theory unworkable here and leave us stuck with our rigid Constitution which is responsible for our deadlocks, confusion, incompetency, and inefficiency. You admit that in a great national crisis it might break down for these very reasons. You offer no hope for adapting our form of government to the real needs of our industrial society. The chances are that in a real national calamity we may see established here a totalitarian government of one kind or another.

Beard: You have said a great deal in a few words. Before I consider the whole bill of doubts, I want to correct one of your statements. When you say that our Constitution is rigid, you repeat an idea about the Constitution which was not written into the document by the framers. It is an idea created by partisan politicians for their own interests and later repeated by foreign critics like James Bryce and by citizens who pick up their views from conversations and stray bits of news and information.

In some few respects our Constitution is rigid. The number of Senators from each state is *fixed* at two. But in vital respects our Constitution is highly flexible. The elastic clause is not the only thing elastic in it. It was intended to be flexible, adapted, as John Marshall said, to the storms of the ages. It is as flexible as American intelligence and character may make it.

A great deal of the rigidity ascribed to it is not in the Constitution itself. It is in the huge body of congressional and executive practices built up under it—precedents and practices not imposed on the country by the Constitution but self-imposed by politicians, sometimes for the very purpose of escaping responsibility and preventing the introduction of efficiency. Our Constitution is encrusted with the accumulated impediments of one hundred and fifty years. If they were scraped off, and if we seized upon the freedom to which we are entitled under the letter and spirit of the Constitution, we could work wonders without altering a line of the document.

Here I should like to qualify another one of your statements. I do not believe that even in a great national crisis we shall necessarily subject ourselves to what you call a totalitarian government of some kind or other. My guess may be wrong, but that is my belief. We passed through the crisis of the American Revolution and the crisis of the Civil War without falling into a totalitarian system, though it was then freely predicted that we would.

This we have already discussed. We may have in a great national crisis a straight military dictatorship under the President or a joint committee of Congress. But I believe that it will prove to be temporary if it ever comes. The idea of our repeating all the mental imagery, ideas, rhetoric, sentiments, and hocus-pocus of totalitarianism in Germany, Russia, or Italy seems to me so highly fanciful as to be purely speculative, for America has not been and never can be Russia, Germany or Italy, through whatever variety of untried being we may pass in the indefinite future.

I agree with you that our fortunes will depend in some considerable measure upon what we do in the way of making our government competent to meet the needs of society, and at the same time efficient in administration. But competence and efficiency, though necessary for the perdurance of a government, are not the sole ends or guarantees of government. Besides, competence in what? In making laws against liberty of opinion, such as the Alien Registration Act of 1940? Efficiency of political police in suppressing liberty of opinion and action?

The end of government in the United States at least is not mere technical efficiency, nor mere competence in specific matters, nor speed of political action, nor instant responsiveness to the will of the majority, nor the unrestricted rule of simple majorities. For us the ends are not only a more perfect Union, the establishment of justice, provision for common defense and general welfare, but also—and don't forget it—the maintenance of the blessings of liberty and the long-run service of American society. Long-run efficiency, competence, action, and deference to temporary majorities or pluralities are devices we believe necessary to achieve the social ends of government.

The philosophy of parliamentary government presents many forms of contradiction to the American system. If we adopted that type of government, we should have to abolish the Senate or reduce it to the status of a mere advisory body, in order to prevent deadlocks between the two houses of Congress. This, I am convinced, is practically impossible, given the tenacity of underlying interests, and undesirable besides. We should also have to abrogate the power of the Supreme Court to declare void acts of Congress trenching upon personal liberty. This, too, I deem undesirable and dangerous.

Under our system, momentary efficiency, speed, or competence may be sacrificed, more or less, and rightly, in the interest of mature deliberation and civil liberty; but it is long-run efficiency and competence that count in the survival of our nation. Parliamentary government puts the great issues of life, liberty, economy, and the pursuit of happiness at stake in single popular elections and places them at the mercy of a majority of the people who take the trouble to vote after the heats and distempers of a campaign.

DR. SMYTH: That lets me out. I should rather endure the risk of incompetence, inefficiency, and confusion than stake the great values of personal liberty on a single throw of the political dice. I am beginning to see that delays, bickerings, and deadlocks in politics may be the price we have to pay for such liberty, justice, and happiness as we have. I suspect also, in view of our political habits, that parliamentary government here would put a premium on factious opposition tactics. It would spur ambitious men in a restless quest for power to intrigues and maneuvers designed to oust the President and the cabinet chosen by Congress and to put members of the opposition in the vacant places of power and patronage.

There is a fine appeal in the logic of the parliamentary theory. But as you once said here, quoting Madison, it is folly to try by a pure ideal the necessities of practical situations—or something like that. In practice there are objections to any system of government, including our own, and the problem at bottom seems to be a question of balancing advantages and disadvantages. I am beginning to doubt whether Americans could be induced to adopt parliamentary government. If they did adopt it, obstructionism, delays, and incompetence might still continue; they might even be worse. *For forms of government let fools contest,* somebody has said.

BEARD: That line about forms of government is from Alexander Pope. The next line is *Whate'er is best administer'd is best.* I do not accept a thing in the couplet. Forms of government are vital to the happiness of the people. Some forms of government are better than others. Our form in general we deem best for us, and efforts to make radical changes in it in the direction of parliamentary or authoritarian government will be and ought to be contested. In my opinion those who lead in that contest would not necessarily be fools, as Pope contends.

While dissenting from Pope's doctrine, I agree with you that there would be obstructionism and factionalism in parliamentary government if it were adopted by the United States. Even Britain is not free from these proclivities of mankind. I have observed it at work in places as far apart as Paris, Berlin, Belgrade, Rome, and Tokyo. I have seen pressing public business delayed for weeks, months, years, while leaders of parties, cliques, and gangs battled and intrigued against the premier and cabinet in power.

You may think that our own factionalism is contemptible: the House fighting the Senate, Congress quarreling with the President, the President lashing out at Congress, the Supreme Court annulling laws duly passed and signed, and all that. Often the way in which these battles are carried on is disgusting. But, suppose that the Supreme Court had no power to annul laws; suppose Congress could at any moment oust the President and his cabinet, would such practices automatically disappear? My answer is, No. And greater evils would probably be added unto these.

Mrs. Smyth: I can well imagine what our Congress would look like and would do, if it had full and constant control over the President and his cabinet and all the jobs in the Executive Department. Add to that putting life, liberty, and the pursuit of happiness at the mercy of mere majorities in single congressional elections. And in such elections the party that polls the most votes does not always get a majority of the seats in the House of Representatives. In 1942 nearly half the voters did not take the trouble to vote, the Republicans received slightly over fifty per cent of the votes cast, and the Democrats got a majority of the seats! As Robert remarked, that lets me out.

Yet the old problems still haunt me. Our Government should be more competent to deal with the needs of our highly industrialized society. It should be more efficient in discharging its duties. The three departments of the Government ought to be engaged in less wrangling, ought to act more responsibly, ought to stick closer to public business.

And it has been pretty well agreed that Congress has, in a dangerous measure, surrendered its legislative function to the President. A limb that is not rightly used withers. Congress seems in peril of the kind of decline that leads to death. If Congress becomes utterly futile, we shall then be in danger of being ruled by the President alone as a sort of Caesar. That would be a sorry outcome for us. So I want to ask this question, Are there not ways of getting more competence, more efficiency, more responsibility in our Government under our Constitution pretty much as it stands now?

BEARD: You have, I think, stated very simply the supreme constitutional issue of our troubled times. I believe that we need again the kind of concentration of talents on this issue that was effected in framing the Constitution in 1787. We ought to return once more to first principles. We ought to clear away in our thought accumulated precedents and practices that hamper the establishment of competence, efficiency, and responsibility in governmental procedure.

But I do not propose to draw up for you a paper scheme for accomplishing these ends. No individual is wise enough to prescribe what is to be done. Such a prescription, like the Constitution itself, should come from the common counsel of experienced and reflective persons. Many paper plans for a new constitution were drawn up before the Convention met in 1787. Various paper plans were presented to the Convention early in its sessions. Those plans were all useful though none of them was adopted as written. The Constitution was a result of the pooling of experiences, the checking and counterchecking of ideas, adjustments, and compromises among realistic interests. So I shall merely list for you a few things which I think *might* be done to make our Government more competent, more efficient, and more responsible. My tentative suggestions are as follows:

There are now great talents in the Senate and the House of Representatives. The organization and procedure of the two bodies should be such as to effect and compel a concentration of those talents on the needs of our society.

For this purpose numerous committees, which disperse talents and waste much time, could be abolished. Some committees could be made joint committees representing both houses, as is done in the Massachusetts Legislature. Thus double hearings could be eliminated.

In each house there could be a grand committee duly elected and put in charge of all the important legislative problems. It might have subcommittees to deal with particular types of bills, but its responsibility for submitting all measures of national significance should be clear and positively fixed in legislative practice and in popular understanding.

This grand committee in each house should have such control over procedure that it could force the due consideration of its proposed measures of law and action.

This grand committee should have at its command a staff of the most competent persons in the country for investigating and reporting on the legislative needs of the nation—the best experts in the several branches of these needs. Thus the outside talents of the nation also could be concentrated on current problems of government. The work of the staff could be supplemented by public hearings on proposed measures—hearings well prepared in advance so as to avoid the meanderings and futilities that mark most of the present hearings and promote a penetrating and comprehensive review of its proposals.

With a view to giving each house ample time to deliberate upon the measures proposed by the grand committee, all petty business and irrelevant airings of opinion should be rigidly excluded by rule. Congress now wastes endless hours on trivial claims against the government, special bills such as pension petitions and other private measures. Such trivial business could all be turned over to appropriate branches of the federal administration, subject, if necessary, to review by Congress under narrow limitations as to verbiage.

There are in ordinary times seldom more than eight or ten great bills of national significance. With the multitude of minor measures out of the way, there would be ample time for full-dress debates on the great bills. By such debates the country, as well as members of Congress, could be interested in and enlightened about public business and talents dedicated to the consideration of it. Thus *competence* could be brought to bear on the issues of our society and on the conduct of government.

Under such a scheme every member of Congress would be free to introduce his own bills dealing with these issues. If he could marshal a majority in favor of his proposals, the grand committee might be compelled to consider and report on them to the house in which they originated.

Some such program would, I believe, squelch windbags in Congress, make necessary a concentration of energies and talents, eliminate the snooping committees, standing and special, and give us a more competent, more efficient, and more responsible Congress.

There remains the question of institutionalizing the relations of Congress and the President; that is making them regular, open, and dignified, instead of irregular, subterranean, and often undignified, vulgar, and capricious.

The hands of the clock on the mantel approach midnight and the subject of legislative-executive relations is as limitless as anybody's realistic imagination. So I shall finish with some mere hints.

A congressional legislative council could be created to conduct relations with the Executive. The council could consist of members chosen from the grand committees of the two houses, or could be otherwise constituted in such a way as to represent the strength of the parties in Congress. The staff of experts associated with the grand committees could also serve the legislative council. The council could sit continuously even between sessions of Congress. Stated days could be set aside for meetings of the council and the President. Apart from the President's formal messages to Congress, his communications with Congress would be through the council. The council would serve as a mediating agency between the Executive and the Legislature, adjusting controversies, working out co-operative measures and projects, and defining issues joined by the council and the President.*

---

* Happy to have support for some of the "theoretical" views I had expressed at our seventeenth seminar and to find a much better statement of the whole case by a Senator of the United States, I wrote to the Smyths as follows:

Hosannah Hill, July 8, 1943.

Dear Dr. and Mrs. Smyth,

If you will look at your current *Atlantic Monthly* you will discover an interesting article by Senator Robert M. La Follette on the very subject of our seventeenth seminar. There he states tersely and comprehensively all that I was fumbling after in our discussion. I enclose a copy of the *Congressional Record* for July 5 which contains an address by Senator La Follette to his colleagues on the need for reform in our federal system and presents a series of concrete resolutions designed to effect such reform. After you have read the article and the address you will see that we were not just wandering around in our own Wonderland.

The recent rains have been bad for hay-making at the farm but I suppose that the roof of your hospital is tight, so that your work goes on without interruption. I saw in the paper that you have fewer automobile accidents to take care of, now that gas is hard to come by.

Sincerely yours,
Charles A. Beard.

Before we begin to tinker with the system established by the Constitution, or talk about borrowing some other system from somewhere, we should have more bold, analytical, creative thought about our Government among members of the Government and the people outside. We should diminish servitude to precedents established under it. The founders of the Republic broke with precedents and set up a highly flexible scheme of government—that is, flexible to informed and daring minds. We should measure up in our times and circumstances, given our changed conditions and needs, to their example.

A great deal might be done by reforming the manners of members of Congress and Presidents—their ways of conducting themselves, using their mouths, and viewing their responsibilities. I should like to see the greatest thinkers in the United States write books on the manners and morals of government in relation to the ends of government and the instruments of efficiency and responsibility. Most of our books on government deal merely with descriptions of political and legal practices. This is the way the subject is usually taught in our institutions of learning. Then we have an abundant literature of abuse, some of which is highly useful.

Unfortunately, we have no truly magnificent works on government comparable to *The Federalist* but adapted to our needs and dealing temperately, realistically, and insistently with all that *ought* to be done to bring our government, in a multitude of ways, closer to the ideal purposes set forth in the Preamble to the Constitution. In this respect our intellectual power seems to have declined. Or has it merely been diverted to specialties such as business, private law or natural science? Can we recover it or return it to this channel?

I could go on indefinitely with the details of proposed ways of increasing competence, efficiency, and responsibility in our system of government. But I have given enough illustrations of what could be done under our Constitution to show that it is wide open to radical changes in the current ways of transacting public business. I put no special value on any of my proposals. I do not advance them as 'solutions' of the problem of competent, efficient, and responsible government. Every one of my suggestions may be fanciful. They indicate, however, that if the talents of the country were concentrated once more on the first principles of such a government, the Constitution as it now stands would give them an almost limitless scope for accomplishing the design of adapting our Government to the needs of our society.

Our troubles lie then, Dr. Smyth concluded, not so much in the rigidity of the Constitution as in our lack of political sagacity.

XVIII

Political Parties as Agencies and Motors

I
T was fortunate, Dr. Smyth opened our exchange of greetings, that last Friday evening you gave us the high-sounding title for our discussion tonight. We did not exactly grasp its meaning at the time, but we smelt something unearthly in the air. Otherwise we should have brought up with us Joe Smedge, our town boss, who is supposed to know party politics from A to Z. Joe is a smart man. For all important purposes he runs both parties, allowing small liberties to his vassals in matters that amount to nothing. He keeps all the varieties of racial tribesmen in both parties in such good humor that they never kick over the traces at election time.

He owns, I am told, the majority stock in both of our dailies, attends directors' meetings, and takes an interest in seeing that the right slant is given to the news and in the editorials. The editors of one of the papers told me, however, that while Joe did not worry much about the news stories in themselves, or the editorials, he watched headlines like a hawk, on the theory that most of his precinct captains read only the headlines, if anything. As soon as women got the vote, Joe beat the Democratic boss to the draw by installing two captains in each precinct—one safe man and one safe woman.

Joe combines business with politics and intellectual interests. In fact, he was a shrewd business man before he became our leading statesman. He was strong for Abraham Lincoln and the Grand Old Party until he got two million dollars for public works out of the Democrats in Washington during the big crash. Then he weakened a little, but he has never lost his grip on the business side of politics.

Not long ago one of the state factory inspectors condemned a safety appliance at our factory and blustered a bit. The foreman, who is one of Joe's precinct captains, settled the matter by telling the inspector that the Company had bought the appliance from Joe's machine works. He is, as I said, a smart man. But I left him down at the Theodore Roosevelt Club rooms playing pool with some friends.

Yet before I left him I asked him to tell me in a few words just what a political party is, and this is his definition: 'A political party is a lot of busy men (and women now) who do for the people everything needed in the way of government and do it soon enough to keep them satisfied.'

How's that for a scientific statement of fact?

BEARD: Ingenious, but not accurate and a little too simple. Joe has given an idealized definition of a political party. Often a party is not as bright as Joe imagines it to be. It fails to guess right on what the people need. Its sense of timing may be bad so that it hands out things too soon or too late. In such a case it may be badly defeated or indeed go to smash, like the Federalists and the Whigs long ago. Joe's theory overlooks the fact that parties sometimes come into existence for the purpose of doing things *to* the people as well as *for* them. His theory is unphilosophic in so far as it assumes that the political party is a kind of free-swinging body of persons, free to do things for and to the people at will. I sometimes think that political parties are more often the victims or agents of forces not of their own generating than independent creative motors in political life. Lincoln more than once gave expression to this idea.

MRS. SMYTH: To come right down to cases, take Joe himself. Many a time in our city he has been compelled by outraged public sentiment to do important things for the town which he had publicly and privately sworn he would never do. His vision is keen, but it is short.

BEARD: That is one trouble with politics in the United States. Too many people suppose that running a nation's government is about the same as running a city government or a factory or a business office. That is one reason why we have so many small-time politicians in Washington. Joe's theory also leaves out of account the composition of political parties—the varieties of interests in American society. It does not cover the relation of the parties to the whole of society and to the movement of ideas and interests in society. Above all, it ignores the role of fate in national history, of fate beyond the power of individuals and parties to control.

DR. SMYTH: Now you are going full steam. I knew that you would take a simple proposition like Joe's definition of a political party and run it into metaphysics.

MRS. SMYTH: Robert, I hoped you had overcome your old habit of bringing up metaphysics every time you encounter a statement that seems a little mystifying.

BEARD: William James once said in effect that metaphysics is what you have when you think long and hard enough about any subject. One of the world's greatest scientists is reported to have declared that if he could understand a grain of sand, he could understand the universe. What you call my metaphysics merely represents, I suspect, my thought about the accumulated facts I have derived from the study of the history of parties—from the factions of ancient Greece and Rome to the congressional elections of 1942 in the United States. These are facts likely to be missed by persons who confine their time-span to today.

It is owing to such facts that I put into the title for our discussion here tonight the words 'as agencies and motors.' By those words I mean that at times and in certain relations the party seems to act as a fated agency of history, of forces behind, in, and through its operations, of forces beyond its control, of forces compelling it to do things that its leaders did not intend to do, did not want to do, were violently opposed to doing. At other times and in other relations a party, or rather its leaders, seem to defy popular sentiments and to act freely, not as mere agents, but in a creative manner; by this I mean that leaders bring into being new institutions and practices despite all the force of countervailing traditions and majority desires.

MRS. SMYTH: I confess that all you have just said sounds highly abstract to me. Won't you make it more concrete by illustrations out of everyday experience, as you have done in such cases during all our study?

BEARD: The history of parties is largely the history of illustrations. I shall offer two examples.

In 1861 the Republican party came to official power in the United States. It represented a minority of the people. In the election of 1860 the Democrats had split, and no party received a majority mandate to do anything. The verdict of the majority was that nothing should be done about slavery in the states where it legally existed. As we have seen, the Republicans with Lincoln's approval were prepared to combine with Democrats and pass a constitutional amendment guaranteeing slavery forever in the South. The Republican party, though expressing some strong anti-slavery sentiments, was in leadership and in rank and file anti-abolitionist and was committed to the policy of letting slavery alone in the Southern states. Then in 1861 came the war.

The voters in the Southern states who voted for secession did not by that act deliberately vote for war. Many—how many we do not know—believed that secession could be peacefully effected and would perpetuate slavery. Whether the majorities in the secessionist states would have voted for secession if they had realized what was coming, that war, defeat and abolition were coming, we do not know. But it seems safe to guess that, if Southern voters had foreseen what was coming, their verdict would have been different.

At all events, in the consciousness of the people in 1860, the issue before the country was not war or peace. Nor was it slavery or abolition of slavery. Relatively few persons then dimly divined the issue in such terms. We now know that war and abolition were to come out of it, but the voters of 1860 did not know it. The joining of issues on war and abolition, it seems to me, took on the character of inexorable fate beyond the intention or understanding of party leaders and party members.

Dr. Smyth: That is all right for ancient history. Give us an illustration of our own time, with which we are more familiar.

Beard: I am not sure that we are more familiar with, or know more about our own time than other times, at least about the fate hidden in our time which will be revealed in coming years. But you can take the Republicans and Herbert Hoover in 1928. Look at their sweeping victory, including the majorities in Southern states. On March 4, 1929, it looked as if the Republicans were in power for an indefinite period, and that their economic policies were rock-founded. In the autumn came the economic crash, which relatively few persons foresaw; and fewer, still, foresaw its devastating course. That crash and its aftermath were in the nature of what I call fate. Had Mr. Hoover and the Republicans in Congress foreseen it, the probabilities are that they could not have prevented it by any measures they could have devised or the country would have sanctioned. The crash came. In the congressional elections of 1930 the Republicans received a terrific beating. I do not have to tell you what happened in 1932 and in the elections since, particularly 1936.

These historical examples show what I mean when I contend that parties may be agencies or victims of fate or forces beyond their knowledge or control.

None of the party programs in 1860 was realized as the outcome of the election. Each proved to be a scrap of paper in a storm which only a few had foreseen as to nature and consequences. No party presented abolition to the voters as a program in 1860. Yet out of the totality of history, including actions taken by voters in that year, came abolition.

DR. SMYTH: That is an awful thought. It is a good thing that you are not uttering it publicly. I suspect that you ought to get hemlock for thinking it privately. You are saying in effect that when our noble voters, all steamed up with patriotism, go to the polls to effect a reform or prevent a reform or save their country, they do not know what they are doing. They think they are plumping for one thing and the consequence is the direct opposite. They are poor boobs and might as well stay at home. According to your statement, Republicans came to power in 1861 promising to guarantee slavery in the South, and ended with destroying slavery throughout the United States. Under that theory the Republicans might now come to power in a landslide of votes on a promise to save the country from the New Deal, or even socialism, and, in an unexpected crash, end in creating a bigger New Deal, or shoving the country into more socialism.

MRS. SMYTH, in unwonted excitement: If what you said about the elections of 1860 is true, if what the Doctor has just said could happen in spite of a majority against it, then elections are a delusion and popular government is also a delusion! If such things are so, then we ought to adopt . . .

BEARD: Adopt what, Mrs. Smyth? And who are we?

MRS. SMYTH: Frankly, I wonder. This brings me to a dead end. I cannot believe it. I have been active in the politics of our precinct and our town. We keep track of what the mayor and council do. We devise programs of municipal reform and we have realized many of our dreams of municipal improvement. Why, the splendid public health program of our city is almost entirely due to the work of public-spirited men and women in an election about ten years ago, when we elected a mayor and a council committed to that program. I have seen the same kind of effective work done in our state, and it was by such hard work that we won national suffrage for women. Now you seem to be saying that we may vote for one thing and get the exact opposite, that fate may compel our elected representatives to do things they never promised or intended to do. You are declaring that things are not what they seem and that the world is turned upside down.

BEARD: Unintentionally, I have led you into some perplexity. Let me rectify my error. Before I make this attempt, let me recall one of your side remarks. In a moment of discouragement you were about to insist that we ought to adopt some other form of government. By we, I suppose, you meant the American people. You gave it up when I asked you what form of government we ought to adopt. You and the Doctor seem to think that I have been introducing a taint of treason into our discussion of popular government by proclaiming the futility of political action through parties. The Doctor implied that such things would be demoralizing if said publicly.

In my opinion, people are not as ignorant as you imagine. Our copybook theory of party politics is that one party offers to the voters its platform of promises, that another party offers another program, that one party receives a majority of votes and, thus victorious at the polls, proceeds to carry that program—and nothing more—into effect. That, I take it, is a theory you both for the moment subscribe to.

DR. SMYTH: I can sing to a harp the words that are on your lips now for the fiftieth time, 'There is something in the theory.'

BEARD: Exactly. There is a great deal in the theory, but on second thought you and all reflective Americans know very well that often you vote for one thing and, though victorious at the polls, get something else and a lot that you did not intend or expect. It is no treason to point out what everybody knows. And it is no condemnation of popular government or popular elections to say it. I believe that Americans are generally aware that sometimes they get what they have voted for, and that sometimes they get things they do not want and have voted against.

Knowing this, they still prefer our system of popular government. I certainly do. I doubt whether we *could* adopt some opposite form of government—whether our spirit and traditions would permit us to do it. Under dictatorial forms of government or any other form that I can visualize, the dominant leaders also are victims of fate and folly and their peoples suffer from the mistakes of leaders. There seems to be no panacea for avoiding such hazards of politics. Americans will do well, I believe, to suffer the ills they have under popular institutions rather than fly to ills they know not of—or know only too well by hearsay.

Under our system, the people have opportunities not offered by other systems. Often by political action they do shape their own fortunes. They are free to work by trial and error to desirable ends and in many cases great and small they do attain these ends. Under our system a pioneer in thought may advance an idea of political or social improvement, gain adherents, do battle for the idea in the forum of politics, and live to see it triumphant through adoption by a political party, and victory at the polls. Sometimes slowly, sometimes rapidly, by straight or devious ways, through our party institutions aspirations of the people are realized. Though, as I believe, many things are fated, are beyond the control of majorities, not all things are fated; and, in the area of freedom, Americans under our system of government work out good fortunes for themselves and their children and children's children. Without quarreling with fate, I rejoice in the freedom.

MRS. SMYTH: Having frightened us by the thought that we may believe in the promises of a party, vote for its candidates, and then get at their hands the exact opposite of what we expect, you owe it to us to give us more fully the other side of the picture if there is one. Of course we are aware on second thought that victorious candidates do not always fulfil their promises after election, but we had been inclined to believe in what you called the copybook theory of American politics. I guess we all like to believe in fairies.

BEARD: I thought it good tactics to tell you the worst first. Frankly, I do not see how our system of popular government could work without parties.

DR. SMYTH: There is no fear on that score. Americans take to party politics like ducks to water. They are the greatest joiners in the world, and at the same time they are always disputing among themselves over everything under the sun. I cannot imagine the United States without political parties. They seem to spring up and flourish like prairie grass on the great plains.

BEARD: In the absence of the silence imposed by the sword, wherever there is freedom of expression, differences of interest and opinion will find vent. That seems to be like a historical law. As James Madison said in Number 10 of *The Federalist*:

> The latent causes of faction are . . . sown in the nature of man; and we see them everywhere brought into different degrees of activity, according to the different circumstances of civil society. A zeal for different opinions concerning religion, concerning government, and many other points, as well of speculation as of practice; and attachment to different leaders ambitiously contending for pre-eminence and power; or to persons of other descriptions whose fortunes have been interesting to the human passions, have, in turn, divided mankind into parties, inflamed them with mutual animosity, and rendered them more disposed to vex and oppress each other than to co-operate for the common good. So strong is this propensity of mankind to fall into mutual animosities, that where no substantial occasion presents itself, the most frivolous and fanciful distinctions have been sufficient to kindle their unfriendly passions and excite their most violent conflicts. But the most common and durable source of faction has been the various and unequal distribution of property.

Then Madison goes on to say that those who have property and those who have none have ever formed distinct interests in society, and that to these are to be added 'a landed interest, a manufacturing interest, a mercantile interest, a moneyed interest, with many lesser interests,' which 'grow up of necessity in civilized nations, and divide them into different classes, actuated by different sentiments and views.' When the sword of a despot does not enforce silence on a people, these propensities, sentiments, and economic interests will find expression in disputes, parties, and factions.

Liberty includes freedom to express these sentiments and interests and to secure governmental actions favorable or gratifying to them. But we as a people have many common bonds which transcend these conflicting interests and help to hold us together—a common language, various common traditions, a common consciousness of many elementary rights and wrongs, and common institutions, including the system of government provided by the Constitution.

And strange to say, the political party in the United States, while often it intensifies conflicts among the people, also acts as a mediatory or conciliatory institution. Our economy and society are highly intricate in composition and in motion. Our economy does not consist of a mere landlord class and a large body of serfs, tenants, and field hands. It does not consist merely of a small capitalist class and a huge proletariat. There are rich and poor. There are large accumulations of wealth and dire poverty. But the gulf between the extremes is filled with graduations. Roughly, we may say, the larger share of manufacturing and financial wealth is in the hands of the Republicans, but it is not all in their hands. Landed property is divided between Republicans and Democrats. The ranks of the Democratic party are crowded by persons from low-income groups, but many a proletarian is a sound Republican.

We have no party that is a purely class party. Jefferson's early Republican party, as he said, represented principally the landed interests, as against the capitalistic interests. Andrew Jackson's Democratic party appealed especially to farmers and mechanics. But as our economy has grown more complex, the economic composition of our political parties has grown more intricate, complex, and various.

In these circumstances, each party becomes an aggregation of interests. Its large campaign contributions may come from one or more principal interests. But its membership includes representatives of many interests, often conflicting interests, large and small.

Thus the political party, or rather its management, may become a *creative force* by drawing together interests which would otherwise be factional and perhaps vindictive, as often happens in Latin-American countries and in Europe. The party so operating becomes more than the mere *sum* of its interested parts, even though one interest may wield great power in its councils. It becomes in itself a power—a power to mediate among and discipline its members, a power to form patterns of political action which are not mere mosaics of the several interests in its ranks. To alter the figure of speech, it brings many little streams of factional power into a common current, mingles them, and becomes something else than its components.

Democrats, for instance, will grant to a Democratic President of the United States measures which they would fight to the last ditch if proposed by a Republican President. They will yield to the management of their party a control over interests which they would defend to the last gasp against the Republican management.

Out of such party coherence come new ideas, legislation, practices, institutions, which otherwise, it is highly probable, would never have been brought into being.

DR. SMYTH: I can see that all right, but these ideas, laws, and practices so created by a party are not necessarily good for the country. They may be bad. Look at the New Deal, a form of state socialism the Democrats had fought against for more than a hundred years.

BEARD: How do you determine for sure whether a law or institution or practice is good for the country or bad? How do you know that what you call a bad creation by a party may not help educate the country and prepare the way for something good?

DR. SMYTH: Let me pass that up, or leave the questions for you to answer.

BEARD: The New Deal is too close to us in time for us to render a dispassionate judgment upon it. That is why I constantly recur to past experience for guidance. Let us take a new deal more remote in time: the Federalist deal which followed the adoption of the Constitution. It put the finances of the Republic on a firm basis. It stimulated manufacturing interests by a discriminative tariff on imports, and other interests by special favors. It created a national bank which facilitated commercial activities throughout the Union. As a good old-line Democrat, Dr. Smyth, you probably regard all that as bad for the country.

DR. SMYTH: I was brought up to believe that it was injurious to the country but, honestly, I do not know enough about it to decide the question in any way, even one convincing to myself. How would you pass judgment on the issue you have raised?

BEARD: Like you, I have my traditional political belief about the issue. Mine is that the Federalist new deal was an advantage to the country. That program certainly helped to cement the Union, to transform the country from a raw-material province of Europe into an independent industrial nation, to enrich our civilization by the diversification of economic activities. I look upon all this as good for the country. But there is another judgment upon the issue. It is the judgment of the Democratic party which once held Federalism to be an evil.

The Democratic party has often been in full power for long periods of time. It has often cursed the protectionism of the Federalist deal. It has occasionally, once at least as I recall, demanded free trade with the world. But it has never established free trade for a single year in all the history of its power. It has at times abolished one piece of Federalism or another, usually only to restore it later; and the economic policies of the Democratic party in our own time embrace the fundamentals of Federalism: protection for American manufacturing industries, a national banking system, the promotion of some industries by special favors, the diversification of our economy, a big navy, a strong army, and all the rest. While adding many things to the Federalist deal, the Democrats today retain most of its great policies. So, I say, the Democratic party has pronounced the fundamentals of Federalism advantageous for the country. Republicans, of course, so pronounce them. The verdict of history is that they were good for the country at the time, and in many respects are still good.

Mrs. Smyth: From that historical record, I presume you might reason that what Robert calls the bad New Deal will receive a favorable verdict in the long time to come. In the funny mixup of politics, I, the daughter of a Republican father, look upon the New Deal with favor, while Robert, son of a true-blue Democrat, condemns it root and branch.

Dr. Smyth: Wait a minute, Beard, before you render a pontifical judgment on the latest New Deal. All this confusion is due to the fact that we no longer have real party divisions in the United States. There are Democrats in the Republican party, and Republicans in the Democratic party, and Socialists in both of them. If we could clean house and get a real line-up, it would be better for the country and we should all know where we stand. Then all the opponents of the New Deal would be together and we could smash it and get back to sanity. Go ahead, Beard, with your argument that the New Deal has merits.

Beard: How far back in our history would you have to go to reach sanity?

Dr. Smyth: I might say, to the New Freedom of Woodrow Wilson, but there was too much labor socialism in it. In a strict sense, for sanity we should have to go back to Grover Cleveland.

Beard: Then the country has been fairly crazy since Grover Cleveland left the White House in 1897? If so, the Democratic party also has been crazy, for it has repudiated in fact about everything that Cleveland stood for.

With that out of my system, I shall merely say this about the New Deal as helpful or harmful to the country. My guess is that if the Republicans come to full power again, they will, despite their promises, keep many fundamentals of the New Deal. Above all they will have to face and will face the great issues President Roosevelt raised and, for a time, grappled with in ways right or wrong—full employment, the elimination of disastrous depressions, social security, and many more. So I propose a paradox as truthful: If the New Deal is as "bad" as you believe it to be, large parts of it may prove to be beneficial to the country. Anyway, America is not going back to Grover Cleveland or Calvin Coolidge or Herbert Hoover. If I know anything, I know that much. But let us return to the thesis respecting parties as creative forces in national life for weal or woe.

DR. SMYTH: First, may I make a little excursion or diversion? After our discussion so far tonight, I confess that there is something in your argument, to use your everlasting maxim, something historically true, if utterly unreasonable. Furthermore, in my present mood, I must declare myself an absolute independent in politics. And there are millions of people like me in the country, millions who have little or no faith, interest, or confidence in any or all of your parties.

BEARD: That is not an excursion or a diversion, Doctor. I was just coming to that myself. As minute studies of political behavior indicate, membership in the two old parties is extensively hereditary. Children in huge numbers inherit party views from their parents and can give no other reasons for the political faith that is in them. But other minute studies seem to indicate that an increasing percentage of our voters is partly or entirely independent.

Party managers, more and more, have to keep their eyes on the independent voters and on third parties that arise from time to time. This necessity is an incentive to creativeness, for party managers want to stay in power or to get into power. Besides running their machines, they act as brokers in opinion, to use a borrowed phrase. The two great party managements, so often evenly balanced, have to bid high for independent votes or lose in campaigns.

DR. SMYTH: How true that is! They would sell their souls rather than get out of office if in, or to get in if out. I say that a party ought to die rather than surrender its principles for mere power and patronage. Party leaders ought to stand squarely on their principles and, win or lose, battle for them to the last ditch.

BEARD: You mean they should stand pat. That is what the Bourbons of old France did, and they lost their heads. If political leaders all stood pat, battling, as you say, for their principles to the bitter end, the country, I have no doubt, would be torn asunder, and the sword would more often be the arbiter in our domestic affairs.

That isn't all. It frequently if not generally happens that men and women who stand pat on what they call their principles are just suffering from mental stagnation in a world which is certainly highly changeful. They may be as dangerous to the civilized way of conducting affairs as the most violent radicals—even the fellows who are willing to meet the test of shooting it out. Standpatters are certain to be outmoded, for our country will change unless it dies. Radicals are likely to be wrong too, but they sometimes have a chance to be vindicated—if they can correctly guess the direction and the velocity of change.

Anyway, it is from the independents, progressives, and radicals that new ideas, inventions, devices, and proposals for the improvement of the individual and society are to be expected. Life is change as well as habit. The spirit of science, so indispensable to our economy, is the spirit of free exploration, free inquiry, and change. From these quarters come the new ideals bidding for acceptance by the American people. Independents take them up first. Sometimes they form third parties, but third parties seldom get very far in the United States. As soon as one of them can muster about a million votes or more, one of the old parties takes the wind out of its sails by adopting more or less of its program.

Thus new ideas work their way up from independents, sometimes through third parties, into the creed of a major party and into the practice of national life. Many of the political ideals and practices now warmly cherished in the United States were once roundly condemned by standpatters, but the ideals rose to power in spite of them. One of the most noteworthy examples is the idea of freedom for chattel slaves. In large part the history of the United States is a story of the rise and progress of ideas. And through the agency of political parties new ideas are often made real in the institutions, practices, and economy of the nation.

DR. SMYTH: The evening draws to a close. As I get the drift of our discussion, we have two broad propositions before us. A party is in some respects an agency of forces outside and inside itself and as such may be driven by fate to actions contrary to the alleged purposes it was elected by the people to accomplish. In the second place, a party may become a kind of creative force or motor, as you call it, by drawing together varieties of ideas and interests and becoming more than the mere sum of these ideas and interests. It seems to me that we have left out of account the role of party leaders, the great figures in history, who inspire and educate their followers. They surely have some effect on the nature and course of parties.

BEARD: There is undoubtedly truth in what you say about leaders, but that involves perhaps the most difficult branch of historical and political thought. Every individual in the world is unique in various respects, however much he may be like other persons in his tribe, clan, or nation. This uniqueness may be a creative force in history. The greater the personality, the more powerful and inventive, the more marked are the qualities of uniqueness. Yet no personality is so unique as to be entirely free from the influence of heredity and environment. The dominating political leader sometimes seems merely to bring to a focus the dominating sentiments of his time and nation.

Jefferson has been called the founder of the Democratic party, and yet he was in many ways an expression of popular forces of discontent and aspiration that existed in the United States independently of his influence. But as a student of history and a thinker gifted in the art of formulating sentiments into striking ideas, he was more than a mere expression of popular tempers and views. In this role, Jefferson developed principles of policy for his party and the nation, which entered into the living heritage of our country.

Yet I am unable to distinguish between what Jefferson was in his uniqueness and what he was as a representative of popular sentiments. I do not agree with Carlyle that history is at bottom merely the work of great men. Nor do I agree with the proposition that history is nothing but the inexorable movement of impersonal forces in which personalities are like pawns in a game or dust in a whirlwind.

MRS. SMYTH: In any case, you leave small fry pretty much out of the picture as more or less futile. We work in the politics of our wards, counties, states, and the nation, hoping to realize our aspirations. A part of the time we are utterly defeated. We win a victory and get the opposite of our expectations and desires. A part of the time we do seem to count, that is, when our views and demands enter into what you call the creative work of a party; but as individuals most of us amount to little or nothing.

BEARD: I fear, Mrs. Smyth, that you are quarreling with the nature of our human world. We are all social beings, not free-swinging beings endowed with independent power. We do our work, such as it is, in society, not upon society. Some, by fate, fortune, and character, achieve greatness of influence in politics. Yet all of us contribute according to our powers to the sum of ideas, sentiments, and aspirations that count in the political government of our country. Sometimes we are defeated even in apparent victory. But a very defeat may become in a larger sense a victory for the nation.

DR. SMYTH: Come, now, how do you make that out?

BEARD: I will repeat an illustration. The majority of the American people certainly voted against the abolition of slavery in 1860. In a few years, in spite of themselves and against their own intentions, they saw slavery abolished. Their expectations were defeated. But nearly all of us now regard this defeat as a victory for our civilization.

MRS. SMYTH: Then politics, small and large, ward or precinct and national, is like life. We strive. We use our powers, or should use them, to the best of our abilities. We often have victories to rejoice in. Sometimes victories turn to sour fruit. Often we have defeats. Some of them are real and terrible. Others in the end happily disappoint us. In politics, by studying the ideas and interests which enter into party conflicts, we may become more and more influential in forming the popular sentiments that do enter into mastery of our national fortunes. As living beings we have to struggle for something or perish. The more we know about the nature of things political and the more we understand what it is we are dealing with, the better equipped we are for our function as citizens. So our evening's debate adds up for me. I feel reassured now.

DR. SMYTH: Sue has a way of trying to bring order out of chaos.

MRS. SMYTH: If I didn't, things would not be so easy for you.

DR. SMYTH: Now you are saying something profoundly true.

BEARD: In the great, the small is often symbolized. Politics is quite a bit like life.

DR. SMYTH, moving rapidly toward the door: If we go on this way we shall soon be like the disputants in Plato's *Republic*. Scholars today cannot tell whether they were concentrating on human justice or headed all the time for a consideration of the immortality of the soul. Your theory of political parties in national life carries me back to my freshman days at college when we discussed freedom of the will and determinism. You brush that scholastic debate aside and say that there are both freedom and fate in politics and everywhere else in human affairs, and you give us a picture of a crazy world in which no sane person would want to live.

BEARD: Come back for a moment, Doctor, and give me your picture of a world not crazy—of a sane world, fashioned to your heart's desire. It is true that I regard debates over either freedom or determinism as futile, and I am convinced that our world is partly free and partly determined and, besides, crowded with what seem to be accidents. Would your sane world be wholly free or wholly determined? Give us your picture of sanity.

Mrs. Smyth looked at her husband intently, as he stood a long time in a meditative mood.

Great God! he burst out. I have never seriously faced that issue. I have gone along through the years calling this or that crazy, criticizing people for being or appearing crazy, without realizing that my words implied some standard or articulate theory of sanity on my own part. Now by demanding my theory of sanity for people and the world, you make it plain to me that I am myself operating on some theory of things. I want to think it over. Give me time.

Before my guests could get their motor started, I shouted from the porch, All the time you want or have.

XIX

The Economic Underwriting of the Constitution

REMEMBERING Dr. Smyth's desire to have Henry Walker, president of the City Trades Union Council, present at our session on the economic underwriting of the Constitution, I took the liberty of bringing John Whiteworth, an industrial magnate, head of a big steel corporation in a neighboring state, into the discussion. Whiteworth built a huge summer mansion on Hilton Mountain overlooking our town, long before he had to pay any federal income tax on his annual earnings. Now he is among what he calls the poor rich. He closes up fifteen or twenty rooms in wintertime and lives in the remaining eight or ten rooms when he comes up for cold-weather outings.

Whiteworth is not exactly in my class, and I had come to know him by a kind of sociological accident. A short time before we first met in 1915, ex-President Taft had delivered a tirade against me before the Pennsylvania Society in New York City, taking my book, *An Economic Interpretation of the Constitution,* as his theme. Whiteworth had heard the speech. Shortly afterward he had encountered a town magnate on the street and redelivered Mr. Taft's charges. The local magnate replied that Taft was right, of course, about that book, but that he knew me and that, while I might be a bit off in the head, I was not a bad fellow. He also suggested that the three of us hold a little party, for the fun of it. Owing to that chance affair, I spent an evening at Whiteworth's place on Hilton Mountain. Having felt out his dogmatic spots and his soft spots, I sidestepped useless debate and told him a string of Indiana stories that seemed to amuse him immensely. Ever since we have been good friends, despite our differences of opinion on many matters.

In introducing Whiteworth to the Smyths and to Henry Walker, I explained to them that I thought we ought to have a man of Whiteworth's experience at our session on economic underwriting, and that he had at first hesitated, but had consented to join us. Incidentally, I added that I had forgotten just why he hesitated. He refreshed my memory.

WHITEWORTH: When you rattled up to my place in your disgraceful old car, Stuttering Kate, and told me that you were going to discuss the economic underwriting of the Constitution, I replied that it was all out of my line. Our law firm, Belton, Holstein, Levy, Antonio and Lasinski, takes care of constitutional matters for us, and as to an economic underwriting of the Constitution, I can't see any sense in it. In the words of our Mr. Belton, it is the business of the Constitution to underwrite economics, that is free business enterprise.

The trouble with you, Beard, is that you get the cart before the horse. Leaders among the framers of the Constitution were, as you have said yourself, businessmen, men of substantial property interests; and they made the Constitution, as you did not say, for the purpose of preventing government interference with business. As our Mr. Belton would put it, they did not think that the Constitution needed any economic underwriting; they thought that free enterprise needed a constitutional underwriting. To quote our Mr. Belton again: 'Until the New Deal dunderheads came along and befuddled the people, everybody in his right mind knew just what the Constitution was for, namely, to protect free enterprise.'

MR. WALKER, labor leader, growing red in the face: I know your Mr. Belton, of Belton, Holstein, Levy, Antonio, and Lasinski very well, Mr. Whiteworth. Away back in 1922, during the railway shopmen's strike, he had a hand in getting the notorious Harry M. Daugherty to extort an injunction from a federal judge. That injunction forbade strikers or their leaders to engage in picketing or to· persuade any person to leave work or refrain from going to work, by word of mouth, telegrams, telephone messages, interviews in newspapers, or any other way. . . .

BEARD: The injunction read 'or otherwise in any manner whatsoever.'

WHITEWORTH: Oh, you would remember the very words! But let that go. Daugherty's injunction is a fine example of what I mean by a constitutional underwriting of rights guaranteed by the Constitution, the constitutional underwriting of free economic enterprise.

WALKER: But what about underwriting the rights of labor to organize and bargain with employers on hours, wages, and conditions of work? Doesn't the Constitution underwrite these human rights of labor as much as it does the rights for your Company?

WHITEWORTH: There isn't a word in the Constitution about the rights of labor, not a word about labor. Not a word. Our Mr. Belton, who knows his Constitution from A to Z, keeps repeating that.

WALKER: Your blessed Mr. Belton may be right on that point. I guess the word labor isn't in the Constitution. But I know the word liberty is, and that's what I am talking about—the liberty of labor to organize and get a square deal for industrial workers.

BEARD: You are both misinformed, gentlemen, about the word labor. It is in the Constitution. Mr. Belton has overlooked it. There is a clause in Article IV which reads:

> No person held to service or labor in one state, under the laws thereof, escaping into another, shall . . . be discharged from such service or labor, but shall be delivered up on claim of the party to whom such service or labor may be due.

There is the word labor three times.

WHITEWORTH: That's my chief quarrel with you, Beard, you are always bringing up irrelevant matters. You know that the clause you have just cited is the provision for the return of runaway slaves, and is obsolete.

WALKER: Of course it is. It never did have anything to do with white labor.

BEARD: I was just joking. You both thought that the word labor is not in the Constitution, and I merely said it is there three times. You agreed that the clause referred only to runaway slaves. You are both wrong again. When the Constitution was framed, there were thousands of white workers, men and women, indentured or bound to labor for their masters for terms of years. This clause covered white servants as well as Negro slaves.

WHITEWORTH: I never heard of that.

WALKER: I never did either.

BEARD: I am not surprised at that. Nor should I blame you at all for complete ignorance of the Constitution and its history if you were not all the time talking about your rights under the Constitution. But go ahead with your rights.

WALKER: I was saying that labor claims its liberty to organize and bargain under the Constitution. The word liberty is certainly in the Constitution, more than once. It includes the kind of liberty that trade unionists are demanding, the same liberty of organization that manufacturers enjoy.

WHITEWORTH: It means liberty for individual human beings. It isn't liberty for labor to form an organization and, through its walking delegates, dictate hours, wages, and everything else to other laborers and to employers. It means liberty for competition among employers and workers to carry on as they please, to improve their conditions, to make a little more money than they are making. The word labor, may be, as Beard says, in the Constitution three times, but the words trade union certainly are not there at all. Are they, Mr. Walker?

WALKER: I suppose not, but I'll bet a dollar that the word company or corporation is not there either.

WHITEWORTH: I've got you there, Mr. Walker! It is true the words company and corporation are not in the Constitution. Our Mr. Belton has often told us that in our conferences. The word person, however, is there, he says, and a company or corporation is, in the eyes of the law, a person, a legal person. Now, Beard, you cannot deny that. You will have to admit that much.

MRS. SMYTH: Watch your step, gentlemen, or Mr. Beard will go to his records and pull out a ton of notes on the origin, history, and meaning of the word person in law, from the most ancient code of Moses down to the latest utterances of Justice Hugo Black.

WHITEWORTH: God forbid! Just let Beard answer one simple, honest question, Is a corporation or company a person at law and entitled to the rights of human persons under the Constitution? Yes or no.

BEARD: No.

WHITEWORTH: Our Mr. Belton declares that it is, and are you going to pit yourself against the best lawyer in the United States?

BEARD: You wanted a Yes or No and I answered your question correctly with a No. Now let me make my own statement. A company or corporation, if duly organized under law, is a person at law for certain purposes and is entitled to certain rights of natural persons, but is not entitled to all the rights of natural persons or citizens under the Constitution.

DR. SMYTH: Hold right there. Otherwise you will be citing all the law cases—Tubbs *v.* Tubbs, Inc., or Bubbs *v.* Bubbs, Inc., and all the opinions of the judges, the concurring opinions and the dissenting and discriminating opinions, until the crack of doom. I have been through it here in this room. It would serve Mr. Whiteworth and Mr. Walker right to have to endure some of it, but let us move along. They are both talking about the rights of organizations, manufacturing corporations and trade union corporations. . . .

WALKER: Pardon me, but a trade union is not incorporated at law like a business corporation and is not subject to the same rules of law. Labor is not a commodity such as manufacturers turn out. A trade union is a society of human persons for the mutual benefit of its members as human beings with rights.

WHITEWORTH: That is correct in a way, Mr. Walker. Your trade union is not incorporated like our Company. You get your charter from the American Federation of Labor or the Congress of Industrial Organizations. We have to get ours from the state government. Our charter is our constitution, and the directors and managers have to obey it. They have to make an accounting to the stockholders and the public for every dollar received and spent, including the salaries paid to officers. Our Company cannot contribute money to campaign funds for the purpose of getting its friends into office. On the other hand, your trade union can spend all the money it likes on influencing candidates and government job holders.* And it is my opinion that every trade union should be incorporated just like our

---

* Aware that Mr. Whiteworth would be pleased to hear that his desire for restraints on organized labor had been partly realized after the discussion at our seminar, I wrote him the following letter:

Hosannah Hill, June 29, 1943.

Dear Mr. Whiteworth,

Enclosed you will find a copy of the Smith-Connally "War Labor Disputes Act" and a copy of the *Congressional Record* for June 25 which contains President Roosevelt's veto message. Section 9 of the Act prohibits, for the period covered by the Act, political contributions by labor organizations. One newspaper columnist declares the President's message to be of high order and another thinks it is so bad that he could not have written it himself. You will doubtless be much pleased with the Act.

With warm personal regards,
Yours sincerely,
Charles A. Beard.

Company, and that its officers should be compelled to obey its charter and account for all the moneys received and spent.

BEARD: That is another way of stating that your Company does not have all the rights of natural persons and many other forms of human organization under the Constitution.

WHITEWORTH: That's correct. Now I understand what you meant when you said that corporations do not have *all* the rights of natural persons. Come to think about it, they do not have, or at least do not get, all such rights as things are now run by the Government. What I want to know of Mr. Walker is this, Why shouldn't every trade union be incorporated and forced to obey its government charter just like every industrial or business company?

WALKER: I explained that before. A trade union is not organized for profit. It is an organization of human beings for purposes of mutual benefit. This mutual benefit is a standard of living for labor which lifts workers out of poverty and gives them the conditions that make for good and independent citizens. It works for what Mr. Beard calls an economic underwriting of the Constitution. Depressed and poverty-stricken citizens can't stand up, assert their rights, and govern themselves in a democratic way. Only citizens who have some economic strength can get the education and conditions of life which are necessary to self-government. Paupers and beggars are not good materials for citizenship.

WHITEWORTH: I don't want to argue all that—merely to say in passing that one of your trade unions recently wrung out of my Company an increase of wages equal to all the profit paid out in dividends to our stockholders that year, and a lot of companies are making no profits at all on account of the high wages they pay to one of your so-called non-profit-making unions of human beings. I think your union people will have to come around and accept incorporation and responsibility to the public for your funds and the way you do business, just like the business corporations. There have been too many rackets and scandals recently in the labor world for you to escape such regulation much longer. Your labor czars don't let members vote freely in union elections and they run their organizations for their own benefit, not for the benefit of the members. Government has tightened down on business corporations recently and it will bring you fellows to terms along with us, unless I miss my guess.

Mrs. Smyth, displaying some rising temper: After listening to you representatives of labor and big business, I have begun to wonder where the consumers come into the picture. Have they no rights as to the prices of products from which both wages and profits are drawn?

Whiteworth: Competition takes care of prices and keeps them as low as the high wages paid to labor will allow.

Walker: It is really the producer that counts. Pay producers good wages, and they can pay good prices. When you are talking about consumers, you are really talking about white-collar workers. Their salaries are often low. If white-collar workers, who complain as consumers, want to have salaries high enough to meet prices, let them organize the way industrial workers do.

Mrs. Smyth: What about small business people, who run millions of little concerns, all necessary to keep our economy going?

Whiteworth: That's what I ask, too. Trade unions are helping to squeeze them to the wall. A big company like mine can fight back and can pass some of the wage increases on to the public. The little fellow is caught between labor and price-cutting.

Walker: Your little business fellows are out to make money. Most of them fail within a year or two. Then they lay their troubles on trade unions. . . .

Whiteworth: And big business?

Walker: That is your lookout. Organized labor does not propose to be ground down by the price-slashing of little business concerns.

Beard: What about farmers? How do they come into your pictures?

Walker: Let them organize and join industrial workers in upholding national standards of life. The trouble with farmers is that most of them are anarchists who will not organize at all, or even co-operate. As a rule they are against organized labor, even though they know that the prices they get for farm produce depend on the high wages which industrial workers manage to win by collective action. If farmers could only see that they are really workers too, and would join labor, they would get their standard of life raised to a higher level.

Whiteworth: Good Lord, Walker, farmers are so well organized now for their game that they almost boss the Government of the United States. If business men and industrial workers do not get together, they will both be run over by the farm bloc, by wild-eyed populists from the West, sons of the wild jackass, as they really are.

WALKER: For years I have been arguing that if management and labor will get together, they can stabilize business and stop the sniping from farmers and gas-station people and little fellows generally. Management and labor! There's the clue to progress in the future.

DR. SMYTH: What you actually mean, then, is that business managers and labor managers are to get together and run the country for yourselves. I read a review of a book on such a managerial revolution. Do you have the book, Beard?

BEARD: Yes, here it is: James Burnham's *The Managerial Revolution,* published in 1941.

MRS. SMYTH: Why, it is all cluttered up with pencil notes and you have put a question mark on about every page. What is the trouble with it?

BEARD: Oh, I just applied the Socratic elenchus to his major statements.

WHITEWORTH: What, in heaven's name, is the Socratic elenchus?

BEARD: In a general way, the Socratic question, Is it true? Or positively, The exact opposite of what you say is the truth of the matter. I just question Burnham's statements and especially his assumptions.

MRS. SMYTH: His assumptions?

BEARD: Particularly, that economic managers have guts enough to make a revolution and could make good afterward, as against the warrior, the statesman, the saint, or the popular hero. With all due respect to Mr. Walker and Mr. Whiteworth, the economic man, as such, is not cast in a heroic mold. Sacrifice, real or nominal, plus political genius, is the secret of revolutionary heroism.

DR. SMYTH: We are clear off the track of the economic underwriting of the Constitution. Whiteworth and Walker have talked about their class rights under the Constitution and have taken it for granted that, if they had their way, everything would be just fine for everybody and the Constitution. From some remarks you dropped, Beard, as we went away last week, I gathered that you meant by the phrase, economic underwriting, that, while the Constitution guarantees certain rights, it depends for its existence and functioning, in part at least, upon certain underlying economic conditions. Did I get your idea? If so, let us consider those conditions.

WHITEWORTH: That is merely Beard's idea of the economic interpretation of the Constitution. Ex-President Taft demolished that. The leading framers of the Constitution, as Beard wrote, were business men, but he is rattle-brained when he claims that their business interests had material influence on their politics. It was an ideal, not their business, that controlled them. The fathers of our country did not believe in class conflicts. Nor did they believe that economics underwrote the Constitution. They believed that under the Constitution, if the government were run according to it, business would be let alone and get the kind of fair deal that would make the country great. Of course, I forgot to say, labor and farmers too would get the same kind of fair deal. In any event, that is the way ex-President Taft, who ought to know, explained it to us in New York City.

DR. SMYTH: What have you to say on that, Beard?

BEARD: Just what all the fathers thought, I do not know. I have some acquaintance with their writings now available to us, and I have never found a scrap of paper indicating that any of them who supported the finished Constitution said anything that gives the slightest countenance to the theory Mr. Whiteworth has ascribed to them, especially the idea of no government interference with economic enterprise. Judging by the records, the leaders among them held opinions exactly opposite to that. The papers of the convention that framed the Constitution show that the members recognized the tremendous influence of conflicting economic interests in American society. If they had talked in terms of an abstract ideal, they could scarcely have agreed on that. They talked almost constantly in terms of conflicting interests, and their Constitution represented compromises among interests.

Madison, for instance, in more than one speech pointed out that the conflict of interests was inescapable. He told the convention that the greatest conflict of all was between those who had property and those who had none. Leaders among the framers wanted, among other things, first, to hold the Union together; second, to set up a government that would protect, regulate, and promote types of economic enterprise; third, to put brakes on the state legislatures which had been attacking the interests of protected classes. All the framers who listened to the debates must have known that conflicting economic interests existed before the Constitution was adopted and would continue afterward. Some of them feared a plutocracy as much as they feared a propertyless majority.

Madison believed that the Constitution, which he had done so much to design, rested on property interests and would endure only as long as property was widely enough distributed to afford a popular support for it, including the safeguards it furnished to property. Jefferson, who has been called the idealist of the Revolution, was convinced that the American Republic could last only as long as the overwhelming majority of the people were farm owners, engaged in agriculture. He declared that mobs in the great cities were sores on the body politic and inimical to republican institutions.

In this direction Madison went beyond Jefferson. The Sage of Monticello foresaw the coming of industrialism, the rise of a vast class of propertyless proletarians, the relative decline of agriculturalists in numbers and influence, and thus a destruction of the economic underwriting of popular government. But he could see no way out of the doom. He thought that the free land would last longer than it did. He was mistaken about that, but that was an incident. He could discover no plan for avoiding the crash, or, if he did, it is not to be found anywhere in his records.

But Madison, writing in 1829-30, hoped there might be a way out of the calamity that would come when the fairly equal distribution of property had given way to a plutocracy on the one side and a propertyless multitude on the other. He thought that the crisis would arrive in about a hundred years, about 1930—which was not a bad guess. Yet he hoped that the tendency to concentration of wealth might be 'diminished and the permanency defeated by the equalizing tendency of the laws.'

In other words, Madison contemplated the use of government to provide an economic underwriting of the Republic by laws designed to control the concentration of wealth and to force a more equal distribution of wealth. For this, he admitted, experience had as yet provided no sure test by experiment. To accomplish the end so necessary to the maintenance of popular government, he concluded, would require 'all the wisdom of the wisest patriots.'

In 1932, as Madison had foreseen, the Government of the United States, under the leadership of President Hoover, began to wrestle with that problem. Mr. Hoover sponsored and Congress passed legislation designed to underwrite home-owners in danger of losing their property, farmers heavily in debt, and railway and other corporations in financial difficulties. President Franklin D. Roosevelt, his successor, carried the work further by seeking to underwrite the millions of unemployed who had no property to live on and no way of earning their bread. Is there anyone in this room who believes that no economic underwriting of any kind or degree is necessary to the existence and continuance of constitutional government?

It is a kind of double-barreled proposition: Without an appropriate economic underwriting, constitutional government could not come into being; and if a constitutional government cannot assure the continuance of a sufficient economic underwriting it will certainly perish.

WHITEWORTH: It sounds pretty theoretical to me. I suppose that you will now try to show that the big purpose of the men who made the Constitution was *not* to protect free enterprise from government interference.

BEARD: To tell the truth, Mr. Whiteworth, I had not thought it worth discussing, for it is a kind of partial truth that amounts to a misrepresentation of fundamental facts in the case.

WHITEWORTH: Oh, why don't you just call it a falsehood and be done with it?

BEARD: For the reason that I do not regard it as a falsehood. You seem to want everything to be either white or black, and I seldom find such a clear-cut division in history. The framers of the Constitution certainly contemplated a large degree of economic liberty for business, industry, and agriculture, as well as a large amount of intellectual and political liberty for the people of the United States. A majority of them wanted to put brakes on the interference of state governments with financial, business, and commercial transactions. But a majority of them intended that the new Federal Government should do a lot of interfering with business as it had been run up to 1789. I know that many Jeffersonian Democrats dispute this. In my opinion they are mistaken, and I do not think that this is merely my old Republican prejudice.

WHITEWORTH: You don't mean to say that you are a Republican!

BEARD: I was brought up by a rock-ribbed Republican father.

WHITEWORTH: I never would have thought it.

BEARD: Well, not all Republicans are as obtuse to facts as you seem to think. Let's go back. I maintained that a majority of the framers of the Constitution intended the Federal Government to interfere with business as it had been run up to 1789. What is my proof? The first two administrations, under President Washington, were largely directed by men who had been members of the Constitutional Convention. As soon as they got under way, they began to enact laws interfering with business as it had been run. They put protective tariffs on a number of imported manufactures. They gave bounties to New England fisheries. They set up a United States Bank. They made discriminations in tonnage and other duties in behalf of American shipping. I shall not bore you with a long list. I covered this subject in my *Economic Origins of Jeffersonian Democracy.*

WHITEWORTH: But that isn't interference with business. That is promotion of business.

BEARD: Let me ask you a few questions. Doesn't a protective duty on manufactures interfere with the business of importing merchants? Doesn't a United States Bank interfere with the business of state banks? Don't discriminative duties on shipping interfere with the importing and the exporting business? Don't duties on manufactures interfere with the business of producing and exporting agricultural products?

WHITEWORTH: They do in a way, I suppose, but they help business more than they interfere with it.

MRS. SMYTH: The point seems to be: Whose business? But time is passing. Could we now discuss how and by whom the economic underwriting necessary to the continuance of our Republic is going to be effected in the future? Mr. Walker and Mr. Whiteworth seem to agree that if management and labor could get together they could guarantee the underwriting. Most people in the United States, I fancy, believe that a disastrous economic crash would spell ruin all around. Do you think that labor and management could provide that underwriting?

BEARD: Certainly not without government intervention and ultimate control. Certainly not without government.

At this point both Whiteworth and Walker exclaimed together, in effect, that they recognized the necessity of some government intervention and control. I replied that capital and labor could not agree at all on the nature of specific measures of intervention and control. Some wrangling occurred as Whiteworth and Walker tried to formulate a single plank in their platform. I turned the discussion to Mrs. Smyth's question.

BEARD: In the first place, these labor-management schemes leave American agriculture entirely out of account and all the millions of farmers, tenants, laborers on the land, all the families living by that mode of economic life. Even if managers and labor leaders could get together, they do not have as such the qualities for government, which is a peculiar kind of art and science, partly economic but also very human. Governing a country takes something more than the kind of interests, habits, and experiences developed in factories, at machines, in offices, and in drafting rooms. The qualities required for successful government are, perhaps, best covered by the word statesmanship, which comprises, in addition to direct experience with business and labor, a knowledge of law and history, a keen appreciation of economic forces in history, administrative experience in public undertakings, the intuitive and practical power of discerning what is necessary and possible in great affairs, many with world-wide implications.

WHITEWORTH: On that point I agree with Walter Lippmann, the most brilliant thinker in the United States outside the business world.

BEARD: Which Walter Lippmann?

WHITEWORTH: What do you mean by that?

BEARD: I mean that in the course of his meanderings he has been on nearly every side of nearly every question, in one way or another, from socialism to world salvation.

WHITEWORTH: I refer to his address to businessmen reported in *Time* for December 21, 1942. There he said that American businessmen hold the world's fate in their hands because the United States alone has 'no governing class which has a social position and political power superior to the business community.' He warned American businessmen to study the respective fates of the French and the British aristocracies. The French aristocrats, Lippmann said, perished because they would make no surrender of their privileges; but the British aristocracy made concessions and continued the work of government. American businessmen hold a commanding position in world affairs, and it is their duty now to exercise that power wisely and effectively. What is the matter with that?

BEARD: Lippmann's allocution is merely one of the terrible simplifications of history that he loves to make. It is not his fault, of course. A man who writes on everything with facility has to simplify in order to get on. Besides, English aristocrats received some education during the Puritan revolution in the seventeenth century.

WHITEWORTH: Judging by your remarks on what you call qualities of statesmanship necessary to govern a great country and your criticism of Mr. Lippmann, you evidently think that businessmen don't have sense enough to run the government. It is my opinion that they have more sense than the politicians and that they could carry on the kind of government which is necessary to let business enterprise do the rest for the prosperity and happiness of the people. It takes nothing but good common sense to run the government as it used to be run before it began to interfere with business in every direction. If we could repeal these laws interfering with business and get back to fundamentals in government, running it would be fairly simple.

BEARD: You have expressed an idea, Mr. Whiteworth, which has wide currency among men of your class. I should like to explore it with you. If I could ask you some questions and get your answers, we might bring our opinions to a head and see what it is we agree upon and differ about. You are not an anarchist, are you?

WHITEWORTH: Heavens, No! How did you get that notion? Why do you ask such a foolish question?

BEARD: I just wanted to get that out of the way. I now know that you believe in some kind of government for the United States. Next, I ask, What kind of government?

WHITEWORTH: Our own kind of government. Our form of government. It is all right. It is only the politicians who run it that disturb me.

BEARD: I shall put aside the question of how you are going to keep our form of government and at the same time secure the election of your right kind of men to take the places of politicians. That might give you a headache. As to form, I take it you would keep the President, the Congress, and the Judiciary. Now we come to things you would have government do. You would have it protect private property, of course?

WHITEWORTH: That is another absurd question. To be sure, it is the duty of government to protect private property. If it did not, we certainly should have anarchy.

BEARD: Would you have everything private property?

WHITEWORTH: I suspect that is a trick question. I would keep government out of business absolutely.

BEARD: Would you abolish laws of inheritance which force the division of a man's property among his heirs on his death and prevent the entailment of estates in the line of the eldest sons?

WHITEWORTH: No. I think that would be unfair to the family. I would keep the laws of inheritance which provide for the division of estates.

BEARD: Would you retain taxes on inheritance?

WHITEWORTH: Yes. Moderate taxes.

BEARD: How moderate?

WHITEWORTH: I should want to think it over.

BEARD: You said that you wanted to keep government out of business absolutely, when I asked you whether everything should be private property. Would you have all transportation privately owned and operated?

WHITEWORTH: Absolutely.

BEARD: Our great system of public highways representing an outlay greater than the capital value of all the railways? Would you turn the ownership and operation of highways over to private parties?

WHITEWORTH: No, of course not. I had overlooked that.

BEARD: Would you turn all the national domain of forests and lands over to private parties, to do as they please with it?

WHITEWORTH: No. A certain amount of conservation is necessary to protect our watersheds.

BEARD: How much conservation?

WHITEWORTH: I should not want to answer that offhand.

BEARD: What about our waterworks and watersheds owned and managed by the city?

WHITEWORTH: That is all right. I would leave it where it is. It is well managed and our rates are low enough. Let us stop this line. There are a lot of things government does own and ought to own. Wherever possible, however, the government should leave operation in private hands.

BEARD: How do you determine what is possible and what is impossible ?

WHITEWORTH: That is just a professor's quibbling.

BEARD: Very well. Do you think that the public interest should be the principle for determining whether anything should be publicly owned and operated or publicly owned and leased?

WHITEWORTH: As a patriotic citizen, I should regard that as a fair principle, but there is danger in it.

BEARD: Danger from whom and in what sense?

WHITEWORTH: Come back to earth and let us have some sensible questions.

BEARD: Would you repeal the Interstate Commerce Act, abolish the Interstate Commerce Commission, and leave all rail, water and pipe-line transportation uncontrolled?

WHITEWORTH: There is sense in that kind of question. I'll give a concise No. When I started in as a manufacturer long years ago, the railways had a free hand to do about as they pleased. They made discriminations in rates between shippers. They gave rebates on freight rates paid to favorite shippers. They issued stocks and bonds that registered water—no values. No, the railways have to be regulated.

BEARD: Would you abolish the Federal Trade Commission? Repeal all laws defining and regulating unfair trade practices?

WHITEWORTH: Never. If all fair practices laws were repealed, the honest and decent businessman would be penalized if not ruined by unscrupulous adulterators and tricksters. Some of the rulings by the Federal Trade Commission are crazy, but we need some control. You are going to ask, How much? But you may as well omit that.

BEARD: I omit it. Mr. Whiteworth, would you repeal the anti-trust laws and leave private corporations and parties free to make combinations according to their interests and otherwise do as they please in conducting their enterprises?

WHITEWORTH: No, I would not repeal all the antitrust legislation, but I would have the government stop hounding business. There are a lot of illegitimate combinations in restraint of trade, formed for the purpose of enriching insiders and skinning the public. But business men are sick and tired of uncertainty as to what they can and cannot do under the laws. Men in my company, with a lot of others, were indicted not long ago and forced into a long lawsuit, which we won at great expense. It was a damned outrage! One morning I picked up my newspaper and read a headline, 'John Whiteworth Indicted.'

I come from an old family of honorable business men, if I do say so. It made me sick to see my name spread all over the front page as a kind of criminal, along with gangsters recently indicted. I felt as if my neighbors regarded me as a sneak thief when I rode on my suburban train to business that day. It was an infernal outrage! It cost us about $250,000 to go through the trial and win the suit. But that did not wipe out the stain of that accursed headline. That Thurman Arnold, the federal prosecutor, is a relentless persecutor. By the way, someone told me during the trial that he once wrote a book in which he made fun of antitrust legislation. Is that so?

BEARD: Yes. Take the book, *The Folklore of Capitalism,* published in 1937, home with you, Mr. Whiteworth, if you want to read it. It is one of the brilliant books of our time. You ought to read carefully Chapter IX on "The Effect of Antitrust Laws in Encouraging Large Combinations."

WHITEWORTH: You may keep it right here on your shelf, or burn it, for all I care. I repeat that business ought not to be hounded.

BEARD: I heartily concur with you on that, Mr. Whiteworth. It is both a preposterous and an outrageous practice, in my opinion too. But, since you are unwilling to repeal all legislation against trusts and combinations, may I ask, What kind of laws would you keep or substitute for the present laws?

WHITEWORTH: I would forbid all combinations in restraint of trade against the public interest. I would forbid all unfair trade practices directed against the public interest. That is clear, isn't it?

BEARD: In principle, yes; in reality, no, until more precisely defined. Would you, for instance, allow all the big concerns in one line of manufacturing to confer and agree on the price scales of their products?

WHITEWORTH: I would, in reason. Let them compete in quality but not in self-destructive competition. Fair competition is all right. Cut-throat competition does nobody any good, not even the consumer, in the long run. But you are just trying to drive me deeper and deeper into what old Professor Sandifell used to call disturbing speculation. By the way, we boys at college named his course on philosophy 'a damned dim candle over a damned dark abyss.' You just want to make everything so complicated that nobody can understand it.

BEARD: If you think hard about it, Mr. Whiteworth, it is complicated. If it is complicated, then we deceive ourselves and the public by pretending that it is simple. An economic theory is an empty abstraction unless you get down to just what comes under it and what is done and said under it.

WHITEWORTH: Oh, I know that, but why don't you get after Walker and his trade unions? They are combinations in restraint of trade, wages, and prices, and some of them are no better than rackets. I was glad to see Arnold go after them.

BEARD: I am willing, if Mr. Walker is. What about it, Mr. Walker?

WALKER: I'll take my turn.

BEARD: Mr. Walker, a while ago you said that every American citizen has the right to work. I suppose you mean by that a right to a job?

WALKER: I do indeed. Unemployment is a shame. It is degrading to human beings to be jobless and breadless. It is demoralizing to the bodies and souls of men and women, especially if it lasts a long time. If you do not believe that, our minds cannot meet.

BEARD: I believe it, Mr. Walker, as warmly as you do. My only question is how to bring full employment about and keep it. One scheme proposed is to cut wages and divide the work evenly among all the workers. That is, let us say, if there are a hundred jobs in an industry and a hundred men are employed at $10 a day while another hundred are unemployed in that trade, the work should be divided so as to employ two hundred men at $5 a day. What do you think of that scheme?

WALKER: That would be ruinous to the American standard of living which trade unions are organized to uphold and advance. That is what Hitler did. He cut wages and divided the work. I am against all schemes for cutting wages, dividing work, and making longer work days.

BEARD: Then you propose that every person in every trade should be furnished a job at wages which he fixes and for the work day that suits him?

WALKER: No. I put it this way: Every person in a trade should be furnished a job at trade-union wages and on trade-union terms as to hours and other working conditions. Surely you are not opposed to that?

BEARD: Not in principle. But by whom and how is that job to be furnished to every person?

WALKER: That is a problem for management or business and the government to solve. The only right way to divide up work is to shorten the work day and give more workers employment at standard wages.

BEARD: Then neither the American Federation of Labor nor the Congress of Industrial Organizations has a plan for guaranteeing everybody in every trade a job at standard wages and in standard conditions. And one more question while we are on this subject, How would you prevent too many workers from rushing into one trade?

WALKER: We have no plans to guarantee jobs to every person at standard wages. It would be the duty of trade unions by apprenticeship and other rules to keep too many workers from crowding into a trade.

BEARD: So you stand fast on the proposition that it is the duty of management or business and government to provide for full employment, jobs for everybody, on the conditions that trade unions prescribe? That is your idea of the right to work?

WALKER: That is my idea of the right to work. I don't say that all trade unionists have it. It is what I mean by the right to work.

BEARD: But suppose that business and government worked out a plan for full employment, and such a plan meant imposing regulations on trade unions such as those prevailing in Russia, would you be willing to make such a surrender of trade-union liberties in the interest of that full employment?

WALKER: Never!

BEARD: Then you prefer to go along as you do now and take the distresses of unemployment for union members and outsiders, as the American Federation of Labor has in the past?

WALKER: If it is a choice between surrendering trade-union gains and adopting such despotic plans for full employment, we will stick by our gains.

BEARD: In that case, what becomes of your right to work?

WALKER: Since you have got a simple proposition all tangled up in your speculation, as Mr. Whiteworth called it, my right to work goes by the board. Still I stick to it. Don't you recognize any rights for human beings?

MRS. SMYTH: We have constantly had that issue of speculation up before us in other relations, Mr. Walker. Charles Beard insists there is no such thing as a natural right, a right guaranteed by nature. He holds that rights are just abstract theories and that no people have any rights in fact except the rights which they have sense enough and competence enough to bring into being, uphold, and enforce in fact, in reality, in practical life and affairs. At first that seemed to me a hard-hearted view of human nature and our world. Now I am beginning to believe that it is true, just a statement of the facts in the case. Isn't that your position, Mr. Beard?

BEARD: You have put it about as I should want to state it. However, I shall add that I believe there is moral power in many abstract ideas of rights. They may inspire and guide us. They become realities to the extent that we have power, intellectual and moral, to give actual effect to them.

DR. SMYTH: A few minutes ago, Mr. Whiteworth and Mr. Walker seemed to be drawing together on the proposition that management and labor could solve the problem of an economic underwriting, including, I take it, that of full employment. Before we adjourn, let us develop their views on this subject.

BEARD: With reference to Dr. Smyth's suggestion, I propose that Mr. Whiteworth, Mr. Walker, and I have a three-cornered conference on what is in our minds as to the management-labor way out of our economic difficulties, as a way of securing an economic underwriting.

[Assent was given.]

BEARD: Mr. Whiteworth, just how do you see the management-labor organization?

WHITEWORTH: In each plant, all workers would be organized in a single union. Everyone of them would be in the union, with one vote. This union would have a constitution, hold regular and special meetings, and elect a council and chairman empowered to carry on all business with the manager of the plant as to hours, wages, working conditions, complaints, and suggestions. It would be agreed that there are to be no strikes until a certain procedure of negotiation had been followed. I could give more details, but this is the sum and substance of the general proposition.

BEARD: Your corporation has many plants scattered over the country. Would you have a separate management-union arrangement for each plant?

WHITEWORTH: Yes, a separate management for each plant.

BEARD: Where do you stand so far on this proposition, Mr. Walker?

WALKER: Bosh, that is just the old company-union game, by which workers are divided into little isolated bodies and made helpless! It gives no special position to skilled craftsmen. It would disrupt the American Federation of Labor and the Congress of Industrial Organizations alike. Any single company could arrange with its hog-tied union to cut wages and undersell competing companies. Then the whole structure of decent wages would go to pieces. If a company had a strike, its workers would receive no help from other workers organized on the national scale. If I should agree to that, I would agree to the complete destruction of organized labor in the United States. It would be suicide for labor.

BEARD: Then what form of management-labor organization do you propose, Mr. Walker?

WALKER: I would keep the present form of national labor organization. There ought to be a merger of the two big national organizations—the American Federation of Labor and the Congress of Industrial Organizations. It's a pity that the split ever occurred. The workers of each plant would choose their committee and chairman to deal with management, subject to fixed union rules about wages, hours, and working conditions throughout the country. Otherwise there would be local anarchy. Besides, officials of national labor organizations would have to have a veto over any arrangements between the local management and the local union, if those arrangements were out of line with labor standards established by national labor organizations.

BEARD: Would you demand the closed shop in every plant and compel management to collect union dues for you?

WALKER: I would have a closed shop wherever we could get it. In any case I would demand preference for union members in every plant.

BEARD: Well, now Mr. Walker. . . .

WHITEWORTH: You need not go an inch further. What Mr. Walker has proposed is the complete subjection of management to some centralized labor authority as well as to the local labor union. Unless you have federal incorporation of all labor unions and national laws giving the rank and file of labor free election of labor leaders, you would, under the Walker plan, turn all American industry over to an irresponsible labor oligarchy in Washington. Just remember that the management of a plant or a single industry throughout the country does not have a free hand to do as it pleases. There are stockholders to be considered. I suppose you will make the usual crack that stockholders count for nothing. That is a form of New Deal or Communist propaganda.

If all the stockholders were thrown out of the window and management did not have to consider them at all, it could not do as it pleased. It is absolutely subject to the price scales and other conditions of the general market in which it buys raw materials and sells its product. It is also subject absolutely to the introduction of new inventions and to technical changes in patents, machines, and processes. It must either adapt plant operations to these pressures from the outside or go into bankruptcy. And organized labor in the plant generally tries to block these changes in the interest of keeping or getting work for its members.

BEARD: But, Mr. Whiteworth, suppose all industry were organized on a national scale to deal with labor organized on a national scale. If power confronted power, organized industry and organized labor, would not a kind of general and equal bargaining power be created?

WHITEWORTH: It is useless to suppose such a case. Yet I will suppose it. Such a management-labor organization on a national scale would be bigger than the Government. One or the other would have to rule. There would be a fight between Government and the management-labor combination. And the Government would come out on top, or perhaps the United States Army. To get such a combination of management and labor, you would have to force all the millions of little business concerns into it and all the millions of industrial workers who now refuse to join labor unions. We may have to face that some day, but that would be a Bolshevik revolution or a Fascist revolution, not a phony managerial revolution. If management and labor did win out against the Federal Government, they would soon begin to fight it out between themselves.

BEARD: There seem to be some formidable difficulties in the way of providing a national economic underwriting by a management-labor combination. But suppose that all industries and all industrial workers were organized in locals and on a national scale. Suppose they could agree on hours, wages, and everything else of significance to them. Suppose all industries and all labor unions were organized and then united in one big holding company, with a monopoly over all conditions of production established by friendly arrangements. Suppose that government, which you both agree must continue to exist, accepts your set-up. Suppose all this. Then let me ask you this question, What about agriculture, that other branch of economy so vital to the life of our nation; what would you do about that?

This question was greeted by a shrug of the shoulders from Mr. Whiteworth, and another from Mr. Walker. A desultory argument followed, in which they admitted that agriculture was vital to the feeding of managers and industrial workers, that they knew little about it, and that they had no plans in their schemes for organizing and adjusting the relations of agriculture to industry.

Then I put another question.

BEARD: Suppose now that we did have a workable plan for agriculture, your monopoly by management and labor would still be subject to fluctuations in the national market. It would be also subject more or less to fluctuations in the international market, even if you or the Federal Government created a national autarchy, that is, adopted a program of national self-sufficiency. You will still have depressions, less violent, perhaps. Is there anything in your management-labor scheme to provide a real economic underwriting, full employment for all workers all the time, on any level or wages?

Another desultory debate occurred, the Smyths taking part in it. The opinion was expressed that fluctuations in business would be less violent, that the level of employment would be somewhere between the depression bottom and boom top. There was no agreement that anything like full employment or even an approach to that ideal could be guaranteed under any management-labor combination. All conceded that heavy responsibility for dealing with unemployment would still have to be assumed by government.

Thereupon I put my final question: What would you do about *new* ideas as to how industry, labor, agriculture, and government should be run—ideas which would continue to arise unless an iron censorship were imposed on all thinking?

That question encountered impatience on the part of Mr. Whiteworth and Mr. Walker. They appeared to regard it as irrelevant or academic, as having nothing to do with their affairs, either management or labor. They fumbled about with the notion that if fair economic conditions could be maintained, people would be contented, and no troublesome ideas in favor of change would come up to bother them. Mr. Whiteworth was not sure that this would prove to be the case. Mr. Walker thought it would be hard to stop agitations in organized labor even under just agreements with employers; that when things were about perfect in this respect, agitators would stir up troubles in their unions and sometimes pull off wildcat strikes on some grounds.

DR. SMYTH: To provide an economic underwriting for the Republic, indeed to keep it going on an even keel, we need a human science more comprehensive than the so-called science of the management-labor combination.

BEARD: I heartily applaud that. So do many of the leading figures in American business, labor organizations, and politics. There is an immense and growing literature on that very subject. Here is a book—George Galloway's *Postwar Planning in the United States*—which gives one hundred and ten pages to listing the organizations and agencies, public and private, engaged in studies and activities connected with economic underwriting; and thirty pages to the titles of books, articles, and other materials bearing on the subject. If you will come into my north library, I will show you groaning shelves full of the books and folders of clippings I have myself collected. For years there has been a striking convergence of American thought on public and associational efforts to provide full employment, expand our productive plant, provide an economic underwriting. The convergence of thought is, in my opinion, an impressive sign of the times—a promise of action to come.

After we had returned to the fireside, Mr. Whiteworth and Mr. Walker soon took their leave, but Dr. and Mrs. Smyth lingered a few moments, evidently impressed by the casual examination of the materials which I had showed them.

MRS. SMYTH, puzzled by the evening's procedure: With all the live, up-to-date books and articles by prominent writers from business, labor, and political circles at your command, why did you wind and twist your way through history and details tonight? Why did you not go right straight at a comprehensive summary of all these plans for getting right down to the work of providing an economic underwriting for the Republic in modern terms?

DR. SMYTH, before I could answer: I suspect Beard of trying to lead us, especially Whiteworth and Walker, all around through the tortuous course of history and petty details for the purpose of tripping us up, tying us in knots, breaking down our assurance, forcing us to define our words, frightening us into believing that something heroic would have to be done to create what he calls an economic underwriting. It is a kind of game borrowed from old Socrates and dressed up in an American garb, that is, with less theory and more facts. Anyway, it worked pretty well.

BEARD: You do me too much honor by associating me with Socrates. I thoroughly appreciate your joke. If I possessed even a hundredth part of his acumen in analyzing ideas, I should be happy. But in another way, I want to steer entirely clear of both Socrates and Plato. In my opinion, Greek metaphysics has done damage, not good, to the Western world and to Christian thought and practice. If modern Europeans had devoted to the study of *The Federalist* the attention they gave to Plato's *Republic,* they would have been far better off in every way.

You ascribe to me far more consciousness of purpose than I was aware of in shaping the direction of our discussion tonight. If I had attacked the subject head-on by summarizing the best contemporary plans for an economic underwriting of our Republic, we should have got into a maze of prejudices and lost sight of the ominous significance of the theme for the future of the nation. At least, I so view the tactics of the occasion.

XX

The Republic in the World of Nations

ON Mrs. Smyth's insistence, to which I bowed with some reluctance, our seminar on foreign policies took the form of a social conclave at her home. I had supposed that she intended to have a small company in for the evening, but when I arrived late, on account of a cold and balky motor, I found her spacious drawing room crowded and a cocktail party in full swing. Already faces were becoming red and voices loud. As I stepped out on the gallery overlooking the scene, I quickly discovered that Mrs. Smyth had deliberately brought together choice members of the intelligentsia from the town and the neighborhood. Some of them I knew personally and others mainly through their writings in the daily papers or their propaganda activities or their lectures to the natives.

Suppressing a lusty desire to escape to my retreat on Hosannah Hill, I slipped into the drawing room by a side door. Mrs. Smyth took me immediately to Professor and Mrs. Tempey, with both of whom I had been acquainted for years. The Professor, who teaches international relations at Berwick University, greeted me a little boisterously and victoriously with: How's the old isolationist? To which Mrs. Tempey added, with a smile intended to be devastating: A bit confused *now,* I suspect?

As I was not selling groceries or peddling intellectual wares at a price, I could express my sentiments freely, and I said: Confused as ever, Mrs. Tempey. I confess that I never have been able to reduce the world and universal history to a simple miniature with no blurred lines in it.

While the Tempeys were profusely commenting on my reply, I secretly turned off my hearing instrument and my mind ran back over the memories of nearly fifty years. The Professor had been an ardent supporter of President Wilson's League of Nations and put the blame for all the troubles that had befallen the world since 1919 on the people of the United States. With the aid of grants from Peace Foundations he had kept up the battle for the League with never-failing optimism, and combined his teaching at the University with lecturing all over the country to foreign policy associations, women's clubs, and every kind of organization that would lend him ears. Whenever I had seen him, he had told me the peace movement was making rapid progress.

The Washington conference for the reduction of naval armaments he welcomed with enthusiasm as a step toward the pacification of the Far East. The Locarno treaties proved to him that he was on the right line. The Kellogg Pact of 1928, by which the nations of the earth renounced war as an instrument of national policy, brought Tempey's zeal to a boiling point. The defeat of the proposal to enter the World Court, by the United States Senate, discouraged him for a moment, but President Roosevelt's Quarantine Speech at Chicago in 1937 revived his spirits and assured him that what he then called collective security was the key to the salvation of mankind. The Atlantic Charter and President Roosevelt's four freedoms for the world made Tempey's cup of joy run over. After Pearl Harbor he immediately gave the following statement to the press:

> At last national unity has been attained, national confusion has been blown away by Japanese treachery. We are now one people, with one mind, with one resolve, namely, that after the Axis powers have been destroyed a new world order guaranteeing permanent peace and the four freedoms to all peoples will be established.

Mrs. Tempey was not less zealous in the advocacy of internationalism than her husband. They had both spent two summers in Europe, on fellowships from a Peace Foundation, studying international affairs. On her return from the second trip, Mrs. Tempey toured the United States, lecturing on America's Duty in the Present Crisis. She had given a course of six lectures in our city auditorium on: The British Commonwealth of Nations, Western Europe, Central and Eastern Europe, The Balkans, The Communist Menace, and The Far East. One of our dailies which had regularly hammered President Roosevelt's New Deal for pauperizing the United States, while praising his foreign policies after 1937, reported Mrs. Tempey's lectures fully, so that I could read them and discover for myself how wonderful they were.

While the Tempeys were alternately praising the glorious times in which we are living, Frank Brooklin joined us, despite signs of disapproval from the Tempeys. Brooklin is a kind of free lance associated with one of our newspapers. I had known him principally through his writings. He had an occasional column on Village Gossip which was undoubtedly clever. He also reviewed books with equal facility. Just for my own enlightenment I kept clippings of them for a year and noted that he reviewed one hundred and twenty-five books, ranging from universal history and political philosophy through geopolitics to scientific progress and modernist fiction. Like Mrs. Tempey's lectures, they were wonderful.

It was rumored around town that Brooklin was or had been a communist, or at least a fellow traveler. At all events he had been active in the Popular Front. After Hitler and Stalin made their pact in 1939, he denounced the conflict in Europe as just another imperialist war. During the life of this pact he fraternized with the Peace Mobilization crowd. Once he tried to enlist my interest in it, but I characterized his proposal as indefensible. As soon as the German army invaded Russia, Brooklin reversed himself as quickly as if he had received commands from a drill sergeant, and blossomed out for 'the people's war' and 'the new democratic world order.'

In a few seconds the Tempeys and Brooklin were deadlocked in a dispute, most of which I managed to miss. Before it closed I heard the Professor tell Brooklin that the United Nations would 'take care of Stalin' 'if he tried to block the right kind of settlement in Eastern Europe and Asia.'

By this time several of Mrs. Smyth's guests had gathered around us. A British professional lecturer and propagandist, who had spent years in scouting in the regions west of the Hudson River, engaged the Tempeys in a discussion over the fate of the British Empire after the war. They favored a liquidation of all empires and a pooling of colonial resources under a system of mandates. He, on his part, insisted that 'it just could not be made to work.'

Another disputant thought that Herbert Agar was the intellectual superman of the times. A young woman, who had read Ely Culbertson's fifty-page plan for organizing the world, explained that it was 'more realistic' than any of the others. One of her companions stoutly maintained that regional organizations throughout the world ought to come first, and that Herbert Hoover should be designated by President Roosevelt as head of a committee to work out the details. 'Of course,' she conceded, 'a world council and a world court would have to be added in order to effect the proper coordination of the several regions.'

From far off on the right came the booming voice of Theodore Laif, chairman of the local Council for Co-operation among Peace Societies. He said that while he approved all the other serious thinkers' ideas, he had, with regret, noted a neglect of the part to be played by the democracy of China in the coming world order. He had been deeply moved, he said, by the profound writings of Pearl Buck and Lin Yu Tang on that point and felt sure that American people, by their neglect, were alienating the affections of the powerful Chinese nation and driving it into the arms of Russia, the arch intriguer on the northwestern frontiers. Just as the Tempeys and Brooklin closed in on Laif, Mrs. Smyth drew me aside and I missed the outcome of the argument.

Mrs. Smyth: I have invited all these people to give colors and tones to our party. Besides yourself, there are to be only four regular speakers. These four guests have positive plans for the coming world order and I hope our discussion can be made to turn on their projects. I shall try to keep the belligerents now gathered around the Tempeys off on the side lines.

The first of my star performers (said Mrs. Smyth) is Doctor Margaret Farebanks, a Doctor of Philosophy in International Relations, from one of our greatest universities. Dr. Farebanks spent several years at Geneva observing the League of Nations in operation and supports a modified League for the world as the best guarantee of permanent peace.

For a thoroughgoing federation of the world, John Lytelton speaks with confidence. A retired lawyer with a keen mind and wide knowledge of federal principles, Mr. Lytelton has devoted a long time to the study of his chosen subject. He has reached a firm conclusion that a league of sovereign nations is bound to fail and, using the analogy of the American Union, he proposes a world federation on the model of our United States.

The third star, Dr. Ryald Hetherson, is the local representative of a union of Protestant churchmen who are working for the Christianization of international relations. Dr. Hetherson has no fixed plans for a world government or order. He is prepared, he says, to support any plan that offers promise of world peace, though he believes that none will be successful unless the peoples and governments of the world are animated by the Christian spirit.

The fourth leading performer is Professor George Winstanley from Carstairs University, a teacher of economics. He is skeptical of politics and politicians and has developed a project for an economic union of nations to precede a political union. He favors, he says, getting down to bed-rock by starting a union of like-minded nations on principles of reciprocal economic advantages.

Having introduced me to her four stars, Mrs. Smyth gave the signal for a march to the dining table. In the seating arrangement I was placed between Mrs. Tempey and Mr. Brooklin and, while they continued in loud tones the debate on the role to be played by Russia in post-war plans for peace, I enjoyed my victuals, marveling throughout at Mrs. Smyth's skill in the management of household economy. From snatches of conversations around the table I gathered the impression that I was not the only person present who suffered from confusion about the coming "world order."

After the meal was over, the proponents of plans, informed of their role by our hostess in advance, drew bundles of papers out of their portfolios.

Mrs. Smyth opened the conference: Since it is already apparent that many differences of opinion exist among us, I suggest that we discover first the fundamental propositions on which we agree before we take up specific plans for the new world order. I suppose that at the outset we can all consent to this statement: The supreme object of American foreign policy ought to be to bring permanent, or lasting, peace to the nations of the earth.

Dr. Smyth, after a silence that seemed to give consent: If you adopt your usual method, Beard, you will want to ask upon what assumptions respecting the universe of mankind that proposition rests. I first thought that inquiring about basic assumptions was just a quirk on your part, but after nineteen sessions I have come to the conclusion that there is some sense in it. So try it on these new innocents.

Beard: This party belongs to you and your wife, not to me. I prefer to remain a listener, or at least to wait until some definite schemes for attaining the objective are before us.

PROFESSOR WINSTANLEY: Surely you agree that such should be the supreme object of our foreign policy?

BEARD: You ask me a direct question, Professor, and I should like to answer it if I could. But I do not understand two terms used in the proposition as stated by our hostess. Mrs. Smyth, are you using permanent and lasting as synonymous? In my mind they are not. Permanent means forever, for all time. Lasting means for some period of time, not necessarily everlasting. It will not help to introduce that other weasel word, durable. It makes a great difference whether you set out to make a permanent or everlasting peace or a peace that will endure for what we hope will prove to be a long period of time, let us say thirty, forty, or fifty years.

MRS. SMYTH: Frankly, I used the terms rather thoughtlessly, in the current fashion. I meant, of course, a permanent peace, that is, putting a final end to war.

[A chorus of approval greeted this clarification of Mrs. Smyth's proposition, but Mr. Brooklin gave me a wink.]

MRS. TEMPEY: Come now and give us your answer, so that we can divide the sheep and the goats.

BEARD: To save time, I will declare simply that I do not believe that the supreme object of American foreign policy should be to bring permanent peace to the nations of the world.

PROFESSOR TEMPEY: Then, what on earth should it be?

BEARD: In my opinion, the supreme object of American foreign policy should be to protect and promote the interests, spiritual and material, of the American people, and, subject to that mandate, to conduct foreign affairs in such a manner as to contribute to the peace and civilization of mankind. Or, to put it another way, to protect and advance American civilization on this continent, the firm earthly basis of our economic and military power, with due reference to relevant international responsibilities.

In order to get on, I was willing to let Mrs. Smyth's proposition stand. But since the question of underlying presuppositions has been raised, I answer that the proposition rests upon four huge assumptions: First, that *the supreme object of our national life* is to bring permanent peace to all nations; a foreign policy directed to the end of permanent peace would be vain unless unreservedly supported by our domestic economy and moral resources. Second, that world peace is desirable or good for mankind or a majority of mankind. Third, that the constitution of our universe makes it possible to effect and maintain permanent world peace for all mankind. Fourth, that it is possible for the Government of the United States to secure at home adequate and continuous support for making and keeping this world peace, a support that will provide all the military, economic, and other sacrifices which it would entail upon our people.

PROFESSOR WINSTANLEY: Surely, you believe that permanent world peace is desirable.

BEARD: As a human being, I share that aspiration, but as a student of history I do not *know* that it is desirable, that it would be good for all mankind. Mankind has never experienced peace throughout the world for any long period of time. There are many writers on politics, history, and biology who contend that prolonged peace would lead to degeneration among some peoples and overpopulation in many countries, particularly in the Orient. But, as I have said, I share the aspiration for world peace and am willing to assume, to take the risk, that it would be desirable.

DR. FAREBANKS: That is a sour note of skepticism, to begin with. You cannot base effective action on anything less than firm conviction that your ends are *feasible* as well as desirable.

DR. SMYTH: I do not see that at all. When I perform a surgical operation I want to proceed on knowledge, not mere conviction. When I encounter a new problem in surgery I want to get some real knowledge about it before I lay open a living body. Beard did not say that permanent peace is *not* desirable. He said he did not know it *is,* on the basis of human experience. But, in spite of that he consents to let you make the assumption that it is desirable. That is what he calls an act of faith.

PROFESSOR WINSTANLEY: But Beard also struck a second note of skepticism by saying that the possibility of world peace also is a mere assumption. Militarists are constantly insisting that there has always been war and there always will be war, that permanent peace is an impossibility. Now a lot of evils once defended as necessary have been abolished. Executions for witchcraft, for one instance. Chattel slavery for another. Defenders of slavery were always citing history, contending that slavery had always existed and therefore always would and must exist. I for one do not propose to be deceived by that type of historical argument. I believe that world peace is a possibility.

DR. SMYTH: Pardon me. You have just said that you believe that world peace is a possibility. You did not say that you *know* it. That is an act of faith on your part. The fact that many evils have been abolished does not prove that this evil, if it is an evil, can also be abolished. Beard agreed to share your aspiration on that point. What you and Doctor Farebanks call skepticism seems to me to be merely caution. Let us take up the fourth assumption, namely, that it is possible for the Government of the United States to get adequate popular support for making a world peace and for all the military, economic, and other sacrifices which it would entail. This is something on which we all, as citizens, at least have opinions. I am inclined to take the affirmative position on that question.

DR. HETHERSON: I am decidedly of the same opinion. War is a barbaric evil. . . .

MRS. SMYTH: You do not include our war with Japan, Germany, and Italy?

DR. HETHERSON: On the contrary, ours is a righteous war against war. I mean war as an institution is a barbaric evil. I believe that the American people, along with most of the peoples of the earth, are heartily sick of war and want to put a stop to it—want to establish institutions to assure permanent peace. Isolationism is dead as a door-nail in the United States. The American people are ready to make any sacrifice necessary to assure a permanent world order. They were ready for it and in favor of it in 1919. If it had not been for tricky and ambitious Republican politicians, the United States would have joined the League of Nations and the present war would not have come about. The recent Gallup polls all show the American people ready and anxious for a settlement after this war that will put an end to war. They are prepared to make all the sacrifices necessary to gain that great end of humanity.

MRS. SMYTH: Is that your understanding of the American spirit, Mr. Beard?

BEARD: Personally, I am in favor of pushing the war against Germany, Japan, and Italy to a successful conclusion. Whether it is righteous in the sight of God I leave to our theologian, Dr. Hetherson. In my opinion, too, there has been a decline in the sheer love of war among many nations. A lot of people in every country become sick of war after they have been in it for two or three years; but the great nations seem to like a war every generation or two. At least they seem to like it enough to get into it. I suspect that there is something in the old adage that when the devil is sick, he would be a saint. Before I agree to the proposition that isolationism is dead, I should like to hear a definition of the term.

DR. HETHERSON: I volunteer to define it. Isolationism is the creed that America owes nothing to other countries and has no moral responsibilities in the world; that foreign wars are none of our business; that the United States should shrink behind high national-ist walls, let the world go hang, and refuse to co-operate in efforts to maintain peace in the world.

BEARD: If that is a correct definition of isolationism, I must say that I never heard of an American of the slightest importance in public life who favors isolationism. If that is isolationism, it is indeed dead; or rather, it never came to life. At least I approve burying the corpse. However, I have no way of knowing that the overwhelming majority of the American people were in favor of our entrance into the League of Nations in 1919. They did not elect Mr. Wilson President in 1916 on a commitment to make a war, or to take the United States into such a League as was set up at Versailles. Just why they elected him, I do not know, but one of the popular slogans in the campaign was that he kept us out of war.

When, in the congressional campaign of 1918, President Wilson called for the return of Democrats to support his policies, the majority of the voters answered him with an emphatic repudiation of his call. I do not maintain that this was a vote against the League of Nations idea, but certainly it is not to be interpreted as a vote for the League idea. Nor do I agree that it was merely tricky Republican politicians who defeated the ratification of the League covenant. I haven't a word to say in defense of the Republican tactics. But President Wilson, by numerous important actions, espe-cially by rejecting compromise modifications, was partly responsible for his own defeat and the defeat of the League.

In any case, if the American people were warmly in favor of the League, as Dr. Hetherson maintains, they had a chance to show it in the election of 1920. The Democrats promised to join the League. The Republicans equivocated. The voters may have been in favor of the League, but they proved in a landslide that they were more in favor of something else. To put the case in another way, there were not enough in favor of the League to elect the men who squarely pledged themselves to put it into effect. Some Republicans said that Harding favored the League, but he merely spoke vaguely of some kind of international association. The weight of evidence, in my judgment, runs against the contention that the majority of the American people ever favored the League intensely enough to force ratification by the Senate.

What efforts and sacrifices in the interest of permanent peace the American people are willing to make or support now is for me problematical. As to the Gallup polls, cited by Dr. Hetherson, they have often been amazingly correct in predicting election returns, but they missed fire badly in the congressional election of 1942, when more than half of the active voters cast their ballots for Republican candidates, and a lot of so-called pre-Pearl Harbor isolationists were successful at the polls.

Hence I am unwilling to base anything serious on a Gallup poll, even relative to election figures. They are worse than useless on matters of opinion. People who would not actually sacrifice a pin for an opinion will say 'yes' to an abstract proposition. Gallup polls, as critics have pointed out, do not measure the *intensity* of opinions or convictions. Intensity of interest, as well as numbers of heads, counts in determining what the American people will support in the way of labor and sacrifice. A majority of the American people may be for an all-out effort to establish and maintain world peace. Though I have grave doubts about it, they may be.

MRS. SMYTH: At this juncture I should like to read the following statement which I have drawn up:

We assume or believe that permanent world peace is desirable and possible; that efforts should be made to establish an international agreement or agreements most likely to effect and maintain it; and that the American people will support such agreement or agreements as general propositions.

Suppose we take a Gallup poll here on this and then consider the specific elements which are to fit into the general proposition.

BEARD: The vote is unanimous, save for my reservation that I am unwilling to accept the formula without an inspection of the agreement or agreements in detail.

MRS. SMYTH: Since we have here representatives of three definite plans for world organization, I suggest that we now have Dr. Fare-banks' statement for the League of Nations, to be modified by amendments. The League is still in existence, and many people are inclined to start with an institution that is not solely new theory. We know something about the League, how it worked, and what its shortcomings were. Mrs. Farebanks has long been associated with our local League of Nations Society, and has observed the League at work in Geneva.

Dr. Farebanks: Nobody can speak with authority for all sup-porters of the League as to modifications in the League regarded as necessary to make it an effective organization for permanent peace. But after a study of many proposals for changes in the con-stitution of the League, which competent authorities have made, I present the following:

1. The states as members of the League must surrender the idea of enjoying henceforward complete sovereignty, and accept a cur-tailment of their sovereignty.

2. The rule of unanimous decision in the Council of the League must be abrogated and provision made for the application of sanctions and force to aggressors on a two-thirds vote.

3. There must be created for the League an executive department strong enough to enforce the decisions of the Council against peace-breakers.

4. It will be necessary to institute an international armed force at the disposal of the League for police work and for putting down aggressors, including insurrectionists.

5. An international Economic Department must be established in the League on the model of the International Labor Office. The Department should embrace representatives of governments, man-agement, and labor. Its duty would be to administer legislation of the League pertaining to world commerce, finance, migration, and living standards.

That a League so constituted could maintain world peace and promote the economic measures favorable to such peace I have no doubt. I shall merely indicate by a single quotation how easily it could work in case of a crisis threatening peace. It is from the address of Prime Minister Churchill delivered to the Congress of the United States on December 16, 1941. 'Five or six years ago,' Churchill declared, 'it would have been easy, without shedding a drop of blood, for the United States and Great Britain to have insisted on the fulfilment of the disarmament clauses in the treaties Germany signed after the Great War.'

In these few words, Mr. Churchill showed how we could have avoided the Second World War. I could enlarge upon the subject, but this is the substance of my case for the new League. Any questions?

BEARD: Would it not have been possible, without shedding a drop of blood, for Great Britain, France and Russia, all members of the League, to have suppressed Hitler in 1933, or Mussolini in 1936, or both of them in 1939? Could they not have done this without the aid of the United States?

DR. FAREBANKS: Unquestionably they had the physical force, but they could not co-operate.

BEARD: What reason have you for believing that the United States, if it had been a member of the League in 1935 or 1936, would have forced co-operation against Hitler and Mussolini on Great Britain, France, and Russia?

DR. FAREBANKS: I think that the United States, being a democratic country and more impartial in respect of Europe, would have been quicker to see the danger to peace offered by the rise of Mussolini and Hitler, and more likely to have insisted on co-operation against them.

BEARD: Is it not true that Great Britain went behind France's back, in violation of the Versailles Treaty, and made a naval deal with Hitler in 1935?

DR. FAREBANKS: Yes. That, I think, was a mistake.

BEARD: Did not Churchill once declare himself in favor of Fascism for Italy, and praise Mussolini? Did not American bankers and investors help to underwrite Mussolini with the aid of a large loan floated in the United States? Is there not evidence that the Tory government in London before 1939 was more eager to turn Hitler against Russia than to form a combination against him and destroy him?

DR. FAREBANKS: I concede that those are the facts. However, I do not see their relevance to the problem of the reformed League of Nations to prevent the repetition of such mistakes.

BEARD: You have admitted that, if the nations of Europe now united against the Axis had really wanted to suppress Mussolini or Hitler at any time before 1939, they could have done it easily without our aid. You have acknowledged that they did not need the help of the United States to effect that end. Have you any more support than your own opinion for believing that, if the United States had been in the League all along, things would have been any different? As between Russian communism and fascism from 1924 to 1939, on which side did American sentiments lie in the main?

Mrs. Smyth: Pardon me for interrupting. Such a discussion of ancient history could go on indefinitely. I suggest that we now have the federation plan from Mr. Lytelton.

Mr. Lytelton: I shall state my case as briefly as possible. The reformed League, as presented by Dr. Farebanks, in my opinion would not be strong enough to overcome the disruptive force of the national sovereignties, even if diminished. Their conflicts over interests, prestige, commerce, colonies, and special priviliges would go on as before and end in another disruption of the world confederacy so constituted. Instead, I propose a real federation of all the nations on the model of the United States of America.

All nations would be equally represented in the Senate or Council. In the lower house or Assembly, they would be represented more or less on the basis of population. There would be an Executive, perhaps of three members. The federation government would have adequate powers, akin to those of the Congress of the United States, over international commerce and finance, and all other common concerns. It would have the power to aid member governments against insurrections and to suppress conflicts among those governments verging in the direction of war. The various national states in the federation would still possess large powers and discharge local functions as the states do now in the American Union.

Why do I believe that such a federation is feasible? The following are my reasons: The world has achieved an economic unity stronger than that of the United States in 1787. Commerce among the nations of the earth is more active and valuable than commerce among the American states in 1787. Rapid transportation has annihilated space and brought the nations of the earth closer together than the states of the American Union were in 1787. Local industries everywhere are more dependent for their existence upon world trade than the local industries in the American states in 1787 were dependent on national trade. Intercommunication among all parts of the world is instantaneous. Nationalism is dead or dying. The state of the world is ripe for federation. If not, why not?

DR. WINSTANLEY: Despite the economic unity which you mention, Mr. Lytelton, there are still grave conflicts of interest among the nations, especially the industrial and commercial nations. I recognize that these conflicts grow out of misinterpretation of national interests and that they are gross violations of the economic laws of the free world market. They are largely induced by politicians who inflame the sentiments of nations by appeals to prejudices. But they undoubtedly exist. It is for this reason that I propose to attack the problem of world peace from the economic instead of the political end.

At this turn of affairs a lively exchange of views occurred, in which the four world-planners took part. Dr. Farebanks was of the opinion that the independent nations were not ready to surrender as much sovereignty as a federation would require. Dr. Hetherson announced that he was ready to support any world plan that promised a lasting peace, while insisting that, unless the spirit of the several peoples of the earth were ready for it, success could not be expected. All the world-planners agreed, however, that Mr. Lytelton's description of the growing economic unification of the world had a close relation to the growing intellectual and spiritual unification of the world.

DR. SMYTH, looking in my direction: Let's have it.

BEARD: Mr. Lytelton makes a far-fetched analogy between the basic conditions of the thirteen American states in 1787 and the basic conditions of the fifty or more independent nations of the earth so utterly diverse in race, history, sentiments, and economy. All I ask you to do, if you want confirmation of my assertion, is to read the first five numbers of *The Federalist*. In America in 1787 more than ninety percent of the whites were of British origin—had a common historical heritage. A common language and the broad principles of a common civil and criminal law prevailed from New Hampshire to Georgia; most of the people were Christians in religious profession; the traditions of the Revolution united their hearts; fear of foreign aggression against the young Republic was a potent force in overcoming their diversities of interest.

The ancient heritages of Europe and Africa and Asia have not been wholly uprooted by the mere adoption and use of the machines and the gadgets of modern industrialism. Nor does a common use of machines make men, women, and children of all nations alike in traditions, habits, sentiments, and values. Moreover hundreds of millions of the earth's people do not have gadgets or machines and are not likely to have them soon, if ever. Nor is the statement, often repeated, that inventions have annihilated space and brought people closer together anything more than a metaphor. Communications are no doubt quicker but the overwhelming majority of people in all the nations have no money or time for extensive traveling and, in space, are as far apart as ever.

If a world federation were formed, conflicts of national interests would go on inside of it. It took a long and bloody civil war to decide the question as to who was to govern the United States of America. A war is no less a war because it is called civil instead of foreign. There is no reason I can fathom for believing that the closer nations are drawn together by commerce and intercourse, the more alike they become intellectually, morally, and spiritually. I suspect that the exact opposite may often be true, as the present state of the world seems to hint. I do not believe that economic practices and relations determine all political relations and sentiments. I do not believe that the politics which Professor Winstanley scorns is all bad or can ever be subdued to purely economic considerations. I sometimes think that politics is more of a determining force in history than economics.

DR. SMYTH: Whew! That is unmitigated pessimism.

MRS. SMYTH: Let us hear from Dr. Hetherson.

DR. HETHERSON: As I have said, I have no precise plan for the coming world order. Some plan is doubtless necessary, but I prefer to leave that to practical persons, like my colleagues, who have spoken for a reformed League and for a new federation. I start from the proposition that war as an institution is barbaric and unchristian; that economic sacrifices must be made by the American people to usher in permanent peace; that Christians must make these sacrifices; that the brotherhood of man is a fact, is a great truth; and that the Christians of the world, in co-operation with Jews, must spread the spirit of brotherhood throughout the earth. I agree heartily with Herbert Hoover and Hugh Gibson, who say in their *Problems of a Lasting Peace:* 'In the end there can be no trustworthy security except by giving the decent elements in a people a chance to co-operate in the work of peace.' In the domain of the spirit lies our hope. God's law of love must reign throughout the earth. When the spirit is ready all obstacles to a lasting peace will be overcome.

During Dr. Hetherson's discourse, here abridged, shadows of impatience occasionally flickered over the faces of the other world-planners. Only Mrs. Smyth listened steadily, with occasional approving glances. At the end, after a long silence Dr. Smyth looked at me with quizzical eyes and inquired: Well?

BEARD: If the peoples of the earth were animated by Dr. Hetherson's spirit, the problems of a lasting peace would be easy of solution. The Christian world-view has been a powerful force in Western history. Its coming destiny I do not pretend to divine. Where conduct squares with that world-view, peace *does* reign.

Mrs. Smyth relieved the tension by calling for Professor Winstanley's project of an Economic Union.

PROFESSOR WINSTANLEY: At this late hour, I can give you only the barest outline. For details I must refer you to Otto T. Mallery's *Economic Union and Durable Peace* or, if you are cramped for reading time, to his 'Typical Plans for a Postwar World Peace' published in *International Conciliation* for November, 1942. My plan differs from his in some ways, but I accept his basic principles. He states them as follows:

1. If goods cannot cross political frontiers, soldiers will.
2. Unless shackles can be dropped from trade, bombs will drop from the sky.
3. Economic bargains, likely to be kept, are preferable to political agreements likely to be broken.
4. Mass unemployment was not overcome by the trade and economic policies adopted by the principal industrial nations during the period between wars, except while preparing for war. Therefore these policies were failures and must be superseded.

It might be well to stop here and consider these principles advanced by Mr. Mallery before we take up concrete plans.

BEARD, after waiting for other comment: Until I have heard the details of your plan I prefer to reserve my remarks on these principles. To me they are not principles at all, but rhetorical flourishes. They consist of two misleading images, one declaration that is historically untenable, and at the end a grand *non sequitur*.

PROFESSOR WINSTANLEY: Of course, if you reject these principles, you will reject the plan of Economic Union based on them. Still, here are the elements of the plan, in my own words, with modifications of my own making:

1. To get full employment and raise living standards for more people of the earth, the benefits of mass production must be extended over larger and larger geographical areas.

2. This extension of mass production cannot be made by any peace conference or by any sudden introduction of free trade. It must be done gradually and mainly by extension of economic agreements among nations.

3. Such agreements cannot be left to politicians. They should be made by agents of management, labor, and governments representing like-minded nations at first and then all other nations.

4. Equal access to raw materials and to the ever-widening international market must be given to the defeated nations in due time.

5. The Economic Union so formed should be governed by an Economic Board representing managers, workers, and governments.

6. The Economic Board, with a Bank at its service, would promote reciprocal trade agreements, aid in giving equal access to colonial raw materials, enforce international fair trade practices, regulate cartels, and promote joint action against depressions.

7. The Economic Union can exist in, under, or alongside any kind of international organization or institutions which may be established. It is a business proposition appealing to capital and labor. By mediation and action it would seek to promote the welfare of all member nations and adjust economic conflicts among them, thus removing the struggles of interests which constitute the main causes of war.

As Mr. Mallery says: 'Our greatest foe is cynicism and fear that what ought to be can never be. Against this fear all plans and planners should present a united front and avow with a calm vehemence that faith is essential to its own realization.'

If I may speak frankly, the kind of cynicism that Mr. Beard expressed at the beginning of our session, which he shares with too many Americans, is the chief barrier to such economic union among nations and to lasting peace for mankind.

BEARD: I do not see that it helps to bring cynicism into our discussion. You have yourself made cynical references to politicians, but I cannot discover in what way references to cynicism advance our knowledge or understanding. We are trying, I take it, to discover ways and means of bringing peace and well-being to the United States and other nations as far as possible and for as long a period of time as possible. In this quest a testing of details by such historical experience and power of reasoning on probabilities as we have at our command seems to me the more helpful method.

So I will venture to take up a few points in the program which has just been presented. What do you mean, Professor Winstanley, by the phrase, equal access to raw materials for all nations? As I understand the words raw materials, they include, besides mineral and organic substances in their raw state, such as copper and timber, also unfinished agricultural products, such as cotton, rice, and tobacco. Various nations, for example, have neither oil nor cotton.

If the United States should give them equal access to its resources, would that allow capitalists and laborers from those countries to enter the United States and exploit our resources for themselves? Since these resources are largely in private ownership in the United States, who is to fix prices for the privilege of exploitation, and how? If foreign capitalists and their workers are not to enter the United States and get this equal access at first hand, how is the equal access to be obtained? Finally, are foreign nations or nationals to pay for the goods they get in the United States, or are they to have them free of charge? If they are to pay, with which specific types of goods are they to pay?

DR. WINSTANLEY: You have a faulty conception of the whole business, Beard. Equal access to raw materials means: (1) nationals and governments of all nations shall have the same and equal right to buy our raw materials in our markets and export them, not the right to enter this country and develop the materials themselves; (2) there shall be no discrimination in our laws against any nation in respect of buying such raw materials; (3) the prices of such raw materials shall be the same for buyers of all nations; (4) all such raw materials are to be paid for, directly or indirectly. This abolition of discrimination would make for equality among the nations —between the haves and the have-nots.

BEARD: That does not differ essentially from the policies historically pursued by the United States, as I understand them. In peacetime any foreign governments or nationals can buy here anything they can pay for, out of cash or credits or money borrowed from American money-lenders. As a general rule, except in wartime, or war emergencies, all countries of the world have been equal in that sense, in American markets. If you are going to require foreigners to buy and pay for the raw materials they want from the United States, then the countries which have the greatest wealth and facilities for paying their bills will be best served in American markets. The have-nots with little or nothing to exchange for our raw materials will be able to get little or nothing here. Their equality of access is thus a mere fiction. Their position will be like that of the poorest people in New York City: they have equal access with the rich to the furs and jewels of Fifth Avenue; their only trouble is that they haven't the money to pay for such luxuries. There is one more point. Suppose the people of the United States wish to conserve their resources for themselves and sell only limited quantities? If they do this, then they will have special advantages as against other nations.

Several years ago, Mary Beard and I had lunch with H. G. Wells and Frank Simonds in Washington, both advocates of equal access to raw materials as a preventive of war. We put to them the very questions which I have put here. When Simonds was asked whether the have-nots were to pay for the raw materials they got in the United States, he answered 'Yes'; but he and Wells went on to argue that an international organization could facilitate exchanges so that the have-nots could pay for their raw materials.

When I pressed the contention that in the long run the have-nots would have to produce and send out real wealth to pay for their raw materials, Simonds admitted that that would be the case. The only important thing we could agree upon was that possibly by international commitments the colonies of various imperial powers might be forced open for the have-nots as well as for the haves to trade with them on equal terms. And Simonds admitted the fact that most of the precious raw materials of the world are to be found in independent countries, not in colonies.

Mr. Wells took the socialist position when Mary Beard asked him where he stood on this issue. He said that, after socialism had supplanted capitalist commercial rivalry, the question of capitalistic trade for profit would disappear and the world brotherhood of man would share and share alike. In his vision, the whole world would be one commonwealth of free people, and goods would flow freely from one part to another. He conceded that there would be exchanges of goods between the parts of the world.

Thereupon Mary Beard asked him whether, for example, the Russian part of the socialist world-commonwealth, having great riches in raw materials, would simply give huge supplies to the Chinese part or the Japanese part, that is, mine or work the raw materials and ship them away free of charge to have-nots of the world commonwealth. At this, Wells threw up the sponge and replied that, when the whole world was operated on socialist principles, such matters as intersocialist trade could be easily arranged. This left me in a fog, and so do Mr. Mallery's specific proposals.

PROFESSOR WINSTANLEY: So you want wars over commerce and raw materials to go on forever? It is generally understood among people who have studied the matter that the struggle for commercial advantages and raw materials is the chief cause of wars, the decisive cause. As Mr. Mallery well says: 'Unless shackles can be dropped from trade, bombs will drop from the sky.'

BEARD: The sentence you have just quoted is, in my opinion, a mere vague metaphor. Men were fighting for centuries before there was any international trade to shackle or unshackle. Recall the endless wars among the ancient Greeks. Were they all on account of shackles on trade? Of course not. Look at the Civil War in the United States. There was free trade from one end of the Union to the other; yet war came, long, bloody, and devastating war. As to what you call the chief cause of wars, or the decisive cause, I confess that I do not know the cause of anything and suspect that you . . .

DR. SMYTH: Hold him, Professor Winstanley! I saw on his desk at his house the other night a manuscript of endless pages, entitled *The Idea of 'Cause' in Natural Science and the Humanistic Sciences.* Come down to earth, Beard.

BEARD: All right, since you seem to think that an effort to be exact in the use of language is unearthly—and futile. What does anybody mean by the metaphor dropping the shackles off trade? I understand, a little bit, the phrase free trade. It means that there shall be no government interference with commerce among nations in the form of protective tariffs, bounties, monetary management, and other discriminative devices. It means that the nationals of all countries shall be free to exchange goods among themselves on terms made by themselves.

Such free trade takes for granted a vast and complicated set of relations respecting property ownership and use and capitalistic production in each nation engaged in this so-called international commerce. It takes for granted also what is called free competition within each nation; that is the absence of private monopolistic controls over resources, patents, and processes in the restraint of trade. It assumes, too, that the United States will not be compelled to safeguard its resources and the devices necessary to the defense of the country or to any wars that it may get into, to say nothing of safeguarding the civilization of the American people.

I am familiar with free trade as promulgated by British industrialists at the middle of the nineteenth century when Britain was the workshop of the world. But I am unable to visualize it as applied to nations, empires, colonies, and protectorates, to the economies of the various nations and empires as now constituted, with all the kinds of government controls and systems of culture and production now in force, from Great Britain to Russia.

Do you actually believe, Professor Winstanley, that countries with managed economies like Russia, or partly managed economies like Great Britain and other first-rate powers, will or can return to the unmanaged economies such as existed fifty or a hundred years ago?

PROFESSOR WINSTANLEY: No, I realize that we are in an age of more or less managed economies and that a return to the conditions prevailing in 1850, or even 1914, is out of the question. As Mr. Mallery says, the economic union 'should begin with a few like-minded nations and not with the whole world.' That would include the countries with the largest amount of free enterprise.

BEARD: Well, American business men are constantly telling us that enterprise is not free here. But, aside from that, name the countries like-minded enough to form your economic union.

PROFESSOR WINSTANLEY: I should say the United States, Great Britain, France, most Latin American countries, Belgium, Holland,

Denmark, Norway, Canada, Australia—in general the democracies.

BEARD: But all the democracies have new deals or managed economies of one kind or another. If any government keeps control over its own currency, it will, in practice, more or less manage its economy and foreign trade. Are you proposing that each country abolish all the controls it has devised to deal with unemployment or to maintain its standards of living? Besides, how do you know what some of those countries will look like after the war?

PROFESSOR WINSTANLEY: I shall reply by repeating Mr. Mallery's words: 'Mass unemployment was not overcome by the trade and economic policies adopted by the principal industrial nations during the period between wars, except while preparing for wars. Therefore these policies were failures and must be superseded.'

I will add on my own account that any country that attempts to raise, or even maintain, its standards of life by managing its domestic economy is doomed to failure and will only end up in lowering its standards. As Cordell Hull has put the argument, no country can lift itself by its bootstraps. If we could get shackles off trade throughout the world, standards of living would automatically rise in all countries enjoying free trade. You would not then have the paradox of one country having shoes to sell and needing wheat, and other countries having wheat to sell and needing shoes—both suffering from unemployment and depressed standards. If they could trade freely, this condition of affairs would not exist.

BEARD: Mr. Mallery is dead right in holding that the measures taken to overcome mass employment by managing economy were not wholly successful, or, for the sake of argument, not successful at all. It does not follow either in logic or historical necessity that therefore these policies *must* be superseded, still less that they be specifically superseded by a world economic union or free trade. Nor does it follow that any expedient of international arrangement will in fact overcome mass unemployment, raise or maintain standards of life for the participating nations.

The very conditions which Professor Winstanley has described as existing between nations now separated by tariff barriers have existed between states of the American Union separated by no tariff barriers. In 1933 there were millions of people with wheat, corn, bacon, and cotton to sell in the West and South and millions of people with shoes, cotton cloth, automobiles, and cooking utensils to sell in the East and North. No trade shackles prevented them from exchanging goods, and yet thousands, nay, millions were suffering in the four sections of the country. What reason is there for believing that unshackling trade throughout the world will do something that unshackling it throughout the United States has not done, does not do? In print and orally I have been asking American economists that question for years and I have got nothing but grunts and contempt from them. One of them took the trouble to write a large pamphlet against me intimating that I am dishonest as well as an ass.

DR. HETHERSON: You are overlooking, in this economic discussion, all ethical questions. The United States is a great power and has the moral responsibilities of a great power. We are a Christian people, besides, and must make all the sacrifices necessary to prevent war and maintain peace and the four freedoms everywhere for everybody. We should not consider these questions in economic terms alone.

BEARD: For years imperialists and internationalists have been asserting that the United States is a great power and must assume the responsibilities of a great power. Of course the United States is a great power, and will be until it has exhausted its oil, coal, and iron, and the morale of the people has degenerated with the exhaustion of economic opportunities at home. Of course it has responsibilities. That is a truism. But what responsibilities? To whom, where, when, and in what form—intellectual, spiritual, and material?

It is not exactly true to say that we are a Christian people. The generalization is too sweeping. There are millions of Jews among us. More than half the population does not belong to any Christian denomination. But, apart from that, do Christians have obligations to help, without limits, Mohammedans, Buddhists, and other pagans that reject the Christian religion and are doing their best to beat back the tide of Christian missionaries?

Since we have been shifted to moral grounds, I want to put up to you a moral question which will test your claims to a higher morality: Are all you world-planners who stand for the brotherhood of man prepared to sweep away all our immigration laws and let your brothers and sisters from every part of the world migrate freely to the United States and settle here?

DR. HETHERSON: Your question is too broad. Some of us would

favor removing many restrictions on immigration and keeping others.

BEARD: Very well, let us take immigration legislation piecemeal. How many would abolish the exclusion of immigrants suffering from loathsome and contagious diseases, advocates of the overthrow of the American system of government, and persons guilty of crimes involving moral turpitude?

A long silence followed. Even Mr. Brooklin did no more than laugh softly.

BEARD: None of you, I take it. How many would abolish the literacy test for immigrants?

More silence.

BEARD: How many would abolish all numerical limits on immigration?

More silence.

BEARD: How many would abolish the quota system which discriminates against the peoples of Southern and Eastern Europe?

Two favored modifying the system at some time in the future. None favored an immediate repeal of the discriminative laws.

BEARD: How many would repeal the exclusion acts directed against the Japanese, Chinese, and millions of other Asiatics?

DR. HETHERSON: I favor putting all Orientals on the quota basis, thus doing away with discriminations, especially the discrimination against the Chinese.

Two others joined Dr. Hetherson in this view. The rest sat mute.

BEARD: The discriminative quota system is still discriminative, a denial of universal equality. How many here believe that it would be possible to induce the Congress of the United States to repeal any of the above laws restricting immigration?

The whole party was mute.

DR. HETHERSON, sadly breaking the stillness: I fear that Congress is more likely to increase the restrictions on immigration than to diminish them, even though such laws stir up ill-will against us in the Orient and in Southern and Eastern Europe.

BEARD: I assume that we all agree on the desirability of maintaining the Republic and our system of self-government and limited liberty. Do any of you think that it would contribute to the strength of the Republic and to the support of popular government, if Congress would admit several million immigrants from countries that have never displayed any zest for self-government and capacity for it?

A desultory discussion followed this question, revealing much difference of opinion. When Mrs. Smyth called for a show of hands, there were only two affirmative votes. One of the two qualified his affirmation by adding: Of course, I should want to apply literacy and other tests, besides that of mere bodily strength.

DR. SMYTH: This immigration question is evidently too hot for us to handle. It is a moral question. From a moral standpoint, from a Christian standpoint, there are objections to our exclusiveness in matters of immigration. Yet I realize that we do have certain precious ways of life which can be kept only by having a population fairly uniform in character. For us these ways are values. If they are values, then it would not help humanity to destroy them by allowing too many unassimilable elements to enter the country. Though I am troubled in my mind about our treatment of immigration, I feel certain of that.

BEARD: The issue is economic as well as moral. At all events organized labor in the United States has for more than fifty years battled for restrictions on immigration, holding the position that free immigration breaks down the standard of life for our industrial workers. Are not Americans in general convinced that a high standard of wages underwrites the good life, or at least works for a better quality of citizenship? Immigration restriction is as much a protective device as a protective tariff on manufactures.

It is, of course, contrary to that free movement of capital, labor and goods usually covered by the term free trade. Once, free immigration made it possible for people to get access to raw materials, land, and other resources. The access was not equal, for many persons wanted to come to America and yet could not raise the passage money; and many who came got little access to our natural resources, except with the pick and shovel as employees of corporations.

Limitations on immigration certainly bottle up American resources against the poor and hungry of other lands, especially those heavily overpopulated, like Italy, China, Japan, and India. Yet it appears that none of you will publicly declare that our responsibilities as a great power include making room for two or three hundred millions of European and Oriental people. Besides, you all know that experience demonstrates the futility of emigration as a solution for the problem of chronic overpopulation where it exists. The issue as I grasp it is one of our having morality without going to such extremes of sentimental sympathy that morality is destroyed in the United States.

MRS. SMYTH: Mr. Beard has played a negative role thus far, on the whole. It certainly would be interesting if not gratifying to learn what the old cynic actually thinks about plans for the post-war world and what he has to offer that is constructive.

BEARD: I thought you knew me better by this time, Mrs. Smyth, than to speak of me as a cynic, even jokingly. I am old obviously. But I resent the application of the term cynic to me, for it implies a low and contemptuous view of mankind and its struggles for civilization—a view I do not entertain. I especially resent it when it comes from this congregation, not a single member of which is optimistic enough, despite all the talk about universal union and brotherhood, to favor a total repeal of our immigration laws and the opening of our gates to the unlimited multitudes of hungry and oppressed men, women, and children in Europe, Africa, and Asia. Even the most optimistic among you are not optimistic enough to believe that the American people as represented in the Congress of the United States will in fact authorize any such repeal and such opening of our national gates. That's that for cynicism.

The discussion of what you call plans for the post-war world meets my personal approval, particularly when it is carried on in an equable temper, with due respect for stubborn facts, and without contempt for those who venture to question the workability of such plans. This discussion comports with the democratic process, which I prefer to characterize as the constitutional process of proposal, discussion, and adoption or rejection.

From the aspirations for the peace and happiness of the United States and the other nations of the world, expressed here, I do not dissent. I am sure of this much: I should like to see the world at peace, a world of highly civilized peoples as nations using their talents and resources to make the true, the good, the beautiful, and the useful prevail more widely.

Nevertheless when Mrs. Smyth asks me what I *think* about plans for the post-war world, instead of being moved to make a string of assertions as they come to my lips, I am shocked into inquiring what one thinks one is doing when one thinks, especially about a matter of the future invisible to us. Since I am no scholastic able to spin out propositions indefinitely by a purely logical process, I cannot proceed to the business of thinking without having some knowledge and concrete realities to work on or with. When I am invited to consider such great public policies as are inherent in a world plan, I am oppressed by the thought that they involve nothing less than knowledge and interpretation of mankind's long history on this planet. This alone is enough to give me pause—and pain. It cramps my facility for voluble expression on the subject.

Now you are asking me what I think about plans for a situation— a combination of order and chaos—hidden from us in the veiled future. Judging by past experiences of history (and I have no other resort for criteria), many contingencies and great events now unforeseen will occur in this unfolding future. There may be shifts in the two coalitions now engaged in war. Unities enforced by war may be shattered when war dies down. Great internal explosions may occur within nations now apparently firm in façade. New combinations of powers may arise.

It takes little knowledge of world history to recall how alliances have been broken, coalitions reformed, eternal friendships forsworn, and the grand designs of the highest statesmen and generals shattered by uncalculated events. For instance, few people early in 1917 could foresee the Bolshevik revolution in Russia and realize that before the end of the war Russia's two allies, Great Britain and France, and her associate, the United States, would be waging unofficial wars on the Soviet Union, north, south and far east. Recalling this bit of history, not merely ancient, leads me to wonder what would happen if Hitler and Mussolini were rubbed out of the picture and relatively limited fascist regimes, such as prevailed in Italy when the Black Shirts first came to power, were established in France, Germany, and Italy, as well as Spain, and new insurrections broke out against them. Many other illustrations of possible contingencies may easily be derived from historical experience, but I forbear citing any more.

Coming home to the United States, I confess that I can see in the midst of the multitude of plans, definite and indefinite, put forth by high officials and eminent citizens and associations, no agreement on fundamentals and details about which to think with any degree of precision and certitude. Nor am I able now to fathom the future of our internal economy, or discern clearly the features of foreign policy which the people of the United States will support persistently and consistently by taxes, army, regimentation, and other sacrifices.

Thus it is impossible for me at this point in time to visualize the complicated situation which you call the post-war world—primary contours and elements of which are hidden from view and must now be mere matters of speculation. What I think about a shadow-land impenetrable to my vision is worthless to me and, I am sure, to others. I suspect, but I do not know, that if the statesmen or military leaders, called upon to draw the terms of the settlement at the end of the war, concentrate on making a durable rather than a permanent peace the results may be more lasting. As to the making of minute plans for the post-war world, I prefer to leave that operation to others who feel that they have a competence to which I cannot lay claim.

Yet I know that someday practical decisions will have to be made on the settlement at the close of hostilities. Speaking as constructively as I can, I should approve, for the present, an effort to hold the United Nations together on practical issues, while striving to adjust grave differences between and within them and to effect agreements among them on points of continuing co-operation during the war. As to the military and territorial settlement at the end of the conflict, I am inclined to the opinion that it should not be accompanied by an elaborate world constitution, full of vague phrases that could be, and probably would be, twisted and turned by governments competing for power. Instead, the settlement should be accompanied by a brief and simple treaty. I would limit the treaty to ten years or more, subject to renewal, and bind the signatory powers to refrain from resorting to violence during that period, and to abide by stipulated methods of arbitration and conciliation in case controversies arise under the terms of the treaty.

The shorter this treaty is, the better; the more concise the terms I have just mentioned, the more likely would be the prospect of observance; the slighter the strain on human nature, the more probable would be whole-hearted willingness to abide by it.

This proposal, I submit, is constructive. It is supported by no little historical experience, including the extraordinary fortunes of our own Constitution which fills only eight pages of print. This program, I believe, would be more likely to realize aspirations for the good of our country and humanity, which we all cherish, than grandiose plans for settling everything and everybody all at once and for all time and for trying to hold millions of people down by police and propaganda. It leaves, as a French statesman once remarked of a short constitution for France, 'something to Providence.'

Having listened without interruptions, if with some impatience, Mrs. Smyth's guests broke up into groups and engaged in animated contentions over the four elaborate plans for the postwar world that had been presented at the table. Taking this as a signal for flight, I escaped to my study on Hosannah Hill, where, for a few minutes, I tried to compose my troubled mind by reading the fifth-century lines of Rutilius to the future of the Roman Empire.

XXI

The Fate and Fortunes of Our Republic

WHAT was on your mind, I asked the Smyths, when you suggested this additional session of our fireside seminar?

MRS. SMYTH: In the course of our discussions, especially at the session on world relations, we were overpowered by the realization that every proposition involved assumptions unprovable but taken for granted; that by assigning a cause to any event we are required, if thoughtful, to make a futile inquiry into the cause of the cause backward along an infinite chain of causes ending in the darkness of prehistory—silence; that all our schemes for a world order come within the sweep of what you call great history; that our institutions, hopes, and plans run up against fate as well as opportunities for action. For your consent to let us have one more conference, and this one all by ourselves, we are grateful.

DR. SMYTH: That's true, Beard. This time we can go straight to your large historical philosophy and your ways of thinking about history. I shall try to have patience with you, though I have not always been successful at the art. Please have patience with me a little longer.

BEARD: There is no reason or pleasure in any other attitude—at least when we are in our right minds. So be as frank as you wish about your present difficulties. Let us go about the business in the freest possible style.

DR. SMYTH: As we told you on the occasion of our first visit last autumn, we had read Spengler or, perhaps it would be truer to say, tried to read him years ago, and we have been deeply interested in his new theory of history. I mean the theory that every nation moves through a kind of cycle from youth to old age and death—spring, summer, autumn, and winter. Just what happens when winter comes, we could not quite make out from Spengler's words, but it seems that at the end of Winter comes Caesar, the man of blood and iron who conquers the man of gold—our urban civilization.

MRS. SMYTH: If Spengler's theory is valid, then it applies to our Republic, to America; and our Republic is fated to perish, to fall under the empire of a Caesar, when its Winter inevitably comes. This is a dreary outlook and makes futile all our talk about constitutionalism, America's place in the world, and the effort to maintain the ideals of liberty and justice which we have discussed during our many sessions together.

If Spengler's new theory is valid, then all that the advocates of world order said the other night at our house goes overboard also. Their propositions were based on the idea that all nations are growing more alike, better ready for world union; that the same civilization will become common around the world; and that all nations will develop together into a peaceful and prosperous future for all time. Spengler dashes such optimistic hopes to earth. We want to know your views on what we may call the larger historical drama in which everything we have talked about has taken place or will take place.

BEARD: That is a tall order. Spengler's theory is really a deterministic theory of our universe.

DR. SMYTH: A kind of Calvinistic theory, then—a theory that all things, events, and persons have been predestined by God or Nature from the beginning of the universe and none of us can do anything about them. It amounts to a species of theology. You probably will want to sidestep it on the ground that you are a historian, not a theologian, and I cannot blame you. As an Episcopalian, I believe in free will, not predestination. But Spengler's theory bothers us, perhaps partly because I read critics who uphold it so stanchly.

BEARD: Pardon me, a moment, for a digression. I do not call myself a historian, but a *student* of history. It is customary for historians, or economists, or what-have-you, to answer, when such a question is raised, 'Oh, that belongs to theology or sociology, or some other learned discipline.' But such a reply really begs the question. It enables the person who makes it to escape the pain of thought about his own field, for his field, whatever it is, actually comes within the scope of that question, however vociferously he may deny it. I am willing to face Spengler's theory of the Universe. Everyone who tries to think his way through the maze of our world must do it. How shall we proceed?

MRS. SMYTH: Suppose you state the theory in your own words and then we can examine it together.

BEARD: Spengler wrote other books and essays besides *The Decline of the West* to which you refer. One of them, the most important for understanding what he was driving at, was *Preussentum und Sozialismus,* which he said contained the germ of his two volumes on *The Decline of the West.* In this little book, which has not been translated, as far as I know, Spengler displayed the Prussian Junker's hatred for the bourgeoisie and indicated a desire to see a union of Prussian state socialism with the socialism of industrial workers. If this could be effected, he evidently believed, it would redound to the strength, glory, and prosperity of Great Germany. . . .

MRS. SMYTH: Was Spengler himself a Junker?

BEARD: Oh, No! he was a small-time professor or schoolmaster in a German gymnasium or technical high school. He taught mathematics before he retired to write his huge book on *The Decline.* Spengler was not a Junker but a petty bourgeois who had taken on the inveterate dislike the agrarian Junker has for the business classes.

DR. SMYTH: That sounds anti-Semitic.

BEARD: The distrust—indeed we may say the contempt—of the agrarian for the urbanite has nothing to do with anti-Semitism. It is thousands of years old. It appeared strongly in Aristotle's *Politics* written in the fourth century B.C. It was not directed by Aristotle against Jews, but against all business classes. After the rise of Christianity in the West, Jews were excluded from engaging in agriculture and forced to enter business. Then they also got the full shock of the old agrarian distrust of and contempt for business, trading, and finance. Spengler was not an anti-Semite, and members of Hitler's party broke with him over that very point.

MRS. SMYTH: Robert, suppose we do not interrupt for a moment, if we can command that restraint, until we get the case of Spengler before us.

[The Doctor nodded his assent.]

BEARD: About ten years after *The Decline of the West* appeared, Spengler published his *Der Mensch und die Technik,* translated as *Man and Technics.* In his work on Prussianism and Socialism,

Spengler was optimistic in the sense that he regarded as possible a union of Prussianism and Socialism which would prove beneficial for Germany if it could be brought about by the intelligence and will of Junkers and industrial workers. In his book on *The Decline,* Spengler had seemed to be dubious as to what would happen when Winter came and Caesar conquered the man of money.

Would it be the establishment of a great and prosperous Empire like that of Rome after Julius Caesar overthrew the Republic and imperial dominion was founded on the ruins of the old constitutionalism? Would an upthrust of peasants, farmers, and strong peoples from below break the death of Winter and start a new Spring?

It is difficult for me to discover what was in his mind on these crucial questions, although I have studied over and over both the German edition and the English translation. But I am convinced that in *The Decline,* Spengler was not wholly pessimistic, had not completely surrendered to the pessimistic belief that all human beings are caught in a web of cruel fate and are powerless to do anything about it. Perhaps he was a black pessimist even when he wrote *The Decline.* Germans who knew him tell me that he was a pessimist even then, but *The Decline* leaves the door of human hope slightly ajar, as I read the lines and between the lines.

In his *Man and Technics,* however, Spengler leaves no doubt as to where he stood at the time of its publication. There he makes man simply a beast of prey. There what he calls 'machine culture' comes to a black and tragic end. Let me read you his final words:

We are born into this time and must bravely follow the path to the destined end. There is no other way. Our duty is to hold on to the lost position, without hope, without rescue, like that Roman soldier whose bones were found in front of a door in Pompeii, who, during the eruption of Vesuvius, died at his post because they forgot to relieve him. That is greatness. That is what it means to be a thoroughbred. The honorable end is the one thing that can *not* be taken from a man.

DR. SMYTH: I call that dithyrambic or lyrical rubbish and a contradiction in its own terms. If all is fated, it is nonsense to talk about bravery, greatness, the thoroughbred, and honor—least of all honor. It is just as if a drop of water in the river that flows through our valley to the sea should rise up and say: 'I am brave; I am great;

I am a thoroughbred; I have honor as, inevitably and will-less, I flow, by the law of gravitation, relentlessly to the sea.' I am willing to let a pessimist believe that man is a mere machine, whose every act, word, thought is fated or predestined as the movement of our river to the sea, but I don't want him to get moral on my hands and proclaim his honor in the circumstances. I am willing to have Holy Willie, in Robert Burns' poem, believe that God sends one to heaven and ten to hell, all for His glory and not for any good or ill they have done afore Him; but I object to introducing moral exhortations to human beings into any such argument. Fatalism is beyond good and evil, honor and dishonor.

MRS. SMYTH: I do not quite believe that. A person may believe in a *good* fate; that mankind is fated to make endless progress toward the good. Some of the advocates of a peaceful and happy world order took that stand at our house last Friday evening.

DR. SMYTH: Yes, but they said that it would not turn out that way *unless* all Americans got busy and forced things to that conclusion. There was an if in their argument: *If* Americans will do their part, the beautiful world order will arrive. In determinism or mechanism, correctly understood, there is and can be no if. To the determinist or mechanist, as a physiologist knows, a thing is or will be, inescapable; it is not conditioned by any if. I can get that point all right, without the aid of philosophy.

Of course, a determinist may say that the machine will work for what we call good, and in this sense he may be optimistic. Even so, he rules out moral choices on our part; his system is beyond good and evil. To tell me that nobody can, by persistent effort, improve his technique in surgery is to fly in the face of my experiences.

MRS. SMYTH: If the American Republic is fated to sink into the death of Spengler's Winter, to be transformed from a system of liberty and self-government into a dictatorial empire, then it is futile, it is nonsense, for American citizens to discuss constitutionalism, liberty, justice, or anything else. I do not believe in any such destiny for us, and I want to ask Mr. Beard to consider two questions before he goes on with Spengler and determinism. Does the study of history necessarily lead to pessimism? If not, what is ahead for our Republic?

BEARD: In fact, Mrs. Smyth, Spengler's theory is very old, not new. The ancient Greeks had cyclical theories of political history. In

Aristotle's *Politics,* government moves from one form to another in succession and back again. His was a kind of tread-mill theory of the necessary fates of governments, let us say, from monarchy to aristocracy, from aristocracy to democracy, from democracy to tyranny, and back again, with slight variations. About 1725, Giambattista Vico, an Italian philosopher and sociologist, developed a cyclical theory somewhat vaguely—from barbarism to what we call civilization and back again—all very much in the style adopted by Spengler.

To pass over other examples, I will cite our own Brooks Adams. In his *The Law of Civilization and Decay,* published first in 1895, the cyclical theory re-appears. According to Adams, nations move from the dispersion of barbarism to the concentration of civilization and back again, with a possible re-infusion of barbarian blood after decay reaches or approaches its climax.

DR. SMYTH: How did Adams get a 'possible' into his fate? A thing is fated or it is not. In fate there is nothing possible, no alternative.

BEARD: Adams got a possible into his cyclical theory for the reason that, like Spengler, he was not sure what would happen when Winter came. For the first edition of his book he had one ending. For the second edition, he had another ending. For the French translation, he had still another ending, and an equivocal one. But it would take too long to go into that. My point is that Spengler's theory is not new. In origins it is old, very old, though it keeps cropping up in modern thought.

MRS. SMYTH: How do you account for the emphasis that has been laid on this cyclical theory in comparatively recent times? How did it get the hold it has over contemporary imaginations?

BEARD: The fortunes of ancient Rome have exercised a powerful influence over strong minds for at least fifteen hundred years. With many weak minds the theme has become a disease. Some of the early Church fathers wrote interpretations of Rome's misfortunes, partly with a view to reconciling the terrible events which marked the breakdown of Roman dominion with the Christian theory of Divine Providence. The renaissance, so-called, the wholesale recovery of Greek and Roman learning after the darkness of the Middle Ages, opened a new world of knowledge and thought to men and women long preoccupied with the Christian theology and world-view. For generations this pagan learning helped to fill the vacuum in secular learning, relatively neglected by theologians—many, not all, for I do not want to fall into the error of depreciating the secular wisdom of the Middle Ages. Meanwhile Western Christianity in development—even Protestant and sectarian—stemmed from the Roman system of thought and practice and, despite efforts to escape to primitive Christianity, has never discarded all of the Roman heritage. And of course the Roman Catholic Church has steadily retained its ties with Rome. . . .

DR. SMYTH: I see that a huge book could be written under the title, The Tyranny of the Roman Tradition over the Western Mind. I don't mean the Catholic tradition, but the whole Roman tradition—rise, growth, decline, and fall. I had never before realized its importance for our thinking about history, including our own history. But, fascinating as the subject is, I wish you would connect this tradition with the cyclical theory of history which exercises a kind of tyranny over modern minds. You don't mind my breaking in?

BEARD: Not at all. You know my tendency to go on and on, and round and round, in dealing with every single point of emphasis in our wide-ranging discussions. As far as I know the first systematic cyclical theory of history, from barbarism through civilization and back again, and over again, was formulated by Vico, the Italian scholar whom I mentioned a few minutes ago. He did not use the word civilization but that idea fairly fits the substance of his thought.

For perhaps a thousand years or more, a tragic sense of Rome haunted Italian thinkers and it still haunts them today. There is nothing mysterious about that. It haunted Vico and he worked out his theory of cycle as a new science.

To jump nearly two centuries, the distinguished Egyptologist, W. M. Flinders Petrie, was captured by the theory of cycle and published one of his own in his *Revolution of Civilization*. Petrie's knowledge of Egyptian history was profound. But his knowledge of universal and modern history was certainly sketchy in important spots. Under the tyranny of the ancient tradition, he was rash enough to talk about the course which every civilization follows.

DR. SMYTH: I take it that you don't think much of Petrie's book.

BEARD: I look upon it as a theory of universal history utterly out of harmony with huge bodies of knowledge at the command of students of universal history. What Petrie did not know about civilization in the United States would fill the Encyclopaedia Britannica. For Americans to base any public policy or private judgment on Petrie's theory would be like basing it on moonshine. Shall I go on with the history of the cyclical theory of history?

DR. SMYTH: It scarcely seems worth while. Sue and I will read more about it at home and not use up all the time tonight on it. But tell us this, Does the study of history necessarily lead to pessimism as to the future of humanity—for our intellectual purposes, in the United States?

BEARD: It does not. Max Nordau bears me out when he says that pessimism or optimism is a matter of temperament, not a matter of philosophy or historical knowledge. Mark Twain who, despite his many sorrows, had about everything that optimism could crave, was a pessimist. The crippled telephone operator at your Hospital has endured poverty and suffering, and yet is about the most cheerful person in our city, a genuine optimist.

The study of history does not necessarily lead to pessimism. Among historians who have devoted their lives to the study of history, some are pessimists and some are optimists as to the future of mankind. The same person is optimistic one day and pessimistic the next. Which day is the right one for classifying him? You answer. Certainly many great, good, marvelous, and delightful persons, events, and things have appeared in history; and many horrible things also. Since the records of history are fragmentary, we can never know enough to strike a balance between the good and the evil in history. Anyway, what would such a balance look like? What features would it have?

It is easy for a pessimist to select innumerable facts to *illustrate* his theory that the world is the home of desolation and sorrow for mankind, and to ignore the countervailing facts. It is easy for an optimist to ignore the pessimist's catalogue and to select just as many facts to illustrate a theory that the world is a place of increasing happiness for humanity. But a multiplication of historical illustrations is not proof.

MRS. SMYTH: Please repeat that last sentence.

BEARD: *A multiplication of historical illustrations is not proof.* I imagine that almost any theory of history could be illustrated in some way. As I understand our intellectual processes, we can formulate three types of propositions: a law, a hypothesis, and a fiction.

A law is something known—the law of gravitation, for instance. Or a mathematical law: if a silo is twenty feet in diameter, its circumference is approximately 3.1416 times twenty feet, always and everywhere.

A hypothesis is a theoretical proposition that can be explored, tested, and proved or disproved. If proved, it ceases to be a theory and comes within the denomination of laws or facts.

A fiction is a different type of theoretical proposition. It is not a law. Nor is it a hypothesis to be proved or disproved. If well grounded in imagination, logic, and knowledge, a fiction is a symbol containing workable truth, but not the whole truth of the reality covered by it. It is not fixed, like the law of gravitation, but changes with the coming of creative thought and action, and the increase of knowledge pertaining to that reality. It remains, however, to the end, partly false, in that it does not embrace all the facts necessarily relevant to it, and it is partly a matter of belief and reasoned conviction.

The theory of the infinite extension of space and the theory of the infinite divisibility of matter are fictions beyond proof and beyond our intellectual grasp; but they have been and are useful fictions in mathematics and physics. All our comprehensive ideas or theories that purport to cover universal history including, for our purposes, American history specifically, are in the nature of fictions, that is, interpretations into which enter elements of knowledge, imagination, and conviction or belief.

As Havelock Ellis says:

> Matter is a fiction, just as the fundamental ideas with which the sciences generally operate are mostly fictions, and the scientific materialization of the world has proved a necessary and useful fiction, only harmful when we regard it as hypothesis and therefore possibly true. The representative world is a system of fictions. It is a symbol by the help of which we orient ourselves. The business of science is to make the symbol ever more adequate, but it remains a symbol, a means of action, for action is the last end of thinking.

DR. SMYTH: I could name a lot of fictions in medicine—theories on which a doctor proceeds when he does not know *all* about the disease he is treating. And a doctor is often successful that way. I should like to know more about fictions as applied to history, public affairs, our Republic, and its future. Can you give me the title of a book which would help me?

BEARD: I'll bring one in—Hans Vaihinger's *Philosophie des Als Ob*. Here is an English translation, *The Philosophy of 'As If.'* Havelock Ellis gives a brief treatment of it, and some criticism, in the third chapter of *The Dance of Life*.

DR. SMYTH: The dance of life! What next?

MRS. SMYTH: Never mind. I am willing to drop the subject—for the moment. To come down to hard cases, do you believe that there will always be an America, our America? Do you believe that our Republic will endure forever? Can we master fate? Must the Republic be turned into an empire, like the Roman Republic, and ultimately dissolve to ruins? With these questions all of our smaller questions reviewed this winter are involved.

BEARD: I shall tackle the third question first and dispose of it. We cannot master our fate. What is fated is fated and is beyond our power of control.

Will there always be an America? I believe that there will always be an America, an America with unique characteristics, however great the changes that will come. I believe that, but I do not know any way by which anybody can *demonstrate* the proposition. A China existed before Rome was founded and China still lives. I do not believe that the United States, with all its primary features, will perish from the earth, any more than China has perished in the course of thousands of years. I believe that our Republic, with authority and liberty constantly readjusted under constitutional principles, will long endure; forever, I hope.

You are entitled to ask: What are the grounds for this assurance? Here we come to human ultimates in thinking about our universe and in reaching convictions about it. What I call a conviction is not just a blind faith. It is a calculation based on knowledge of numerous relevant facts well established by a consensus of competence in critical scholarship, and it is formulated with reference to the highest degree of probability that seems warranted by these facts. The possibility of error is by no means excluded from this operation, but if there is a more efficient way of arriving at informed and reasoned assurance, I have never come across it in my years of searching under Pascal's mandate: *chercher en gémissant*.

After the prelude, I give you the grounds of my assurance respecting the fortunes of our Republic. My first is that the analogy of Rome and other societies which have perished is utterly inapplicable to the United States. What is called the fate of Rome, as a prophecy for modern nations, is a fancy of European pessimists—the offspring of their pessimism, not the source of their pessimism; or it is a thesis of special pleaders with a cause of their own to sustain. The serious application of biological, physical and historical analogies to current human affairs as if they were laws is, in my view, a sign of intellectual weakness and displays ignorance of the true nature of history.

Now I come to the second ground of my belief in the future of our Republic: History does not repeat itself. The proposition that it does repeat itself is false to the facts in the case. Rome did not repeat the history of Egypt, Babylonia, or the Alexandrian empire. No European nation has repeated the history of Rome in the course of the last four or five hundred years. America has not repeated and cannot repeat the history of any European nation.

The spring-summer-autumn-winter theory of national histories is nothing but delusive rhetoric. Rome, as a political state, rose, expanded, was transformed, declined, and dissolved. Rome at its height was not a nation, but a congeries of nationalities ruled by Roman officials headed by an emperor, a commander in chief with unlimited power. All along her northern borders were barbarian hordes who could make and use weapons about as destructive as Roman weapons. Rome decayed and the Roman empire dissolved. Never again has the posture of human affairs been identical, even similar. Many nations, still thriving, are old enough to be mature—whatever these words may mean—are old enough to be in their autumn or winter time, if there were anything whatever in the seasonal theory of history.

England as a united nation has existed for nearly nine hundred years and is still full of vitality and promise. When China was a thousand years old, it was still young. It is really rhetorical to speak of nations as young or old. When a man reaches three score and ten he knows very well that he is old. How many years does it take to make a nation old? A hundred years or five hundred years or a thousand years? If so many people did not talk solemnly and pontifically in such terms, it would be silly for us to discuss them. The chief reason for considering the cyclical theory of history is to dismiss it to the limbo of historical lumber.

America is not fated to repeat the history of Rome or any other nation in the world. There is fate—things necessary and inescapable —in our history, I have no doubt, including the fate to be distinguished from the histories of all other countries. America is fated to be America, and all the pulling and hauling of world-planners cannot alter that fact.

But according to my world-view, our universe is not all fate; we have some freedom in it. Besides fate or determinism, there is *creative intelligence* in the world, and there is also *opportunity* to exercise our powers, intellectual and moral. America is well endowed with such powers. I find no evidences of general decline in them, at least of any such decline as marked Rome in the fifth and sixth centuries A.D. Unwise leadership may lead to a sad wastage of these powers. But our resilience is great. The destruction of great cities and vast agricultural equipment during wars, in countries less favorably endowed than the United States, has been followed in modern times by a complete reconstruction on better lines within ten years.

Calamities may come upon America or be brought upon the country by demagogic leadership. Civil storms may shake the United States. Temporary dictatorships may be set up. But the vast accumulation of physical, biological, and social knowledge that distinguishes the modern world from all antiquity, we may be fairly certain, will not be destroyed. Even in the midst of the worst imaginable domestic calamities, it is highly *improbable* that all our sciences, arts, skills, liberties, aspirations, institutions, laboratories, libraries, museums, industries, and farms will be utterly devastated. Enough of our Republic will be kept intact to restore, rebuild, and go ahead. Of this I *feel* sure.

I am not merely dreaming. Nor am I teaching the pleasing theory of the Victorian optimism which believed in straight-line, uninterrupted and everlasting progress. I am allowing for calamities enough to please the sourest pessimists. Yet, I have confidence in the tenacity of civilization, always in conflict with its foe, barbarism, and I hold to the conviction that it will not be extinguished on the earth. While I reject middle-class utopianism, I also reject the utopianism of communism—the spring into endless freedom and peace. I do not expect the United States ever to be as well-ordered as a Sunday

School. Still less do I expect the world of nations ever to be as well-ordered as a Sunday School. The universe does not seem to be "planned that way." But civilization in the United States, I believe, will continue for long centuries to come.

Such is the nature of my faith in the Republic, in American civilization, in the future of America. There are immense and varied opportunities in which we can work for the good, the true, the useful, and the beautiful. For us to belittle or fail to use our intellectual and moral powers for this work is to belie the best in our natures. To depreciate and neglect the exercise of these powers is as great a folly as to overestimate and overstrain them. The little that the strongest of us can do may seem small, but surely the unresting spirit of Americans will endlessly strive to carry on the values in their heritage, to improve upon them, to create new arts and sciences of living, to sustain and make better the Republic.

If this combination of faith and knowledge be not the workable truth of the business before *us,* what is it?

DR. SMYTH: Leave it there. It is the kind of well-seasoned pessimism that I like. Under it I can keep faith in our Republic, discharge my duties as a citizen with more discrimination than hitherto, and work harder than ever in the place where I seem fated to work at preventing and curing human ills with the aids afforded by modern science.

MRS. SMYTH: No! That is the kind of well-reasoned optimism under which I can go on working where I seem fated to work, with renewed strength.

BEARD: Have it either way or both ways. You asked for my human ultimates and I have given them to you.

In this mood we shook hands and brought our long student communion to a close.

CONSTITUTION

OF THE

UNITED STATES OF AMERICA

Constitution of the
United States of America

PREAMBLE

We, the People of the United States, in Order to form a more perfect Union, establish Justice, insure domestic Tranquility, provide for the common defence, promote the general Welfare, and secure the Blessings of Liberty to ourselves and our Posterity, do ordain and establish this Constitution for the United States of America.

ARTICLE I.

Section 1. All legislative Powers herein granted shall be vested in a Congress of the United States, which shall consist of a Senate and House of Representatives.

Section 2. The House of Representatives shall be composed of Members chosen every second Year by the People of the several States, and the Electors in each State shall have the Qualifications requisite for Electors of the most numerous Branch of the State Legislature.

No Person shall be a Representative who shall not have attained to the Age of twenty-five Years, and been seven Years a Citizen of the United States, and who shall not, when elected, be an Inhabitant of that State in which he shall be chosen.

Representatives and direct Taxes shall be apportioned among the several States which may be included within this Union, according to their respective Numbers, which shall be determined by adding to the whole Number of free Persons, including those bound to Service for a Term of Years, and excluding Indians not taxed, three-fifths of all other Persons. The actual Enumeration shall be made within three Years after the first Meeting of the Congress of the United States, and within every subsequent Term of ten Years, in such Manner as they shall by Law direct. The Number of Representatives shall not exceed one for every thirty Thousand, but each State shall have at Least one Representative; and until such enumeration shall be made, the State of New Hampshire shall be entitled to choose three, Massachusetts eight, Rhode-Island and Providence Plantations one, Connecticut five, New-York six, New Jersey four, Pennsylvania eight, Delaware one, Maryland six, Virginia ten, North Carolina five, South Carolina five, and Georgia three.

When vacancies happen in the Representation from any State, the Executive Authority thereof shall issue Writs of Election to fill such Vacancies.

The House of Representatives shall choose their Speaker and other Officers; and shall have the sole Power of Impeachment.

Section 3. The Senate of the United States shall be composed of two Senators from each State, chosen by the Legislature thereof, for six Years; and each Senator shall have one Vote.

Immediately after they shall be assembled in Consequence of the first Election, they shall be divided as equally as may be into three Classes. The Seats of the Senators of the first Class shall be vacated at the Expiration of the second Year, of the second Class at the Expiration of the fourth Year, and of the third Class at the Expiration of the sixth Year, so that one-third may be chosen every second Year; and if Vacancies happen by Resignation, or otherwise, during the Recess of the Legislature of any State, the Executive thereof may make temporary Appointment until the next Meeting of the Legislature, which shall then fill such Vacancies.

No Person shall be a Senator who shall not have attained to the Age of thirty Years, and been nine Years a Citizen of the United States, and who shall not, when elected, be an Inhabitant of that State for which he shall be chosen.

The Vice-President of the United States shall be President of the Senate, but shall have no Vote, unless they be equally divided.

The Senate shall choose their other Officers, and also a President pro tempore, in the Absence of the Vice-President, or when he shall exercise the Office of President of the United States.

The Senate shall have the sole Power to try all Impeachments. When sitting for that Purpose, they shall be on Oath or Affirmation. When the President of the United States is tried, the Chief Justice shall preside: And no Person shall be convicted without the Concurrence of two-thirds of the Members present.

Judgment of Cases of Impeachment shall not extend further than to removal from Office, and disqualification to hold and enjoy any Office of honor, Trust or Profit under the United States: but the Party convicted shall nevertheless be liable and subject to Indictment, Trial, Judgment and Punishment, according to Law.

Section 4. The Times, Places and Manner of holding Elections for Senators and Representatives, shall be prescribed in each State by the Legislature thereof; but the Congress may at any time by Law make or alter such Regulations, except as to the Places of choosing Senators.

The Congress shall assemble at least once in every Year, and such Meeting shall be on the first Monday in December, unless they shall by Law appoint a different Day.

Section 5. Each House shall be the Judge of the Elections, Returns and Qualifications of its own Members, and a Majority of each shall constitute a Quorum to do Business; but a smaller Number may adjourn from day to day, and may be authorized to compel the Attendance of absent Members, in such Manner, and under such Penalties as each House may provide.

Each House may determine the Rules of its Proceedings, punish its Members for disorderly Behaviour, and, with the Concurrence of two-thirds, expel a Member.

Each House shall keep a Journal of its Proceedings, and from time to time publish the same, excepting such Parts as may in their Judgment require Secrecy; and the Yeas and Nays of the Members of either House on any question shall, at the Desire of one-fifth of those Present, be entered on the Journal.

Neither House, during the Session of Congress, shall, without the Consent of the other, adjourn for more than three days, nor to any other Place than that in which the two Houses shall be sitting.

Section 6. The Senators and Representatives shall receive a Compensation for their Services, to be ascertained by Law, and paid out of the Treasury of the United States. They shall in all Cases, except Treason, Felony and Breach of the Peace, be privileged from Arrest during their Attendance at the Session of their respective Houses, and in going to and returning from the same; and for any Speech or Debate in either House, they shall not be questioned in any other Place.

No Senator or Representative shall, during the Time for which he was elected, be appointed to any civil Office under the Authority of the United States, which shall have been created, or the Emoluments whereof shall have been increased during such time; and no Person holding any Office under the United States, shall be a Member of either House during his Continuance in Office.

Section 7. All Bills for raising Revenue shall originate in the House of Representatives; but the Senate may propose or concur with Amendments as on other Bills.

Every Bill which shall have passed the House of Representatives and the Senate shall, before it becomes a Law, be presented to the President of the United States; If he approve, he shall sign it, but if not, he shall return it, with his Objections, to that House in which it shall have originated, who shall enter the Objections at large on their Journal, and proceed to reconsider it. If after such Reconsideration two-thirds of the House shall agree to pass the Bill, it shall be sent, together with the Objections, to the other House, by which it shall likewise be reconsidered, and if approved by two-thirds of that House, it shall become a Law. But in all such Cases the Votes of both Houses shall be determined by Yeas and Nays, and the Names of the Persons voting for and against the Bill shall be entered on the Journal of each House respectively. If any Bill shall not be returned by the President within ten Days (Sundays excepted) after it shall have been presented to him, the Same shall be a Law, in like Manner as if he had signed it, unless the Congress by their Adjournment prevent its Return, in which Case it shall not be a Law.

Every Order, Resolution, or Vote to which the Concurrence of the Senate and House of Representatives may be necessary (except on a question of Adjournment) shall be presented to the President of the United States; and before the Same shall take Effect, shall be approved by him, or being disapproved by him, shall be repassed by two-thirds of the Senate and House of Representatives, according to the Rules and Limitations prescribed in the Case of a Bill.

Section 8. The Congress shall have Power: To lay and collect Taxes, Duties, Imposts and Excises, to pay the Debts and provide for the common Defence and general Welfare of the United States; but all Duties, Imposts and Excises shall be uniform throughout the United States;

To borrow Money on the credit of the United States;

To regulate Commerce with foreign Nations, and among the several States, and with the Indian Tribes;

To establish an uniform Rule of Naturalization, and uniform Laws on the subject of Bankruptcies throughout the United States;

To coin Money, regulate the Value thereof, and of foreign Coin, and fix the Standard of Weights and Measures;

To provide for the Punishment of counterfeiting the Securities and current Coin of the United States;

To establish Post Offices and post Roads;

To promote the Progress of Science and useful Arts, by securing for limited Times to Authors and Inventors the exclusive Right to their respective Writings and Discoveries;

To constitute Tribunals inferior to the supreme Court;

To define and punish Piracies and Felonies committed on the high Seas, and Offences against the Law of Nations;

To declare War, grant Letters of Marque and Reprisal, and make Rules concerning captures on Land and Water;

To raise and support Armies, but no Appropriation of Money to that Use shall be for a longer Term than two Years;

To provide and maintain a Navy;

To make Rules for the Government and Regulation of the land and naval Forces;

To provide for calling forth the Militia to execute the Laws of the Union, suppress Insurrections and repel Invasions;

To provide for organizing, arming, and disciplining the Militia, and for governing such Part of them as may be employed in the Service of the United States, reserving to the States respectively, the Appointment of the Officers, and the Authority of training the Militia according to the discipline prescribed by Congress;

To exercise exclusive Legislation in all Cases whatsoever, over such District (not exceeding ten Miles square) as may, by Cession of particular States, and the Acceptance of Congress, become the Seat of Government of the United States, and to exercise like Authority over all Places purchased by the Consent of the Legislature of the State in which the Same shall be, for the Erection of Forts, Magazines, Arsenals, dock-Yards, and other needful Buildings;—And

To make all Laws which shall be necessary and proper for carrying into Execution the foregoing Powers, and all other Powers vested by this Constitution in the Government of the United States, or in any Department or Officer thereof.

Section 9. The Migration or Importation of such Persons as any of the States now existing shall think proper to admit, shall not be prohibited by the Congress prior to the Year one thousand eight hundred and eight, but a Tax or duty may be imposed on such Importation, not exceeding ten dollars for each Person.

The Privilege of the Writ of Habeas Corpus shall not be suspended, unless when in Cases of Rebellion or Invasion the public Safety may require it.

No Bill of Attainder or ex post facto Law shall be passed.

No Capitation, or other direct, Tax shall be laid, unless in Proportion to the Census or Enumeration herein before directed to be taken.

No Tax or Duty shall be laid on Articles exported from any State.

No Preference shall be given by any Regulation of Commerce or Revenue to the Ports of one State over those of another: nor shall Vessels bound to, or from, one State, be obliged to enter, clear, or pay Duties in another.

No Money shall be drawn from the Treasury, but in Consequence of Appropriations made by Law; and a regular Statement and Account of the Receipts and Expenditures of all public Money shall be published from time to time.

No Title of Nobility shall be granted by the United States; And no Person holding any Office of Profit or Trust under them, shall, without the Consent of the Congress, accept of any present, Emolument, Office, or Title, of any kind whatever, from any King, Prince, or foreign State.

Section 10. No State shall enter into any Treaty, Alliance, or Confederation; grant Letters of Marque and Reprisal; coin Money; emit Bills of Credit; make any Thing but gold and silver Coin a Tender in Payment of Debts; pass any Bill of Attainder, ex post facto Law, or Law impairing the Obligation of Contracts, or grant any Title of Nobility.

No State shall, without the Consent of the Congress, lay any Imposts or Duties on Imports or Exports, except what may be absolutely necessary for executing it's inspection Laws: and the net Produce of all Duties and Imposts, laid by any State on Imports or Exports, shall be for the Use of the Treasury of the United States; and all such Laws shall be subject to the Revision and Control of the Congress.

No State shall, without the Consent of Congress, lay any Duty of Tonnage, keep Troops, or Ships of War in time of Peace, enter into any Agreement or Compact with another State, or with a foreign Power, or engage in War, unless actually invaded, or in such imminent Danger as will not admit of delay.

ARTICLE II.

Section 1. The executive Power shall be vested in a President of the United States of America. He shall hold his Office during the Term of four Years, and, together with the Vice-President, chosen for the same Term, be elected, as follows:

Each State shall appoint, in such Manner as the Legislature thereof may direct, a Number of Electors, equal to the whole Number of Senators and Representatives to which the State may be entitled in the Congress: but no Senator or Representative, or Person holding an Office of Trust or Profit under the United States, shall be appointed an Elector.

The Electors shall meet in their respective States, and vote by Ballot for two Persons, of whom one at least shall not be an Inhabitant of the same State with themselves. And they shall make a List of all the Persons voted for, and of the Number of Votes for each; which List they shall sign and certify, and transmit sealed to the Seat of the Government of the United States, directed to the President of the Senate. The President of the Senate shall, in the Presence of the Senate and House of Representatives, open all the Certificates, and the Votes shall then be counted. The Person having the greatest Number of Votes shall be the President, if such Number be a Majority of the whole Number of Electors appointed; and if there be more than one who have such Majority, and have an equal Number of Votes, then the House of Representatives shall immediately choose by Ballot one of them for President; and if no Person have a majority, then from the five highest on the List the said House shall in like Manner choose the President. But in choosing the President, the Votes shall be taken by States, the Representation from each State having one Vote. A quorum for this Purpose shall consist of a Member or Members from two-thirds of the States, and a Majority of all the States shall be necessary to a Choice. In every Case, after the Choice of the President, the Person having the greatest Number of Votes of the Electors shall be the Vice-President. But if there should remain two or more who have equal Votes, the Senate shall choose from them by Ballot the Vice-President.

The Congress may determine the Time of choosing the Electors, and the Day on which they shall give their Votes; which Day shall be the same throughout the United States.

No Person except a natural born Citizen, or a Citizen of the United States, at the time of the Adoption of this Constitution, shall be eligible to the Office of President; neither shall any Person be eligible to that Office who shall not have attained to the Age of thirty-five Years, and been fourteen Years a Resident within the United States.

In Case of the Removal of the President from Office, or of his Death, Resignation, or Inability to discharge the Powers and Duties of the said Office, the Same shall devolve on the Vice-President, and the Congress may by Law provide for the Case of Removal, Death, Resignation or Inability, both of the President and Vice-President, declaring what Officer shall then act as President, and such Officer shall act accordingly, until the Disability be removed, or a President shall be elected.

The President shall, at stated Times, receive for his Services, a Compensation, which shall neither be increased nor diminished during the Period for which he shall have been elected, and he shall not receive within that Period any other Emolument from the United States, or any of them.

Before he enter on the Execution of his Office, he shall take the following Oath or Affirmation:—"I do solemnly swear (or affirm) that I will faithfully execute the office of President of the United States, and will, to the best of my Ability, preserve, protect and defend the Constitution of the United States."

Section 2.   The President shall be Commander-in-Chief of the Army and Navy of the United States, and of the Militia of the several States, when called into the actual Service of the United States; he may require the Opinion, in writing, of the principal Officer in each of the executive Departments, upon any Subject relating to the Duties of their respective Offices, and he shall have Power to grant Reprieves and Pardons for all Offences against the United States, except in Cases of Impeachment.

He shall have Power, by and with the Advice and Consent of the Senate, to make Treaties, provided two-thirds of the Senators present concur; and he shall nominate, and by and with the Advice and Consent of the Senate, shall appoint Ambassadors, other public Ministers and Consuls, Judges of the Supreme Court, and all other Officers of the United States, whose Appointments are not herein otherwise provided for, and which shall be established by Law: but the Congress may by Law vest the Appointment of such inferior Officers, as they think proper, in the President alone, in the Courts of Law, or in the Heads of Departments.

The President shall have Power to fill up all Vacancies that may happen during the Recess of the Senate, by granting Commissions which shall expire at the End of their next Session.

Section 3. He shall from time to time give to the Congress Information of the State of the Union, and recommend to their Consideration such Measures as he shall judge necessary and expedient; he may, on extraordinary Occasions, convene both Houses, or either of them, and in Case of Disagreement between them, with Respect to the Time of Adjournment, he may adjourn them to such Time as he shall think proper; he shall receive Ambassadors and other public Ministers; he shall take Care that the Laws be faithfully executed, and shall Commission all the Officers of the United States.

Section 4. The President, Vice-President and all civil Officers of the United States, shall be removed from Office on Impeachment for, and Conviction of, Treason, Bribery, or other high Crimes and Misdemeanors.

ARTICLE III.

Section 1. The judicial Power of the United States shall be vested in one Supreme Court, and in such inferior Courts as the Congress may from time to time ordain and establish. The Judges, both of the Supreme and inferior Courts, shall hold their Offices during good Behaviour, and shall, at stated Times, receive for their Services, a Compensation, which shall not be diminished during their Continuance in Office.

Section 2. The judicial Power shall extend to all Cases, in Law and Equity, arising under this Constitution, the Laws of the United States, and Treaties made, or which shall be made, under their Authority;—to all Cases affecting Ambassadors, other public Ministers and Consuls;—to all Cases of admiralty and maritime Jurisdiction;—to Controversies to which the United States shall be a Party;—to Controversies between two or more States;—between a State and Citizens of another State;—between Citizens of different States;—between Citizens of the same State claiming Lands under Grants of different States, and between a State, or the Citizens thereof, and foreign States, Citizens or Subjects.

In all Cases affecting Ambassadors, other public Ministers and Consuls, and those in which a State shall be Party, the Supreme Court shall have original Jurisdiction. In all the other Cases before mentioned, the Supreme Court shall have appellate Jurisdiction, both as to Law and Fact, with such Exceptions, and under such Regulations as the Congress shall make.

The Trial of all Crimes, except in Cases of Impeachment, shall be by Jury; and such Trial shall be held in the State where the said Crimes shall have been committed; but when not committed within any State, the Trial shall be at such Place or Places as the Congress may by Law have directed.

Section 3. Treason against the United States, shall consist only in levying War against them, or in adhering to their Enemies, giving them Aid and Comfort. No Person shall be convicted of Treason unless on the Testimony of two Witnesses to the same overt Act, or on Confession in open Court.

The Congress shall have Power to declare the Punishment of Treason, but no Attainder of Treason shall work Corruption of Blood, or Forfeiture except during the Life of the Person attainted.

ARTICLE IV.

Section 1. Full Faith and Credit shall be given in each State to the public Acts, Records and judicial Proceedings of every other State. And the Congress may by general Laws prescribe the Manner in which such Acts, Records and Proceedings shall be proved, and the Effect thereof.

Section 2. The Citizens of each State shall be entitled to all Privileges and Immunities of Citizens in the several States.

A Person charged in any State with Treason, Felony, or other Crime, who shall flee from Justice, and be found in another State, shall on Demand of the executive Authority of the State from which he fled, be delivered up, to be removed to the State having Jurisdiction of the Crime.

No Person held to Service or Labour in one State, under the Laws thereof, escaping into another, shall, in Consequence of any Law or Regulation therein, be discharged from such Service or Labour, but shall be delivered up on Claim of the Party to whom such Service or Labour may be due.

Section 3. New States may be admitted by the Congress into this Union; but no new State shall be formed or erected within the Jurisdiction of any other State; nor any State be formed by the Junction of two or more States, or Parts of States, without the Consent of the Legislatures of the States concerned as well as of the Congress.

The Congress shall have Power to dispose of and make all needful Rules and Regulations respecting the Territory or other Property belonging to the United States; and nothing in this Constitution shall be so construed as to Prejudice any Claims of the United States, or of any particular State.

Section 4. The United States shall guarantee to every State in this Union a Republican Form of Government, and shall protect each of them against Invasion; and on Application of the Legislature, or of the Executive (when the Legislature cannot be convened) against domestic Violence.

ARTICLE V.

The Congress, whenever two-thirds of both Houses shall deem it necessary, shall propose Amendments to this Constitution, or, on the Application of the Legislatures of two-thirds of the several States, shall call a Convention for proposing Amendments, which, in either Case, shall be valid to all Intents and Purposes, as Part of this Constitution, when ratified by the Legislatures of three-fourths of the several States, or by Conventions in three-fourths thereof, as the one or the other Mode of Ratification may be proposed by the Congress; Provided that no Amendment which may be made prior to the Year One thousand eight hundred and eight shall in any Manner affect the first and fourth Clauses in the Ninth Section of the first Article; and that no State, without its Consent, shall be deprived of it's equal Suffrage in the Senate.

ARTICLE VI.

All Debts contracted and Engagements entered into, before the Adoption of this Constitution, shall be as valid against the United States under this Constitution, as under the Confederation.

This Constitution, and the Laws of the United States which shall be made in Pursuance thereof and all Treaties made, or which shall be made, under the Authority of the United States, shall be the supreme Law of the Land; and the Judges in every State shall be bound thereby, any Thing in the Constitution or Laws of any State to the Contrary notwithstanding.

The Senators and Representatives before mentioned, and the Members of the several State Legislatures, and all executive and judicial Officers, both of the United States and of the several States, shall be bound by Oath or Affirmation, to support this Constitution; but no religious Test shall ever be required as a Qualification to any Office or public Trust under the United States.

ARTICLE VII.

The Ratification of the Conventions of nine States, shall be sufficient for the Establishment of this Constitution between the States so ratifying the Same.

done in Convention by the Unanimous Consent of the States present the Seventeenth Day of September in the Year of our Lord one thousand seven hundred and Eighty-seven, and of the Independence of the United States of America the Twelfth. In witness whereof We have hereunto subscribed our Names, Attest

WILLIAM JACKSON
    Secretary

G° WASHINGTON—Presid^t
               and deputy from Virginia

New Hampshire—JOHN LANGDON, NICHOLAS GILMAN.

Massachusetts—NATHANIEL GORHAM, RUFUS KING.

Connecticut—W^m SAM^l JOHNSON, ROGER SHERMAN.

New York—ALEXANDER HAMILTON.

New Jersey—WIL: LIVINGSTON, DAVID BREARLEY, Wm PATERSON, JONA: DAYTON.

Pennsylvania—B. FRANKLIN, THOMAS MIFFLIN, ROB^t MORRIS, GEO. CLYMER, THO^s FITZSIMONS, JARED INGERSOLL, JAMES WILSON, GOUV MORRIS.

Delaware—GEO: READ, GUNNING BEDFORD, jun. JOHN DICKINSON, RICHARD BASSETT, JACO: BROOM.

Maryland—JAMES MCHENRY, DAN OF S^t THO^s JENIFER, DAN^l CARROLL.

Virginia—JOHN BLAIR, JAMES MADISON, Jr.

North Carolina—Wm BLOUNT, RICH^d DOBBS SPAIGHT, HU WILLIAMSON.

South Carolina—J. RUTLEDGE, CHARLES COTESWORTH PINCKNEY, CHARLES PINCKNEY, PIERCE BUTLER.

Georgia—WILLIAM FEW, ABR BALDWIN.

In Convention Monday September 17th 1787.

Present The States of New Hampshire, Massachusetts, Connecticut, Mr Hamilton from New York, New Jersey, Pennsylvania, Delaware, Maryland, Virginia, North Carolina, South Carolina and Georgia. Resolved,

That the preceeding Constitution be laid before the United States in Congress assembled, and that it is the Opinion of this Convention, that it should afterwards be submitted to a Convention of Delegates, chosen in each State by the People thereof, under the Recommendation of its Legislature, for their Assent and Ratification; and that each Convention assenting to, and ratifying the Same, should give Notice thereof to the United States in Congress assembled.

Resolved, That it is the Opinion of this Convention, that as soon as the Conventions of nine States shall have ratified this Constitution, the United States in Congress assembled should fix a Day on which Electors should be appointed by the States which shall have ratified the same, and a Day on which the Electors should assemble to vote for the President, and the Time and Place for commencing Proceedings under this Constitution. That after such Publication the Electors should be appointed, and the Senators and Representatives elected: That the Electors should meet on the Day fixed for the Election of the President and should transmit their Votes certified, signed, sealed and directed, as the Constitution requires, to the Secretary of the United States in Congress assembled, that the Senators and Representatives should convene at the Time and Place assigned; that the Senators should appoint a President of the Senate, for the sole Purpose of receiving, opening and counting the Votes for President; and, that after he shall be chosen, the Congress, together with the President, should, without Delay, proceed to execute this Constitution.

By the Unanimous Order of the Convention

Gᵒ Wᴀꜱʜɪɴɢᴛᴏɴ Presid^t

W. Jᴀᴄᴋꜱᴏɴ Secretary.

Aᴍᴇɴᴅᴍᴇɴᴛꜱ.

Aʀᴛɪᴄʟᴇꜱ in addition to, and Amendment of the Constitution of the United States of America, proposed by Congress, and ratified by the Legislatures of the several States, pursuant to the fifth Article of the original Constitution.

Aʀᴛɪᴄʟᴇ I.

Congress shall make no law respecting an establishment of religion, or prohibiting the free exercise thereof; or abridging the freedom of speech, or of the press; or the right of the people peaceably to assemble, and to petition the Government for a redress of grievances.

ARTICLE II.

A well-regulated Militia, being necessary to the security of a free State, the right of the people to keep and bear Arms, shall not be infringed.

ARTICLE III.

No Soldier shall, in time of peace be quartered in any house, without the consent of the Owner, nor in time of war, but in a manner to be prescribed by law.

ARTICLE IV.

The right of the people to be secure in their persons, houses, papers, and effects, against unreasonable searches and seizures, shall not be violated, and no Warrants shall issue, but upon probable cause, supported by Oath or affirmation, and particularly describing the place to be searched, and the persons or things to be seized.

ARTICLE V.

No person shall be held to answer for a capital, or other infamous crime, unless on a presentment or indictment of a Grand Jury, except in cases arising in the land or naval forces, or in the Militia, when in actual service in time of War or public danger; nor shall any person be subject for the same offence to be twice put in jeopardy of life or limb; nor shall be compelled in any criminal case to be a witness against himself, nor be deprived of life, liberty, or property, without due process of law; nor shall private property be taken for public use, without just compensation.

ARTICLE VI.

In all criminal prosecutions, the accused shall enjoy the right to a speedy and public trial, by an impartial jury of the State and district wherein the crime shall have been committed, which district shall have been previously ascertained by law, and to be informed of the nature and cause of the accusation; to be confronted with the witnesses against him; to have compulsory process for obtaining witnesses in his favor, and to have the Assistance of Counsel for his defence.

ARTICLE VII.

In Suits at common law, where the value in controversy shall exceed twenty dollars, the right of trial by jury shall be preserved, and no fact tried by a jury, shall be otherwise re-examined in any Court of the United States, than according to the rules of the common law.

Article VIII.

Excessive bail shall not be required, nor excessive fines imposed, nor cruel and unusual punishments inflicted.

Article IX.

The enumeration in the Constitution, of certain rights, shall not be be construed to deny or disparage others retained by the people.

Article X.

The powers not delegated to the United States by the Constitution, nor prohibited by it to the States, are reserved to the States respectively, or to the people.

Article XI.

The Judicial power of the United States shall not be construed to extend to any suit in law or equity, commenced or prosecuted against one of the United States by Citizens of another State, or by Citizens or Subjects of any Foreign State.

Article XII.

The Electors shall meet in their respective states, and vote by ballot for President and Vice-President, one of whom, at least, shall not be an inhabitant of the same state with themselves; they shall name in their ballots the person voted for as President, and in distinct ballots the person voted for as Vice-President, and they shall make distinct lists of all persons voted for as President, and of all persons voted for as Vice-President, and of the number of votes for each, which lists they shall sign and certify, and transmit sealed to the seat of the government of the United States, directed to the President of the Senate;—The President of the Senate shall, in the presence of the Senate and House of Representatives, open all the certificates and the votes shall then be counted;—The person having the greatest number of votes for President, shall be the President, if such number be a majority of the whole number of Electors appointed; and if no person have such majority, then from the persons having the highest numbers not exceeding three on the list of those voted for as President, the House of Representatives shall choose immediately, by ballot, the President. But in choosing the

President, the votes shall be taken by states, the representation from each state having one vote; a quorum for this purpose shall consist of a member or members from two-thirds of the states, and a majority of all the states shall be necessary to a choice. And if the House of Representatives shall not choose a President whenever the right of choice shall devolve upon them, before the fourth day of March next following, then the Vice-President shall act as President, as in the case of the death or other ꞈonstitutional disability of the President.—The person having the greatest number of votes as Vice-President, shall be the Vice-President, if such number be a majority of the whole number of Electors appointed, and if no person have a majority, then from the two highest numbers on the list, the Senate shall choose the Vice-President; a quorum for the purpose shall consist of two-thirds of the whole number of Senators, and a majority of the whole number shall be necessary to a choice. But no person constitutionally ineligible to the office of President shall be eligible to that of Vice-President of the United States.

Article XIII.

Section 1. Neither slavery nor involuntary servitude, except as a punishment for crime whereof the party shall have been duly convicted, shall exist within the United States, or any place subject to their jurisdiction.

Section 2. Congress shall have power to enforce this article by appropriate legislation.

Article XIV.

Section 1. All persons born or naturalized in the United States, and subject to the jurisdiction thereof, are citizens of the United States and of the State wherein they reside. No State shall make or enforce any law which shall abridge the privileges or immunities of citizens of the United States; nor shall any State deprive any person of life, liberty, or property, without due process of law; nor deny to any person within its jurisdiction the equal protection of the laws.

Section 2. Representatives shall be apportioned among the several States according to their respective numbers, counting the whole number of persons in each State, excluding Indians not taxed. But when the right to vote at any election for the choice of electors for President and Vice-President of the United States, Representatives in Congress, the Executive and Judicial officers of a State, or the members of the

Legislature thereof, is denied to any of the male members of such State, being twenty-one years of age, and citizens of the United States, or in any way abridged, except for participation in rebellion, or other crime, the basis of representation therein shall be reduced in the proportion which the number of such male citizens shall bear to the whole number of male citizens twenty-one years of age in such State.

Section 3. No person shall be a Senator or Representative in Congress, or elector of President and Vice-President, or holding any office, civil or military, under the United States, or under any State, who, having previously taken an oath, as a member of Congress, or as an officer of the United States, or as a member of any State legislature, or as an executive or judicial officer of any State, to support the Constitution of the United States, shall have engaged in insurrection or rebellion against the same, or given aid and comfort to the enemies thereof. But Congress may by a vote of two-thirds of each House, remove such disability.

Section 4. The validity of the public debt of the United States, authorized by law, including debts incurred for payment of pensions and bounties for services in suppressing insurrection and rebellion, shall not be questioned. But neither the United States nor any State shall assume or pay any debt or obligation incurred in aid of insurrection or rebellion against the United States, or any claim for the loss or emancipation of any slave; but all such debts, obligations and claims shall be held illegal and void.

Section 5. The Congress shall have power to enforce, by appropriate legislation, the provisions of this article.

Article XV.

Section 1. The right of the citizens of the United States to vote shall not be denied or abridged by the United States or by any State on account of race, color, or previous condition of servitude.——

Section 2. The Congress shall have power to enforce the provisions of this article by appropriate legislation.—

Article XVI.

The Congress shall have power to lay and collect taxes on incomes, from whatever sources derived, without apportionment among the several States, and without regard to any census or enumeration.

Article XVII.

The Senate of the United States shall be composed of two Senators from each State, elected by the people thereof, for six years; and each Senator shall have one vote. The electors in each State shall have the qualifications requisite for electors of the most numerous branch of the State legislatures.

When vacancies happen in the representation of any State in the Senate, the executive authority of such State shall issue writs of election to fill such vacancies: *Provided,* That the legislature of any State may empower the executive thereof to make temporary appointment until the people fill the vacancies by election as the legislature may direct.

This amendment shall not be so construed as to affect the election or term of any Senator chosen before it becomes valid as part of the Constitution.

Article XVIII.

Section 1. After one year from the ratification of this article the manufacture, sale, or transportation of intoxicating liquors within, the importation thereof into, or the exportation thereof from the United States and all territory subject to the jurisdiction thereof for beverage purposes is hereby prohibited.

Section 2. The Congress and the several States shall have concurrent power to enforce this article by appropriate legislation.

Section 3. This article shall be inoperative unless it shall have been ratified as an amendment to the Constitution by the legislatures of the several States, as provided in the Constitution, within seven years from the date of the submission hereof to the States by the Congress.

Article XIX.

The right of citizens of the United States to vote shall not be denied or abridged by the United States or by any State on account of sex.

Congress shall have power to enforce this article by appropriate legislation.

Article XX

Section 1. The terms of the President and Vice-President shall end at noon on the 20th day of January, and the terms of Senators and Representatives at noon on the 3d day of January, of the years in which such terms would have ended if this article had not been ratified; and the terms of their successors shall then begin.

Section 2. The Congress shall assemble at least once in every year, and such meeting shall begin at noon on the 3d day of January, unless they shall by law appoint a different day.

Section 3. If, at the time fixed for the beginning of the term of the President, the President elect shall have died, the Vice-President elect shall become President. If a President shall not have been chosen before the time fixed for the beginning of his term, or if the President elect shall have failed to qualify, then the Vice-President elect shall act as President until a President shall have qualified; and the Congress may by law provide for the case wherein neither a President elect nor a Vice-President elect shall have qualified, declaring who shall then act as President, or the manner in which one who is to act shall be selected, and such person shall act accordingly until a President or Vice-President shall have qualified.

Section 4. The Congress may by law provide for the case of the death of any of the persons from whom the House of Representatives may choose a President whenever the right of choice shall have devolved upon them, and for the case of the death of any of the persons from whom the Senate may choose a Vice-President whenever the right of choice shall have devolved upon them.

Section 5. Sections 1 and 2 shall take effect on the 15th day of October following the ratification of this article.

Section 6. This article shall be inoperative unless it shall have been ratified as an amendment to the Constitution by the legislatures of three-fourths of the several States within seven years from the date of its submission. [The text followed above is that of the 'Literal Print' edition issued by the Department of State in Washington, D. C., 1933.]

Article XXI.

Section 1. The eighteenth article of amendment to the Constitution of the United States is hereby repealed.

Section 2. The transportation or importation into any State, Territory, or Possession of the United States for delivery or use therein of intoxicating liquors, in violation of the laws thereof, is hereby prohibited.

Section 3. This article shall be inoperative unless it shall have been ratified as an amendment to the Constitution by conventions in the several States, as provided in the Constitution, within seven years from the date of the submission hereof to the States by the Congress.

ARTICLE XXII.

Section 1. No person shall be elected to the office of the President more than twice, and no person who has held the office of President, or acted as President, for more than two years of a term to which some other person was elected President shall be elected to the office of the President more than once. But this article shall not apply to any person holding the office of President when this article was proposed by the Congress, and shall not prevent any person who may be holding the office of President, or acting as President, during the term within which this article becomes operative from holding the office of President or acting as President during the remainder of such term.

Section 2. This article shall be inoperative unless it shall have been ratified as an amendment to the Constitution by the Legislatures of three-fourths of the several States within seven years from the date of its submission to the States by the Congress.

ARTICLE XXIII.

Section 1. The District constituting the seat of Government of the United States shall appoint in such manner as the Congress may direct:

A number of electors of President and Vice President equal to the whole number of Senators and Representatives in Congress to which the District would be entitled if it were a State, but in no event more than the least populous State; they shall be in addition to those appointed by the States, but they shall be considered, for the purposes of the election of President and Vice President, to be electors appointed by a State; and they shall meet in the District and perform such duties as provided by the twelfth article of amendment.

Section 2. The Congress shall have power to enforce this article by appropriate legislation.